CONTRASTS IN EMERGING SOCIETIES

Map 1. South-Eastern Europe in 1900

Contrasts in Emerging Societies

Readings in the Social and Economic History
of South-Eastern Europe in the
Nineteenth Century

Selected and translated by

G. F. CUSHING
E. D. TAPPE
V. de S. PINTO
PHYLLIS AUTY

and edited by

DOREEN WARRINER

INDIANA UNIVERSITY PRESS

BLOOMINGTON 1965

To the Memory of

REGINALD ROBERT BETTS

PREFACE

OUR object in combining to compile a book on the life of the peoples of these four countries of South-Eastern Europe during the nineteenth century was in the first place to help fill the gap left in general economic histories of Europe by the neglect of its eastern half. Since this neglect is largely due to the barrier of languages, we hoped that a collection of extracts translated from contemporary sources might provide a means of overcoming it.

In the second place, our object was to make comparisons between the four countries considered as emerging societies, and so to enable further comparisons with societies emerging in our own time. Now that historians as well as economists are turning towards the study of the under-developed world, the past history of Eastern Europe gains in interest through its comparability with agrarian countries in other continents. Above all, this is true of its land tenure systems and its nineteenth-century agrarian reforms. Backward farming, wasteful use of land, recurrent famine, were problems in this region, as they are in the under-developed continents today; so too was the extinction of old crafts and once prosperous domestic industries, not replaced by the growth of factory employment.

The experience was very varied, and should be studied from contemporary sources, because the diversity and intricacy of the social fabric may easily be obliterated by modern methods of condensing or packaging history. The advantage of approaching the subject through the eyes of contemporaries is that their eyes were fresh; they observed detail and diversity. Powers of observation were undimmed by academic disciplines; minds were uninhibited in making judgements of value.

Our selection illustrates the range of the material. Some extracts are taken from the works of well-known writers—Cantemir, Vuk Karadžić, Petőfi, Jireček, Vlaykov, Caragiale, Illyés; others from writers who played a part in the development of the economy, such as Széchenyi and Geshov; others illustrate concern with the problems of backwardness, such as the passages quoted from Demian, Ghica,

K. Bobchev and Grünberg. The reasons for including English texts in a volume primarily intended as a way round the language barrier are that two are from unpublished sources, several are little known and specially interesting, while some, notably Paget and Gardner Wilkinson, are indispensable.

To allow of comparison, the arrangement of the extracts follows the same pattern for each country, so far as the material allows. Each country section includes introductory passages broadly descriptive of the agricultural background, types of farming, and land use. Social life follows as the central content of each section, with the relationship between landlords and peasants forming its hard core, illustrated by the texts of major laws where possible. Other classes and groups appear more briefly, to illustrate their functions in society and economy. General economic conditions are illustrated by extracts describing markets, fairs, trade, agricultural and domestic industries, and communications. The extracts are arranged chronologically, by subjects, divided into periods in the sections on Hungary, Rumania and Bulgaria, and into regions in the section on Yugoslavia.

Subject to this general outline, the choice of the extracts and their translation has been the responsibility of the individual specialist. As three of the four contributors are 'language and literature' men, their selection includes extracts from memoirs and documentaries, which give the feel of social life so much better than sources by convention regarded as historical. In this region, where literature was always *engagée*, the choice requires no justification.

We owe much gratitude to Professor Rudolf Bićanić, of the University of Zagreb, for advice on the Yugoslav sources, and to Mrs. Sonia Bićanić, D.Litt. Oxon., Docent in the same University, for the translations from Serbo-Croat. To Mr. S. E. Mann, Reader in Czech and Albanian Languages and Literatures in the University of London, we are indebted for the translations from Jireček included in the Bulgarian section. To Dr. Bernard Lewis, Professor of the History of the Near and Middle East in the University of London, we owe thanks for advice on the transliteration of Turkish words; to Mr. B. H. de C. Ireland, Miss Barbara Kerr, Miss Mary Lauterbach and Mr. H. D. Warriner for advice on the selection of extracts and for help in translation; and to Dr. R. L. French, Lecturer in the Department of Geography, University College, and in the School of Slavonic Studies, for guidance in the preparation of the maps, which were drawn by Mr. K. Wass of University College London.

The compilation of the volume began under the general editorship of Professor R. R. Betts, from 1946 until his death in 1961 Masaryk Professor of Central European History in the University of London. Much of the material was used in papers read at a seminar under his unifying leadership. We have done our best to complete, however inadequately, the task which he did not live to fulfil.

School of Slavonic and   G. F. C.
East European Studies,   E. D. T.
University of London   V. de S. P.
April 1964   P. A.
                                           D. W.

CONTRIBUTORS

PHYLLIS AUTY

M.A., B.LITT., Lecturer in the History of the Danubian Lands in the School of Slavonic and East European Studies

SONIA BIĆANIĆ

D.LITT. (Oxford). Docent in English Literature in the University of Zagreb

G. F. CUSHING

M.A., PH.D., Lecturer in Hungarian Language and Literature in the School of Slavonic and East European Studies

V. DE S. PINTO

M.A., PH.D., Lecturer in Bulgarian Language and Literature in the School of Slavonic and East European Studies

E. D. TAPPE

M.A., Reader in Rumanian Studies in the School of Slavonic and East European Studies

DOREEN WARRINER

B.A., PH.D., Reader in Social and Economic Studies of Eastern Europe in the School of Slavonic and East European Studies

CONTENTS

Rumania
E. D. TAPPE

CONTENTS

Agriculture

Social Life

Trade, Industry and Transport

Bulgaria
V. de S. PINTO

Yugoslavia
PHYLLIS AUTY

I. SERBIA

II. INTERNATIONAL TRADE

CONTENTS xix

18. Need for Agricultural Progress 355
Dr. Bleiweiss, 1856.

19. Help for Home Industries 358
Official Enquiry into Agricultural Conditions, 1884.

20. Causes of Agricultural Depression 361
G. Pirc, 1894.

V. DALMATIA

21. Trade and Agriculture 364
Sir John Gardner Wilkinson, 1848.

22. Benefits of Tobacco Cultivation 365
Anon., 1894.

VI. MONTENEGRO

23. Village Life and Trade 367
Sir John Gardner Wilkinson, 1848.

VII. BOSNIA-HERCEGOVINA

24. Undeveloped Resources 372
Anon., 1821.

25. The Land Question, 1878–1910 374
(a) The Existing Land Tenure System. (b) Official Policy and the Kmet Strike.
K. Grünberg, 1911.

Note on Weights, Measures and Currency 387

Indexes
Persons 389
Place Names 391
Subjects 397

MAPS

1. South-Eastern Europe in 1900 *frontispiece*
2. Hungary in 1900 28
3. Rumania in 1900 116
4. Bulgaria in 1900 206
5. The Territories of Yugoslavia in 1900 282

PLACE NAMES

In the translation of the extracts, the place names used by the author have generally been retained. The modern equivalent is given in a footnote when each name is first mentioned. The Place Name Index includes all versions.

On the country maps, place names are given in the language of the country represented. Where maps overlap, one place may appear in two versions (e.g. the river Tisza in Hungary is Tisa in Yugoslavia).

On the general map, the names are those most likely to be familiar to the modern reader.

FOREIGN WORDS

The versions of foreign words used by the authors have been retained. The same principle has been followed in the transliteration of words borrowed from the Turkish, which accordingly appear in different versions in different extracts, e.g. *chitluk* in translation from Serbian and *chiflik* in translation from Bulgarian.

General Introduction: Contrasts and Comparisons

DOREEN WARRINER

THE four countries of the Lower Danubian region, whose recent social and economic past is illustrated in this book, gained national independence mainly during the nineteenth century. Hungary, unlike the rest, never came completely under Turkish suzerainty, although a great part of its territory was conquered by the Turks and occupied by them until 1686. In the nineteenth century the Hungarian state plays a double role, subordinate to Austria until 1867, while itself ruling subject nationalities in its outlying territories. The three others won freedom by stages. Serbia rebelled suddenly and violently against Turkish rule in 1805–13 and 1815, to gain autonomy within the Ottoman Empire in 1830 and full independence in 1878. Rumania became independent at the same date, the vassal principalities of Wallachia and Moldavia having united in 1859 to form an autonomous state. Bulgaria in 1878 emerged as an autonomous state nominally under Turkish suzerainty, in reality independent, though formal independence was not proclaimed until 1908. The rest of the Southern Slavs remained under alien rule until 1918, when they united with Serbia to form the new state of Yugoslavia.

With the political history of how national independence was attained, and the long intricacies of 'the Eastern Question', this book is not concerned. Its theme is the economic and social foundations of the movement towards national independence, and the problems encountered by these different societies in reforming their institutions and developing their economies in a Europe composed of more advanced and more powerful states. In these problems there are evidently many analogies with those encountered by emerging societies in Africa and Asia today. To the European political consciousness of the nineteenth century, this region was the underdeveloped world, a ferment of aspirations and a permanent source of potential conflict between the Great Powers.

B

The Early Nineteenth Century

The first and more obvious similarity with the contemporary under-developed world lies in the fact that these countries at the beginning of the century were mainly agricultural, and remained so during the century, with a significant shift in the balance of occupations only in Hungary. But unlike agrarian societies in the modern world, they had one immense advantage: at the beginning of the century, they still had large reserves of fertile land. Southern Hungary and Slavonia, after centuries of devastation, had been re-settled during the eighteenth century, and in the early nineteenth century were still sparsely settled and only partly cultivated (Y 8).[1] According to Paget, one-quarter of the agricultural land of Hungary was uncultivated in 1839; the Great Plain was still mainly pastoral at mid-century (H 17 and 25a). In fertile Wallachia, crushing taxation and shortage of labour were responsible for neglect of cultivation during the eighteenth century; in 1820, Wilkinson estimates that in Wallachia and Moldavia only one-sixth of the plain land is cultivated; even after independence, proposals for colonization by German or Swiss farmers are canvassed (R 4, 17, 19 and 22). In Serbia, Bulgaria, Bosnia, Montenegro, and the mountainous parts of Rumania, farming was still mainly pastoral. The sources quoted under the first heading of each country section all stress the great agricultural potential of the plains and the factors which cause its neglect: taxation, tribute, indolence, insecurity, ignorance.

During the course of the century, as the population grew, the greater part of the cultivable area was gradually brought under the plough. Maize became the main cereal crop in the dry regions: potatoes were introduced in the hills with their moister climates. The farmers of the Balkans slowly turned from shepherding towards the cultivation of the arable land, and at the same time the zadruga (the extended family or 'long house') holdings broke up into independent single family farms (Y 1b, 13, B 15). Certain districts excepted, farming remained extensive, with grain as the main product and livestock still relying largely on grazing. At the end of the century, signs of population pressure were apparent in the mountain regions, because in Turkish times they had been comparatively densely populated, but the plains were still short of labour. By the nineteen-thirties, however, agricultural over-population had, to a greater or lesser[2] degree, become a problem in all these countries.

[1] References are to the numbers of the extracts in each country section; H indicates Hungary, R Rumania, B Bulgaria and Y Yugoslavia.

[2] In Hungary the problem was not serious, because it had lost the over-populated regions through the post-war territorial settlement.

Their former agricultural potential had not been used to promote general economic development on a sufficient scale to raise the rural living standard to any demonstrable extent, or to invest in industrial production sufficiently to cause a large expansion of industrial employment. The fertile plains of the Danube basin never rivalled the American Middle West as a stimulus to general expansion.

In the inter-war period, agricultural over-population in Eastern Europe seemed such a striking and unusual condition, by comparison with Western Europe, that models of 'under-development' have been based on it, often with exaggerated precision in the calculation of the extent of the labour surplus. From the standpoint of economic theory, this method of approach is of course legitimate, but such analysis can be deceptive if the abstract model is regarded as a description of an historical process. It may then convey the sense that the past was stagnant and monotonous—a mere filling up of empty land on a subsistence economy basis, in the uniform 'mud from Vladivostok to Trieste'.

But as the following sections show, the past was neither monotonous nor uniform. In the early nineteenth century, the volume of trade, both external and internal, was probably larger in relation to the volume of agricultural production than it was in the inter-war years. Domestic industries and crafts were flourishing and widespread. Economic life was more diversified and dynamic and social life more lively than broad generalizations about backwardness suggest.

In considering the causes of the backwardness of the region, much weight must of course be given to the agrarian policies of the ruling powers, since they influenced the course of development during the long period of emergence. These policies were not by any means universally oppressive. Many of the extracts illustrate their direct or indirect effects, and comparison shows that the agrarian policies of Austria, Hungary and Turkey were strongly contrasted.

Austria's agrarian policy appears on the whole to have been enlightened. In the eighteenth century, indeed, it was pre-eminently so. The Urbarium of Maria Theresa of 1767 and subsequent legislation were genuine agrarian reforms, far in advance of their time. Though the legislation did not abolish feudal dues, it defined the rights and obligations of the serfs, and so protected them against extreme exactions of labour and produce; by fixing the total area of peasant land it protected peasant holdings from absorption by the landowner. It laid a solid foundation for serf emancipation by ensuring that some proportion of the land was in peasant occupation when serf obligations were abolished. Its motives were threefold:

politically it was an insurance against the recurrence of peasant risings; economically, it provided a basis of tax assessment; socially, it was humanitarian and paternal.

This great contribution of Austria to rural welfare has been stressed in the selection of the extracts, since in works by English historians it has generally been obliterated by nationalist recriminations in the period of the Monarchy's decay. It is true that the agrarian society established by the reforms of Maria Theresa and Joseph II was hier-archical and stratified, without a trace of equality, liberty or fra-ternity; but as compared with agrarian society in England, France, Russia, Prussia or Turkey in the same period, it had the great merit of offering the peasants a measure of economic security. If they were at the bottom of the social structure, their tax liability was at least fixed, as in the Balkan countries it was not; and if they could not rise in the hierarchy, at least they were not liable to sink and lose their livelihood by expropriation, as they were in England.

The significance of these reforms can best be appreciated in Hungary. Although the urbarial legislation was only partly enforced, since landowners could and did exact from the peasants more labour than the law laid down, it appears to have been effective to a certain extent, in that it guaranteed the peasants a share in the land, varying from district to district, but not, generally, inadequate at that time (H 4, 5, 6, 23). In Transylvania, where there was no urbarium, the conditions of the peasants were far worse than in the rest of Hungary (H 10). Conditions were also worse in Croatia, because the legislation was not enforced (Y 9a).

Apart from the urbarial legislation, Austrian paternalism is also strikingly displayed in the peculiar tenure system of the Military Frontier, where there were no aristocratic landowners, and all the land was held by peasant farmers in large family holdings, on condi-tion that the men should perform a period of military service. The extracts quoted are critical of backward farming methods in military Croatia and Slavonia rather than of the tenure system of these provinces, which was socially better than that of civil Croatia and Slavonia (Y 7 and 8b).

Agriculturally, Austrian policy was progressive; for a land-locked Empire, mainly rural, the encouragement of intensive farming and quality production—originating from the eighteenth-century physio-crats—made good sense, both socially and economically. Slovenia is a good example, and so is Dalmatia—in the 1890s, though at an earlier time there had been complete negligence (Y 18, 20, 21 and 22). Apart from the tragic failure to reform the land system in Bosnia in the late nineteenth century, so vehemently denounced by a Viennese professor (Y 25), Austria's agrarian policy indubitably encouraged technical and social progress in this region.

Hungary's agrarian policy was double-edged. On the one hand, it was hostile to the Austrian urbarial reforms. 'Lusimus Mariam Theresiam' said the magnates, opposed to reform from above as well as from below (H 23). On the other hand, the Hungarian revolutionaries of 1848 certainly exerted an influence on the emancipation of the serfs in Hungary and Croatia (Y 12). Agriculturally, state policy was constructive, particularly as regards the regulation of the Danube and the reclamation work in the Alföld, carried out by Count Széchenyi and his successors (H 25a).

The Ottoman land tenure system had been oppressive and paralysing from the sixteenth to the eighteenth centuries (B 1); but the reforms of the 1830s were effective, at least in parts of this region. One of the main causes of the Serbian risings of 1804–13 and 1815 was Turkish land-grabbing (Y 1a). As a direct consequence of the rebellion, the long-obsolete spahi system was abolished in 1831 throughout the Empire. In fact the ex-spahis could convert their former conditional property into absolute ownership, and remained as landowners, though no longer entitled in law to exact tithes or labour service. These old oppressions vanished in Thrace and the Danube plain region of Bulgaria, but lingered on in the remoter districts of Bulgaria and in the parts of Serbia which remained under Turkish rule until 1878, while in Bosnia similar exactions continued until 1918 (B 8a, 13c, Y 25).

Rumania did not experience the Turkish land tenure system; the effects of Turkish policy on the peasants were felt indirectly, through the crushing burden of taxation, and compulsory export of grain to Constantinople at a price one-quarter of the market value (R *Introduction*, 3 and 17). The legacy of privilege and corruption was a more intractable and intangible burden than Turkish landownership, which could be removed by a sudden military operation; the 'milch cow' attitude to the peasants could not be so easily abolished (R 24).

Agriculturally, Turkish land policy was a great obstacle to progress. The tithe on field crops discouraged arable cultivation and encouraged livestock over-grazing and deforestation. In Bulgaria, however, there was an effort during the fifties to improve methods of farming, and incidental benefits were derived from the Turkish market, since the demand from Constantinople stimulated intensive cultivation of roses (for rose essence), tobacco, sesame, rice and vegetables, crops well suited to the semi-tropical climate of the Maritsa valley, which became and remained Bulgarian specialities.

The skills acquired in growing them were later exported by the migrant gardeners (B 2, 7, 16).

Foreign travellers saw rich land, poor people; and drove home the paradox. They lacked the concepts of a subsistence minimum, or an adequate living standard, and such indeed were inapplicable. In the first half of the century, the Serbian peasants were free and well-fed (Y 1b). In military Slavonia, peasant farmers had too much land, secure tenure and no obligations except military service; they could, presumably, live fairly well (Y 8). But elsewhere there was dire poverty due to poor soil and bad farming, even in the most civilized parts; in the Western Croatian military districts, and in Slovenia in the late eighteenth century, there was recurrent famine (Y 7 and 16). Social oppression might be offset by the bounty of nature. The peasants of Rumania were oppressed to the utmost, and yet not starving. 'I should have declared the Moldavian peasants the most wretched farmers in the world', wrote Cantemir in the early eighteenth century, 'if the fertility of the soil and crops did not, as it were, save them from poverty against their will'; by a later writer they are likened to 'the worm in the radish' (R 1 and 9).

So in the early years of the century the two main factors influencing the rural living standard were the tax and tenure system, and the productivity of the soil. Peasant poverty was general, but its causes were not everywhere the same.

The extent to which trade was a dynamic influence is difficult to assess; the sources disclose much activity. During the eighteenth century there had been a big expansion of trade between Turkey and Austria-Hungary, handled through Zemun by the Cincars and Greeks, and also an increase in grain exports from Slavonia and Croatia by river and state highway to Trieste and Fiume (Y 5 and 6). But the Danubian plain, in spite of its backward farming, produced more grain than could be sold. In Hungary, Townson found 'cellars full of wine and granaries full of corn, and one common complaint, the lack of a market'. Wyburn refers to 'the necessity of throwing away whole magazines of damaged corn' in Wallachia, and Demian mentions grain stock-piling on estates in Slavonia. The internal market was restricted by the poverty of the peasants, lack of communications and the small population of the towns, the external market by high costs of transport; landowners' inertia in seeking a market was also a factor, particularly in Hungary.

The liveliness of internal trade, illustrated by descriptions of the great fairs at Pest in Hungary, Uzunjova and other towns in Bulgaria, strikingly confutes the view that these were subsistence economies. The products of domestic industries, such as Slovakian linen, Bulgarian cloth, lace and braid, are staple commodities (H 16b, B 9, 10, 11). Merchants play an important part in the economy: the Cincars are financiers with a wide international network. Only in Bulgaria was there a native middle class (B 6). Elsewhere the traders are Jews, Armenians, Greeks, Germans or Russians. Of their trade in Rumania Colson acutely observes, 'It will not grow up' (R 18), i.e. no capital was thereby accumulated.

Domestic industries and crafts still flourished at mid-century. The evidence is most plentiful for Bulgaria, where crafts were well-organized in guilds and domestic industries widespread, having been encouraged from an early date by Turkish policy, in this respect highly beneficial, in contrast to its agricultural effects (B *Introduction*, 6d, 7, 10). Vlaykov's account of the life of Pirdop in the 1860s recalls Defoe's description of Yorkshire written nearly two centuries before (B 11). But by comparison with Britain many West European countries would appear similarly backward: in Germany, it should be recalled, domestic industries in the 1850s still employed more manpower than the factories. As to Slovenia, modern parallels spring to mind, for official circles in the 1880s were discussing means of encouraging these industries to provide supplementary earnings for the distressed peasantry—as they do in Japan today, while other Asian countries endeavour to promote them for the same purpose.

Thus in the first half of the nineteenth century there seemed to be fair prospects for future development: good land in plenty, great scope for progress in farming methods; much commercial enterprise and some trade expansion; and traditional industrial skills. The main drawbacks were lack of the nineteenth-century basic industrial raw materials, coal and iron, which Hungary alone possessed, though Bosnia had iron; poor communications; and land tenure systems which (with exceptions in the Austrian territories) discouraged better farming and kept peasants poor. Once these hindrances had been abolished, the way to progress seemed open. The drawback of insufficient basic raw materials could be overcome, if exports of agricultural produce expanded sufficiently to allow coal and iron imports.

The Land Reform Period: 1830–1880

Up to this point, we have considered some of the main factors influencing the economic and social life of the four countries, and have noted some of the broad similarities from comparison of the texts. But the extracts also make it abundantly clear that there were great contrasts between the countries, in Yugoslavia even between the different regions which later composed the independent state. Each country had a strongly marked individuality, associated with a national way of life based on the structure of agrarian society. The main contrasts between the countries arose from the way in which the traditional systems of landownership were abolished or reformed in the period 1830–80.

These traditional systems are described by Marxist historians as 'feudal'; the word nowadays is much overworked. To avoid confusion, it should be pointed out that in the sources quoted the term is used in two quite different senses. For nineteenth-century historians feudalism meant tenure in fief, i.e. the grant of land to a vassal on condition that he should perform military service. (Modern West European historians generally use the term in the same sense, though not consistently, since sometimes they take it to include the relationship between lord and serf in the domainal or manorial economy, as well as the vassal relationship.)

Using the term to mean fief tenure, the land system was feudal in origin in three out of the four countries. But this aspect of the land system was no longer significant. When Jireček, describing the origins of the Ottoman land system, says that 'Up to 1839 the old Turkey was a feudal state' (B 13c), he means that the landowners' privileges had survived their original obligation of military service, which in practice had not been enforced since the early seventeenth century. In Hungary, the great estates had a similar origin, but long before the nineteenth century constitutional law had become the basis of landownership and the rights associated with it. By the Code of 1517,[1] known as the Tripartitum, landowners had been given absolute power over their serfs. This absolute power Austria in the eighteenth century strove to restrict by the urbarial legislation mentioned above, without much success. As to Rumania, the origins of the boyars are obscure. Cantemir would like to think that the nobles of Moldavia had originally received their lands as gifts from the Prince; but another authority declares roundly that 'Feudalism has never existed in Rumania. Every man is fully the owner of his real estate' (R 1a and 9). Whatever the historical origin, by the nineteenth century the landowners' obligation to bear arms was obsolete. As Petőfi said, the ancestral sword was rusty (H *Introduction* and 13).

The Marxist conception of feudalism as a mode of production means that it is identified with serfdom. This usage is illustrated in

---

[1] Strictly speaking, the Code was never enacted, for though it was approved by the Diet and the king, it did not receive the royal seal; in practice nevertheless it had all the authority of constitutional law.

the extract from an article on the emancipation of the serfs in Croatia in 1848 (Y 12), which unravels an intricate political story, and emphasizes the part played by the peasants themselves. Certainly serfdom was the outstanding characteristic of society up to that date, and the advantage of this definition is that it emphasizes its abolition as a major social turning-point. Its disadvantage, however, is that it overstates the extent of economic change involved in the political event, a point discussed further below.

In this region of Europe, to use the word feudal in either sense to the exclusion of the other fails to convey the real nature of the land systems. In medieval Western Europe fief tenure and serfdom were related aspects of the same social order. Tenure in fief implied an element of social obligation on the part of the landowner, since income and privilege were granted in return for military defence, an essential function when the power of the central government was weak, and an economic function also, since the land could not be brought into cultivation without it. But in South-Eastern Europe the element of obligation was lacking; either it had lapsed, or had never existed, while serfdom continued.

On this point there is an apparent conflict of evidence. The English travellers in Hungary, liberals schooled in the tradition of *The Wealth of Nations*, observed wasteful and arbitrary oppression. Bright found that 'the peasant is considered by the government, much more than by the landlord, in the light of a slave; . . . his situation is, not only in appearance, but in reality, oppressive' (H 6). Yet the former landless serf remembers a time when the gentry were real gentry, not bothering about money, ready to slaughter an ox for the serfs to eat to their health (H 29). For reasons explained below, the two views are not necessarily opposed, since Bright was describing conditions before 1848. On the whole, however, the consensus of opinion is that oppression was not mitigated by any sense of obligation. 'Why should this divine creation have to live in slavery?' asks the Wallachian boyar Golescu, '. . . the reason is that the Princes and we boyars never see these men' (R 8). 'Best crying', according to Tkalac, summed up the attitude of the—mainly alien—nobility of Croatia towards the peasants; Desprez in 1845 is struck by the extremes of wealth and poverty (Y 9a, 10). In the Turkish provinces, there was certainly no common bond between landowner and cultivator (B 1a, b). Jireček, in his perceptive description of the attitudes of Turkish landowners and Bulgarian peasants in 1880, observes a sharp class division (B 13c).

At the beginning of the century, the majority of the cultivators of the land were serfs in the sense that they were subject to the payment of produce rents, in the form of tithe or various levies, and the performance of compulsory labour, in return for the land they occupied: they were the taxpayers. For the most part they were not legally tied to the land, as they still were in Russia. In Austria-Hungary, legal bondage had been abolished in the eighteenth century, as also in Rumania (R 2), while in the Turkish Empire serfdom had never existed in law. As Townson points out, the distinction between bonded and free had little significance (H 4). The labour of the peasants had to support both the State and the privileged class.

The agrarian history of the four countries during the century turns on the struggle of the peasants for ownership of the land in freehold, in the first place for emancipation from serfdom. It was a struggle for economic independence, and for political and social equality. In Serbia and Bulgaria, the victory was sudden and complete: the traditional Ottoman system of land tenure was abolished by the expulsion or expropriation of the Turkish landowners, and with national independence a new social structure came into existence, based on small peasant ownership. In Hungary and Rumania, there was no such victory. Serf emancipation in 1848 and 1864 respectively brought a significant change in the status of the peasants, but it was in no degree comparable with the genuine revolutions in Serbia and Bulgaria, since the large estates continued to dominate economy and society. In these countries, as also in Bosnia, the struggle against the landowners continued into the twentieth century, smouldering on in the form of agrarian socialism in Hungary, and breaking out in the Rumanian peasant rising of 1907 and the Bosnian *kmet* strike of 1910 (H 30, R 26, Y 25).

This variety of experience has some bearing on agrarian reform questions in our time, because similar types of oppressive landownership still exist in other continents. Large half-cultivated latifundia worked by quasi-serfs, not so unlike those of nineteenth-century Hungary, can be found in most Latin American countries; extravagant landowners, taking extortionate rents, like the Rumanian boyars, prevailed in the Middle East until very recently, while the small parasitic agas of Bosnia have counterparts in several Asian countries. For this reason a comparison of the economic effects of large estates and peasant ownership in the four countries can throw some light on what agrarian reform can be expected to achieve, and how best to achieve it.

Those who believe in the efficiency of large-scale enterprise in agriculture may be inclined to attribute the more rapid rate of economic growth in Hungary to the predominance of the great estates. Yet the texts offer little or no evidence to suggest that they made any positive contribution. The rigidity of the social structure fascinated the English travellers, accustomed to more fluid class distinctions, but to their liberal way of thinking it loomed large as an obstacle to progress.

Before 1848, the barrier between nobles and non-nobles was absolutely fixed: only nobles and clergy could own land; only non-nobles paid taxes. The extraordinary inheritance law of *aviticitas*, abolished in 1848, kept the barrier almost impenetrable; Baron Sina's wealth may have been the exception which proved the rule (H 3, 4, 5, 6, 7, 11). Both above and below the barrier there were gradations in prestige and wealth, with little mobility between them: above, 'gorgeous magnates', the gentry, the poor 'peasant nobles'; below, well-to-do urbarialists, cottagers with small holdings and the mass of the landless. Serf emancipation benefited the half-million urbarial peasants, who in the south-east became owners of farms of substantial size, forming a farming middle class. To the landless serfs, the abolition of the robot brought a brief interval of sunshine in the fifties and sixties, which the former serf recalled as the happier past (H 29). For a time food was plentiful and livestock and poultry could be grazed on the pastures; but with the coming of the railways and the imposition of taxation, the landowners became more grasping, and squeezed out the poorer peasants by depriving them of their rights of grazing by bringing pastures under the plough; at the same time, food grew shorter as the railways opened markets and peasant farms grew smaller as they were subdivided on inheritance. Thus the change in labour conditions resulting from serf emancipation brought no fundamental change in in the strata of the rural social hierarchy, which persisted until 1944–5, though it did change the relationship between rich and poor.

Foreign observers comment on the landowners' extravagance, indolence and indifference to agriculture, and provide no evidence of technical progress, almost precluded, indeed, by the 'Extra Hungariam non est vita' attitude. The view that 'the apathy and wealth of the Hungarian magnates prevent development' is re-iterated at intervals through the century (H 1, 24, 28). Large estates were for the most part worked as large enterprises, managed by an army of agents, stewards and bailiffs, some with technical training in farming, who presumably introduced better livestock breeding and better cultivation; there was also sub-letting to peasants. Possibly the grossly unequal distribution of income from agriculture may to some degree have stimulated investment of large estate profits in the expanding agricultural industries, but since the main source of industrial investment was Austrian and German capital, it cannot be argued that the wealth of the landowners played much part in developing industry. The incentives to investment in better farming and better marketing might well have been greater, if the large estates had been smaller and the peasant farms larger.

Yet though the attitude of the magnates was an obstacle to progress, there were individuals among them who undertook improvements, such as the school of agriculture founded by Count Festetits (H 14). Moreover, it must be remembered that Count Széchenyi was a magnate; only a magnate, indeed, could have laid the foundations for economic development through the reform of the credit system, the big public investment programmes in land reclamation, the regulation of the Danube, and the planning of the railways.

Rumania shows large landownership in a far more unfavourable economic light. The boyars, unlike the Hungarian nobility, were not an exclusive or stable aristocracy; they were merely rich, and in Wallachia absentees as early as the fifties (R 10). Fortunes were squandered quickly; Green, possibly exaggerating, states that 'there is hardly an estate in the country which has been for three generations in one family' (R 21). There was the same broad class division between privileged and under-privileged as in Hungary, but without class loyalty; the barrier was less rigid and could be crossed by climbers into the ranks of the tax-free, created as supplementary nobility by rulers wishing to increase their revenues, and so cheapening rank.[1] These *ciocoi* 'lend themselves to the most disgusting abuses in the exercise of public functions', especially in exacting labour from the serfs, yet they also infiltrated revolutionary ideas (R 9, 10). They evidently embodied the curious mixture of corruption and liberalism that pervaded the Rumanian social climate then and long afterwards.

In the first third of the nineteenth century, the peasants of the Principalities were probably the most wretched in the region. They were certainly far worse off than the Bulgarian peasants under Turkish rule, and probably worse off than the serfs in Hungary, for though serf obligations were lighter, taxation was cruel. Sources otherwise in conflict agree on this evil. Wyburn sees the Wallachian as a robust, well-fed fellow, often beaten up by tax-collectors; Golescu, more sensitive and cognizant, paints a black picture of flight in terror, while Colson, referring to the peasants of Moldavia, says that 'Their hollow eyes, which they dare not raise, proclaim their slavery and absence of well-being' (R 7, 8, 19). Under the

---

[1] The practice has parallels in British history; James I sold baronies for £10,000. See Anthony Sampson, *The Anatomy of Britain*, London, 1962, p. 6.

Organic Statutes, enacted under the Russian occupation in 1831–2, which, like the Austrian urbarial legislation, defined serf rights and duties, the peasant was entitled to receive ten acres of land, and obliged to work for the landowner for twelve days, cart wood and pay tithe; but as Codru Drăgășanu points out, the dues imposed were in practice heavier, and peasants could no longer escape (R 9). Through the Russian occupation one great relief came to the peasants, the reform of the tax system, substituting a single direct poll tax for the many arbitrary exactions; but in the forties the old abuses slipped back again (R 10).

The agrarian reform law of 1864 (R 20), enacted by decree after Prince Cuza had dissolved the hostile assembly of boyars, was the law of serf emancipation, parallel to the laws of 1848 in Austria-Hungary and 1861 in Russia. The law allotted small holdings in freehold ownership to all peasants who had occupied land as serfs under the Organic Regulations and other legislation enacted in the eighteen-fifties, in the same way that serf emancipation in Hungary granted land to the urbarial peasants; but in Rumania the peasants occupying land were a larger proportion of the farm population, so that the effects of the law were wider.[1] The landless cottagers, who in Hungary received no land under the emancipation, were in Rumania to receive farms on the State domains, the enormous monastery estates taken over by the State in 1863. The size of the holdings allocated was to depend on the number of livestock held by the peasant, an interesting reflection of the extent to which the economy was still mainly pastoral. Landowners were guaranteed compensation at the rate of ten times the annual value of the abolished servitudes, two-thirds of which was to be paid by the peasants and one-third by the State from the revenues of the State domains. According to Green (R 21), it was the prospect of raising cash on the bonds that induced the boyars to accept a law so damaging to their interests. But in the event they were not so passive. Cuza was expelled from the country within eighteen months; the law was the cause of his downfall. Thereafter the landowners found ways of evading the application of the law—as they do in under-developed countries today.[2]

The effects of the reform have been much disputed, on the whole with emphasis on its negative results; some Rumanian liberal historians condemn it because it did not give enough land to the peasants and produced 'neoserfdom'; others criticize its failure to produce efficient peasant farming of the West European type (rather

[1] See R 21, pp. 187-8, footnote.
[2] For example, India, Egypt and Syria.

absurdly, since in 1864 this type of farming had not made its appearance, even in Denmark). Both criticisms involve too much hindsight
to be convincing. By comparison with Hungary, the law appears as
a great and genuine manifestation of liberalism, in spite of the injus-
tices in its execution.

It is true that the reform created rather than solved 'the land
question'; it was in fact the first step in the peasants' struggle for
freehold ownership. By the end of the century the greater part of
the land of the large estates was sub-let to the peasants by detested
middlemen. Through ownership of small holdings, growing smaller
with subdivision, and tenancy of small lots on the big estates at
ever-increasing rents, the peasants grew hungry for more land, and
expressed their desire in 1907 with revolutionary violence, as
Caragiale with masterly simplicity explains (R 26). After the First
World War, this desire, in alliance with traditional liberalism,
became the driving force behind the land reform policy of the
National Peasant Party.

Rumania was thus socially more progressive than Hungary, but
economically far more backward. Primitive methods of extensive
grain cultivation prevailed on large estates and peasant farms alike.
No Széchenyi emerged from the ranks of the boyars, just as no Cuza
could have emerged from the ranks of the magnates in Hungary.
Ghica could only deplore the neglect of the land, together with
forest spoliation proof of enduring lack of concern with the economic
future (R 22, 25b). Even though grain production and exports increased rapidly towards the end of the century, there can be no
doubt that the large estates were an obstacle to development.

The same is true of the land system of Bosnia, a special local
variant of the Ottoman system in decay. A precise account of the
way in which *kmet* tenure prevented agricultural progress is included
in the extract quoted from Grünberg, whose views were later
strikingly vindicated by the expansion of arable cultivation which
followed the abolition of the system in 1918 (Y 25).

Did the peasant states fare better in combining social satisfaction
with economic progress? The Serbian experience is interesting,
because the texts quoted show the results of reform over a long
period, by soundings taken at different dates. The law of 1830, a
conscious choice of peasant proprietorship in preference to a new
form of fief tenure, produced an agrarian reform successful from
every angle, because the conditions were ideal. First, peasants were
not encumbered by debt. Second, there was sufficient land for all
to receive adequate holdings. Third, there had been an expanding

market for pigs in Vienna for at least half a century before the reform, so that there was a strong incentive to increase output in the type of farming best suited to the natural and human conditions of the country. The large family households had enough capital in land and livestock to live well in the traditional style, and the supply of family labour was adaptable to the various labour requirements of cattle grazing, arable cultivation, and home industries.

The result was an independent, stable and equal society. At mid-century, an anonymous author (presumably French) stresses its merits; considered as workers, the people of Serbia were undoubtedly better off than the pauperized working class of Western Europe (Y 3). But by the end of the century the standard of comparison has changed. The German-educated author of the survey of Serbian agriculture considers his countrymen as farmers, and so stresses their primitive tools and cropping, the false starts in agricultural education, and the lack of a credit system. The co-operative movement was weak, and depended much on stimulus from outside the peasant class; when the priest or the teacher goes away or dies, the society often dissolves—a comment often found in registrars' reports on co-operative societies in Africa today (Y 4). Altogether, Serbia appears to have been a society without economic dynamism, though politically it was dynamic enough.

Serbia had perhaps been too satisfied with its achievement, and was not providing for the future as its population growth required. Yet in spite of technical backwardness, maize yields were as high as in Hungary. Most certainly the peasant standard of living in Serbia was higher than that of Hungary's dwarf peasants and landless farm workers.

Bulgaria's agrarian reform, like that of Serbia a direct consequence of national independence, was carried out in much less favourable conditions. Most of the Turkish landholdings were purchased immediately after the war by the peasants jointly, and then divided up, usually into very small holdings: these purchases were made by borrowing money or selling livestock, and in consequence the new owners were subsequently burdened by debt (B 13a, 19). The law of 1880 legalized the process by giving share-croppers and farm labourers freehold rights to land which they had cultivated for ten years. The semi-serf tenure still prevalent in Kyustendil gave rise to a special problem, on which the new government, lacking the simple self-confidence of the Serbs, requested expert advice. Many an 'outside expert' in under-developed countries today will appreciate Jireček's exasperation with the government's failure to act on his recommendations; by modern standards, however, they were carried out rather quickly, though the landowners were compensated at an excessively high rate (B 13d).

As in Serbia half a century earlier, there was sufficient land for all claimants to receive a farm, though holdings were mostly small, and in the mountains minute; they were distributed apparently to individual families, since the large family households were in dissolution (B 15). The intensively cultivated special crops of the Maritsa valley were well suited to small-scale farming, though the extensive corn-growing of the Danubian plain was not, and presumably for this reason the government, in a spurt of modernization, imported machinery, with the result of reducing the wages of the migrant harvesters from the mountains (B 13b). Low prices for cereals in world markets in the eighties and poor communications meant that there was less incentive to increase production than there had been in Serbia in the early days after the reform.

On the other hand, because there were these difficulties, both peasants and governments were more alive to the need for better agricultural organization than they were in Serbia. Agricultural credit was better provided, owing to Turkish initiatives in the 1850s, and to the extension of the savings banks after liberation (B 7 and 19). As is evident from extracts B 16 and 17, co-operative partnership among artisans and gardeners was a spontaneous indigenous growth, requiring no state encouragement or outside stimulus; the methods used show an extraordinary combination of hard work and skill with tiny amounts of capital. Perhaps because it had been so banked down under the Turks, enterprise formed these ingenious outlets; perhaps the guild tradition also helped (B 6d). Peasants too proved co-operatively minded and later used agricultural co-operation for credit and marketing as a springboard for agricultural progress; in this respect, Bulgaria was far more dynamic than Serbia.

As to the effect of the land reform on the rural standard of living, the evidence suggests no material change. Three accounts of peasant life in Bulgaria, by Walsh, Barkley and Dicey, in 1829, 1877 and 1894 respectively, are strikingly similar: good home-made clothes, warm and clean though smelly houses, enough food—'rude comfort' is the keynote. Barkley considers that Bulgarian peasants are better off than 'the labouring poor of England and Ireland'. Dicey finds that the Bulgarians are free and happy and have ground to thank the causes that have made them a nation of peasants; the gain in security was immeasurable.

Thus comparison of the four countries shows that the large estates did not promote progress, because the landowners preferred extravagance to investment. The Serbian experience shows that a satisfied peasant society may vegetate on the standard it considers adequate. But the experience of Bulgaria proves that a satisfied peasant society may none the less evolve its own methods of advance, through co-operation, and that this impetus needs to be encouraged by government policy.

So far as the growth of industry is concerned, lack of capital was a general obstacle common to both types of social structure: Széchenyi emphasizes it in Hungary at mid-century, Dicey in Bulgaria at the century's end. But in Hungary lack of capital was of course a direct consequence of the landowners' attitude to investment, since otherwise the size of their incomes would have encouraged capital accumulation, while in Bulgaria the difficulty of mobilizing capital was largely caused by the indebtedness of the peasants incurred through land purchases. Another general obstacle was the stagnation of the internal market. Here the peasant economies, in spite of their high degree of income equality, provided no greater stimulus than the large estate economies, since peasant living standards were frugal and the pattern of consumption highly conventional (B 14, 19).

In no country except Hungary was there any general expansion of industry which quantitatively deserves the name of industrial revolution. By the end of the century, only 66 per cent of the population was occupied in agriculture in Hungary proper (excluding Croatia and Slavonia) as compared with about 80 per cent in the other countries. Hungary had many advantages to counterbalance the celebrated Magyar indolence: coal and iron; after 1867 access to the urban markets of industrialized Austria; a banking system; a high level of education; skilled German workers in its early manufactures; and above all an influx of Austrian and German capital. As the railways and Danube steamships opened up export markets, agricultural processing industries, such as flour mills, distilleries and timber works, were founded in the 1860s and 70s in Hungary proper and Croatia-Slavonia (Y 14, 15). Engineering and textiles were concentrated in Budapest, as were also most of the agricultural processing industries (H 27).

As contrasted with this broad general development, with agricultural industries constituting the 'leading sector' generating further expansion (as in the United States at the same period), there was another type of industrial expansion, extremely one-sided, concentrated on mining and financed by large foreign firms. Austrian capital was invested in the Zenica iron mines in Bosnia; still more

C

important was the investment of German, British, Dutch and Belgian capital in Rumanian oil. The impact of this type of foreign investment resembled that in modern lop-sided economies, such as the Middle East oil-producing states, or the Congo and Rhodesia, where foreign capital investment produces an extraordinarily rapid growth of the national income through the expansion of the most profitable sector, while leaving the rest of the economy backward and short of capital. The mining industries in this region did not give much stimulus to general economic development, for they employed little labour; and since most of the profits were taken out of the country they did not provide a source for further capital investment, as in modern policies for ploughing back profits from the main industry into other sectors.

Domestic industries on the whole followed the standard industrial revolution pattern, though here too there were contrasts. Some suffered from the competition of factory production, as, for example, Slovakian linen and the Slovenian domestic industries, though some of the latter developed into modern factories. The decline of domestic industries was gradual, because the pace of industrialization was slow; such industries were still producing in the 1930s. In all parts of the region peasant crafts were still carried on in conjunction with agriculture and were valuable in providing part-time employment.

In Bulgaria, however, the sudden impact of foreign factory competition produced a crisis. With the achievement of national independence, the previously flourishing and widespread domestic industries lost their protected market and were killed by the competition of foreign imports. Bulgaria had few advantages for industrialization other than its celebrated industriousness; there were no valuable mineral resources, and apart from a little French capital there was not much foreign investment; factory production grew slowly. Independence benefited the peasants more than the middle class (who as merchants had played a much greater role in the economy under the Turks), and made the country more agricultural than it had been in the past (B *Introduction*, 18, 19). To this pattern the obvious modern analogy is India, where domestic industries were destroyed by the competition of British factories in the early nineteenth century, and factory production could not develop, so that the population grew on the land.

Apart from Hungary, what plainly failed to occur in these countries was the *general* rise of a capitalistic class, capable of transforming social attitudes and acting as a dynamic force. Even in Hungary the growth of capitalistic industry did not undermine or rival the power of the landowners. Clearly the pattern of growth was different from that of Western Europe, where trade had been the great solvent of the domainal economy, and townspeople and merchants had taken the side of the peasants against the feudal landowners. In South-Eastern Europe, trade had a directly contrary effect: it benefited the large landowners who exported grain. They benefited also by the indemnities paid for serf emancipation, by the coming of the railways, and by the opening of export markets. Peasants also benefited as agricultural producers by the coming of the railways, though they were injured in so far as their earnings from the carrying trade were wiped out, a result illustrated only for Slovenia (Y 18, 19), though doubtless general. Towards the end of the century grain yields were improving and grain exports from the whole region increased as world prices rose. By 1909–13, annual exports of grain averaged one million tons from Hungary, three million from Rumania, and half a million tons each from Serbia and Bulgaria.

The Late Nineteenth Century

To survey development in the last twenty years of the century we need some standard of comparison. Progress, in contemporary opinion, there undoubtedly had been; it was attested by social equality, even by happiness (Y 3, B 19); by better education, urban sanitation, peasant living standards, and the discipline of the army; or by railways, shipping and oil (R 24, 25). But today these standards seem vague; we are lost without the yardsticks of gross national product or Marxist periods.

It is, however, difficult to fit the history of these countries into the patterns of packaged history which are now in vogue. At first sight, Rostow's pattern, a boldly empirical classification of the stages of growth, seems obviously relevant, since its central principle is the need for abolishing or reforming a traditional society before sustained growth can begin. This traditional society, the starting-point or first stage in economic growth in Rostow's conception, does not exclude economic change, resulting from fluctuations in trade, 'different degrees of political or social turbulence', and so on; but it does exclude development, because owing to the absence of technical innovation the level of productivity remains low. The second stage is marked by the appearance of the preconditions of growth: technical changes raising the levels of productivity in industry and agriculture; new men prepared to mobilize savings, take risks, modernize and invest: an expansion of trade; and 'here and there' the beginnings of modern manufacturing industry. These changes are slow, and come up against 'the habits and institutions, the values and vested interests of the traditional society'. When the forces of modernization make a decisive break-through, expand and come to dominate the society, the economy enters the third and crucial stage, the 'take-off into sustained growth'.[1] During this interval, the rate of investment rises, one or more leading export industries grow rapidly, the national income increases fast, and the proportion of the population in agriculture declines considerably. After the take-off comes the fourth stage, 'the drive to maturity', a long broadening-out of the industrial base from the pioneer industries, which culminates in the fifth stage, 'economic maturity', characterized by a shift of the leading sectors towards consumer durables and services.

This typology of growth is derived from the experience of the advanced countries, but is intended to provide rather more than an historical generalization, since it assumed that all growing economies will pass through these stages. Superficially, at any rate, the conception of the traditional society seems to reflect the situation in South-Eastern Europe in the first half of the nineteenth century, though of course the traditional societies then in existence, being based on serfdom, were much more rigid in their structure than Great Britain, for example, before its eighteenth-century take-off. Uneven spurts characteristic of the 'preconditions stage' can be observed in Hungary, Croatia-Slavonia, Slovenia, after mid-century, though not to the same extent in the rest of the region. Thus the vital questions are whether the reforms carried out in the middle of the century were a condition of economic development, and how far there is evidence of the beginnings of take-off towards the century's end.

On this standard, our four countries make a poor showing. Two, Serbia and Bulgaria, broke with the traditional society as sharply and completely as possible in 1830 and 1878; but found thereby no great impetus to economic growth, though they certainly won satisfaction. Of course it might be said that the two new states jumped the gun, and that national independence did not represent a breakthrough of economic forces making for change so much as an extreme degree of 'political and social turbulence'. Yet national independence *was* preceded by development, in Serbia through the expansion of the pig trade before the rebellion, in Bulgaria by the growth of the domestic industries which prospered the middle class into feeling economically superior to their Turkish masters (Y 2, B 8b). Preconditions of growth certainly existed: to steer a quarter of a million pigs on their long walk to Vienna required the elaborate

---

[1] W. W. Rostow, *The Stages of Growth*, Cambridge, 1960, p. 4. This stage is 'tentatively and approximately' dated between 1783–1802 in Great Britain and 1890–1914 in Russia; in Western Europe, the U.S.A. and Japan, take-off is dated within various periods between these two extremes (p. 36).

commercial organization evolved in Zemun in the eighteenth century (Y 5), while the prosperity of the Bulgarian middle class was rooted in old-established social formations (B 6). At any rate, the two small countries surged forwards from these backgrounds, and broke through; and then, for reasons already discussed, found further growth difficult, although they were carried forward by the expansion of grain exports.

Rumania, on the other hand, came to no such decisive moment, passing flaccidly through a series of events, the freeing of trade, the reform of taxation and the emancipation of the serfs, all of which doubtless might be regarded as preconditions of growth (R 19). But the progress made after independence seems out of all proportion to the extent of social change. Noted in 1888 as outstanding in Europe for the rapid development of its resources and the improvement in its social conditions, Rumania in the first decade of the twentieth century became Europe's second largest oil producer (Russia being the first); and by 1914, when it was exporting about 40 per cent of its grain production, ranked fourth among the world's grain exporters, only a little behind the United States. No national income figures are available for this period, but it is obvious that the rate of growth must have been fast. Yet Rumania can hardly be considered to have entered the take-off stage, since apart from oil there was little industrial development, and four-fifths of the population was still in agriculture. With its rich natural resources, all that was needed for take-off was a more efficient mobilization of internal savings; but, as we have seen, this was prevented on the one hand by the extravagance of the landowners, on the other by the transfer of oil profits outside the country.

As to Hungary, the discrepancy between social change and economic growth is even more striking. Notwithstanding the spending habits of the aristocracy, many of the conditions for take-off were fulfilled. As listed by Rostow, these include: 'the emergence to political power of a group prepared to regard the modernization of the economy as serious, high order political business'—surely an apt description of Széchenyi and his followers; 'the build-up of social overhead capital'—mainly the result of their efforts; and 'a surge of technological development in industry and agriculture'—true of industry, though in agriculture there was only a ripple. Between 1890 and 1914, almost all the features of take-off were displayed; swift expansion of industry, with food processing and engineering as the leading sectors; a higher rate of investment due to the influx of foreign capital; and a considerable reduction of the proportion of the population in agriculture. Between 1899–1901 and 1911–13, national income increased by about 75 per cent, per capita income by about 70 per cent.[1] In this period, if not earlier, it might well be claimed that Hungary did in fact begin its take-off, although there had been nothing which could be described as a break-through of forces making for progress. However, Rostow would not allow Hungary even to sit for the examination, since he asserts that before the First World War 'the Austro-Hungarian Empire was in the early preconditions stage, a rural-based society breaking up'.[2]

While growthmanship thus puts our four countries right out of the picture and understates their progress, the use of the Marxist version of packaged history has the opposite effect: it exaggerates the extent of economic change and blurs the contrasts between the countries. For Marxist doctrine, as currently interpreted in Eastern Europe, feudalism ends at a fixed date, that of serf emancipation, and capitalism clocks in. The effect of this sharp transition from one economic system to another is artificial and mechanical, for, as we have observed, much of the old order remained in Hungary and Rumania, where the emancipation of the serfs turned landowners into capitalistic employers, but not into capitalistic investors. Moreover, the arbitrary fitting of Marxist categories to periods, by analogy with the classical examples of Britain and Germany, leaves a sense of omission, since it fails to explain why capitalism did not bring about a similarly rapid expansion of industry. The impression left by Marxist history textbooks is that of faint carbon copies of the Western European pattern of development. That the pattern *was* different is implicitly recognized by Marxist historians when they call the large estate régimes 'feudal-capitalism', by the hyphen wiping out the bourgeois revolution and substituting a more indefinite class struggle for that of the proletariat. So the Marxist packages, like the five stages of growth, tend to burst at the seams when the history of this region is crammed into them. Nevertheless, the Marxist interpretation has the merit of underlining the importance of serfdom, as classless growthmanship cannot, and helps to explain why peasant discontent should have come out into the open in the prosperous first decade of the twentieth century.

[1] Friedrich Hertz, *The Economic Problem of the Danubian States*, London, 1947, p. 41.
[2] *Ibid.*, p. 118. This verdict is not in itself surprising, since Austria's case, like that of Hungary, does not fit into the typical sequence of stages; the rate of growth of national income before 1914 cannot be explained if it is assumed that modernization must dominate before sustained growth can begin. What is puzzling, however, is that Russia is judged to have completed take-off by 1914, while Austria-Hungary is not considered even to have begun it by that date, although on most indices Austria-Hungary was much more advanced than Russia, in spite of Vienna's misleading pre-economic charm.

Since the typologies of economic growth derived from the history of the advanced countries are at best a clumsy fit when applied to this region, must it be concluded that these four states in the late nineteenth century were really under-developed countries, in the same sense that the 'Third World' of today is under-developed? The 'Third World' is vastly heterogeneous, a conglomeration rather than a concept; the condition of under-development can be defined only in the most general terms, mostly negative. The under-developed countries are those which have not undergone an industrial revolution; where levels of productivity in agriculture are low; and where the expansion of trade does not raise the rural standard of living or weaken the power of the landowners, so that the question of agrarian reform is of central importance. For this reason, as we have seen, the agrarian history of South-Eastern Europe can be relevant to modern land reform problems, and since there is this broad similarity, it is not surprising that in the modern world it is possible to find analogies to illustrate one facet or another of the past history of South-Eastern Europe.

But of course it would be wrong to suppose, on the basis of such partial analogies, that these small European states, the actual living organisms which came to independence during the nineteenth century, were really like the *societies* emerging in our own time. On one fundamental point, there is no parallel whatsoever. Their peasants were not poor, as peasants in under-developed countries today are poor. A hundred years ago there was not the enormous gulf between their standards of living and those of the more advanced countries that there is between the standards of rich and poor countries today. Foreigners might well think that Balkan peasants were better off than the pauperized working class in Western Europe or 'the labouring poor of England and Ireland', for it should not be forgotten that England at the time of its 'technical maturity' (1850) was an ugly sight. By the nineteen-thirties, of course, as compared with the highly productive peasant farmers of Western Europe, the peasants of Eastern Europe certainly seemed poor and primitive—yet in retrospect their standard of living seems almost luxurious, if compared with that of villages in the present-day Middle East.

Another fundamental difference lies in their economic setting. In the late nineteenth century the world economy was expanding, offering wider markets for grain and meat, capital on easy terms, and jobs in North America, so that production could grow without planning. In the nineteen-sixties, when prices of primary produce tend to fall, capital is hard to get and migration is blocked,

development has to be tackled mainly through national policies—
and is infinitely more difficult.

Then, as now, national independence was the first great desideran-
dum. It meant European statehood, not a seat in the United
Nations; the framework was different, the gain in status the same.
The political form was more definite; parliamentary democracy was
adopted as obligatory, embodying ideals of social equality and justice, and it was not until the inter-war years that dictatorship
became the rule.

The Emerging Societies

As to the kind of societies these were, the purpose of this collection
is to allow the reader to judge, through minds which are both channels and reflectors. In judging, it must be remembered that they
were very old societies, European to the core of their culture,
returning to a civilization which in spirit they had never left. The
opinion-makers, preoccupied with the future, are worth reading for
their factual and frank recognition of backwardness. Yet it seems
clear that economic development was not desired as an end in itself;
if Geshov, for example, takes a touching pride in the achievements
of the migrant market-gardeners, it is not really on account of their
contribution to the gross national product. Prestige attached to the
past, because under the alien dust-sheet the peoples had conserved
traditions in religion, language and legend. Some fossilized institutions, such as Hungary's incapsulated medieval social structure, had
also been conserved through the centuries. Scholars dwelt lovingly
(and tediously) on the imagined beauties of the zadruga, because
they believed it to be peculiar to the Southern Slavs. On this survival, readers may like to compare different angles (in Y 1b, 7, 13,
B 15, a, b); the anthropologist will appreciate Jireček's comment
that 'people did not like talking about it'. Peasant life, the micro-
culture with do-it-yourself values, can also be observed from different angles, comparing Illyés with Caragiale, or Vuk Karadžić,
the insider, with the outside views of priggish Germans, sensible
British and emotional French.

Modern governments in under-developed countries are, on the
whole, more aware of the need for development, less inclined to
cherish the past. Following the example of the revolutionaries of
1789, they often describe their land reform policies as 'the abolition
of feudalism'. The phrase, though ambiguous, has value; it concen-
trates the intention of creating a freer and more equal society. Yet
lamentably little has so far been achieved; two or three countries
excepted, within the last decade there has been almost no progress

in land reform. It would be hard to find any country, which, like Serbia and Bulgaria, has thrown off foreign rule and landlordism at the same moment. The liberal ideas behind serf emancipation have almost lost their power. Agrarian unrest there is in plenty, no genuine peasant risings. In recent years the peasants have not been a revolutionary force, though promises of reform may secure their support; nor does the urban middle or working class identify itself with the efforts of governments to reform the land system from above. Time is not on the peasants' side, as it was in South-Eastern Europe during the nineteenth century.

From this standpoint, the most interesting outcome of these comparisons between the four countries is to show how great a role the peasants played in history. Often they are believed to be no more than passive spectators, strong only in the continuity of endurance, as Alun Lewis wrote:

> Across scorched hills and trampled crops
> The soldiers straggle by.
> History staggers in their wake.
> The peasants watch them die.

On a certain kind of history, particularly that usually associated with 'the Eastern Question', that is fair comment. But looking below the surface, it seems that the peasants' own actions helped to attain the kind of society they desired. There was nothing primitive in the institution of peasant ownership. On the contrary, its evolution was the result of many influences: the reform policies of the Austrian enlightenment, the liberal and revolutionary ideas of the nineteenth century, as well as peasant risings.

Today in the under-developed countries the peasants' desire for ownership is no less strong. Yet modern governments aiming at land reform are inclined to regard it as out-dated, and seek to clothe their policies in more modern dress, perhaps because economic development has become fashionable as an end in itself, or because they seek guidance from 'experts' rather than from their own people. If the past experience of this region of Europe has a lesson to teach, it is simply that economic development is a long slow process, much impeded by large landownership, and not easy for peasant economies, which need help to create their own institutions to encourage investment and education. Because the process is difficult and slow, that is all the more reason why people should in the meantime achieve a quality of life which fulfils their aspirations.

Hungary

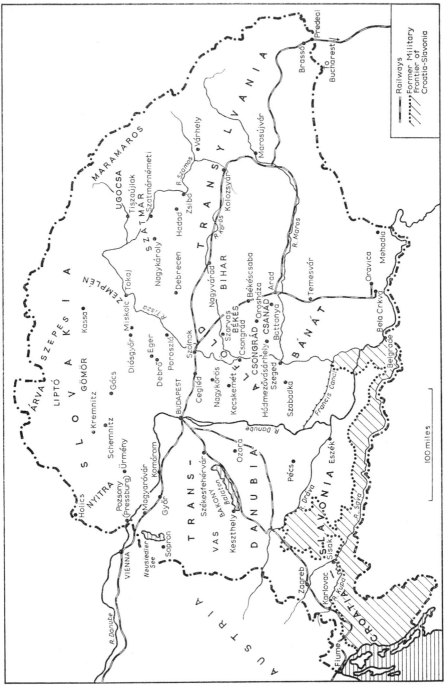

Map 2. Hungary in 1900.

Hungary : Introduction

G. F. CUSHING

THE nineteenth century was one of the most exciting periods of Hungarian history. Politically, Hungary forced her way from stagnation through violent national revolution to partnership, however uneasy, with Austria. Immense progress was made in the cultural field, where the development of the national language was closely bound to political advance. Industry and trade, which had been largely confined to the fulfilment of local needs in 1800 and suffered severely from Austria's tariff policy throughout the first half of the century, suddenly made rapid progress after the *Ausgleich* of 1867; it is noteworthy that half of the rolling-stock required for the Piccadilly tube in London at its inauguration in 1906 was manufactured in Hungary. Yet agriculture has always been the basis of the Hungarian economy, and here the story is a gloomy one, of brilliant suggestions spasmodically applied or ignored completely, chiefly because they also affected the rigid social structure of the country.

The clear division between noble and non-noble vitiated all attempts at reform. 'Outside Hungary there is no life; if there is, it's not like life here'[1] aptly expresses the general attitude of the nobility. Their self-satisfaction and indolence were deep-rooted. They were 'the Hungarian nation'; they managed the country without paying taxes, although they were required to rise in her defence (as they did for the last time, somewhat half-heartedly, against Napoleon in 1809). They were virtually above the law, which in any case they administered. They could, and did, amass large debts with impunity. As long as the lands they owned provided them with sufficient income, they were not interested in their improvement. It was the non-nobles who carried all the burdens of tax, tithes, feudal dues and services. They maintained the roads and provided transport as well as working the land they could not possess, and had little chance of obtaining redress for their grievances against their all-powerful overlords. 'There's no sadder creature than the peasant, for his miseries

---

[1] Extra Hungariam non est vita; si est vita, non est ita.

are greater than the sea'[1] runs the refrain of a Hungarian folk-song.

This division had its origin far back in history. It was enshrined in the code known as the *Tripartitum* of István Werbőczy, published in 1517, a mere three years after the savage suppression of György Dózsa's peasant revolt and consequently full of punitive clauses. By its provisions, the peasant was bound to the land and subjected absolutely to the whims of his landlord. Although various attempts were made to alleviate his lot, it was not until 1767 that Maria Theresa, doubtless prompted by the succession of peasant risings during her reign, published her *Urbarium*, which placed limits on the feudal services that could legally be required of him. She also decreed that peasant-occupied land might not be added by the land-lord to his own holding. The *Urbarium* was issued without the ap-proval of the Diet or of the nobility, whose attitude was well ex-pressed in a poetic epistle written by an apostle of enlightenment:[2]

I remember how, when the *Urbarium* was published,
As we danced in your house, we wept over the fall of our land.

The immediate effect was to curb the rapacity of those landlords whose estates were near enough to Vienna for their serfs' complaints to be heard there. Custom, however, has always been stronger than the letter of the law in Hungary and in much of the country little change was felt. Yet by defining the rights and obligations of the serfs and by fixing the area of peasant land, the *Urbarium* paved the way for the reforms of the nineteenth century. Moreover travellers were quick to note the difference between Hungary and Transyl-vania, which was not included in the *Urbarium*, and where the plight of the peasants was far worse.[3] A wide-scale revolt there in 1784, followed by risings in Hungary, prompted new decrees by Joseph II in the following year. They were largely ineffectual, owing to the determined opposition of the nobility. When the majority of his measures were repealed (though with the exception of these peasant-decrees) on his death in 1790, a further revolt in north-east Hungary provoked anxious deliberations in the Hungarian Diet, then meeting for the first time since 1764. The Diet finally agreed on a com-promise which included provisions from both the *Urbarium* and Joseph II's decrees, and set up a commission to work out further reforms. Here again the new dispensation was hailed as a triumph

[1] Nincs boldogtalanabb a parasztembernél,
   Mert nyomorúsága nagyobb a tengernél!
[2] Ábrahám Barcsay, *Két nagyságos elme költeményes szüleményei*, Pozsony, 1789, vol. ii, p. 232.
[3] See Paget's account, p. 54 below.

of common sense over privilege, and once more the general situation remained unchanged, for the new king, Francis I, was opposed to all reforms. Nevertheless, the existence of a serious social problem had been acknowledged in the highest court of the country, and from this time until the emancipation laws of 1848 the claims of the non-nobles were put forward by political reformers and writers. Hungarian literature, indeed, played a very important role in plans for reform; enlightenment from France and Germany brought increasing awareness of the backward state of Hungary and the necessity of improving the lot of the peasant. Acknowledgement that literature was not for the privileged only came as early as 1825.[1]

There were distinctions within the two main social groups. The nobility included both the wealthiest magnates in the land and 'sandalled noblemen', who were often as poor as the peasants they scorned, but clung grimly to their privileges.[2] The peasants consisted of both landed and landless serfs; these latter outnumbered the landed peasantry, yet were consistently forgotten in all legislation, including the emancipation laws of 1848, which mark a turning-point in the history of the country.

Trade and industry before 1848 were undeveloped. 'Austria regards us as a sponge which she squeezes when necessary', wrote Gergely Berzeviczy in the eighteenth century. Hungary supplied the raw materials for Austria to make up, and any attempts to enter the Austrian market with manufactured goods were frustrated by high tariffs. Thus only local requirements were met by such industries as the cloth-factory established by Count Forgách at Gács in Upper Hungary (Slovakia). Communications were poor. The Danube was extremely dangerous until systematic clearing of the main stream was undertaken in the nineteenth century, and even with the introduction of steamboats, the journey from Vienna to the Black Sea was full of hazards.

Comment on the economic and social life of Hungary during this period can be found chiefly among foreign writers, although some Hungarians had discovered that life outside Hungary was indeed very different from that to which they were accustomed. Such was the eighteenth-century priest, Sámuel Tessedik, who founded an agricultural academy at Szarvas on the Great Plain and toiled hard until he despaired of overcoming the ignorance of the peasants and the indifference of the nobility. Gergely Berzeviczy, his contemporary, wrote of local problems in Slovakia. Others, like Pál Magda

---

[1] József Bajza, the critic, insisted that 'Literature is an eternal republic' (letter to Ferenc Toldy, 1825).
[2] See p. 58 below.

and Demian, incorporated the findings of these earlier writers in
their geographical textbooks. None of these, however, achieved
recognition in their day. Not until the appearance of three works by
Count István Széchenyi[1] was national interest aroused. Széchenyi
possessed both wealth and an honoured name which forced attention; he not only wrote, but instigated schemes for improvement of
communications, the introduction of steam power and the regulation
of the rivers Danube and Tisza. He was responsible for the first
permanent bridge over the Danube between Buda and Pest, and
struck at the roots of privilege by insisting that all who used it were
to be liable to tolls. No other Hungarian succeeded in accomplishing
so much for the economic progress of his country; his aphorism
'many think that Hungary has been; I like to believe that she will
be'[2] expressed his firm belief in her future at a time when romantic
pessimism was more general than hope for the future.

Other problems faced these early writers. Ferenc Kölcsey, the
poet, critic and politician, complained of the utter unreliability of
official statistics. In his account of the taxpayers of his own county
of Szatmár, he remarks on the wild differences in three calculations
of the area he administered.[3] All figures, whether of population,
land-measurement or weight, varied according to the purpose for
which they were required, and where the interests of landlord and
peasant clashed, it was not uncommon for deliberate mismeasure-
ment to occur.

The accounts of foreign travellers provide the most interesting
observations on life in Hungary before 1848. During the eighteenth
century Hungary had become a land of dark mystery, from which
intending visitors were repelled by the fearful accounts of savagery
emanating from Vienna. German travellers, with few exceptions,
liked to stress the odd and oriental aspects of Hungarian life; their
views were heavily coloured by political considerations. The French
did not 'discover' Hungary until later in the century, although certain specialists visited the country for specific studies. It is the British
who provide some of the most valuable information at this time, a
claim borne out by modern Hungarian historians who quote their
views extensively. They also had an early reputation in Hungary for
accuracy; a reviewer, commenting on an indifferent account of
Hungary in German, ostensibly by an anonymous Englishman,
remarks that the author was undoubtedly masquerading as British,

---

[1] *Hitel* (Credit), 1830; *Világ* (Light), 1831; *Stadium*, 1833.
[2] Sokan azt gondolják: 'Magyarország—volt; —én azt szeretem hinni: lesz'
(*Hitel*, p. 270).
[3] They varied from 86 to 110 square miles.

but that his work was not worthy of that name. Their importance was often grossly exaggerated by Hungarians and foreigners alike, who saw them as emissaries of the British government. Friedrich List, the German economist, wrote: 'Wherever there is a full wool-sack to be traded for a case of manufactured goods, there John Bull sends his apostles, who then write books . . . in which they place the native government in the shade, make laughable and despicable objects of the Germans, and praise the happiness of a trade connection with England.'

Of the English travellers, the irritable Townson was a mineralogist and Bright a medical doctor. Paget, whose two volumes on Hungary and Transylvania remain one of the best sources of information, married and settled in Transylvania, though after the appearance of his work. Miss Pardoe adds the interest of a woman's viewpoint; she was impressionable, and adopted the views of her mentor, Gábor Döbrentei, one of the less reputable literary characters of the age, but her pictures of country life are unusually vivid. All these travellers needed interpreters, yet they complete the picture of Hungarian life in a way which no official statistics or even native authors can surpass. The lack of communication between Britain and Hungary at this period, and consequent ignorance of her institutions, may well have prompted the careful observations found in these works. The visitors are generally pleased with what they see; most of them, on discovering that many of the tales they had heard in Vienna were false, tend to be anti-Austrian like their hosts.

1848 was the turning-point in the history of the country. The attempt to seize political independence failed, but the laws emancipating the serfs and altering the conditions of land-inheritance remained. It is ironic that these were enforced by decree in 1853, at the height of the absolutistic régime imposed by Austria. The emancipation laws, as already noted, applied to less than half of the serfs, and these, some 550,000 of them, received for the most part holdings so small that they were often compelled to go back to the large estates to work as before. Moreover, with the development of the railway system and high corn prices, the large estates began to become very profitable holdings. The new landowners, whose only experience had been in local markets, could not hope to compete with them, even if the necessary capital had been available. When steam power was widely adopted on large farms, the demand for labour fell; add to this some years of disastrous harvests and finally the arrival of cheap corn from America, and the extent of damage to the small, ill-equipped peasant farms can be imagined. Nor did the large estates escape; ignorance and indolence were still

D

widespread among the nobility. They were satisfied as long as they could obtain high prices for their produce, but when faced with severe competition they were at a loss. Agricultural studies had never flourished; only 1,534 students had passed through the agricultural academy of Magyaróvár in 37 years, and most of these were employed as farm bailiffs, and were not, as might have been the case, the sons of the landowners. 'The land remained as before,' writes Gyula Szekfű, 'handled in an old-fashioned, patriarchal manner, while the pleasures of the gentry were increased by better communications with the west, which brought greater luxury to their country houses.'[1]

Once again there were insurrections, some of them supported by the new agrarian socialist movements which were especially strong in the Great Plain, and once again belated remedies were applied in the form of insurance plans, co-operatives, seed-distribution and promises of protected wages. But now there were ways of escape from the land, first to industry, whose swift development required increased labour, and secondly to America. The emigration figures, rising from 16,014 in 1882 to 114,847 in 1900 and 206,011 in 1903, tell their own story, particularly when the relatively sparse distribution of population is taken into account.

A much brighter picture emerges from the development of industry, particularly after the *Ausgleich* of 1867, which made credit available in the country, and ensured stable political conditions to attract foreign capital. At first this came mainly from Austria, the Creditanstalt of the Rothschilds financing the largest transport enterprises, collieries and ironworks. After the financial crisis of 1873, however, German investments in Hungary grew rapidly, and an ever-increasing number of German firms opened branches there, completely eclipsing other foreign ventures. By 1904, for example, ten times as many preference shares in the Hungarian railway network were held by Germans as by Austrian investors. Pest, already the largest commercial centre in Hungary, became the largest industrial city, whose population (together with the twin city of Buda) rose from 271,000 in 1869 to 717,000 in 1900. Not only agricultural equipment, but iron and steel goods and heavy machinery began to be manufactured in Hungary, to which a large number of foreign firms was attracted. There were many problems to be overcome, and in many respects Hungarian industry was primitive, for example in the use of lignite for smelting, when other countries had long turned to coke. In 1898 almost half of the industrial output was concerned with food products and milling.

[1] *Magyar Történet* (History of Hungary), Budapest, 1933, vol. vii, pp. 339-40.

It is notable that the second half of the century, with its improved communications, saw the arrival of more superficial visitors to Hungary. She was less interesting than in the time when she was virtually cut off. The Hungarians themselves began to publish information for distribution abroad, and willingly arranged tours to visit the best model estates and institutions, which were indeed very good but not typical of the country as a whole. A statistical office was set up in Budapest in 1869, and figures regularly published on economic aspects. Some foreigners, however, penetrated into the country and maintained individual views; among these Patterson and the extreme anti-Hungarian Paton are outstanding, while the comments of de Gubernatis and Recouly might well have been written at a much earlier period.

The extracts which follow have been limited to certain aspects of Hungarian economic and social history, and naturally concentrate on the social problem which still remained as a hindrance to development at the end of the nineteenth century. That there was a less gloomy side to life can be seen in the account by Beudant of a visit to Keszthely, in the report on education by Eötvös, and most surprisingly in the reminiscences of one of the 'forgotten' landless serfs. How much more exciting the history of Hungary might have been had the ideas of the reformers been carried out!

I. Hungary before 1848

1. APATHY AND WEALTH

Marcel de Serres, *Voyage en Autriche*, Paris, 1814, vol. iii, p. 262.

ALTHOUGH Hungary is a fertile country, the inhabitants have no idea how to extract the riches of the soil that is theirs to cultivate. Ignorant and superstitious, the Hungarians are bad agriculturalists and equally little attracted to trade. Moreover, despite the great extent of Hungary, she has only some 7,224,207 inhabitants, an average of only 1,887 per square mile.

The lack of progress in Hungarian agriculture must be ascribed to a number of causes which also prevent the increase of the population. Thus the proportion of grazing land is far too great in relation to the cultivated fields because the Hungarians, naturally indolent, prefer pastoral to agricultural life. Again, animals provide excellent food for the country-dweller, but cannot support a large population. It must be confessed that the Hungarian peasants, receiving none of the benefits of landownership, show little interest in improving agriculture, since they would gain no advantage from it. Almost all the land in Hungary belongs to the clergy or the nobility, and the peasants are scarcely even allowed to lease it. This province will never make any effective progress until the peasants have the right to possess the land. The apathy and wealth of the Hungarian magnates also prevent development. Content with their huge estates, they make virtually no efforts at all to improve them. But it must be admitted that as a result of ideas now in vogue in Austria, some landed proprietors in Hungary have recently begun to interest themselves in agriculture.

Marcel de Serres (1783–1862), French, judicial and administrative officer in Illyria and Dalmatia, wrote his book as a guide for the French governors of the regions of Austria occupied by Napoleon's troops. It is based on wide research.

2. A Typical Large Estate

Sándor Újfalvy, *Emlékiratok* (Memoirs), MS of 1854–5, ed. Z. Jékely, Buda-pest, 1955, pp. 64–6.

(The author describes the estate of Baron Miklós Wesselényi the elder as it was on his death in 1809.)

The estate was in a very poor condition when it was passed to Wesselényi's widow and son. Apart from a large stud-farm, nothing was properly equipped; even the horses brought in the least possible income owing to the way in which the stud was handled. Dealers could only visit the stud as an exception, and they came very rarely, for the price of a horse to one would be a sack of thalers and to another a bushel of gold. The proper price of a good mount would be pushed up from 10,000 forints to 50,000 forints. So it was usually old age or sickness, and only very infrequently horse-dealers, that carried off the horses at Zsibó. And even when a sale or two had been completed, Wesselényi would be upset and bad-tempered. He would regret his action for weeks afterwards and become thoroughly annoyed with himself, for he thought it a terrible weakness to part with such a noble animal, however high the price.

Yet the stud grew despite the lack of attention given to it, although it was a waste, and brought in no profit. In 1816 disease reduced it from 350 to 50, and the young Wesselényi had to build it up again. This he did in 1822, when he brought thoroughbreds from England.

The most productive parts of the Zsibó estate were overrun with scrub, watery thickets and useless willow-groves. It was, however, a mortal sin to touch these, because a few pheasants happened to roost among them. The state of the ploughlands and hayfields was beneath all criticism. They never saw manure, of which huge dumps, sixty to eighty years old, stood in various places around the castle. For decades not a single cartload had been removed.

There were very few cattle, sheep, pigs and bees, and even these had been acquired through taking over serf-holdings which reverted to the owner after the family had died out, or through the usual tithes paid by the serfs. As they had been acquired, so were they treated and gradually wasted away. In any case, the estate could not possibly flourish when there was never any permanent and expert farm-manager. None of those who came could put up with the exceptionally heavy burdens and troubles of service there for even a year at a time. The serfs, whose daily treatment was severe enough, were ordered away from the most urgent summer work to go hunting, and in this way they performed their statutory labour, while the vines and maize remained untended, and the wheat and grass went to waste. True, an occasional farm-manager would take precautions to have the maize-fields scythed at the edges by the road where the master liked to drive or ride, but within the fields the crops were stifled by weeds, the manager knowing full well that by the time they were fully ripe he would no longer be in service there.

The house and garden were similarly treated. The baroness normally kept the keys of the granary and cellar, but never visited either. So the experienced and trusted major-domo made full use of his opportunities; the worst corn went to his mistress, and he kept the best for himself. The fine old wines in the cellar became undrinkable. The baroness kept the seal for the barrels, and the major-domo merely kept away from them when he did not fancy them. The pantry was usually empty; the man in charge of the pigs preferred to fatten his purse and allowed very little of the rich lard to reach the house. Thus more money was demanded for food—in fact it was doubly paid for. Yet the late Wesselényi, a very generous man, would order a barrel or two of wine or a cartload of corn or straw for this person or that, when his own granary, cellar and pantry were completely empty. Moreover his orders had to be carried out, because in his vocabulary the words 'There isn't any' and 'It can't be done' did not exist.

Sándor Újfalvy (1792–1866), Transylvanian landowner, gives a vivid picture in his Memoirs of the great reformers and the problems they had to face. He was particularly friendly with the 'great Wesselényi', Széchenyi's companion, who inherited this estate.

3. Classes at the End of the Eighteenth Century

J. A. Demian, *Statistische Darstellung des Königreichs Ungarn* (Statistical Description of the Kingdom of Hungary), Vienna, 1805–6, vol. i, pp. 84–6.

(a) The Nobility

In the kingdom of Hungary the nobility are partly Slav and partly Hungarian in origin. The family names show this distinction clearly. This class comprises counts, barons, landowners of noble rank (*nobiles donatarii*) and those who have been granted patents of nobility (*nobiles armalistae*). In law the clergy also belong to the Hungarian nobility. This kingdom contains the largest proportion of nobles in all the lands of the Emperor of Austria. In 1785, according to the census of Joseph II, the secular nobles numbered 162,947 males. Now if the number of females of noble rank is estimated to be the same, the total Hungarian nobility (including those of Croatia and Slavonia also) is 325,894, which means that in the whole of Hungary there is one nobleman to every 21½ of the population.

(b) The Burghers

According to Schwartner, in[1] the year 1796 the population of the 48 royal boroughs (including those of Croatia and Slavonia) was 366,000.

(c) Privileged Settlers

The Jazygians and the Cumanians[2] come between the nobles and the peasants. There are 42,357 of the former, while the Cumanians number 38,326.

(d) The Peasants

This category includes all the inhabitants of the lowlands who are not numbered among the nobility, students or military. The census of Joseph II shows a total of 509,823 landed serfs and 788,993 classed as landless, servants, etc. Together they number 1,298,816. In his *Statistik*, Schwartner estimates the total of peasants engaged in agriculture in the strictest sense of the word at 451,052, of whom 217,018 occupied a whole session of land belonging to the king, the clergy or the nobility.

For biographical note see p. 324 below.

4. THE URBARIUM

Robert Townson, *Travels in Hungary in the year 1793*, London, 1797, p. 108; pp. 131–6.

THE Empress Theresa in 1764[3] made known her *Urbarium*; which, though published without the knowledge of the states, has been received as law. Nevertheless, Seventeen Hundred and Sixty-four must be considered as forming an epoch in the history of the

---

[1] Martin Schwartner (1759–1823), statistician and from 1788 librarian of the University of Pest. His *Statistik des Königreichs Ungarn* (1798) was widely used by nineteenth-century writers.

[2] The Jazygians (Jászok) and Cumanians (Kunok) were early non-Magyar settlers, who still retained special privileges and vestiges of their original tribal organization. They inhabited the north-west of the Great Plain.

[3] The correct date is 1767.

amelioration of the state of the peasants, not only by more accurately fixing the reciprocal obligations of the lord and his peasants, but by shewing that the latter were thought worthy of the protection of government.

By this ordinance the reciprocal rights of the peasants and their landlords are determined, and it appears, that the Hungarian peasant pays to his lord, for twenty-five acres of arable land (each containing about twelve hundred square fathoms), and twelve days mowing of meadow land, a ninth of the produce of the soil, of the lambs, kids and bees, and about one hundred and eleven days labour, two shillings for rent, and three shillings for fowls, butter, etc.

This I conceive to be no hard contract for the peasant. I have been informed by several great landed proprietors, that they did not receive upon an average, taking all their dues together, more than equal to a gulden,[1] or about two shillings English, for an acre. The hardship lies chiefly in the nature of the contract: this is a reciprocal hardship, as inconvenient for the landlord as for the peasant. It chiefly arises from receiving labour for payment; yet this kind of payment is always used in similar cases, in the first stages of improvement. This compels the landlord to keep a great part of his lands in his own hands, to employ the labour of the peasants, however he may dislike rural economy. The law must entrust him, as I have lately said, with great authority over his peasants. He requires a great many stewards, bailiffs, and overseers to assist him, and to these he must delegate a part of his authority over them. From hence arise complaints from them, on the hardship of their fate, and of the severity of their masters; and from these no less complaints of the perverse, obstinate, idle and discontented disposition of their peasants; who by not being interested in the labour they perform for their lords, first are slothful in the performance of this, and then through custom become slothful in their own: and thus a bad state of husbandry pervades the lands.

The right of the peasantry to leave their landlords, did manufactures and the industry of towns flourish in this kingdom, would be sufficient soon to make them find their just value in society, and get rid of unreasonable humiliations: though indeed peasants are little inclined to change their occupations, and they often remain cultivators of the soil on which they are bred under many hardships, rather than become mechanics; and a peasant who should leave the estate on which he was born, and should apply to another landlord, would meet but with little encouragement; and as a certificate must first be obtained from his last landlord, some hindrances can still be

[1] See Note on Weights, Measures and Currency, p. 112.

thrown in the way of those who wish to better their lot. —Such then is the connection between the peasantry and their landlords.

To the public, of which the peasantry here forms no part, they have obligations likewise; for, the great aristocratic body being as I lately said exempt from bearing any part of the public burthens, these naturally fall upon the citizens and peasants, who are emphatically styled in the public acts the *misera contribuens plebs*.

These pay a tax which is called a *contribution*, part into the military chest, and part into the county chest, or *cassa domestica*; from the first, the military stationed in the province are paid, and from the latter, the expences of the government of the county, the repairs of the roads and bridges, and the damages sustained by the peasants by fire, storms, and inundations; and likewise the expences of the deputies or representatives of the county, that is, *of the nobility*, when attending the Diets. It is assessed on the ability and opulence of the peasants, in the following manner:

	Deca[1]
The peasant is valued at	1
His 2 Sons capable of working	1
4 Daughters ditto	1
4 Farming Servants, men	1
8 Ditto ditto, women	1
2 Draught or fat oxen	1
2 Milk cows	1
4 Horses	1
4 Young oxen	1
8 Calves	1
16 Hogs	1
32 Young pigs	1
Winter corn, of a whole farm	2
Summer, ditto, ditto	2
Meadows producing six *fuders*[2] of hay	2
A still	1

Sheep and bees according to the profit arising from them.

If the peasant is besides a shoemaker, tailor, weaver, smith, etc., this makes an additional deca. What is paid for a deca I am at present not able to inform my readers; but I hope to do so in an Appendix.[3] That part paid into the *cassa domestica* must vary, according to the expences of the county.

Robert Townson, British traveller, had studied medicine at Göttingen, but was chiefly interested in geology. His book, written after five months' travel in Hungary, contains much acid, but refreshingly realistic comment.

[1] See Note on the System of Taxation before 1848, p. 113.
[2] See Note on Weights, Measures and Currency, p. 112.
[3] There is no trace of this.

5. RIGHTS AND DUTIES OF THE PEASANTS

Pál Magda, *Magyarországnak és a határőrző vidékinek legújabb statisztikai és geographiai leírása* (The Latest Statistical and Geographical Description of Hungary and the Military Frontiers), Pest, n.d. (1819), pp. 153–8.

ACCORDING to the census of 1805, there were 1,426,579 peasant families in Hungary, or rather more than 7,000,000 peasants. This great multitude, excluding children, works in order that the land owned by 70,000 noble families may flourish and bear fruit, that it may enrich its owners and feed the labourers. Although these seven million are indeed conscious of the burden of their status and are made to feel their inferiority, their lot is no longer so miserable as it was of old. For we read in Article 26 of Ferdinand I's decree of 1547:

> The avenging wrath of the Lord has clearly been shown in both early and later ages upon nations which have sinned grievously. Nothing appears to have harmed Hungary more than the oppression of the serfs, whose cries of woe have justly ascended into the presence of God. Wherefore at the request of their king, the Estates of the Realm resolve that the liberty of the oppressed and wretched serfs, taken from them in recent years for whatever reason, be restored to them.

In other words, the peasant depended entirely upon the whims of his landlord, whose attitude was by no means always merciful and humane. The peasant was an unavoidable necessity to the nobleman unless he himself wished to follow the plough, yet the nobleman did not even think of making a contract with him. So the peasant, who neither knew nor felt his human dignity or his natural rights, was driven by humility, necessity, custom, law and other circumstances to abase himself and to give himself as a chattel to his lord, who at least preserved him from starvation. 'The duties of the peasants were defined neither in a common contract nor in writing, but depended upon the will of the lord and upon custom.'[1]

Times have changed. The lot of the Hungarian peasant has been eased partly by the Urbarium and partly by the spread of humanity through enlightenment, though even now it is impossible to deny the truth expressed by the humane author Berzeviczy, himself a nobleman and landlord, when he writes, 'A savage master has at hand a thousand means of oppressing his subjects.'

---

[1] Gergely Berzeviczy, *De conditione et indole rusticorum Hungariae*, [*recte in Hungaria*], 1807 (*Author*).

Although Maria Theresa caused the Urbarium of 1767 and 1773 to be introduced in very many places by her commissioners, and although the noble orders agreed to these provisions at the Diets of 1791 and 1792, thus greatly improving the state of the peasantry, there are still very great differences in the rights and duties of the peasants in various parts of the country. For having regard to the size of the population and to other circumstances, in some places a peasant to whom one whole plot of land is due receives only 16 *hold*[1] of ploughland, while in others he is given 40, and in Békés county 50. So the condition of the peasant who works to produce oats on 40 *hold* of poor rocky soil in Árva county must differ greatly from that of his fellow-countryman who reaps the best wheat from 50 *hold* on the fertile plains of Békés. It should also be noted that the *hold* itself varies in size from 1,200 to 1,300 or even more square *öl*[1] in different places. Moreover in some areas the pasture is plentiful and good, while in others it is scanty and poor; in one place there are many trees, in others few. Finally the amount of services to be rendered by the serfs to their lords is regulated in one place by the Urbarium, and in another merely by the wishes of the lord; thus some peasants carry a tolerable burden, while others are very greatly oppressed. Nowhere, however, do the peasants still wear the chains of slavery.

The Rights of the Hungarian Peasants

1. The peasant who is deemed to possess one whole plot has 1 *hold* where he lives and apart from this has at least 16 *hold* under cultivation (up to 40 *hold* in some areas, and 50 in Békés), and from 6 to 22 *hold* of grassland. The landless serf has no land outside his own plot, and very many have not even this.
2. Where there is wood, the peasant receives varying amounts free, for both kindling and building.
3. Where there are vineyards, a village is permitted to sell wine for six months of the year; where there are none, for three months.
4. The peasant may leave his plough and pursue another mode of life; he may study and thus become a great man.

The Duties and Burdens of the Peasants

1. The peasant who owns a whole plot owes his landlord 52 days' labour with animals or 104 without them. The landless serf owes 18 days' labour if he has a house, and 12 if he has none.
2. He owes 1 *forint*[1] hearth-tax and 2 forints for a brandy-still.
3. He owes 2 hens, 2 capons, 12 eggs and 1 *itce*[1] of melted butter.

---

[1] See Note on Weights, Measures and Currency, p. 112.

4. He must chop and transport 1 *öl* of wood for his lord. He must also make one long journey for him and hunt, etc.

5. He must give one-ninth of all produce to his lord, including every ninth lamb and beehive; if he does not possess nine of these, he must pay 3–6 kreutzers[1] for each one he possesses.

6. He pays one-tenth of all his produce to the Catholic priest; in addition he pays the stipends of the priest and of the schoolmaster.

7. The peasants together with the inhabitants of towns bear the burdens of the state. They pay to the military treasury the tax of 5,000,000 forints decreed for the upkeep of the regular army and for the payment of the chief state officials. For the collection of this tax the whole kingdom (except for Croatia) is divided into 6,210$\frac{3}{4}$ so-called *portae*.[2] Of these the royal free cities account for 555$\frac{4}{4}$ portae. For the year 1807 the payment demanded from each porta was 814 forints 51$\frac{1}{8}$ kreutzers.

8. Even more than this is paid into the so-called 'domestic treasury',[3] from which the salaries of the county officials and servants are paid, public buildings and bridges are erected, prisoners are fed, etc. The taxpayers are rightly termed at law 'misera plebs'.

9. The peasants must give both money and labour for the construction and repair of roads.

10. The peasants also supply recruits for the defence of the country, as do the townsfolk. (In 1805 there were 339,000 non-noble conscripts between 17 and 40 years old under arms in Hungary. Of these 190,453 were either unmarried or widowers.)

The following regulations also concern the status of the peasant:

The peasant, like the commoner, may not possess or own noble real estate. He may not occupy any official post, high or low, with the exception of the village or town magistracies and similar offices. If he has sufficient cause, he may leave his master and choose another ('He is not bound to the land; he has freedom of movement'), but his landlord too may take away his land and give it to another. What the peasant acquires for himself is his own. If he has children, this is inherited by them; if he has none, he may leave two-thirds of it to whom he will, but the remaining third belongs to the landlord. If he dies intestate, his whole estate goes to the landlord. The peasant has no right to approach county or higher officials. In his own name he

---

[1] See Note on Weights, Measures and Currency, p. 112.
[2] See Note on Taxation before 1848, p. 113.
[3] In 1768:   71,603 forints 13 kreutzers

1773:	939,242	,,	40	,,
1775:	1,114,956	,,	55	,,
1815:	6,508,748	,,	32	,,

may not go to law against his own landlord (except for contractual matters) or against any other person. His immediate judge is his own landlord, even in lawsuits involving the latter. 'It is clear', says Berzeviczy, 'that the peasants have neither common human nor any personal rights.' And this is the state of 7,200,000 folk in Hungary. There is no question of the representation in the diet of the non-nobles and peasants as there is, for example, in Switzerland.

Pál Magda (1770–1841), Hungarian teacher of geography, studied at Jena, then held various teaching posts in Hungary. His textbook is based on earlier sources, but well seasoned with his own enlightened ideas.

6. State of the Peasants

Richard Bright, *Travels through Lower Hungary*, Edinburgh, 1818, pp. 111–15.

THE peasants on these estates were formerly bound to perform indefinite services, on account of the supposed grants and privileges, likewise little understood. Maria Theresa put the whole under certain regulations, which left less arbitrary power in the hands of the Lord. She fixed the quantity of land upon each estate, which was to remain irrevocably in the possession of the peasantry, giving to each peasant his portion, called a *session*,[1] and defining the services which should be required of him by his Lord in return. The only points determined, however, were, first, the whole quantity of land assigned to the peasants; secondly, the relation between the quantity of land and the quantity of labour the Lord should require for it. The individual peasants are not fixed to the soil, but may always be dismissed when the superior finds cause; nor is it of necessity that the son succeeds to his father, though usually the case. The peasant has no absolute claim to a whole session;—if the Lord please he may give but half a session, or a third; but, in this case, he cannot require more than one-half or one-third of the labour. The quantity of land allotted to a whole session is fixed for each *comitatus* or county. In the county of Neutra, where Ürmény is situated,[2] it varies, according to the quality of the soil, from twenty to thirty joch, each equivalent to 1·46 acres, or nearly 1½ English statute acre; and of these sixteen or twenty must be arable, the rest meadow. The services required of the father of the family, for the whole session, are one hundred and four days of labour during the year, if he work without cattle, or fifty-two

[1] See Note on Taxation before 1848, p. 113.
[2] The estate of Count Hunyadi, visited by the author. Now Urmín, near Nitra in Slovakia.

days if he bring two horses or oxen, or four, if necessary, with ploughs and carts. In this work he may either employ himself, or, if he prefer and can afford it, may send a servant. Besides this, he must give four fowls and twelve eggs, and one pfund[1] and a half of butter; and every thirty peasants must give one calf yearly. He must also pay a florin for his house,—must cut and bring home a klafter[2] of wood,—must spin in his family six pfund of wool or hemp, provided by the landlord,—and, among four peasants, the proprietor claims what is called a long journey, that is, they must transport twenty centners,[2] each one hundred French pounds weight, the distance of two days' journey out and home; and besides all this, they must pay one-tenth of all their products to the church, and one-ninth to the Lord.

Such are the services owed by the peasant, and happy would he be were he subject to no other claims. Unfortunately, however, the peasant of Hungary has scarcely any political rights, and is considered by the government, much more than by the landlord, in the light of a slave. By an unlimited extension of the aristocratical privilege, the noble is free from every burthen, and the whole is accumulated upon the peasant. The noble pays no tribute, and goes freely through the country, subject to neither tolls nor duties; but the peasant is subject to pay tribute, and although there may be some nominal restrictions to the services due from him to government, it can safely be said, that there is no limit, in point of fact, to the services which he is compelled to perform. Whatever public work is to be executed,—not only when a road is to be repaired, but when new roads are to be made, or bridges built,—the county meeting gives the order, and the peasant dares not refuse to execute it. All soldiers passing through the country are quartered exclusively upon the peasantry. They must provide them, without recompence, with bread, and furnish their horses with corn, and whenever called upon, by an order termed a '*forespann order*', they must provide the person bringing it with horses and means of conveyance. Such an order is always employed by the officers of government; and whoever can in any way plead public business as the cause of his journey, takes care to provide himself with it. In all levies of soldiers, the whole falls upon the peasant, and the choice is left to the arbitrary discretion of the Lord and his servants.

Taking a general view of the situation of the peasant, we may be satisfied, that it is not only in appearance, but in reality, oppressive. The appearance of oppression constantly imposing on the sufferer a consciousness of his humiliation, is of itself an evil hard to bear; but in the present case there is more than apparent hardship; for, even

[1] Pound.   [2] See Note on Weights, Measures and Currency, p. 112.

supposing that the return made to the Hungarian peasant for his labour by his Lord were an ample recompence, still the unlimited demands of service from government would prevent his deriving advantage from it. It is certain that the whole system is bad. Neither the Lord nor the peasant is satisfied. The benefit derived by the latter is by no means proportionate to the sacrifice which the land-lord is called upon to make. The quantity of land appropriated to the peasant is enormous, and still he labours always unwillingly, and of course ineffectually, under an idea that he works from compulsion and not for pay. In order to do all the farming work on a given estate by the peasants, it is no wild assertion, that nearly one-half of the land capable of cultivation is portioned out amongst the labourers. Owing to local circumstance, however, the proportion between the estate and the peasants belonging to it varies very much. When the Empress Maria Theresa made the distribution, she was guided, in a great degree, by the actual number then existing on each estate, to all of whom she gave lands, apparently without considering how the change would apply to individual cases. And, besides this original inequality, subsequent divisions of estates, and the cultivation of lands at that time wholly neglected, have rendered the dis-proportion in some cases, glaringly absurd. Thus, I have heard of estates, of which every acre was occupied by the peasants, the land-lord receiving nothing but the tenths and other casual services from them, unless he had occasion to transport them to labour on some other of his estates. On other properties, again, there are no peasants, —and this appears to be the state of things most desirable to the proprietor,—and so much so, that, even where peasants have been upon an estate, instances have come to my knowledge, in which the Lord has almost neglected to demand their services, finding his labour better performed by hired servants.

But, if the landlord have reason to be little satisfied, still less can the peasant be supposed to rejoice in his situation. It can never be well, to make the great and actually necessary part of society,—the labouring class,—dependent on the chances of a good or bad harvest for its existence. A man of capital can bear, for a year or two years, the failure of his crops; but, let a cold east wind blow for one night,— let a hail storm descend,—or let a river overflow its banks,—and the peasant, who has nothing but his field, starves or becomes a burthen to his Lord. Of this I have seen actual proof, not only in the wine districts of Hungary, in which the uncertainty of the crop is extreme, but in some of its richest plains, where I have known the peasantry, full three months before the gathering in, humbly supplicating the landlords to advance them corn on the faith of the coming harvest.

These are evils always liable to occur, supposing the peasant were allowed to cultivate his lands without interruption. But is this the case? The Lord can legally claim only one hundred and four days' labour from each in the year; yet who can restrain him if he demand more? There are a multiplicity of pretexts under which he can make such demands, and be supported in them. The administration of justice is, in a great degree, vested in his own hands. There are many little faults for which a peasant becomes liable to be punished with blows and fines, but which he is often permitted to commute for labour. In fact, these things happen so frequently, and other extorted days of labour, which the peasant fears to refuse, occur so often, that I remember, when in conversation with a very intelligent Director, I was estimating the labour of each peasant at 104 days,— he immediately corrected me, and said I might double it. If, however, the Lord, or his head servants, have too much feeling of propriety to transgress against the strictness of the law, they can at any time call upon the peasants to serve them for pay; and that, not at the usual wages of a servant, but about one-third as much, according to an assessed rate of labour. Add to all this, the services due to the government,—remember, too, that cases occur in which a peasant is obliged to be six weeks from his home, with horses and cart, carrying imperial stores to the frontier,—and then judge whether he is permitted to cultivate, without interruption, the land which he receives, as the only return for his labour.

Richard Bright (1789–1858), British physician, after whom Bright's disease is named, travelled widely in Europe and took a keen interest in customs and habits of other peoples. His record of Hungary is one of the most accurate and perceptive accounts of the time.

7. The Law of Inheritance

Richard Bright, *Travels through Lower Hungary*, Edinburgh, 1818, pp. 110–11.

THE manner in which land is possessed and distributed in this country is very singular. No man can possess lands who is not a noble of Hungary. But, as all the family of a nobleman are also noble, it is supposed that, in every twenty-one individuals in the nation, one is of this class. The lands descend either entire and undivided to the eldest son, or are equally divided amongst the sons, or, in some cases, amongst the sons and daughters; so that many of the nobles become, by these divisions, extremely poor, and are often obliged to discharge all the duties of the meanest peasant. If any of these nobles wish to sell an estate to a stranger, however high in rank, even to a noble of the Austrian empire, application must first be made to the surrounding proprietors, to learn whether they wish to purchase at the stipulated price; if they decline, the stranger may purchase it for a period of thirty years; at the end of which time, any branch of the family which sold it, however distantly related, may oblige the stranger to surrender his bargain. This goes so far that, in many cases, though the purchaser be an Hungarian noble, the family of the former possessor can reclaim it after thirty years, on payment of the original price, together with expences incurred in the buildings and improvements which have been made during that period. The litigation, ill-will, and evils of every kind to which such laws give rise, are beyond calculation.

8. THE TAXPAYING PEOPLE OF SZATMÁR

Ferenc Kölcsey, *A szatmári adózó nép állapotáról* (On the State of the Taxpaying People of Szatmár). Speech delivered at the County Assembly, Nagykároly,[1] 1830. *Kölcsey Ferenc összes művei* (Collected Works), Franklin, Budapest, n.d., pp. 1033–46.

OF all our deficiencies, none is greater or more troublesome than the lack of bread cereals, for in three-quarters of the county only the richest of the landed proprietors can sell them. It follows that the little money carefully scraped together by the inhabitants of Szatmár goes to other counties to purchase this staple article of food. Not a little money is taken out of the county by craftsmen who come from other places to inundate our little markets with their wares. Now the money thus spent on bread, clothing and agricultural implements far exceeds that which comes into the county from the sale of brandy distilled every three years from the plums in the orchards by the rivers Tisza and Szamos, from the few apples transported down the Tisza on the pine-log rafts from Máramaros, and from honey and tobacco, of which we allow one or two foreign traders to have a perpetual monopoly. The cattle-trade is almost entirely in the hands of the Jews who lease the slaughterhouses, except for a dealer or two who occasionally drives a few cattle to the smaller markets. The Jews also run the majority of our poverty-stricken inns—and these account for the whole of our internal trade in wine and spirits. We may add that the Tisza is the only one of our numerous rivers which can be used as a trade route by some of the smaller villages in the

---

[1] Now Carei, Rumania.

Szamosköz district. All the others are unnavigable, and there is no way of compensating for the immense losses they cause when they overflow their banks. It is not enough that they cannot be used for communications, but for half the year they block the overland routes to two-thirds of the county. They burst asunder the laboriously constructed dykes and cover the fields, first delaying the sowing of crops and then destroying all hopes of harvest. This applies chiefly to the Kraszna and Szamosköz districts; meanwhile those who live on the hills in the Bánya region sow their seed for the benefit of the mice, and in the Nyír district seed is mostly sown on soil so sandy that it is swept away by the first north wind. The only area to boast of more fortunate circumstances is the small region of Nagykároly. Here, however, the circulation of money is tiny and there is no large town to consume the produce, which is therefore worth considerably less than in Debrecen, where the surrounding countryside is immeasurably richer. Apart from this, Nagykároly lies close to the border and can offer trade only to a very small part of the whole county, while Szatmárnémeti[1] is beyond the range of the whole area by the Tisza. So the products of this region, which has a common boundary with Ugocsa county at Tiszaújlak, depend entirely upon the selfish, profit-seeking outlook of the treasury officials, and the land is kept permanently inactive.

This is the situation of the taxpaying community which every year pays into the domestic and military treasuries alone a sum of some 90,015 silver forints. Those of them who buy their bread keep a very small number of cattle in proportion, and since they find the means of trade completely blocked wherever they turn, they usually obtain the money for their taxes from handicrafts. There are over 17,000 landless serfs, gardeners and similar folk in the county, and more than 3,000 of these have no home of their own. This figure might well be increased. They have neither land nor cattle, and for most of their lives cannot bake bread. Even the smallest piece of food is gained from others by daily labour. The uncertainty of this means of obtaining food was shown in the fearful consequences of 1816 and the next year. Even when food is cheaper and their need less obvious, we may well be disturbed by the thought that these unfortunate peasants have not been allowed to escape the burden of the *portae*,[2] and that the county authorities have been compelled to levy the same amount from the richest landed peasant and the very least landless serf. It is easy to see that the very poor cannot carry as great a burden as the rich, and it is desirable that the county should reduce its demands to relieve them. Such measures are all the more

[1] Now Satu Mare, Rumania.　　[2] See Note on Taxation before 1848, p. 113.

necessary, for the two taxes already mentioned form only part of the whole burden of the taxpayers. The royal tithe, paid partly in cash and partly in kind or by service, and the provision of relay mounts may be reckoned to cost 5,100 silver forints per year. There was a loss of 4,645 silver forints on the bread rations supplied for military use in the year 1827–8; the amount lost on oats and hay may be estimated at about the same. What must the total losses have been in such years as 1816 and 1817, when the price of maize was 50 forints and that of wheat 80 and 120 forints? Now since the taxes are shared out among the villages by the county authorities, and then are handled by the local officials whose whim alone determines any further division, does it not inevitably follow that the peasant is burdened with more than his statutory taxes? To put it mildly, he pays at least a tenth more than the rate levied by the county. And apart from this, each little village has its own local expenses, which must all be paid from the taxpayers' pockets. I should like to see someone more expert than I compile a proper list of these dues; I am sure that the result would be wellnigh incredible.

Even so, none can fail to see at a glance that if the total taxes due to the two treasuries reach such a high figure, the addition of all the other items mentioned makes the burden of the taxpayers not merely great, but intolerable. Here I must add that since this sum cannot be covered by the produce of their own land, and cattle-grazing and trade are severely restricted, the peasants can fulfil their obligations only by the sacrifice of their own possessions, not even through the income from them; and in many cases where they have no possessions to sacrifice, they can only resort to manual labour.

I am fully aware that the county authorities would be glad to lighten the load of the people administered by them, and to make their life easier. But there are many causes other than those I have mentioned which combine to force the taxpayers into poverty. Let me mention but one. There are many villages in the county where for various reasons the peasant frequently changes his plot of land for another. This means that urbarial lands remain uncultivated. Such cases occur all the more frequently because in very many places the buildings on the plot belong to the landlord, so that there is nothing to keep the peasant in one spot. This migration ruins the productivity of the land, as does the fact that there is nothing to prevent the peasant from selling off the use of his land either for a yearly rent or merely to cover his debts, thus plunging himself into utter poverty. There is nothing more natural than for a poor man in financial trouble to borrow small sums from others; but in my experience these loans are far more iniquitous than those made by the most grasping moneylenders in the large towns. I have seen a peasant hand over as interest on a loan of 50 forints a plum orchard which in one single harvest brought in more than the original loan. I have seen a cartload of maize paid yearly for almost twenty years as interest on ten or twelve forints. I have seen lands capable of producing at least two quintals[1] given over to creditors for several years as interest on 15 forints, and there are many other such cases which ought to be taken up publicly.

I have already referred to one of the greater burdens of the tax-payers, namely that the allotment of individual taxes out of the amount levied upon each village is entrusted solely and without further instructions to the local authorities. These authorities are also solely responsible for the compilation of the figures used to assess the *dica*.[2] Thus the more astute inhabitants, who are either in authority themselves or in league with the assessors, lighten their own burdens at the expense of the less fortunate. Their estimates, which can so easily become the source of selfish profit, are nowhere more harmful than in the classification of land, which in any case is extremely difficult to determine accurately. . . .

I should like to bring one further point to your attention. There can be no more dangerous source of poverty than the Jews, whose numbers are increasing. The census of 1804 listed 2,290 male Jews; that of 1826, 2,872. Thus the Jewish population increased by 582 males; if we count females, the total community must have increased by at least 1,164. During the same period, if there are no serious errors in the figures, the total number of Christian taxpayers decreased by 16,000. None of the members of the council here can fail to recall the fate of Galicia, where the Jews likewise increased. Far be it from me to conjure up the fearful visions spread by Eisenmenger and others, but I must mention the terrifying sketch given by Pr. Schulze of the degradation of Galicia through their activity. He rightly declares that any country where the Jews proliferate is on the brink of material disaster. . . .

Ferenc Kölcsey (1790–1838), Hungarian poet and critic, spent most of his life in the county of Szatmár, both managing his small estate and serving as notary. He was elected to the Diet (1832–4) and gained a reputation for powerful oratory on the side of reform.

[1] See Note on Weights, Measures and Currency, p. 112
See Note on Taxation before 1848, p. 113.

9. EFFECT OF THE ROBOT SYSTEM

John Paget, *Hungary and Transylvania*, London, 1839, vol. i, pp. 305–7.

THE system of rent by *robot* or forced labour—that is, so many days' labour without any specification of the quantity of work to be performed,—is a direct premium on idleness. A landlord wishes a field of corn to be cut; his steward sends out, by means of his Haiducks,[1] information to the peasants to meet at such and such a field at such an hour with their sickles. Some time after the hour appointed a great part of them arrive, the rest finding some excuse by which they hope to escape a day's work; while others send their children or their wives, declaring some reason for their own absence. After much arranging they at last get to work; a Haiduck stands over them to see that they do not go to sleep and between talking, laughing and resting they do get something done. Where horses are employed, they are still less inclined to hurry lest they should tire them for the next day when they use them for their own purposes.

But how much does the reader suppose such workmen perform in one day? Count S[zéchenyi][2] says, just one-third of what the same men can do easily when working by the piece; and he has accordingly compounded his peasants' one hundred and four days' robot for a certain amount of labour, which they generally get through in about thirty-four days.

Another evil of the robot is the ill-will it begets between the masters and the workmen: their whole lives seem to be a constant effort on the one hand to see how much can be pressed out of the reluctant peasant; and on the other, how little can be done to justify the terms of the agreement and escape punishment. Mutual injury becomes a mutual profit; suspicion and ill-will are the natural results.

John Paget (1808–92), British physician, travelled widely in Hungary between 1835 and 1837, then married Polyxena Wesselényi and settled in Transylvania, where he lived, apart from a short break after the revolution of 1848, until his death. His book is one of the standard works of the period, full of accurate reporting and enthusiasm for reform.

[1] Attendants, messengers.
[2] The great reformer, whose plans for the improvement of agriculture, industry and commerce appeared first in *Hitel* (Credit), 1830.

10. PEASANTS IN TRANSYLVANIA

John Paget, *Hungary and Transylvania*, London, 1839, vol. ii, pp. 311–12;
313–17.

WE found the peasants of Transylvania in a far worse condition, and
much more ignorant than those of Hungary. When Maria Theresa
forced the Urbarium on the nobles of Hungary, she published certain *Regulations Punkte*, founded on nearly the same principles, for the
government of the peasants of Transylvania. Whether it was that
these *Punkte* were not adapted to the state of the country, or whether
its greater distance from the central power allowed the nobles to
evade their adoption, it is certain they never obtained the same
force as the Urbarium, nor have any succeeding attempts to improve
their condition met with a better result. The Transylvanians say
they are ready and anxious to do everything that is right and just,
provided only it is done in a constitutional form, through the intervention of the Diet.[1] In the meantime the state of the peasantry is a
crying evil, and one which, if not speedily remedied by the nobles,
will be remedied without their consent, either by the government or
by the people themselves; and I fear the sympathy of Europe will
scarcely be in favour of those who oppose such a measure of justice.

Among the greatest evils of which the Transylvanian peasant has
to complain, is the absence of any strict and well-defined code of
laws to which he can refer, and, in consequence of that deficiency,
his almost entire subjection to the arbitrary will of his master, against
which he has nothing but custom to urge in defence. The peasant-
land too, has never been classed here as in Hungary, according to
its powers of production, nor has the size of the peasant's portion, or
fief, been ever accurately determined. The amount of labour therefore, cannot be fairly and legally proportioned to the quantity and
value of the land. Nor is the amount of labour itself better regulated.
In some parts of the country it is common to require two days a
week; in others, and more generally, three are demanded; and in
some the landlord takes as much as he possibly can extract out of the
half-starved creatures who live under him. Here, too, the flogging-
block is in full vigour; every landlord can order any of his tenants or
servants, who may displease him, twenty-five lashes on the spot, and
it is generally the first resource which occurs to him in any disputes
about labour or dues. But it is in the hands of the underlings, the
stewards, bailiffs, inspectors,—a flock of hawks which infest every

[1] The Diet of 1837 nominated a commission to prepare an Urbarium for
Transylvania, but I cannot yet (1839) hear that anything has been done (*Author*).

Hungarian estate,—that this power becomes a real scourge to the poor peasant. It is the custom to pay these officers an exceedingly small sum in ready money, as a salary, so small indeed that it would be impossible for them to live decently upon it; it is consequently obliged to be made up by the addition of some land, or by the permission to feed a certain number of cattle, or horses, or to sell a certain quantity of corn on their own account. Now to cultivate this land, or to carry this corn to market, labour is required, and this they generally manage to get out of the peasantry without payment, either by threats of punishment for slight or imaginary offences, or by applying for themselves what ought to be given to their masters. Generally both these means are used—the master is robbed, and the peasant ill-treated.

From the manner in which estates are commonly divided in Transylvania, it is nearly impossible for the landlords to escape from the clutches of these bailiffs. Every son has an equal share in the male estates, and every child in the female estates of a family. This equality of right in each individual estate is often the cause of great inconvenience, for the same person might have a few acres only in twenty different villages, when the expense and difficulty of management would exceed the revenue. Of course, the most natural remedy is an equitable division among members of the family themselves; and, where this can be effected, it is well; but, where it cannot, their only remedy is cultivating in common and dividing the profits. In such cases almost the entire management rests in the hands of the stewards, and this complication, together with the endless lawsuits to which it gives rise, is one of the greatest evils to which the landlord and peasant of Transylvania are subject.

The ignorance of the Transylvanian peasant is of the deepest dye. He is generally superstitious and deceitful, the two greatest signs of ignorance. These qualities are most conspicuous in the Wallack peasantry, but the Magyars are by no means free from them. Schools are extremely rare. It is only here and there that they have been established by the good sense and liberality of the Seigneur, and even then they have often failed for want of a little caution and perseverance in those who have conducted them. The peasants belonging to the Greek church are undoubtedly the most ignorant, those of the Unitarian and Lutheran churches, the best educated.

We entered some of the Magyars' cottages at Hadad,[1] and though they were superior to the Wallack huts of Várhely, they were still very inferior to those we had visited in Hungary. It is rare that the

[1] On the estate of Baron Miklós Wesselényi, into whose family Paget later married.

Transylvanian peasant's cottage has more than two rooms, some-times only one; his furniture is scanty and rude, his crockery coarse, and those little luxuries, which in the Hungarian denoted some-thing beyond the needful, are rarely seen in Transylvania. There is an air of negligence too about his house; his fence is broken, his stable out of repair, and everywhere there is a want of that thrifty look which declares that a man thinks he has something worth taking care of, and hopes to make it better.

11. Magnates in Debt

Julia Pardoe, *The City of the Magyar*, London, 1840, vol. ii, pp. 287–92.

THE besetting sin of the Magyar is vanity. He is proud of his nation, of his liberty, of his antiquity, and above all, of his privileges. In short, he admits no superior, and scarcely an equal, when he has high blood, a long pedigree, and an apparent rent-roll. I say apparent, for perhaps Europe cannot present collectively so pauper-ized a nobility as that of Hungary, when their circumstances and positions are thoroughly understood. From the gorgeous and princely Esterházy, with his debt of two millions sterling, to the minor Mag-nate who rattles over the pavement of Pesth behind his four ill-groomed horses, there are not twenty nobles in the country who are not *de facto* bankrupts.

This is a startling assertion, but one which can be easily borne out; and hence the great difficulty (greater than those originated by the jealousies of the Austrian Government) to the establishment of a solid and serviceable foreign commerce. The Hungarian noble sacri-fices everything to show, and luxury, and ostentation: and thus his necessities ever outrun his income, and he is compelled to dispose of the productions of his extensive estates to a swarm of Jews and traders, who profit by his inconsiderate prodigality.

'The idea of a commercial treaty with England is at best a bubble for the present' said one of the most intelligent of the Magnates with whom I was one day conversing on this subject; 'We have still much to do ere it can be brought to bear. The Magyars have not yet learnt to be traders; and as to the nobles—we one and all prefer sitting quietly upon our sofas, and disposing of our produce for a given number of years to an accommodating individual who will pay down the price *argent comptant*, even though it be at a loss of fifty per cent, to having the trouble of speculating, calculating, and waiting, in order to rid ourselves of the sacrifice.'

Of this fact I have had ample verification since I have been in the country; and Baron Sina,[1] the great Greek Banker, may truly be said to be the King of commercial Hungary, for I have been assured that he is the creditor of every Magnate in the nation. How far his engagements with Austria may leave him untrammelled in his other speculations is not for me to decide; but it is certain that no undertaking here can be carried through without him. His money has served to rebuild most of the good houses ruined by the inundation[2]—the wood from his estates, as well as his gold, is to aid the construction of the bridge over the Danube—in short, no speculation has lately been undertaken without Baron Sina, whose wealth has purchased his nobility, and whose name is an *open sesame* which here at least cannot easily be resisted.

The great national misfortune of this state of affairs is, that as in Hungary there is no law of imprisonment for debt, and that even if there were, it could not affect the nobles, whose privileges would exempt them from the penalty, the excesses of the Magnates entail ruin upon the trading classes, who are unable to contend against the enormous losses contingent on the defalcation of the higher orders; and thus the whole commerce of the country is crippled by the follies of a few.

That I am supported in my opinion is proved by the fact that the Jews, who transact all immediate traffic with the nobles, will not trust a penny to the personal pledges of a Magnate, nor to the protection of the Hungarian law; and that they nevertheless purchase at a ridiculously low price all the products of the land, such as wool, corn, wood, etc., by merely paying in advance; and thus enabling the nobles to continue their career of extravagance, for which they would otherwise need funds.

The obvious result of this miserable arrangement is simply this— that while they keep the proud Magnate who seems to spurn them from his path in a state of actual moral subjection, they endanger the progress of agriculture, commerce, and industry; for the peasant labours grudgingly for the greedy Israelite; who, in his turn, looks not beyond the harvest which he is himself to garner, caring little for the neglect which may ensue; and meanwhile, as I have before remarked, many of the bankrupt lords could barely meet all the demands upon them by disposing of their whole estates.

When a difficulty of this nature becomes extreme, the great landholder is placed under 'sequester', as it is technically called; that is, his property (which cannot be sold) is placed under a legal

---

[1] For the origin of the Sina family, see p. 317 below, footnote 1.
[2] The great flood of 1838, which destroyed 2,281 houses in Pest.

administration totally independent of his influence, and he receives annually from the proper authorities in charge, one-twelfth of the revenues, until the remaining eleven parts of his debts are paid.

Let it not be believed, however, that they are discharged on the principle of 'an eye for an eye, and a tooth for a tooth'. Far from it. The administration generally commences its duties by a lawsuit with the creditors; disputing every debt, impeaching the opposing party of usury; when, can it be proved that he has realized, or rather striven to realize, more than six per cent, he loses all claim upon the estate of the debtor; and tendering to others the moiety of the claim, *pendente lite*; to which conditions they frequently accede rather than run the risk of an action at law which may endure for years, and entail an outlay so considerable as to render the ultimately beneficial effect of the result extremely doubtful.

Julia Pardoe (1806–62), British traveller and contributor to many journals, twice visited Hungary. Although her work often reflects the opinions of Gábor Döbrentei, who was an ambitious but dull hanger-on of Széchenyi, she includes much good observation and comment.

12. PEASANT NOBLES

Julia Pardoe, *The City of the Magyar*, London, 1840, vol. i, pp. 134–6.

THE herd of cows, as it left the village, amounted to some hundreds, and it was strange to reflect that although as many as forty or fifty head of these cattle belonged to the same individual, that individual was probably not possessed of as many shillings in specie had you searched his whole dwelling; and this is the secret of Hungarian poverty. The finest cow of the herd might have been purchased for a pound, and at that price the owner would gladly have parted from her; but who was to give it? A neighbour could but barter sheep or pigs or grain or whatever other stock he possessed—money there is none among the small landholders, or *bocskoros nemesek*[1] as they are called, a species of petty nobility who, while their shadowy rank exempts them from taxation, tolls and all compulsory assistance in public works and gives them the privilege of transmitting their possessions in the male line, are nevertheless mere peasants in their habits and modes of life; and very frequently cannot even read or write. Thus their very riches are poverty, for where they need money

[1] 'Sandalled noblemen', a name derived from the half-shoes strapped over the instep, which they wear in common with the peasantry (*Author*).

for any particular purpose, they have it not, nor can they procure it by the sale of their produce.

The fact is evident that they might find a market by driving their cattle or carting their grain to Vienna or any other trading city, but how are they to provide against the contingencies of the journey? And when it is made, the expenses defrayed and the heavy tax exacted at the Austrian frontier on the admission of Hungarian produce paid, what remains to the agriculturalist? Simply the conviction that the first sacrifice is the most easy, and that he had better live on from day to day amid his herds and his fields, shearing his own sheep for clothing and slaughtering his own cattle for food, than risk absence from his family and his avocations on a merely speculative attempt at improvement which too frequently proves a failure.

13. THE HUNGARIAN NOBLEMAN

Sándor Petőfi, *A magyar nemes* (The Hungarian Nobleman), poem of 1845. *Petőfi Sándor összes művei* (Collected Works), Akadémiai k., Budapest, 1951, vol. i, p. 340.

> My ancestors' old bloodstained sword
> Hangs on the wall, with rustmarks scored.
> Rusting, tarnished—let it lie:
> A Magyar nobleman am I!
>
> Nought but idleness is life.
> I'm idle, therefore I'm alive.
> Peasants work until they die:
> A Magyar nobleman am I!
>
> Serf, repair that road! Your horse
> Has to carry me, of course.
> Walking's not for me—and why?
> A Magyar nobleman am I!
>
> Shall I then a scholar be?
> Scholars live in poverty.
> I can't write or read, or try,
> A Magyar nobleman am I!
>
> One science I've made all my own;
> In it few rivals have I known—

Food and drink that satisfy!
A Magyar nobleman am I!

Tax I do not pay; that's fine!
Few the lands that I call mine,
But debts enough to reach the sky:
A Magyar nobleman am I!

For my country nought I care,
Nor her thousand troubles share.
Soon her woes away will fly.
A Magyar nobleman am I!

Ancient hall and ancient rights
Bound my life, till angel flights
Bear me heavenward when I die.
A Magyar nobleman am I!

Sándor Petőfi (1823–49), the most widely known Hungarian lyric poet of the
nineteenth century, was also one of the most revolutionary writers of his age.
His portrait of the typical nobleman, while couched in fierce language, is
not unjust.

14. THE GEORGICON AT KESZTHELY

François-Sulpice Beudant, *Travels in Hungary in 1818*, translated from the
French. London, 1823, pp. 122–3.

IN lieu of making mineralogical excursions about Keszthely, I intended visiting the different establishments of rural economy which
Count Festetits had created on his estate. These required a particular
attention both from the manner in which they are conducted, and
from their being an inlet for the introduction of agriculture into
Hungary. This was the first object I was eager to explore next
morning, and the count and his son accompanied me, to detail the
particulars. Among these, I was most struck with the Georgicon, or
school of agriculture, designed to qualify young persons for the
superintendence and management of estates. It is intended, also to
provide the peasants with such instruction as may make them expert
in gardening and farming. This establishment is maintained entirely
by the count, who has endowed it, for the purpose, with a considerable farm; there being different professors for different courses of

study. These, for such as are to become officers of economy, include what is necessary in geometry, mechanics, the art of drawing, and, more especially, architecture, with the designing and construction of plans, etc. In the latter part of their time the pupils are practically employed in various concerns about the establishment, as keeping accounts, and, alternately, through a round of other duties. Some part of their time is devoted to botany, and to the acquiring of some knowledge of physics and chemistry. On finishing their studies, the young persons either return home with certificates of their proficiency, good behaviour, etc., or are disposed of by the count, on his own domains, or transferred to other lords that may stand in need of their services. The young peasants intended for gardening and farming, are taught reading, writing, and accounts; nor is instruction in religious duties neglected. They attend to all such improvements in cultivation, generally, as may be suggested in the modes of rearing cattle, in models of the different implements for plowing, of which there is a complete assortment on the establishment. Every department of the school appeared to be well adapted and conducted; what is essential to be known is taught, and nothing further. In the gardens are collections of various kinds of kitchen vegetables, cereal plants, fruit and timber trees; utility being the object to which everything is directed. There is also a small botanical garden.

F. S. Beudant (1787–1852), French professor, geologist and mineralogist, travelled through Hungary in 1818 and published his researches some four years later. His observations are narrow in range, yet careful and accurate.

15. TRADE AT THE END OF THE EIGHTEENTH CENTURY

Robert Townson, *Travels in Hungary in the year 1793*, London, 1797, pp. 194–200.

WHEREVER I went I was led into cellars full of wine and into granaries full of corn, and I was shown pastures full of cattle. If I felicitated the owners upon their rich stores, and of articles never out of fashion, I heard one common complaint—the want of a market, the want of buyers.

Some of its natural productions are rivals to the natural produce of other parts of the Austrian dominions, as its wines. The exportation therefore of this article is checked by imposts and custom-house formalities and expenses.[1]

The local situation of Hungary is unfavourable: it is chiefly surrounded with countries which stand in no need of its produce. It has fine rivers, but these run in a different direction from the course of its commerce, the Austrian provinces, which are the markets for four-fifths of its exportation; whilst they run toward Turkey. And land carriage is rendered very expensive by the badness of the roads, and territorial tolls; a thing severely felt upon raw produce.

An Hungarian writer says that good wine is bought for six shillings, has an additional expense upon it of eight shillings when it reaches the port of Trieste; and that corn which is bought for two shillings, an expense of six; tobacco that costs twelve shillings a hundred weight, likewise an addition of six.

The annual exports, according to the following list, are above sixteen millions of guldens, or 1,600,000 pounds sterling; and its imports eleven millions, or 1,100,000 pounds sterling; which gives a balance in favour of Hungary of half a million sterling.

In 1778 there was exported 14,262,800
            And imported 10,390,328
                          ───────────
                           3,872,472 balance in favour of
                                              Hungary.

In 1787   Exported 17,800,000
               Imported 13,800,000
                         ───────────
                          4,000,000 balance in favour of
                                             Hungary.

This balance in favour of Hungary, of about five millions of guldens, or half a million sterling, is not the consequence of its

---

[1] Duties on Hungarian produce entering Austria compared with the duties of the produce of Poland, taken from notes of the Committee. By Poland I believe is meant that part of it belonging to Austria, Galicia, etc.

		Hungarian	Polish
Beer, per *eimer**		12 creutzers	5 creutzers
Butter per cwt.		40	32
Raw sheep skins, the 100	Flor.	2·0	1·36
Wheat the Presburg measure		4	3
Rye		3	2
Millet		4	3
Calves skins, ten pieces		2	1·36
Mead per *eimer*		48	19

N.B. Sixty creutzers are one florin, and one florin two shillings (*Author*).

* See Note on Weights, Measures and Currency, p. 112.

exported manufacture, but of its great exports of raw produce, as the following table from De Luca,[1] for the year 1783 will show.

Horned cattle	3,670,000	
Hogs	780,000	
Sheep and cattle	540,000	
Other animals	70,000	
		5,060,000
Flour	1,060,000	
Wheat	990,000	
Rye	640,000	
Oats	350,000	
		3,040,000
Wine		1,040,000
Wool		2,810,000
Other goods		11,950,700
		15,019,100
Of which there was exported to		
Austria		9,000,000
Moravia		2,600,000
Inner-Austria		1,300,000
Bohemia and Silesia		1,130,000
		14,030,000
Transylvania		427,000
(Therefore to the hereditary dominions)		14,457,000
Foreign countries		2,225,000
Total exports		16,682,000

Why there is no mention of tobacco in the preceding list I know not. It is a staple produce and article of exportation. Professor Miller, of Gross Wardein,[2] in his *Schedium Fabricarum*, etc., gives the export of it at eight hundred thousand florins. Nor does this list account for the 16,682,000 florins of exportation, only for 15,019,100. But it is sufficient to shew that its exports are almost entirely raw produce.

Several attempts have been made to increase the markets by forming commercial companies and by establishing agents in foreign countries: but none of these schemes have succeeded, and the blame, as usual, is laid on the Austrian government.

[1] Ignaz de Luca, *Geographie des Königreichs Ungarn* . . . , Vienna, 1791.
[2] Nagyvárad, now Oradea Mare, Rumania.

16. The Fair at Pest

(a) In 1793

Robert Townson, *Travels in Hungary in the year 1793*, London, 1797, p. 85.

The Pest fair happened whilst I was here. It is the greatest in the kingdom, and lasts eight or ten days: many shop-keepers came from Vienna, and brought their merchandise with them. But the chief articles were the natural productions of Hungary, and the principal of these, horses. These are driven to market in flocks like horned cattle, from the great *Pusztas* or commons: they are quite wild, and have never had a halter about their heads. When they come to market, they are driven into folds. In this manner they are shewn and sold. . . . The smaller kind of horses, such as are in use among the peasants, sold for about four or five pounds; those for the army, from seven to twelve pounds.

Another staple article are oxen. A pair of fat oxen sold for nine or twelve pounds: not fattened, for eight or nine pounds. Wool, from the Hungarian breed of sheep, from thirty-six to forty-four shillings per hundred weight of Vienna; which I believe is about an English hundred weight of 112 pounds. The wool of these sheep is often sold by the pair of fleeces, at about two shillings the pair. The wool of the common German breed was about double this price. That of the mixed breed of German and Spanish fetched from five to six pounds the 100 lb.

Tobacco is likewise a staple article: that from Fünfkirchen[1] sold at ten shillings per 100 lb. of Vienna: that of Szegedin at fourteen shillings; and the best, which is from Debroe, at sixteen shillings.

Besides these staple articles there were many cart-loads of hides and Knoppern. These latter are a kind of gall, which grows upon the calix of the acorns of the common oak; and are used as a substitute for galls, and for oak bark, in tanning. The quantity of common earthenware was surprising. A great many Jews, Greeks and Armenians, who have most of the commerce of the kingdom in their hands, attended the fair.

(b) In 1837

J. G. Kohl, *Austria*, translated from the German. London, 1840, pp. 208–12.

As geographical centre of the country, Pest is also the centre of the Hungarian trade. It has four great markets or fairs which, from

[1] Pécs.

their importance, might be called the royal fairs of Hungary. The most considerable is that beginning at the end of August, at which time all the channels of communication are in their best state, the Danube free, the roads dry, and at this time it is that the great purchases are made for the winter. The principal places occupied by the fair are first the Danube Quay, on which is erected a row of shops and along which the vessels lie; secondly the Jews' quarter, where every corner swarms with goods and buyers and sellers; thirdly the market-places in the interior of the town, which are covered with booths; and fourthly all the open spaces in the Joseph's suburb.

The Danube Quay is very broad and over a German mile long, having on the side opposite the river a row of handsome houses, the ground floors of which only are used as shops. On the morning of the fair it was filled with thousands of busy traders and the river was crowded with vessels of all kinds, including steamers. There were vessels from Austria, or the lower Danube as far as Belgrade and Semlin,[1] and from different parts of the Theiss.[2] The largest and most solid vessels seen in the middle Danube carry from 10,000 to 12,000 metzen[3] of wheat. They also go up the Theiss as far as Szegedin, where many of them are built. Others are built at Eszek[4] on the Drave, where is to be had the fine hard oak chiefly used in their construction. They generally last with repairs as much as five-and-twenty or thirty years. Besides large vessels there are others of a smaller size, broad and flat built, which carry furniture and manufactured goods to Turkey. . . . I could not make out very accurately the relative proportions of land and water traffic at Pest, but I believe the latter is at present increasing much more rapidly. Near the Quay was the pottery market, and never in my life did I see together so many pots and pans and clay vessels of every possible variety.

The people who came with the goods I have mentioned for sale were mostly Slavonians and Magyars: but there were also many Germans, colonists from the distant parts of Hungary. The weekly provision market of Pest is almost entirely supplied by Germans, as there are many German colonies in its immediate vicinity; these men are so disguised in their Magyar costume that one does not always recognize them. One of them, coming from the Bakony forest, who had brought various wooden wares, spoons, shovels, rakes, tubs, etc., confirmed to me the satisfactory information concerning the cultivation of potatoes, which I had collected on the

---

[1] Zemun, Yugoslavia.   [2] Tisza.
[3] See Note on Weights, Measures and Currency, p. 112.
[4] Osijek, Yugoslavia.

F

Neusiedler Lake. The people are becoming everywhere reconciled to
them, although here, as elsewhere, they were at first received with
violent dislike. Thirty, nay twenty years ago, the Hungarians attributed every possible mischief to potatoes, scarcely deeming them
good enough even for pigs. At present, however, he added, they were
raised everywhere in the Bakony country.

One of the most abundant articles in the market, and one of
genuine Hungarian manufacture, was soap, of which the quantities
truly were astonishing. This is all made on the Hungarian steppes,
principally on the Theiss, and in Debrecen and Szegedin. The best
has much the appearance of Limburg cheese, and comes from
Debrecen, where there are no fewer than a hundred soap-boilers.
There also are made the true Hungarian tobacco-pipes; and, according to the recent statistical tables, eleven millions of them are manufactured every year, which would give one for every man, woman
and child in the kingdom. In general whatever is regarded as
peculiarly Hungarian is to be found about Debrecen—for example
the finest and largest melons. . . . A prize melon I saw exhibited by
the Agricultural Society weighed sixty pounds. The gourds also
grow to an immense size, one of them often weighing as much as a
hundredweight, and occasionally even twice as much. The common
people eat them in slices, roasted like chestnuts.

The fair at Pest is not only important to the different parts of
Hungary, as giving an opportunity for the interchange of commodities among themselves, but also to the neighbouring provinces
of Turkey in the south, and of Germany and Poland in the north.
Hungary is rich in the raw productions of nature, and the German
provinces, as well as Austria, Moravia, Silesia and the western part
of Galicia, have surrounded this land of raw produce with a chain
of industrial towns, busied in the manufacture of leather, wool, cotton and silk. The principal articles which they come to look for at
Pest are wool, tobacco, cotton, skins, corn, wax, wine and others of
less importance. The persons principally engaged in Pest, as agents
from these provinces, are Jews; and the greater part of the business
is therefore carried on in the Jews' quarter, which is perhaps the
busiest scene in the fair. Skins are brought thither in great waggons,
drawn by four, six or eight horses; whilst behind comes a reserve
team, either for relief or for occasional sale. In the inner courts of
the houses where the wares are unpacked, is a scene of litter and
dirt, uproar and confusion that cannot be described, but which may
be conceived if we reflect that among the chief articles bargained for
are stinking hides and bed-feathers and that the bargainers are
Slavonians and Polish Jews.

Crossing the feather market, we abandoned ourselves unresistingly to the pressure of the masses, who were at this time flowing out of the town towards a large open space, covered with men and animals of all nations and races—not less, certainly, than thirty thousand persons being present. The ground was very uneven, and on one little hill some women had established a market for eggs and live fowls. Another hill was covered with droves of pigs, on the plain were vast troops of horses and the valleys were covered with sheep. In some places were long rows of linen merchants from Slavonia. . . . At the entrance to the market was a cohort of dealers in paprika, of which astonishing quantities are eaten by the natives. One might think that everything in Hungary grew seasoned with paprika, bread being the only exception.

The Slovaks are the principal dealers in linen, which they manufacture themselves in the north-western parts of Hungary, bordering on Silesia and Moravia, and this branch of industry has spread thence to other countries. As the Slovaks are the greatest manufacturers, the Hungarians are chiefly occupied in the breeding of cattle and horses; and in the energy with which they devote themselves to the latter, it would seem as if they had not quite forgotten the ancient mode of life of their forefathers on the Asiatic steppes.

J. G. Kohl (1808–78), noted German cartographer, travelled extensively in Austria-Hungary and was particularly interested in economic activity. He was a keen observer and vivid writer.

17. Prospects of Trade with England

John Paget, *Hungary and Transylvania*, London, 1839, vol. ii, p. 607; pp. 612–14.

For the erection of the new chain-bridge at Pest, it has been found cheaper to have the iron-work cast in England, sent by water to Fiume or Trieste, and from thence by land to Pest, than to have it manufactured either in Hungary or in any other part of the Austrian dominions. Such is the advantage which commercial habits and scientific knowledge give over cheap labour. I have heard it stated that the iron of Hungary possesses qualities superior to that of any other part of Europe, except Sweden, for conversion into steel; yet it is so badly wrought that worse cutlery cannot exist than that of Hungary. Hungarian iron is quite unknown in the English market. . . .

Wool is at present one of the chief articles of Hungarian commerce, chiefly because its exportation is untaxed. It is scarcely twenty years since the Merino sheep has been introduced into Hungary; and the quantity of fine wool now produced may be judged from the fact that at the last Pest fair there were no less than 80,000 centners offered for sale. The greater part of this wool is bought by the German merchants, and much of it is said to go ultimately to England, after having passed by land quite across Europe to Hamburg. Of late years a few English merchants have made their appearance at the Pest fairs, which are held four times in the year; but I have not yet heard of any wool being sent to England by the Danube and Black Sea. Besides the Merino wool, there is a considerable quantity of a long coarse wool grown, which is chiefly sold for the manufacture of the thick white cloth worn by the peasants, and which might be found very serviceable for our carpet fabrics.

A still more important article of Hungarian produce is corn, and it is one from which, it is to be hoped, England ere long, by the abolition of her corn laws, will enable herself to derive the full benefit. At present the quantity of grain annually produced in Hungary is reckoned from sixty to eighty millions of Pressburg metzen.[1] This calculation, however, is of little importance, as at present scarcely any is grown for exportation; but, were a market once opened, it is beyond doubt that the produce might be doubled or trebled without any difficulty. I have heard it stated by one well able to judge, that at the present time one quarter of the whole country is uncultivated, although the greater part of it is capable of furnishing the richest crops at a very slight cost. The wheat of Hungary is allowed to be of an excellent quality. Where the land has little value for other purposes, and the labour costs nothing, it is difficult to see how it can be produced anywhere at a cheaper rate than here.[2]

[1] See Note on Weights, Measures and Currency, p. 112.

[2] In an article in a late number of the British and Foreign Quarterly, it is stated that Hungarian wheat from Fiume can be brought to England at a lower rate than from any other country. I quote the statement as it stands, without being able however to vouch for its accuracy:

	Fl.	kr.	s.	d.
The price of Hungarian wheat fit for shipment to England is at present, *per metzen*, at Sissek:* (N.B. At other times it is 30 or 40 per cent less.)	2	45	5	6
Expense of transport from Sissek to Karlstadt† by the River Culpa‡	0	10	0	4
Expense of transport from Karlstadt to Fiume by land	0	50	1	8
	3	45	7	6

(*Author.*) * Sisak. † Karlovac. ‡ Kupa.

18. MANUFACTURES

Michael J. Quin, *A Steam Voyage down the Danube*, London, 1838, p. 22.

THE manufactures of Hungary are very limited, consisting chiefly of coarse linen, cotton, an indifferent kind of paper, spirit which is obtained from grain, plums or other fruits, and oil which is obtained from linseed, the seeds of the rape, the poppy and the sunflower. Tobacco and snuff are produced in great abundance. At Odenburg[1] and Fiume sugar-refineries are established. The manufacture of clothes and woollen stuffs has made no great progress as yet in Hungary; flannels are made in Stuhlweissenberg[2] and many parts of the Zips, and heavy waterproof cloth for cloaks as well as other coarse articles, is woven by the Croatians and Slavonians. Attempts have been made to grow and manufacture silk at Grosswardein,[3] Pressburg,[4] Alt-Ofen,[5] Pesth and other places, but hitherto without success.

The articles fabricated in gold and silver are not sufficient to supply the home consumption. Iron is produced in considerable quantities in Gömör, Zips and Liptau;[6] the steel of Diós-Győr is excellent; nevertheless the chief supplies of these articles are furnished by Vienna and Styria. Several manufactories of common glass and pottery are distributed throughout the country. Debretzin[7] is famous for its tobacco-pipe heads. Holitsch[8] is highly esteemed for its earthenware, but here terminates the list of Hungarian manufactures. The principal resources of that country are to be found in her mines, her vineyards, her harvests and her flocks, and these are so abundant that she needs but greater facilities for exportation to become one of the richest states in Europe.

According to Schwartner the annual vintage of Hungary may be estimated at eighteen millions of eimers. The principal vineyards are those of Syrmien,[9] Buda-Pesth, Tokay and Grosswardein. Its produce in grain is said to amount to 60 million Pressburg metzen, excluding Indian corn and rice. Its improved sheep are calculated at six million, its unimproved at four million, the whole of which are constantly feeding in the country and yield large annual returns to their proprietors. Extensive droves of horned cattle and swine are sold in all the fairs and markets.

Sulphur has been procured in many parts of Hungary from copper pyrites. Traces also of coal are scattered throughout the country, but

[1] Sopron.
[2] Székesfehérvár.
[3] Oradea Mare (Nagyvárad).
[4] Bratislava (Pozsony).
[5] Óbuda.
[6] Liptov, Slovakia.
[7] Debrecen.
[8] Holič, Slovakia.
[9] Srem, Yugoslavia.

veins hitherto discovered are of no great value. Peat also abounds in Hungary; salt is found there in the greatest profusion, as well as considerable quantities of soda, saltpetre and alum.

M. J. Quin (1796–1843), British writer, visited Hungary in 1834 at the time of the first notable reforms, of which he obtained information from Széchenyi. Much of his work savours of a lesson well-learnt.

19. MINING

(a) Salt

Robert Townson, *Travels in Hungary in the year 1793*, London, 1797, p. 231.

IN the morning we continued our route to Poroslo,[1] on the banks of the Theiss; this was only about an hour's ride. Here are the salt magazines for landing and depositing the rock-salt which comes from the county of Maramaruss;[2] it is brought down the river on floats of pine-trees, on which it is piled up like bricks, in great pieces of fifty pounds to a hundred weight. In wet weather there is a considerable deficit. The quantity annually landed here is very great; last year it amounted to 118,000 cwt.: but this is not the only place of debarkation. The quantity of salt annually dug from the mines in the county of Maramaruss is estimated in the Hungarian Magazine at 600,000 cwt. From hence it is sent to the royal magazines in the towns, where it is sold to the public. A great many carts were waiting for loading on this business: twopence halfpenny per cwt. is given for carting it to Erlau,[3] and sevenpence halfpenny per cwt. to Pest. The Maramaruss salt, which lies on this side of the Carpathian chain, is like that of Wielitzka on the other side; it is of a sparry texture, and must, without doubt, form great beds, as it does at Wielitzka. As the floats are here broken up and sold, Poroslo is likewise a depository of wood; one of the finest pines sells for about three shillings.

(b) The Salt Mines of Marosújvár[4]

John Paget, *Hungary and Transylvania*, London, 1839, vol. ii, pp. 356–63.

THE chief part of the salt mines is formed by three vast subterranean chambers. Before we had reached six feet from the surface, the salt

[1] Poroszló, now on a branch of the Tisza.
[2] Máramaros, now Maramureş, Rumania.
[3] Eger.   [4] Ocna Mureşului, Rumania.

was already perceptible. After passing some new workings, we descended to the lower workings.

We entered at one end of a vast hall—two hundred and seventy feet long by one hundred and eighty wide, and two hundred and ten high,—with a Gothic arched roof, dimly lighted by the candles of the miners. At the opposite end to that by which we entered was a huge portal, reaching nearly to the top of the chamber, and affording entrance to a second, and that again to a third hall of equal extent with the first. On a signal being given, a sudden blaze burst forth in each of these chambers, and lighted up the whole space with a brilliant illumination. It was the grandest sight I had ever beheld. The walls were of solid rock-salt, which, if not so dazzling as writers are generally pleased to describe it, was extremely beautiful from the variety of its colours. It resembled highly polished white marble veined with brown, the colours running in broad wavy lines.

The whole floor of the chamber was covered with workmen employed in detaching and shaping vast masses of salt rock preparatory to its ascent. It is cut by means of sharp hammers into long blocks of about one foot in diameter, which are afterwards broken up into masses, weighing from fifty-eight to fifty-nine pounds each, and in this form it is brought to market. The accuracy with which they can measure the weight is extraordinary. After shaping his block above and on the sides, the miner calls to two or three of his neighbours to aid him in detaching its base from the rock. This is effected by repeated blows of very heavy hammers on the upper surface, the most exact time and equality of force being maintained. This is the severest part of their labour, but it lasts only a few minutes at a time.

The number of workmen employed here is about three hundred. Among these are Magyars, Wallacks and Germans. . . . The miners begin their work at three o'clock in the morning and leave it at eleven, and the average rate of wages for eight hours' labour is about ten pence. The employment is far from unhealthy, and even children often apply themselves to it very young.

The quantity of salt annually produced from these mines is six hundred thousand centners, all of which, with the exception of about thirty thousand used in the neighbourhood, is sent to Hungary.[1] In this calculation I believe the *dust salt*, or broken particles produced

---

[1] The east of Transylvania is supplied from mines in the Szekler land, and the North of Hungary chiefly from Velicska and the Marmaros. In a small work on Transylvania, published by M. Lebrecht in 1804, the amount of salt furnished by Transylvania is stated at above a million centners. The price was then one fifteenth of what it is at present. The population has increased and the consumption fallen off. Is not the elevation of price the cause? (*Author*).

by the hammering, is not included. Many thousand centners of salt are thrown into the river every year. For each of the masses of fifty-eight pounds which we have mentioned above, the miner receives two and a half kreutzers (twopence). With all the expenses, however, the centner is delivered at the pit's mouth for about twenty-four kreutzers *c.m.*, or tenpence. It is sold in Transylvania at three florins and a half, or seven shillings, the centner. The greater part is sent by the Maros to Szegedin, at an expense of about tenpence more each centner. It is sold there at seven guldens and a half, or fifteen shillings, the centner!

There has been so much complaint against this price of salt in the Diet, that we must say a few words more about it.

A monopoly of the sale of salt is one of the royal privileges, acknowledged as such by the nation, and enjoyed by the crown for a long succession of years. It can hardly be supposed, however, that the right of the crown can extend to raising the price of one of the first necessaries of life to any amount it may think fit; for this would be the admission of an indefinite and irresponsible right of taxation on all classes. To go no farther back than 1800, the price of salt was half a florin (one shilling) per centner. The long and exhausting wars, which brought on two national bankruptcies within a few years of each other, were an excuse for raising this price to three florins and a half in Transylvania, and seven and a half in Hungary. Even during the continuance of the war, complaints enough were heard against this augmentation, and since that time they have become every year more angry and more just. . . .

But the most extraordinary part of the affair is that the Government incurs this obloquy, and runs the chance of this loss, all to no purpose. The whole line of the frontier, from the Adriatic to the boundaries of Russia, is beautifully adapted for smuggling; and bulky as the salt is, I can assure the reader it is smuggled in along the whole of this frontier. If I am asked from whom I have obtained this information, I can only answer from some of the Government salt officers in Hungary, who told me that they themselves bought their salt from the smugglers.

I have been shown the salt smugglers' paths on the frontiers of Wallachia, where they often come over with whole troops of laden horses. I have heard from the county magistrates, that it was ridiculous to attempt to oppose them; that they had the sympathy of the peasantry with them, and were not only able to bribe the border guard, but that they came in such numbers, and so well armed, that they did not dare even to make a show of resisting them. I doubt if there is one great proprietor in the south of Hungary, who uses Government salt, except in such quantity as decency requires to blind officers who do not wish to see. . . .

The foreign trade, of course, is entirely lost by the increase of price; and Wallachia, Moldavia, and Servia, which formerly drew their salt from Hungary, now, as we have seen, return the compliment.

(c) The Gold and Silver Mines of Schemnitz

John Paget, *ibid.*, vol. i, pp. 333-4; 341-3; 344-5.

SCHEMNITZ[1] may be considered as the mining capital of Hungary. The mines are divided, from their position, into four districts, the Schemnitzer, Schmölnitzer, Nagy Bányaer and Banater; of which the first is by far the most considerable. Each district has its government, and its separate establishment of smelting-houses; but all send their produce to Kremnitz,[2] in the Schemnitzer district, to have the gold and silver separated and the crude metal coined.

A school of mining in imitation of that of Freyburg in Saxony, was founded at Schemnitz in 1760, and has attained considerable celebrity. It now contains about two hundred students, who receive their education free of cost, many of them being assisted with an annual donation of from twenty to thirty pounds for their support, and all being supplied with drawing-paper and pens, etc., at the expense of the Government.

The lectures are entirely in German, and indeed most of the students are German or Slavackish. The professors give a very favourable account of the state of the school and the industry of its scholars. The students have access to a good library, where every new work of importance bearing on the subjects studied may be obtained, and where a considerable number of French and German periodicals are received.[3]

The students give rather a different account. The younger students, they say—of course my informants were seniors—are generally better acquainted with the coffee and billiard rooms than with the halls of their professors; and the public examination is a farce, as it is well known that anyone can purchase the *primam classem* (the highest certificate) by a bribe to the professors. How far these statements may be true I know not; but I am inclined to believe that Schemnitz not only does not lead, but is far behind Freyburg and

[1] Hu. Selmecbánya, now Banská Štiavnica, Slovakia.

[2] Hu. Körmöcbánya, now Kremnica, Slovakia.

[3] To the disgrace of Schemnitz be it spoken, there is no good collection of minerals, either public or private; that of the college is below criticism. There is no dealer in minerals in the place (*Author*).

indeed most other schools, in the adoption of modern scientific improvements. A strong proof of this is the very bad manner in which the Austrians' mining establishments are said, by those who understand the subject, to be conducted in almost every part of the Emperor's dominions, and particularly in Hungary.

The students wear a neat uniform of dark green cloth turned up with red. The jacket has padded sleeves from the shoulder to the elbow, to protect the arms from the sides of the mines, with buttons bearing the crossed hammer and pick-axe. Behind is a large piece of leather, something like the tails of a coat, strapped round the waist, and forming in fact a posterior apron. In full dress they have gold epaulettes and a sabre. . . .

Austria has not yet learned that it is good economy to pay her servants well. The salaries of the mining officers, which even in reformed England would run from £100 to £1,000 a year at least, do not average more than from £50 to £100; and though provisions are cheap in Hungary, yet the clothes which the station of these officers obliges them to wear cost as much there as here. Where so much gold and silver slips through the fingers, it is not wonderful that some has occasionally stuck to them. A few years since a well-conceived and long-undiscovered scheme of robbery was laid open, in which six of the government officers of Schemnitz were concerned, and by which they had defrauded the State to a large amount.

The common miners, amounting in Schemnitz to twenty thousand, are exposed to the same temptation. They are not allowed to gain more than three florins per fortnight or three shillings per week! As if it were to check any disposition to industry, it has been reckoned how much the miner can do comfortably in the fortnight, working eight and sometimes six hours in the day. This quantum he is bound to perform, but he is allowed to perform no more, the government finding him in oil, gunpowder and instruments. This gives the miner many opportunities of peculation in these articles, which do not tend to improve his honesty, though rather a useful quality where gold and silver are in the case. The loss sustained in these articles alone, by the united rogueries of the labourer and his superiors, is said to be considerable. The method of paying the miner is not less defective: he is sometimes paid according to the amount of the material brought out without regard to quality, in which case he defrauds his employers by working where it is most easy to himself; sometimes according to the quantity of the metal produced, when he is apt to work the mine unfairly, taking only the richest parts and leaving much good material behind. In either case a premium is offered for roguery. . . .

About one half of the Schemnitz district is in the hands of private individuals or companies, who are said generally to lack capital and spirit. The laws of Hungary respecting mining are exceedingly liberal. Any one, on applying to the Kammer (as the exchequer is called) may receive permission to work any mine which does not interfere with other workings, no matter on whose estate it may be, paying only a moderate sum to the proprietor for the land used for buildings or necessary works. Likewise any mine already worked, if left unworked for fourteen days, may be taken up by anyone else. One tenth of the clear produce is payable to the Crown, and generally speaking, though I do not think necessarily, the ore is smelted in the government smelting-houses, for which a deduction is also made. The metal must all be coined in the country.

20. THE SCHUTZVEREIN

(J. Palgrave Simpson), *Letters from the Danube*, London, 1847, vol. i, pp. 255-7.

ONE of the most important and at the same time the most striking results of Hungarian national spirit may be found without a doubt in the establishment of the Society for the Protection of National Trade and Manufactures, the purposes, progress and probable issue of which you may have heard mentioned and discussed as the Hungarian *Schutzverein*, in Magyar *Országos védegylet*.

The members of this institution, although they take no oath to observe its regulations, yet give their word of honour to adhere to all its principles, and to obey its commands for a space of six years— the term allotted to give the society fair play and prove its efficacy— that is to say, to wear nothing but Hungarian manufactures, to consume nothing but Hungarian products—in short, to be national, entirely national, as far as is possible.

It is a pity that the words 'possible' and 'impossible' should exist in any man's moral dictionary; for they have such unlimited latitudes of interpretation in many minds that they finally have no meaning left in them at all. And thus fair ladies will subscribe the regulations of the society, excepting several items, such as foreign laces and similar adornments, as things 'impossible' to live without; and some fine gentlemen will except foreign cigars, as luxuries 'impossible' to be dispensed with, and yet support existence. . . . At all events the extent to which the society has spread itself is extremely remarkable, seeing that it was only established two years ago or thereabouts. The results of this national league are to be found to a very striking degree in the establishment of so many manufactories throughout the land and in the thriving condition in which they flourish under the auspices of a separate company, maintaining a close connection with the Sch_utzverein; and the progressing development of the national manufactures may be every day witnessed in the wares exhibited at every shop-window, not only in the capital but through-out the country, proudly ticked with the announcement that they are 'honi' (native) or 'nemzeti' (national).

The political results of this great national league for the protection of the national industry have been also very apparent. Established in order to prove a check to the painfully restrictive system of the Austrian custom-house as regarded the commercial relations be-tween Hungary and Austria, it was at first held up to ridicule by the latter country as a childish folly, incapable of any effect of solidity or worth. But the change of opinion has been great in the short period since its institution: its consequences are now looked to as important; and this importance has been strikingly proved by an offer on the part of Austria to make a change in its system of com-mercial relations with Hungary,—still more perhaps in the refusal of the Hungarians to accept *now* a change which, however it may propose a system of free trade between the two countries, no longer offers the same advantages to the rising manufactures of Hungary, as long as the outward restrictions of Austria in its dealings with other lands remain the same. . . .

J. P. Simpson (1807–87), British writer and dramatist, first visited Hungary in 1846. His 'Letters' are notable for their colourful description of village life.

21. CREDIT

Count István Széchenyi, *Hitel* (Credit), Pest, 1830, p. 88; *Stadium*, Leipzig, 1833, pp. 49, 54.

(Count István Széchenyi's three main economic works, *Hitel* (Credit), *Világ* (Light) and *Stadium*, cover similar ground. Their common theme is that radical alterations must be made in the financial, legal and social system if Hungary is to make proper use of her potentialities.)

THE absence of credit is the reason why nobody can improve his lands as much as should be naturally possible. . . . It is natural that an estate of 50,000 *hold*[1] in Hungary cannot today bring in an income of half a million pengő[1] but that it should not produce more

[1] See Note on Weights, Measures and Currency, p. 112.

than 30 or 40,000 pengő without endangering it is utterly unnatural
—yet this is how matters stand.

At the moment credit in Hungary is nothing but a mockery, for
in general the only folk who have it are those who are not in dire
need of it; those who need it most have none. The result is—and I
am prepared to demonstrate this—that in many parts of the country
an estate cannot flourish for lack of capital, while next door to it,
and again for lack of credit, money lies profitless in another. . . . Thus
the landowner languishes without money, while elsewhere money,
agriculture and labour go to waste. So death, not life, dwells on the
surface of the earth.

Our system is the chief offender here, in that our credit laws do
not apply to noble and non-noble alike, and that they generally
protect the bad farmer and hit the good one. . . . There is scarcely
anywhere in Hungary where despite all impediments and difficulties
10 per cent could not be gained by proper investment. This is certain
—and the profit would be 100 per cent in certain low-lying areas if
ditches were dug and the land drained. So let us have a system of
credit if we wish to reap profits. . . . In a country where practically
1,000 square miles of productive land are under water, where there
are really no internal communications, where there is a noble river
with an outlet to the Black Sea yet hardly used by shipping, where
not one single estate is even half utilized, where the inhabitants are
youthful and nature untamed, there are boundless riches to be
tapped. But let us not always think about the setting of our sun, but
rather its rising.

Count István Széchenyi (1791–1860), Hungarian magnate and reformer,
was termed 'the greatest Hungarian' by his political rival, Kossuth. After
extensive travels in the west, he both wrote and acted to improve the
economy of Hungary; he was responsible for books on economics, the first
permanent bridge at Budapest, steamboats, the regulation of the Tisza and
Danube and the creation of the Academy. The modern railway network is
also based on his plans.

22. DANUBE SHIPPING

Julia Pardoe, *The City of the Magyar*, London, 1840, vol. ii, pp. 307–14.

THE increase of traffic on the Danube is slowly but surely working
out the prosperity of Hungary; and were the financial circumstances
of the landed proprietors less trammelled than they are generally

admitted to be, there is no country in Europe with which the trading interests of England might be so closely and profitably united.

The Steam-Packet Company have established a dockyard on a small island opposite to Old Buda, which is a perfect model, with its workshops, forges and dry-docks. There are two stone-sheds, the one covered in and the other preparing for its roof, under which the new vessels are to be erected; the first ever built there being now in progress of completion, to be called the Nádor, and to replace the vessel of that name which has plied since the formation of the Company. An iron boat of one hundred and twenty horse power is also under construction. The carpenters are principally from Trieste and the smiths from Venice.

The engine-house is under the control and superintendence of an English engineer, assisted by several British and Scotch workmen; the rope-walk is a hundred and ninety toises[1] in length, and entirely under cover; and, as well as all the other buildings connected with the establishment, and the depot of wood used in constructing the vessel, they are encircled by a ring fence; and the whole of this compact and substantially-built dockyard has been erected since the month of April 1839 under the direction of a talented Italian, Captain Virgilio Bozzo.

There are at present ten steamers on the Danube and seven on the Black Sea. The dimensions and tonnage of those on the river itself are as follows:

	Length of deck Feet	Breadth Ft.	Ins.	Tonnage
Erős	179	25	0	525
Árpád	180	23	0	467
Zrínyi	167	23	0	405
Marianna	147	22	0	339
Francis	139	22	0	318
Nádor	138	18	2	212
Pannonia	132	17	2	180

In the year 1837, the aggregate number of passengers conveyed by the company was 47,436; in 1838 it had augmented to 74,584 (making an increase of 27,148) and in 1839 it was 66,800.

The amount of merchandise carried during the same period was, in 1838, 211,919 bales and 320,614 cwt.; and in the previous year only 151,402 bales and 246,623 cwt., also showing a considerable increase. In 1839 the freightage was 240,000 cwt.

[1] See Note on Weights, Measures and Currency, p. 112.

II. Hungary after 1848

23. THE EFFECTS OF THE EMANCIPATION

Arthur J. Patterson, *The Magyars, Their Country and Institutions*, London, 1869, vol. i, pp. 318–35.

THE emancipation of the land[1] was effected by Article IX, which abolished the *robot* or forced labour of the peasants for the landlords, as also of the dues they had to pay, whether in money or in kind; by Article XIII, which abolished the payment of tithe to the Roman Catholic clergy; and by Article XV, which abrogated the institution of *aviticitas*.[2] The first set of measures freed the lands of the peasantry, the last that of the nobility, from feudal burdens and restrictions.

Up to 1848 land in Hungary was either 'noble' or 'non-noble'. The first was not subject to the payment of direct state taxation. The land-tax was wholly raised from the non-noble land. In spite of the occasional efforts of the nobles to establish the principle *'onus non inhaeret fundo'*, which meant that, if a tax-paying noble occupied peasant-land, he was not obliged to pay the land-tax for it, the Government successfully resisted this encroachment. Of 'noble' land, the lord was the sole and only proprietor. In 'non-noble' land, three distinct parties had an interest,—the noble landlord, the State, and the tax-paying copyholder. It is obvious that the crown domains and the lands belonging to free districts or to royal free cities did not, strictly speaking, fall under either of these categories. They paid taxes to the State, but no dues to a subordinate *feudal lord*. Noble land was not necessarily occupied by nobles. On the contrary, they often gave it out in allotments to peasant tenants. This class of tenants was called 'contractualists' or 'curialists', to distinguish them from the older tenants, who were called *'jobbagyiones'*, 'subjects' and also 'urbarialists'. By a somewhat loose and incorrect use of the word, the tenure of these latter tenants has been called 'feudal'. They were, in fact, a sort of copyholders. The dues which they had to pay to the landlord had been determined by immemorial custom. To protect

[1] See also R. Bićanić, 'The Liberation of the Serfs in 1848', p. 335.
[2] See Richard Bright, 'The Law of Inheritance', p. 48.

these tax-paying peasants against any encroachments on the part of their tax-free landlords, Maria Theresa had a general manorial survey of the whole country taken in 1767–73. This survey is generally known by the name of *Urbarium*, whence the tenants whose rights and burdens it defined were called 'Urbarialists'. In contradistinction to these, the more modern class of tenants were called 'contractualists', because they had made a special contract with the lord as to the terms on which they were to hold their land, and 'curialists', because the land they occupied was 'curial', as forming part of the *curia* or 'court' of a nobleman. The curialists paid the capitation-tax; the urbarialists paid both.

The Urbarium of Maria Theresa corresponds to the 'Inventory' described by Mr. Shirley in his book on the *Russians of the South*. The great manorial survey was so closely associated with the queen who had ordered it to be made that '*Lusimus Mariam Theresiam*' passed into a proverb among the Hungarian squires for a successful evasion of its provisions.

The Hungarian peasant experienced to a certain degree the advantages of serving two masters. When the desert lands in the south of Hungary were resettled after the expulsion of the Turks, the government took care, first of all, to allot the best fields to the tax-paying peasant, while the tax-free nobleman only got a share of the fields of inferior quality. Even now the Banat land has two prices, according as it was noble or not (*Herrngründe* or *Bauerngründe*); the latter being the dearer. The Government in its anxiety to keep up the number of taxpayers and the area of taxable land regarded with extreme suspicion the conduct of the lord towards his peasantry. He was not allowed to evict them except for certain definite reasons set down in the law. These copyholds were hereditary. Should, however, the copyholding family die out or be evicted, the lord was not allowed to occupy the holding himself, but was obliged to give it to another non-noble tenant. A peasant who held a whole *sessio* was called a 'whole peasant'. This session varied in different parts of the country from sixteen to forty *Joch*[1] of arable land and from six to twenty-two *Tagewerke*[2] of meadow. A session might be divided into four parts, and so generally was it thus divided into quarters that a 'quarter peasant' may be taken as the average of his class in the better parts of the country. The same paternal interference of the authorities not only limited the subdivision of these peasant holdings, but also restricted their accumulation. A peasant might not hold more than one session in an urbarial estate in which the number of

[1] See Note on Weights, Measures and Currency, p. 112.
[2] = *Joch* or *hold*. See p. 43.

sessions did not exceed forty. In like proportion he might acquire two, three and even four sessions; but four sessions was the maximum of land he was allowed by law to acquire, however large might be the urbarial estate (*dominium*) to which he belonged.

In spite of these regulations it very often happened that a landlord could not find a tenant who would take a vacant quarter of a session. In such a case, after a certain lapse of time, he obtained on application to the authorities permission to break it up into smaller allotments, which he assigned to *zsellérek* or cottagers. Of this class there are a great number in Hungary, but many of them doubtless date from a period antecedent to the *urbarium* or are settled on curial land.

As an instance of the minuteness of legislation on this subject I may observe that the lord was not only allowed but even required by the urbarial law of Maria Theresa to set fire to the roof of such urbarialists as remained in the vineyards after the vintage had been gathered in. . . .

In 1848 the Hungarian liberals, considering that the peasant had acquired a claim on the state by having borne for so many centuries a disproportionate share of the public burdens, determined to indemnify him by converting his copyhold farm into a freehold estate, at the same time compensating the landlord out of the public treasury. Indeed during the many years' agitation which preceded the reforms of '48 many landowners enabled their subjects to buy their freedom at a moderate price. In so doing they were certainly actuated by motives of the purest patriotism and philanthropy and their conduct had doubtless a very beneficial effect in preparing the public mind for the general measures of emancipation. At the same time it cannot be fairly disputed that the massacre of the Galician landlords in 1846 by their peasantry at the instigation of some Austrian officials contributed its part towards impressing upon the Hungarian landlords a sense of the untenableness of their position.[1]

When the urbarial tenants were thus converted into freeholders, the curialists, whose relations to the lord seemed to them so similar, not to say quite identical, thought that they also should be allowed to keep their holdings without fulfilling the terms of their contract. During the troubles of 1848–9 many of them did so. It was only after peace had been re-established by the complete triumph of the Austrian Government that the landlords could commence suits in the civil courts to enforce the payments of their dues by the curialists; which suits took a long time to decide. In 1862 a small landed proprietor who had had recourse to the Austrian courts in this matter and had gained his suit told me that since 1859 when the prestige

[1] See p. 336.

G

of the Austrian Government was weakened and the more excitable portion of the population expected Garibaldi, his curialists again began to refuse payment. 'And now', said he, 'I will leave them alone; for it is better that I should lose my rents than that they should set my house on fire over my head.'

Indeed not the tenants only, but the landlords also confused from interested motives the two classes of urbarial and curial cottagers. Although the Government paper given them as compensation for the land was not actually equal to it in value, they preferred to take it rather than to run the risk of having continually to have recourse to the law courts to compel refractory and litigious peasants to fulfil their obligation. As for the tenant himself, he naturally made no objection to the substitution. Provided he got his land rent-free, he cared not under what title he was relieved from his burdens. So that nobody suffered, unless it was the Government and the tax-paying public—the parties who everywhere, but especially in the East of Europe, are the least able to defend themselves against fraud.

No unprejudiced observer can have any doubt as to the permanent advantage to the country at large from the emancipation of the peasant-lands. There can be little doubt that the class of 'noble' landlords suffered severely, as the great majority of them were perfectly unprepared for the change. In the slovenly system of agriculture which was fostered in both lord and peasant by the institutions of *robot* or forced labour, which formed the greater part of the rent of these copyhold farms, the lord had not only no experience of what paying regular wages meant, but he had not even enough draught cattle or agricultural implements. These he had to buy as best he could, for his stock of ready money was, generally speaking, very small. He was compensated for the land taken away from him and given to his former 'subjects' by Government bonds bearing interest. Of these a large mass were at once thrown upon the money-market and sold considerably below their value. Many landed proprietors were besides in debt through their passion for what they called 'extension', that is, the purchase of additional land, if not through even less excusable forms of extravagance. To all this were added the pecuniary losses caused by the War of Independence, patriotic loans, military requisitions and, after the final defeat of the Hungarian armies, fines, confiscations, imprisonments and forced military service. Who can reasonably wonder that so large a proportion of the Hungarian gentry are involved?

It was fortunate for the country at least that the reforms of 1848 had abolished the institution of *aviticitas*. The estates of a Hungarian nobleman were, before those reforms, but imperfectly alienable. As they had been granted to a family for ever, they could be pledged only in perpetuity, and that only to another nobleman. Jews were incapable of acquiring any real property whatsoever, nor could peasants or burghers become the real owners of the fee simple of noble lands. When the family died out, the fief returned to the Crown. When land changed hands, it was the custom to set down in the deed of sale as the purchase-money a sum twice as large as was actually paid. For at any time the descendant of the vendor could redeem the estate of his ancestor by repayment of the purchase-money plus the estimated value of the improvements effected by the capital of subsequent owners. Under this institution the title to land was even more uncertain in Hungary than it is in England. Scarcely any landed proprietor could feel sure that a lawsuit might not instantly be brought against him to oust him from his estate. One very common ground for such a suit was the allegation that an ancestor of the proprietor, or an ancestor of someone from whom the estate had been in any way previously acquired, had been concerned in one of the many insurrections of the seventeenth century, and had been branded with the *nota infidelitatis* (stigma of treason) which involved confiscation of his property. Fortunately the arsenal of Hungarian chicanery furnished as many weapons of defence as of offence, so that the actual proprietor would defend himself for at least twenty years. Whatever services this institution of *aviticitas* may have rendered the aristocratical constitution, it of course could not be allowed to survive it for a single day, and this abundant source of obstinate lawsuits was abolished by the Article XV of the laws of 1848, which ordered the Ministry to lay before the next Diet a new code of real-property law. This new code was prepared and imposed upon the country by the Austrian Government of Bach. . . .[1]

Commassatio is a technical word requiring explanation. Before 1848 the peasants in a village were in some respects tenants in common of the lord. Nor was the lord necessarily a single person. The lordship might be held by several noble proprietors (*compossessores*), not separately, but in common. The forests and pastures were regarded as the property of the lord, as in fact was the arable land too. His peasant tenants, however, had a recognized right to the use of them. When the arable land was converted from the copyhold to the freehold estate of the subject-peasant, his right to the use of the pastures and woods remained to him unchanged, except that it was relieved from all claim for rent or dues on the part of the lord. Before 1848

[1] Baron Alexander Bach (1813–93), Austrian Minister of the Interior 1849–59, whose name is associated with the severe absolutist rule imposed upon Hungary after the collapse of the revolution of 1848–9.

the latter had not perceived the many inconveniences arising from this joint tenure on his part with the peasants. As soon, however, as he had to pay wages and taxes, he found it incompatible with profitable farming. Nor was this joint tenure the only thing that dragged the cultivation of the land down to the level of that of the peasants. Owing to circumstances connected with the original allotment, or rather allotments of the peasant holdings, they were intricately mixed up with the land reserved by the lord. The process of *commassatio* was the remedy provided by the legislation of the Hungarian Diet shortly before 1848.

On the petition of either the lord or the majority of his former tenants, a commission might proceed to 'commass' the urbarial estate. It valued the former holdings of the peasants, as also of the residue reserved by the lord, field by field, and proceeded to do the same with the woods and pastures. It then grouped together on the one side the arable land that belonged to the lord and on the other what belonged to each several peasant. This proceeding would be in the eyes of most English agriculturalists an unmixed good, since it would save the waste of time and labour involved in moving from one small plot of ground to another in a different part of the estate. Nevertheless this process of *commassatio* has been, in the great majority of cases, entered upon at the petition of the landlord and not of his former tenants. The latter are firmly persuaded that self-interest is the motive of all men's actions, and suspect their former landlord of a design to get more than his fair share either in quality or quantity of the ploughed fields by the help of lawyers and surveyors, who are themselves *kabátos emberek*, people who wear coats. Besides this the Hungarian peasant sees two distinct objections to commassation. The first is that as time and labour appear to him commodities of but little value, he sees no advantage in having his arable land collected into one or two plots instead of ten or fifteen, especially when he has to pay the expense of commassing it. On the contrary, he thinks it his interest to have his patches of land at some distance apart, so that if the crop fail in one situation it may succeed in another. His second objection is at once more important and less honourable. When the commissioners had commassed the arable land they proceeded to divide the common woods and pastures. Now as long as the pastures remained undivided the peasant could practically feed, to the detriment of the lord, as much livestock as his purse enabled him to buy. In like manner, as long as the woods were held in common, it was difficult or impossible to prevent the peasant from cutting down more than his fair share of the timber. Consequently the peasant objected to the commassation, as it furnished the lord with an opportunity of putting an end once for all to the encroachments of his former tenants.

As far as I could judge the relations between gentry and peasantry in Hungary are fairly good. The Hungarian aristocracy and landed gentry always assured me that they are beloved by the peasantry. But it is, at least, significant that such assurances were always most unqualified in the mouths of landlords of high rank or large estates. The middle class of freeholders often expressed themselves to me in terms most unfavourable to the peasant with regard to his moral character, especially his honesty and sense of justice. This may have been because they lived in more constant and immediate contact with the class below them. Or it may have been the result of that worst form of oppression, 'a poor man that oppresseth the poor'. . . . Nor can we, in justice to the peasant, disguise the fact that the equality proclaimed by the laws of 1848 has not been accepted by Hungarian society without all *arrière pensée*. In the villages proclamations are stuck up forbidding smoking in the streets for fear of the straw-thatched cottages catching fire. Yet the 'gentlemen' may be seen lighting their pipes there, explaining to the stranger as they do so that 'the laws are made for the peasants'.

Arthur J. Patterson (1835–99), British scholar who visited Hungary first during the years before the *Ausgleich* of 1867. He studied the language, and later taught English at Budapest University. His comments are careful and balanced.

24. THE INDOLENCE OF THE MAGYARS

A. A. Paton, *Researches on the Danube and Adriatic*, Leipzig, 1861, vol. ii, pp. 16–18.

THE tendency to civilization visible in Pesth is entirely and exclusively from the large influx of German artisans, and from the German education of the superior classes. The fine streets and houses are all the product of German architects, builders, smiths, carpenters and cabinet-makers, assisted to a moderate extent by the Slovacks of the northern counties, who, inhabiting a poorer soil, are far more industrious than the Servians and Croats of the south; but here in Szolnok, where there are no Germans or Slovacks, you might imagine yourself to be in a village of Central Asia, so unlike is it to Europe, nothing being visible but filth and barbarism. Here and there a few logs of wood are thrown lengthways in the streets to prevent one getting over the ankles in mud; and in a town of

12,000 inhabitants, I have seen no house with a first floor, except the convent attached to one of the churches.

I find the Magyar character to have a great resemblance to that of the Turks who followed them out of Central Asia. They are generous to profusion; they are naturally very courageous, and like all foreigners that enjoy a supremacy through the valour of their forefathers, much more sincere than the Servians or Wallachians. Their defects are also the Asiatic defects—pride and indolence. The Magyar is uncivilized because he feels no desire to be better; he is on perfectly good terms with himself; he has no internal desire to labour, to improve, to take pains, and to persevere until he arrives at a great future result. Even if the common Magyar go to Pesth or Vienna, you find him a waiter in a tavern, a barber, or any light sauntering employment, but rarely in a trade that requires severe labour or long apprenticeship. If he stay at home, and devote himself to agriculture, he is equally remarkable for a spirit of antique, incurable Asiatic indolence.

Of the value of manure they have not the least idea, or rather they set too much store by it, for it accumulates in the towns so as to breed a fever from time to time. . . . The ploughs here are of the rudest description, and are all of wood, except a coarse ploughshare, which turns aside the earth so insufficiently that all the ploughing is done with six oxen, when in a modern plough, a pair of stout oxen is quite sufficient for the heaviest land. The harrows look as if they had come out of Noah's ark, being entirely of rude branches of trees, pegged together in the most inartistic manner, and do their work so imperfectly that a considerable part of the seed-corn is blown away.

When harvest-time comes, the wheat, instead of being reaped, is mowed down like grass, the mower receiving an eighth of the whole for his trouble in mowing. The corn is heaped up in stacks, and often lies on the ground until the outside grows green again. There is no threshing, except in the model-farm of a wealthy magnate here and there, and even with them, if a wheel goes wrong there is nobody in all the country round who can repair it, and a man must be sent for from a large town. The grain is trodden out by horses in the open air, at an immense loss, and the substitute for the granary is no doubt the same as between the Lena and the Oxus before the time of Arpad.[1] A hole is dug in the earth, narrow at the top and broad below, and here the corn is deposited. To exclude the damp, the mouth is so narrow, and the cavity so deep, that the man that takes it out is let down by a rope, like Joseph into the pit; and, after half a

---

[1] The first Hungarian ruler, and founder of the Árpád dynasty, who led the Magyars into Hungary. He died in A.D. 907.

year, the corn gets so earthy a flavour, that the bread has an unavoidable *goût*, which every traveller in the back settlements of Hungary can remember.

A. A. Paton, British correspondent, found little to admire in Hungary, which he visited after the revolution of 1848. His critical observations are well-founded.

25. REGIONAL CONDITIONS

(a) Problems of the Alföld

Arthur J. Patterson, *The Magyars, Their Country and Institutions*, London, 1869, vol. i, pp. 74–95.

FROM Pest to the borders of Transylvania, from Tokay to Belgrade, stretches one vast alluvial plain, here sandy, here dry, here marshy, but on the whole remarkably devoid of trees and still more of stone. . . . This Great Hungarian Plain is 70 German miles[1] from the north-east to the south-west. Its breadth from the mountains of Transylvania on the east to the hills of Bakony and Vertes on the west is about 30 German miles and the whole extent of the plain is at least 1,700 German square miles. It extends on both sides of the Danube, the Theiss[2] and the Maros.

The utter absence from the Great Plain of wood, stone and all other materials for road-making, has conduced in no small degree to cripple its agricultural development. . . . The struggle between the agriculturalist and water is at best a long and toilsome one, but it becomes nearly hopeless when the ambiguous element appears in the form of subterranean waters. Now, unfortunately, water on the Alföld almost always takes a subterranean form. There is perhaps no European country which has so few brooks as the Hungarian lowland. . . . In seasons of drought the moisture in the land drains into the rivers—a phenomenon not peculiar to Hungary, but what is unfamiliar to us is that in wet seasons the reverse takes place, and the waters of the rivers soak through their banks into the adjacent country, reappearing perhaps at a great distance off in the form of pools or swamps. . . . The *pontes sine aqua* were bridges thrown over the hollows in this way, which, although dry during the summer, are after heavy rains filled with water which comes down from the mountains and wanders through these slight depressions in the plain.

The soil of the Alföld is, for the most part, of exuberant natural

[1] See Note on Weights, Measures and Currency, p. 112.   [2] Tisza.

fertility. . . . But this is not the result of geological conditions alone. Before 1848 the Alföld was a country without roads or railways; the population was sparse and trade and commerce at their lowest ebb. Consequently but little more corn was grown than was required for the cultivator's own consumption. Immense tracts of land, the so-called *pusztas*, naturally better adapted for crops of wheat and maize, served only as pastures for immense flocks of sheep and herds of long-legged, long-horned, cream-coloured oxen and of half-wild horses. These animals could be more easily sent to the market across those tracks of summer's dust and winter's mud, which, by a misuse of language, were called roads. This state of negative passivity has been to a great measure put an end to by the advance of civilization, by the partial introduction of railways and canalization of rivers, and last but not least by the terrible pressure of taxation introduced by the Austrian government after the war of 1849. Before that year the Hungarian peasant's favourite mode of investing his money was in flocks and herds, especially in oxen and horses, which he consequently called *jószág*, 'property', without any explanatory cause or epithet. This 'property' he was obliged to part with in order to satisfy the demands of the 'German' tax-gatherer. The peasant had, in fact, to pay at least double the amount which he had paid before 1848 and this, though he then bore the whole burden of taxation, whereas since that year he has shared it with his 'noble' compatriots. If, however, we consider not merely what the peasant paid during those two periods, but compare the total amount of taxes paid by the country at large, the figures will be perhaps even more startling. In the years 1843–5 Hungary, Croatia and Slavonia, without Transylvania or Dalmatia, paid thirty-four and a half million florins, whereas in 1864 the same countries paid one hundred and twenty-one and a half million florins. In the first period it is calculated that about eight millions passed definitely out of the country; in the second, however, forty-eight millions. These figures show how it is that the country has not benefited so much as might have been expected by the emancipation of the land in the year 1848.

When the peasant had parted with his livestock, he had still before his eyes the prospect of ever-recurring demands on the part of the 'German'—demands which rather increased than diminished as time went on and the difficulties which beset the Viennese government became more pressing. In order to meet them it became necessary to plough up some of the old pasture land and sow it with corn. The natural consequence of this increase in the production of wheat and maize was a fall of prices. This necessitated still further encroachments on the *puszta*. A tourist has observed of the country around Madrid that Spain is the only country in which 'cultivated deserts' are to be found. If he had ever travelled from six o'clock of a summer morning until four in the afternoon along the *Theiss Eisenbahn* from Pest to Nagyvárad or Gross-Wardein, he might have seen cause to modify his statement. There the traveller passes from station to station on a plain as level and as well-cultivated as La Beauce.

Before 1848 there prevailed over this vast extent of country a system of agriculture which Dr. Ditz[1] calls 'extensive', as opposed to the 'intensive' system which prevails in more highly civilized countries. Here the effects of natural causes are hardly modified by the efforts of the cultivator. Consequently the general production of the country and the result of any particular harvest depend almost entirely on natural causes. Of the natural fertility of the soil we have already spoken; the climate, however, is so bad as almost to counterbalance that advantage. . . . It is marked by frequently recurring droughts, by occasional violent floods, extreme heat during the summer and equally extreme cold during the comparatively brief winter, both occasionally diversified by violent storm-winds. . . .

But the peculiarities of the climate of the Alföld as regards temperature are not so disastrous as those which relate to moisture. Some persons are of the opinion that the periodical droughts which afflict that region are becoming more frequent. For this they assign two reasons. Dr. Ditz produces some very good arguments for supposing that the Alföld was formerly not so destitute of trees as it is at present, and that the original forests have been rooted by the recklessness of the Magyars themselves. A second and more recent cause is the great amount of land-drainage effected during the present century by Count Stephen Széchenyi, his associates and successors. The great work of the regulation of the Theiss reclaimed to cultivation 217 geographical square miles of swamp. Before that time the river was continually overflowing its banks, and as the waters retired they left behind them pools in the hollows of the plain, which did not dry up for three or four years, and mitigated by their exhalations the excessive aridity of the Alföld summer. The bad effects upon the climate of this extensive drainage are the less to be disputed as its good effects are even more evident. . . .

Two measures have been recommended by the commission appointed to inquire into the possibility of increasing the rainfall of the Alföld. The first and most important is the construction of canals which should serve the double purpose of navigation and irrigation. . . . Surveys have been made for the construction of a canal from

---

[1] Heinrich Ditz, *Die ungarische Landwirtschaft*, Leipzig, 1867.

Pest on the Danube to Csongrád or Szeged on the Theiss. The second measure recommended was an extensive plantation of trees, which has, indeed, been to some extent adopted. . . . The lack of trees is not only injurious in its effects on the climate in diminishing the rainfall of the district and increasing the violence of the winds, it tends to impoverish the soil by compelling the inhabitants to burn for fuel what ought to be returned to the ground as manure. . . .

The vast and desolate character of the *pusztas* is enhanced by what Dr. Ditz calls the 'Asiatic husbandry' of the Alföld Magyar. In its original form this Asiatic husbandry was characterized by the minimum of farm buildings. The Hungarian language bears witness to the fact that a covered stall was an innovation borrowed from Germany. It is called *istálló*, a word derived from the German *stall*. Originally the Magyar confined his cattle in an unroofed fold, *akol*. Nor did he want a covered threshing floor, as his corn was trodden out on the field by horses or oxen, almost as soon as it was cut. The corn was then laid up in bottle-shaped holes, narrower at the top than below, which were excavated in the ground, burnt dry, and lined with straw. These were his granaries. When filled they were covered with straw, and above that with earth, so as to make it even with the ground. During the Russian invasion in 1849 the Cossacks, accustomed to a similar system of agriculture, showed a fatal ability for discovering these subterranean granaries by probing the ground with their long lances. The extreme difficulty, not to say utter impossibility, of finding building materials over the greater part of the Alföld gave rise to these arrangements.

(b) *Natural Wealth of the Bánát*

A. A. Paton, *Researches on the Danube and Adriatic*, Leipzig, 1861, vol. ii, pp. 28–9.

THE Bánát is the cornucopia not only of Hungary but of the whole of the Austrian Empire;—even Lombardy, highly favoured as it is by nature, must yield precedence to the Bánát of Temesvár; and one must go to the delta of the Nile to find a similar soil. . . . This produces wheat of a quality nowhere else to be found in the imperial states. But the eastern part being hilly, is rather fitted for wine culture. . . . The mineral wealth of this part of the Bánát is no less remarkable. In the vale of Mehadia, our talented and ingenious countryman, Count General Hamilton, a soldier of the school of Prince Eugene, rediscovered in 1736, after a lapse of more than 1,000 years, those sulphurous springs renowned through all the

Roman Empire for their power and efficacy; and in the extensive coal mines of Oravicza,[1] near Weisskirchen,[2] the king of Hungary possesses a treasure more valuable than all the gold of Schemnitz and Kremnitz, having become, as proposed, the terminus of the great railway which a few years later stretched over Central Hungary to Temesvár.[3]

(c) The Jews in Transylvania

Raymond Recouly, *Le Pays Magyar*, Paris, 1903, p. 8.

IT would seem that with the best will in the world nobody could extract any profit from such wretched folk as these. But it can be done, for right in their midst and living solely upon them is the Jewish innkeeper who grows rich and prospers. I have seen all the villages in the district, and there is not one without its Jewish inn-keeper. Over the inn-sign, always accompanied by the words 'Wine, Beer and Spirits', the name one finds is invariably Solomon, Isaac or Nathan. Now this Jew, as often as not the only one of his race in the village, is not merely the innkeeper, but the grocer, haberdasher, hardware dealer, etc., as well. He sells to the peasants all they need, and from them he buys eggs, fruit and goose feathers as well, if geese are bred in the district. In short all the small trade of the village passes through his hands, and some of it stops there. Trading is not enough, so he adds banking to his business. He makes loans to the peasants. Here Mr. T., the lord of the manor, once had the right of keeping an inn, and he put it to good use; when the state took over this right, along came the Jew, who is now firmly entrenched. His house is built of stone and has two floors, and his wife wears a hat.

I hope that nobody will read into these lines the least traces of foolish anti-Semitism. I have merely stated what I saw with my own eyes. If the Jew prospers so rapidly, there is no doubt that he owes his advance to the carelessness and improvidence of the poor peasants who surround him. He also owes much to his own quick mind and energy. Usually he arrives in the village with all his worldly posses-sions knotted in a handkerchief on the end of a stick. Once arrived, he falls to work with unbelievable tenacity and invincible obstinacy.

Raymond Recouly, French writer, visited Transylvania in 1902. At that time, he was sympathetic towards the Hungarians; his later writings are more critical.

[1] Oravița, Rumania.   [2] Bela Crkva (Fehértemplom), Yugoslavia.
[3] Timişoara, Rumania.

(d) Szeged and Danube Shipping

A. A. Paton, *ibid.*, vol. ii, pp. 24–7.

SZEGEDIN is an interesting place. It has not European civilization like Presburg or Pesth, nor is it barbarous like the villages of the interior. It is a rough, home-spun, busy, prosperous money-making place and, as I should imagine, like a town in the Ohio, a place of mills and boats, grain warehouses and general stores; not an ultimate emporium that stands in contact with the luxurious consumer, but the initial market that takes its tone from the laborious producer. . . .

All round the fort is the civil part of the Palanka, or central town, which is inhabited by the merchants and tradespeople, with a great inequality of architecture. Some of the houses are large, lofty and modern, in the style of Vienna, and side by side an old Hungarian house of one story, that perhaps stood there when there was a Turkish pasha in the fortress. Most of the shop-signs in the public place of the Palanka have German names, but the designation of the trade and baptismal names is in Magyar. During the mania for Magyarization, none were so keen to identify themselves with the Magyars as the small German shopkeepers. Most of the highest and wealthiest nobility being Magyars, Magyarism was very naturally more or less associated with the idea of aristocracy and supremacy, and while the Croats and Servians, and the great majority of Slovacks, much to their honour, were rather proud of their national- ity than ashamed of it, these German tradesmen, anxious to purify themselves from a supposed identity of blood with Schiller, Goethe and Beethoven, and roused to an enthusiasm with the greater ser- vices Attila[1] and Arpad[2] had rendered to civilization, were anxious to throw off their own names and adopt Magyar ones. Not one, two or three, but hundreds of such instances occurred.

The lower town, or Alsó-város, is mostly inhabited by land culti- vators; and is composed of long streets with the houses considerably apart, each having a kitchen-garden, and being mingled with ponds and marshes, is neither town nor country. A portion of the inhabi- tants of the lower town are ship-builders and mill-wrights; for here the best and cheapest boats in Hungary are built, as well as the best floating-mills. These floating-mills are a peculiarity of the river, there being no less than three hundred of them on the Theiss; for small water power being scarce from the flatness of the country, the only power sufficient for turning a mill is on the large streams. The

---

[1] Attila the Hun was by legend and tradition the ancestor of the Magyars.
[2] See note, p. 86 above.

boats are for the most part built of oak and come from the '*Tisza Hat*', or so-called back of the Theiss, being a part of the Theiss between Tokay and the Carpathians. These boats are not only employed on this river, but on the Save and Danube, and are remarkable for their strength and neatness.

The Felső-város, or upper town, is not much higher than the lower town. . . . The principal manufacture of the upper town is soap-boiling; there being above 20 of these establishments here, in which common laundry-soap is made, much of which is exported to Pesth and Vienna; the low places in the sandy plains between Ketskemet[1] abounding in soda. Formerly any one could gather this alkali, but since the trade has become extended these places have become private property. These manufactories are carried on in a very primitive but economical manner. The father of the family acts as traveller, attends the fairs of Pesth and Debreczin, and takes his orders in Vienna and the other large towns; while the operations of manufacture are performed by his wife, daughters, and servants, there being no workmen at wages in the establishment.

The upper town is also the residence of the principal boat-owners, and some of them are so extensively engaged in navigation and transport as to possess 50 or 60 boats, worth each when new about £400. Comorn[2] and Szegedin are, in pacific times, the two towns in Hungary which are the seats of the river shipping interest, as well for building as for ownership. The principal freights upwards were corn and rape-seed from the Banat, and tallow brought down the Maros from Transylvania; which, along with the soda on the spot, enables the soap manufacture to thrive. The returns from above are the cottons of Bohemia, the cloths of Moravia, and coarse fancy articles from Vienna. Considerable quantities of wood and wine also come from Tokay and the upper Theiss, to the Francis canal, which leads into the Danube, thus saving the considerable détour by the confluence; it was then dragged up to Raab[3] and Wieselburg,[4] which latter town is the great granary of Vienna. But railways have now revolutionized communications in Hungary.

[1] Kecskemét.
[2] Komárom.
[3] Győr.
[4] Moson.

26. The State of Elementary Education

Baron József Eötvös, *A VK Miniszternek az országgyűlés elé terjesztett jelentése a népiskolai közoktatás állapotáról* (Report of the Minister of Education to Parliament on the State of Elementary Education), Pest, 1870.

(In 1868 school attendance was made compulsory for children from six to twelve, and 'repetition' courses from twelve to fifteen. The Minister, Baron József Eötvös, immediately ordered an inquiry into the state of education in Hungary, and presented his findings to parliament in 1870, together with far-sighted recommendations, few of which were ever implemented. The following extracts are from his report.)

(a) The Actual State of Elementary Education

REPORTS have arrived from all the public authorities in Hungary and Transylvania, and of the 11,903 parishes only 83 have not sent in their statistics. These show the following:

1. There are 1,615,181 children (boys and girls) between 6 and 12 years old, and 669,560 between 12 and 15, a total of 2,284,741 children of school age. Of these there are 1,928,679 (987,626 boys and 941,053 girls) in Hungary proper and 356,062 (185,544 boys and 170,518 girls) in Transylvania.

2. In Hungary proper 526,269 boys and 434,769 girls actually attend school. Apart from these 40,003 boys and girls attend other educational institutions. Thus 1,001,041 children attend school, 50·88 per cent of the total school population. In Transylvania 86,902 boys and 58,964 girls attend elementary schools and 5,208 children go to other institutions. Thus 151,074 attend school, 40·37 per cent of the total school population.

From these figures it will be noted that 1,132,626 children, i.e. almost half of those of school age, grow up without any schooling at all. These figures give an even sadder picture of the previous state of education when we take into account the favourable effect of the new law, for partly as a result of the increased interest in education and partly due to the new law and measures taken to implement it, far more children were at school throughout the country during the year 1869–70 than at any time during the last decade. Another factor to note is that a large proportion of the children recorded as attending school does so only during the winter. We must also realize that most of the children in the 12–15 age-group do not attend school, and that of the 1,132,626 children shown as absentees, there will be a large number who have learnt something up to the age of 12. As far as we can calculate, some 68·53 per cent of the children in Hungary between 6 and 12 do in fact attend school.

3. The number of schools is as follows:

Of the 9,630 parishes in Hungary proper, 1,367 have no school. The remaining 8,263 parishes have 11,144 schools. In Transylvania 349 parishes are without schools, and in the other 1,924 parishes there are 2,654 schools.

Of the parishes which have no school, 779 state that the children attend schools in neighbouring parishes. This leaves 933 (in Hungary 869, in Transylvania 64) where there is no instruction whatsoever.

The proportion of existing schools to area and population is as follows:

In Hungary, there are 2·9 schools per square mile and 1·0017 per thousand of the population. In Transylvania there are 2·8 schools per square mile and 1·2630 per thousand of the population. These figures show that the number of schools is still far too small.

4. In Hungary there are 12,802 regular and 1,560 assistant teachers in the state and denominational schools. Of the total of 14,362, 220 are women. In Transylvania there are 3,166 regular and 264 assistant teachers, a total of 3,430, including 25 women. The proportion of teachers to children of school age is as follows:

In Hungary there is one teacher to 135 children, or to 70 who actually attend school, while in Transylvania there is one teacher to every 104 children of school age, or to 44 actually at school. These proportions, however, are much less favourable in reality, for in many small villages there are only 25–30 children to one teacher, while in larger parishes and towns one teacher has to take a class of 120–200.

The average salary of teachers at present is 208 forints 87 kreutzers in Hungary and 120 forints 47 kreutzers in Transylvania.

5. In the whole country there are 36 denominational and 14 state training colleges for teachers. In the former the course lasted for only two years (except in the case of one or two Protestant colleges), and some 1,500 men and 130 women have studied there. In addition to these some 200 students have gone each year from theological colleges and secondary schools to teach, in most cases only temporarily, i.e. for two or three years.

In the state colleges there are altogether 405 men and 86 women students. There are two reasons for these small figures. First, the announcement of their opening was delayed, and secondly hostel accommodation was not mentioned in the relevant law, so that insufficient provision was made for board and lodging. Since the poorer students who wish to teach can hardly afford to live outside college, many of them went elsewhere before enrolment had been completed.

(b) The Main Deficiencies in Elementary Education

There is no doubt that the greatest deficiency and worst obstacle to progress is the unsatisfactory ratio of schools to children, and to this must be added the lack of suitable buildings. According to the reports of the inspectors, some counties have a surprisingly large number of parishes without schools. Thus in Vas 297 out of 646 parishes are without schools, and of these only 97 state that their children attend neighbouring schools. In Bihar there are 120 Greek Orthodox parishes alone without schools. In Alsó-Fehér 62 parishes have no school, while in 64 more the school buildings cannot be used.

An even greater deficiency is to be noted in the larger parishes which possess schools, but insufficient rooms and teachers. In these not even half of the children of school age can be accommodated, so that in some places every year several thousand children are compelled to go without schooling. It is unfortunate that these are usually the more prosperous, populous and cultured towns. In Szabadka[1] there are altogether 29 classrooms, which according to law may take only 2,320 children. Last year 3,000 children attended —but there are 10,000 children of school age in the town. It is easy to see why the last census revealed that 32,000 of the 56,000 inhabitants of Szabadka could neither read nor write.

The situation is similar in Szeged, Arad, Kecskemét, Nagy-Kőrös, Debrecen, Czegléd, Pozsony,[2] Temesvár,[3] Kassa[4] and Kolozsvár.[5] From this it is easy to see that the lack of schools is not to be measured merely by the number of parishes that have none.

All these figures prove that the most essential part of the Education Act of 1868, i.e. general compulsory education, cannot be implemented in the greater part of the country, even with the best will in the world, since if all parents were to send their children to school, either there would be no room for them, or there would be no place to which to send them.

The majority of classrooms now in use do not fulfil the requirements of the law. Some are tumbledown and out-of-date; others are so dark, cramped, low and damp that in normal circumstances they should never be used for educational purposes. From my own experience I may say that the children who spend at least half a day in most of the schoolrooms in Hungary suffer greater harm to their health than profit from the education they receive.

A second great obstacle to progress is the lack of properly trained teachers. According to estimates already made, we need 10,767.

[1] Subotica, Yugoslavia.   [2] Bratislava, Slovakia.   [3] Timişoara, Rumania.
[4] Košice, Slovakia.   [5] Cluj, Rumania.

Even if the government were to open all the requisite training colleges immediately, it would take at least 15 years for all the posts to be filled. This lack of teachers—and the unsatisfactory nature of their training—is proved by the hurried despatch to schools of second-year and even first-year students during the present academic year.

Nor are there sufficient candidates offering themselves for training. In the last three years the number has decreased, since with the restoration of constitutional life, many previously closed or new careers have been offered to youth, and intelligent and capable young folk will not enter a profession which is neither profitable nor designed to offer any great advancement.

A further problem is the poor quality of a large number of present teachers. Since I have been concerned with elementary education I have been astonished at the lack of culture of very many of them. Some of them are so unfitted for their task that they can scarcely keep their present knowledge alive. Not only have they no idea of the proper methods of teaching, but they do not possess positive knowledge of those subjects which they must teach, according to the law. Several sad cases show that some teachers possess not even the most elementary knowledge—in Zemplén there are 17 teachers in denominational schools who cannot even write.

These failings can be attributed to the following main causes:

1. Many posts have been filled by untrained teachers, who at most have learnt the ritual of the church and a few hymns.

2. The majority of training colleges have been established only during the last 20 years, and they have been so poorly organized that far too little attention has been paid to anything other than religious instruction, ritual and singing.

3. The salaries of the teachers are often so low that well-trained folk will not enter the profession. Even if they do, they are compelled to augment their salaries by undertaking non-educational work. And their poverty often prevents them from buying necessary equipment, so that they do not even know of the existence of suitable books.

4. Very many teachers are cut off from educated society and their own status is low.

Finally it is a serious drawback that so many teachers in denominational schools are at the same time precentors and parish clerks, so that they can devote only a small amount of time to teaching. How can a teacher educate himself and others when he has a large family, occupies the offices of precentor and parish clerk, and on top of this has at least 150 children to educate? And for all this work he receives so little pay that he is compelled to undertake agricultural labour too in order to keep alive.

H

Although there is often enthusiasm for elementary education, the efforts of the government are often undermined by the indifference of parents, parishes and other local authorities. The indifference of parents is shown in their failure to send their children to school and in their unwillingness to provide them with books and equipment. Frequently they not only fail to send them to school, but keep them at home on the slightest pretext, and in the towns they send faked medical certificates to the teachers. While in Transylvania the Saxons send their children to school until they are 18, in the rest of the country parents do not want their children to be educated after the age of 10–12. Indeed, from spring till autumn they take their children away from school, so that even today it is virtually impossible in most places to ensure their education during the summer months.

The main obstacles to schooling in the summer months are as follows:

(a) Tending animals, particularly geese, for which children of 6–8 are used. Those of 11–14 are used to guard horses and cattle.

(b) Taking lunch to parents working in the fields—but this need not prevent them from attending school from 7–10 in the morning.

(c) Looking after young children while the parents are working in the fields. This can only be overcome by the provision of adequate day-nurseries as soon as possible.

Baron József Eötvös (1813–71), Hungarian author and statesman, was one of the most enlightened political and social writers of his age. He was th founder of modern education in Hungary.

27. INDUSTRY IN BUDAPEST

(a) In 1859

János Hunfalvy, *Pesth und Ofen* (Pest and Buda), Pest, 1859, pp. 197–8.

PEST is the centre of industry and commerce in Hungary. In these, there have been very marked developments during the last few years. At the end of the eighteenth century there were very few industries in Pest; some ships were built here, and there were leather and parchment factories which were quite well known. To these must be added the silk factory of Thomas Valero, erected in 1770, which gained a wide reputation for its products. The main stimulus to industrial activity, however, is of recent origin, and many of the means adopted were undoubtedly mistaken; nevertheless the results are plain. In 1846 there were some 40 industrial establishments in Pest; more recent events, however, curbed and paralysed their development. A general shortage of money became acute after the revolution, when virtually all working capital was lost. This shortage has not yet been overcome, and hinders the various branches of industry.

The number of agricultural machinery factories has recently increased to seven; in these various types of machine are produced as well as certain necessary implements.

One of the largest factories is the Joseph Mill, rebuilt after destruction by fire in August 1850. Here there are three steam engines of 60, 40 and 10 H.P. respectively. In 1856 some 300,000 *metzen* of corn were ground. Other steam mills are to be found in Ofen (Buda), while on the river there are floating mills which work for 8–9 months of the year.

Close to the Joseph Mill is the sugar refinery, erected in 1845. Although well-equipped, it has never prospered.

Much more flourishing is the recently established sawmill and cabinet works, which produces a wide variety of wooden articles. Even larger is the brickyard of Alois Miesbach, situated about an hour's distance from the town. Here the eleven kilns produce over 15 million bricks yearly.

János Hunfalvy (1820–88) was an eminent Hungarian geographer, who from 1870 held the chair of geography at Budapest University. His description of the difficulties of industry during the Bach régime makes an interesting comparison with the account of Lukács less than forty years later.

(b) In 1893

Béla Lukács, 'Industrie und Handel in Budapest' (Industry and Commerce in Budapest), *Die österreichisch-ungarische Monarchie in Wort und Bild*, Vienna, 1893, vol. iii, pp. 467–80.

THE visitor approaching Budapest from the north along the Danube immediately realizes that he is nearing a very large commercial and industrial centre. From some distance away he notes the grey haze peculiar to large cities, and in the outer suburbs he sees slender factory chimneys and long unbroken lines of industrial premises on both banks of the river. At Óbuda and Újpest there are shipyards. Then follow quays piled with planks and firewood, paving and building stone, and then there are the heavy machinery factories which fill the ear with their din. . . . If one approaches from Belgrade and the Iron Gates, it is the factories on the plains of Kelenföld and the endless row of industries on the Pest bank that offer the first welcome. Then the visitor sees the trains rumbling over the south railway bridge and the long lines of wagons in the State Railways goods depot on the river-bank, with the municipal grain-elevator and its group of warehouses in the background. Then come the customs halls and the flood of commercial life to be seen on the quayside. All this shows that the Hungarian capital is the centre not only of political life, but of industry, commerce and transport. The same impression is gained by the rail-traveller, whether he approaches the city from Transylvania, Fiume, Constantinople or Bucharest; he is first greeted by the turmoil of industrial activity, smoky factories, long goods trains and wagons of all shapes and sizes standing on tracks which lead to breweries, distilleries, oil refineries and other plants.

Industry is scattered throughout the capital and may still be found in areas which, according to the latest town-planning schemes, are reserved for blocks of flats and office-buildings. In general, industry is slowly being forced into the suburbs. It is not long since the site of the Danube Corso, the most elegant promenade in the city, was occupied by a row of small factories and tanneries; huge piles of refuse from these littered the river-bank where now there are stone quays and landing-stages. The river itself was sprinkled with hundreds of little water-mills, which did their work cheaply and without competition from the powerful steam-mills. . . .

Almost all the industries of Budapest are new. The city cannot look back upon centuries of industrial and commercial development; these have been fostered by the political importance and natural location of the capital. It was the introduction of steamboats that provided the first stimulus; later the development of a railway network with Budapest at its centre brought rapid progress. . . .

Some idea of the extent of this progress is given by the municipal accounts. The city has a budget of some 12 million gulden, of which several millions are spent on the maintenance of roads, water-mains, warehouses, slaughter-houses, cattle-markets and various commercial enterprises. According to the statistics of 1890, some 30 per cent of the population of Budapest are engaged in commerce and industry. 110,142 were employed in industry alone, in the strict sense of the word. . . . Not counting shops, commercial or transport undertakings or credit institutions, there are 371 factories and industrial plants within the city boundary.

Flour-milling is one of the oldest and most extensive industries in the city, largely due to the distinctive quality of Hungarian wheat, which has won the highest awards in international exhibitions. The Joseph rolling-mill, built at the end of the forties and since improved and extended, must be regarded as the pioneer steam-mill, although the first one in the country—a short-lived experiment—was at Sopron in the west. Today there are 15 steam-mills in the city, with 3,200 employees. From 5–6½ million metric centners[1] of grain they produce annually 4–4$\frac{8}{10}$ million metric centners of flour. The corresponding figures for 1870 were 3 million metric centners of grain and 2½ of flour.

Another flourishing industry is that of distilling and refining spirits. This occupies 10 large factories, which owing to the good rail and river connections receive raw supplies from all parts of the country and are never short of them. The larger distilleries export extensively to both east and west. Cattle and pig fattening, important by-products of this industry, are also well-developed.

The manufacture of machinery has grown considerably, especially milling equipment and agricultural machines. Steam threshing machines, made by the State Machinery Factory, were first constructed in 1879, since when over 1,000 have been made. Other heavy machinery factories in the city manufacture railway equipment, iron bridges, locomotives, boilers, stationary steam engines, gas engines, marine engines, milking machines (which have achieved a fine reputation) and turbines. The large turbines for the electric power station by the romantic Tivoli waterfall near Rome have been ordered from Budapest. Various hydraulic machines, firefighting equipment, cast-iron wheels and railway track are also made.

A new industry which has quickly entered the export market is the manufacture of electrical machinery and equipment. The lighting plants which supply Venice, Karlsbad, Monaco, the Tsar's palace at Tsarskoye-Selo and the Bulgarian capital were all made in Budapest. A special product is mobile lighting equipment, which can be used for a short time and then taken elsewhere; this is useful for festivals or for the entrainment by night of large bodies of troops.

The leather industry is flourishing. In Budapest and the industrial suburb of Újpest there are six large factories, one of which dates back to 1815. . . .

As for chemical products, there are two large dyeworks, a tar-factory, limeworks, an artificial manure factory, several plants for the manufacture of oils and an extensive factory which produces perfumes and pharmaceutical articles. By the station at Ferencváros there are two large oil refineries which obtain crude oil from Russia and Rumania via Fiume and Predeal.

Three gasworks supply the city, whose rapid growth can be measured by the production figures; in 1860, there was one

[1] See Note on Weights, Measures and Currency, p. 112.

gasworks, which produced 1,753,000 cubic metres, while in 1890 the three works produced 18,511,000 cubic metres. Recently, however, electric lighting has begun to replace gas, which was first used in 1856. 800 workers are now employed, and the gasworks produce coke, tar and other by-products.

Another active industry is shipbuilding. Two large dockyards attached to the Óbuda works of the Donaudampfschiffahrtsgesellschaft build 25 new ships every year. In 1890 the total number of new ships built in Budapest was 60.

The wagon works of Budapest are also well known. In the four largest factories some 900 wagons are built each year, of which a considerable proportion goes to the orient. . . .

The brickyards on the outskirts of the city cannot keep up with the demand, although they are at work continuously. They produce 110–115 million bricks annually, and these are used for the erection of large blocks of flats, public buildings and town houses. A speciality of Budapest is the 'Keramit' brick with which some of the streets are paved. The growth of the building industry has also affected cabinet-making, carpentry and allied trades. . . .

Mention should also be made of the manufacture of telegraphic apparatus and telephones, the paper mills and playing-card factories. Then there are tobacco and match factories, and several small plants for the production of luxury articles. Armaments are also manufactured in the city. There is an extensive jute-factory, while india-rubber, gutta-percha and asbestos are all made here. . . .

This sketch, though necessarily given in broad outline, is nevertheless sufficient to show that industrial development in Budapest is extremely active.

Béla Lukács (1847–1901), Hungarian economist, became a director of the State Railways and Minister of Trade. He was responsible for the Hungarian exhibition in Paris in 1900. His account, while obviously intended as an advertisement, nevertheless gives a good picture of the astonishing growth of industry in Pest.

28. The Aristocracy at the End of the Nineteenth Century

Angelo de Gubernatis, *La Hongrie Politique et Sociale*, Florence, 1885, pp. 261–3.

THE majority of the aristocracy have been reduced to the status of mere landed proprietors. But here too their lack of education makes itself felt. Agricultural science is a novelty despised by certain Hungarian aristocrats. Moreover, since they have done nothing to improve the land and have failed to adopt modern and rational systems of agriculture, they are gradually being forced to realize that their lands, newly burdened with various dues, are bringing in less income. But instead of trying to find remedies for this state of affairs, they are letting matters slide from bad to worse, and proving quite incapable of stemming the advance of the middle classes who are encroaching upon them from all sides.

In an age when the landlord had no need to share his income with either the state or the labourers, and always had more than enough money, agricultural industry and commerce were unnecessary. Now, however, life has become more complicated. Luxury has increased, the hand that labours must be duly paid, and the State demands its contribution—a large one—from the landlords. The only landowners to save themselves are those who have realized the necessities of modern life and have sensed its dangers. These are trying to defend and improve their sadly-menaced position by means of active and intelligent work. . . .

The fortune of numerous Hungarian magnates is on the edge of disaster, which industry alone can help to avoid. But in order to save itself from entering into dangerous enterprises, the aristocracy must take up practical life and learn its secrets. Dilettantism in speculation always leads to ruin. 'He who sits on the ground cannot fall' runs the Hungarian proverb. But the Hungarian aristocrat who repeats this to his comfort may well die of starvation among the sacks of wheat he is unable to sell. The magnates no longer have to brandish their ancestral swords to defend their soil; their right to possess it is guaranteed by that same state which taxes them. The soil is still their greatest strength and, in a way, their indestructible privilege, but they must draw from it all that it can yield. The consideration they will be able to demand and their influence in society will be proportional to the production they obtain from this part of the national riches that fate and the merits of their ancestors have entrusted to them.

Angelo de Gubernatis (1840–1913), Italian scholar, visited Hungary in 1885, and wrote a general work on political and social conditions there. His views on the aristocracy might well have been written at any time during the century.

29. REMINISCENCES OF A LANDLESS SERF

Gyula Illyés, *Puszták népe* (People of the Pusztas), Budapest, 1936, pp. 55-7.

(Gyula Illyés describes the life of the landless serfs of Transdanubia in his book *The People of the Pusztas* (1936). His own family belonged to this class, which always outnumbered the landed peasants, yet was consistently overlooked in any proposals for land reform.)

NATURALLY the past was always better than the present. At first I listened with enthusiasm to the old folk as they talked, then, with the customary superiority of youth, I doubted them. Later, however, I thought they were right: the past they talked about was indeed better.

How many shirts has a hired farm-lad today? When my grandfather from Nebánd got married, he had in his trunk 16 ordinary pairs of wide trousers, six pairs with fringed edges and 16 round-necked shirts. In addition he had two pairs of top-boots, a real silver cane and a sheepskin cloak which would still be good today, had it not been struck by a chance flash of lightning and burnt up together with the wooden arm of the well where it had been left. What do the people of the pusztas[1] eat nowadays? In grandfather's time the labourers' wives took lunch out to their menfolk in wooden bowls so immense that they could scarcely keep their heads upright under their weight. At about 11 o'clock a long caravan of women would leave the labourers' dwellings, and the sheepdogs would raise their heads a good mile away as they sniffed the paprika stew, whose scent floated like a glimmering ribbon through the thousand smells of the field. For in those days everything was to be had. There was even fish. 'There were no poor folk then.' The beggars rode in carts. The only thing lacking was lamp-oil, for that cost money—and there was no money in those days either.

Truth to tell, however, there was no real need of money. Grandfather was satisfied. 'That's what the world of serfdom was like', he mused—the age which by his reckoning lasted up to the eighties, and whose passing he mourned with sad shakes of his head. This disturbed me. Was grandfather not glad that serfdom had disappeared? 'Ah, those were the good old days', he sighed, and recalled summers and autumns full of merriment, while I was astounded to calculate that these had occurred during the sad years of national oppression. 'Well, grandfather, weren't you emancipated?' I asked. He looked at me in astonishment. He knew nothing about the struggle for the

---

[1] In Transdanubia, *puszta* means the collection of labourers' lodgings, stables and barns on a large estate.

freedom of the press, nor had he ever really thought about the ending of robot, tithes and urbarial dues.

The name of Kossuth caused grandfather's heart to stir as little as that of anyone else on the puszta. Kossuth, 1848, liberty—all these were regarded as the concern of village-folk, like parliamentary elections, when carts going from one parish to another were sometimes seen dashing across the estate with swaying wine-bottles and fluttering national flags. True, Kossuth forgot them too; in general everybody forgot them in every age until it had become a custom. Not only statesmen, but scholars too passed them over. Thus there are even fewer 'genuine' details of their past than of their present. Where had they come from? I could no longer be satisfied with the words of the old folk, who as a rule could only say of their grandparents, 'He was a very poor old man, God rest his bones', but did not know where the poor old man was buried.

'The serfs were liberated'; for a long time I pictured this in the same way as I did the Hungarian nation. It had happened somewhere afar off, in some happy land, and not at all where I was living. The serfs had got their land, they became their own masters and free citizens of Hungary. . . . How was it then that as far as my eye and imagination could see, the lands in all directions around me belonged to unknown potentates whose power was kept more secret than that of the medieval war-lords? At very rare intervals their emissaries visited the big house in a coach-and-four, and the common people bowed to them, stiff with fright, and whipped off their hats; they looked neither independent nor free. . . . Why had these folk not been emancipated? Feverishly I began to look for the mistake, and after much trouble, I came upon it. . . .

After 1848, these folk were just as much serfs as before it or during it. They were not stirred by speeches. . . . We need not be surprised that they were untouched by the great changes. Could they move freely? From the frying-pan into the fire. Were they beaten any more? They were. If their fortunes changed at all, it was not due to the long words uttered in Parliament or at the street-corner.

Grandfather ascribed the change to the trains, and he was quite right. And then there was men's greed, that mad thirst for money which gripped the nobility from one day to another. Grandfather was no lover of change; for as long as he could remember, each change had brought trouble. What had it been like before? Then the people of the pusztas had been shepherds, lying around in the stable or in the sun, not bothering to stir themselves. The estate produced as much corn as its dependents needed. 'When I was a boy, there was hardly any ploughland round here. I knew a lot of folk who never held a hoe in their whole lives.' Scythes? Even he had never held one, except to try it. 'There were sheep and cows, and so much manure that they didn't even bother to cart it all out on to the land; they used it for fuel. There was grazing land everywhere.' The labourers could keep as many animals as they could obtain. 'Nobody ever asked, "János, what's your cow been eating to make her so fat?" or "What are your wife's ducks and hens eating?" ' There was food, and in plenty. Had an ox gone lame? 'Slaughter it and divide it among the labourers; have it for nothing, to my health!' For then even the gentry were real gentry. One of the counts Zichy refused to give his bailiff a pension, saying, 'He could have amassed it himself, I didn't stop him!' Every year grandmother sold 300 forints worth of butter, chickens, eggs and lard at the market at Ozora, and she had been known to drive 25 sucking-pigs to market. Cattle-dealers who visited the estate looked first at the labourers' animals, because they were always better than the landlord's. After all, it is common knowledge that the landowners learnt all about intensive animal-breeding from the labourers. From them too they learnt how to fatten pigs, breed cows, keep bees, and more recently, sell eggs. People themselves were better. There wasn't so much bad language, and no damned putting on airs. One suit or one dress sufficed a grown man or woman their whole life through. Only the sick slept inside—for there was good health too in those days. But then the trains came. . . .

It is true that the first few decades of the second half of the nine-teenth century brought some temporary alleviation to the puszta-dwellers in parts of Transdanubia, if nowhere else. Robot came to an end on the big estates, and agricultural production, now geared to profit, demanded more and more labour. The claims of the labourers were scarcely greater than in the times of slavery; they lived in half-buried mud hovels and made their own clothes. Their cultural needs were amply fulfilled by folk songs and folk art. Even the smallest improvement was regarded as a blessing from heaven. The land-owners took very little notice if one or two of their cleverer labourers began to spread their wings a little. All they needed for their animals was a band of trustworthy, faithful workers, and they were absolutely faithful.

But this happy age had to come to an end some time. The railway came, and now not only live cattle but corn too could be taken away to be sold. Good prices came in, as yet without competition from overseas, and production rose to make more profit. Grazing lands were ploughed up, and machines arrived. Meanwhile even the peasants began to realize that freedom had dangerous side-effects—

free competition was sprung upon them. For decades it was they who had ploughed the estate lands, they who had reaped and they who had threshed in the huge threshing barns right up to Christmas in most places. Now steam ploughs began to turn the land. The peasant plots were divided into ever smaller portions, and more and more of their children were forced to become landless or work in the pusztas. The number of estate labourers grew, and the more they grew, the more the earth cracked and broke beneath them, like thin ice under the weight of a crowd. They tried to struggle, they tried to save each other, sometimes with heroic devotion and self-sacrifice, but all in vain. History again betrayed them; they sank inevitably to where they had been at the beginning of the eighteenth century. In the 1900s the total income of a family under all possible heads came to 200 forints. They recalled the good old days with sighs, and did not realize that they had been but a brief glimpse of the sun.

Gyula Illyés (1902–), Hungarian poet, novelist and playwright, won immediate recognition with his dispassionate yet powerful book, *The People of the Pusztas*, in 1936. It remains the finest account of the life of the landless peasants in Hungary.

30. AGRARIAN SOCIALISM

Selected from

(1) Péter Simon, *A századforduló földmunkás- és szegényparasztmozgalmai 1891–1907* (Movements among the Agricultural Labourers and Poor Peasants at the turn of the Century, 1891–1907), Budapest, 1953, pp. 36–8; 63–4; 154.
(2) Geoffrey Drage, *Austria-Hungary*, London, 1909, pp. 315–17.

THE main agrarian socialist movements in Hungary took place in the last decade of the nineteenth century in the counties of Békés, Csanád and Csongrád, together known as the 'Storm Corner'. There were, however, peasant risings before this. In 1848 there was an attempt to distribute land in Orosháza, and the government had to suppress the movement by calling in military aid. Those who took part in it were landless serfs who had not acquired land under the emancipation decree. It was here, too, that Mihály Táncsics[1] was elected to parliament in 1869; he was greatly loved by the folk of Orosháza, who read and carefully preserved the books he wrote on socialism.

[1] Táncsics (1799–1884) was one of the earliest and most prolific writers on socialism and popular education. He served numerous prison sentences, notably in 1847–8, from which he was released on the first day of the revolution.

In 1889 socialism took a more active form, when organized agitation was set on foot in the provinces and a regular system of correspondence commenced, partly as a result of the International Workers' Congress held in Paris in that year. 'The party organizers,' notes a police report, 'realizing that their movement cannot struggle to any importance in an agricultural state like Hungary so long as it is confined to factory and industrial workers, aim to bring farm labourers also inside the movement.' Orosháza was one of the main centres of activity.

When the Social Democratic Party held its foundation congress at the end of 1890, the agricultural workers were represented by two delegates. In the debate on the state of the agricultural labourers, the delegate from Orosháza declared that 'official' statistics were false. The labourers in Békés, he said, spent two-thirds of the year in unemployment. Only during threshing were they able to earn two forints per day, and this employment only lasted two weeks. Most of them were compelled to keep their families on 100 forints per year.

In the spring of 1891 there were serious risings at Orosháza, Békéscsaba and Battonya, and these were followed by further riots elsewhere, despite the heavy sentences imposed on the leaders. Then there followed a lull of three years, during which propaganda went steadily forward. On 22 April 1894 a very serious riot occurred at Hódmezővásárhely, where the town hall was stormed by a large crowd of peasants who had been stirred to action by the seizure of books and documents belonging to the local 'General Workers' Reading Union'. Police and military forces had to be summoned to restore order, and the government ordered a state of siege throughout the Alföld, at the same time forbidding the holding of all meetings.

Once again there was a lull in the countryside, but military units were used to break a wave of industrial strikes in various parts of the country in 1895. These involved miners, factory hands, bakers and postmen.

The Social Democratic Party now began to show signs of disintegration. In 1896, István Várkonyi began to publish *Földmívelő* (Agricultural Labourer), a newspaper which dealt specifically with agricultural problems and soon earned the disapproval of the party leaders, who swiftly convened the first Agricultural Labour Congress to formulate specific demands. These included a twelve-hour working day to be reduced later to eight hours, the abolition of unpaid labour, payments in cash, equal wages for men and women and the end of child-labour under the age of 14. Várkonyi promptly held a rival meeting of the 'Independent Social Democrats' as they were now called, and formulated a very similar programme with the important addition of the distribution of land and common ownership. His movement spread rapidly through the Alföld, and at the first congress of the new party in September 1897 there were 239 delegates from 123 districts.

Meanwhile a large strike was organized in support of the agricultural workers' demands. During the summer of 1897 it spread rapidly through the Alföld, involving some 60 communities. The government retaliated by forming a reserve contingent of workers, chiefly Slovaks and Rumanians from Transylvania, but these frequently sympathized with the strikers and were of doubtful value. There was a poor harvest, and this together with the strike meant dearth and distress; the income of many peasants dropped to 50–60 forints for the whole year.

The government now took stronger steps to suppress the growing unrest. Várkonyi's paper was banned in February 1898, and he himself fled the country; he was later caught in Vienna and brought back to face seven charges concerning contravention of the press laws. He was duly imprisoned for nine months. At the same time the Minister of the Interior ordered strict watch to be kept on all socialist movements, adding that preventive action and if necessary force should be used to maintain order. A new law, 1898 II, which soon earned the title of 'The Slave Law', regulated with the utmost strictness the working conditions of the agricultural labourers. Strikes, meetings and even complaints were forbidden, on penalty of severe fines or imprisonment.

After these measures, the agrarian socialist movement waned. Várkonyi's party decayed, although he himself almost reached parliament in the elections of 1901; instead he was imprisoned for alleged offences during his campaign. A new split occurred in the official Social Democratic Party when Vilmos Mezőfi, a bizarre journalist, formed a 'reorganized' party in 1900. His programme differed little from that of the official party, except that it stressed patriotism and the political leadership of the Hungarian nation. He succeeded in winning over the majority of Várkonyi's supporters. It was not until 1905 that any of these parties succeeded in achieving parliamentary representation; in that year Mezőfi and András Áchim, who then founded the Independent Socialist Peasant Party, were elected to represent constituencies in the 'Storm Corner'.

Geoffrey Drage, British author, was particularly interested in social problems and compiled numerous reports to the Royal Commission on Labour. His work on Austria-Hungary is based on the best sources and contains a wealth of information.

31. HUNGARY AT THE BEGINNING OF THE TWENTIETH CENTURY

R. Vargha, *Hungary*, Budapest, 1906.

Area: 324,851 sq. km.
Population (1900): 19,254,559
Density of population: 59·3 per sq. km.

Increase of population between 1869 and 1900	%
Country areas	19·2
Free Towns	32·5
Municipalities	77·3
Budapest	164·7

Occupations	%
Agriculture	68·6
Mining and Industry	13·4
Commerce and Trade	4·1
Domestic Servants	4·4
Day Labourers	3·3
Professional	2·4
Pensioners, etc.	1·6
Armed Forces	1·5
Other Occupations	0·7

In Hungary proper 65·9 per cent are engaged in agriculture
19 per cent are engaged in industry
In Croatia/Slavonia 84·3 per cent are engaged in agriculture
9 per cent are engaged in industry

Emigration: 168,000 left for America alone in 1906.

Agriculture

In 1900, 4,234,051 men and 1,821,339 women were employed, representing 68·6 per cent of the total working population. In 1890 the figure was 72·5 per cent.

There were five agricultural colleges, one veterinary and one forestry college, with a combined total of 1,307 students in 1905–6. Considering the great preponderance of agriculture as a branch of occupation, this number is decidedly small: Hungarian society is not yet conscious of the fact that a successful farmer demands special professional training, hence the majority of the owners of 'intermediate' and 'large' properties (*v. infra*) do not attend agricultural colleges, but are content to obtain legal qualifications offered by the universities and colleges of law. The statistics prepared in 1895 on the agriculture of Hungary mention the existence of 2,795,885 landed properties (farms), distributed as follows:

Type	No. of farms	% of whole	Area (hectares)	% of whole
Dwarf (0–5 hold)	1,459,893	52·3	1,467,533	6·15
Small (5–100 hold)	1,311,218	46·82	11,574,860	48·44
Intermediate (100–1,000 hold)	20,797	0·74	3,399,401	14·22
Large (Over 1,000 hold)	3,977	0·14	7,451,640	31·19

Types of Land, 1906

	Hectares	% of whole
Ploughland	13,531,028	41·63
Garden	421,705	1·30
Meadow	3,349,806	10·31
Vineyard	234,182	0·72
Pasture	4,092,882	12·59
Forest	9,060,888	27·88
Reed-beds	75,042	0·23
Non-productive land	1,734,261	5·34
	32,499,794	

Note on Weights, Measures and Currency

1. *Weights*

The *Centner* of Vienna = 56 kg. or 123·48 lb.

The *Metric Centner* or *Quintal* = 100 kg. or 220·46 lb.

The *Metze* (*Mérő*) of Austria-Hungary, used for grain, varied with locality. Most of the extracts cite the *metze* of Vienna, which = 61·5 litres, 45 kg. or 99 lb. The *metze* of Pressburg (Pozsony) = 62·5 litres.

The *Eimer* was a liquid measure = 56·6 litres.

The *Itce* or *Icce* of Hungary was a liquid measure = 0·85 litres.

The *Fuder* (Extract 4) was a hay measure; it was sufficient to fill a cart pulled by two horses.

2. *Measures of Length and Area*

The *Mile* generally referred to in the texts is the German mile of 7·5 km. or 4·6 statute miles. The Austrian post mile = 4·98 statute miles, and the Hungarian mile = 8·3 km. or 5·2 statute miles.

The *Square Mile* (in extracts from Demian) contained 10,000 *joch* = 22·24 English square miles.

The *Klafter* or *Toise* (*Öl*) = 1·89 metres or 6 feet (*Fathom*).

The *Joch* (*Hold, Jutro*) varied with locality and type of land from 1,000–2,000 square klafters.

The *Hungarian joch* (1,200 sq. klafters) = 0·43 hectares or 1 acre.

The *Small joch* (1,000 sq. klafters) = 0·36 hectares or 0·8 acres.

The *Cadastral joch*, standardized in 1875 (1,600 sq. klafters) = 0·57 hectares or 1·4 acres.

3. *Currency*

In the late eighteenth and early nineteenth centuries:

1 Thaler = 2 Forints (Florins).

1 Silver Forint, sometimes loosely termed Gulden (Extract 4) or Pengő (Extract 21) = 60 Kreutzers: the silver forint was $\frac{1}{20}$ of a mark of pure silver = 2 English shillings.

In Hungary, after 1761, 1 Forint = 100 Fillérs.

After 1857:

1 Silver Forint = 100 Kreutzers: the forint was now reduced to $\frac{1}{21}$ of a mark of pure silver.

After 1892:

1 Gold Korona (Gulden) = 100 Fillérs. The korona contained 0·305 g. of gold.

For a considerable time, however, there was an unofficial rate of 1 silver forint to 2 gold koronas.

NOTE ON THE SYSTEM OF TAXATION
BEFORE 1848

The Diet agreed on the number of *portae* into which the country was to be divided for tax purposes. By the eighteenth century, the *porta*, originally a feudal 'gate' on which fixed tax was due, had become merely a notional figure. The *portae* were divided among the counties and towns who had to collect the tax due. From 1791 to 1849 Hungary and Croatia together were assessed at 6,346⅛ *portae*.

The county authorities themselves decided on the amount of tax to be paid by parishes and individuals, and for their purpose the *dica* (*deca*) was invented. The serfs themselves, their families, crops, animals and holdings were all assessed at so many *dicas*, and these were about the same throughout the country. The tax paid per *dica*, however, varied from county to county.

The basis of this assessment was the *sessio* (*telek*), reckoned as one whole peasant-holding registered or regarded as subject to feudal dues and services. The *sessio* normally consisted of about 1 *hold* pertaining to the house, yard and garden (inner *sessio*), and arable and meadow land (outer *sessio*) which varied from 22 to 60 *hold*. The *sessio* could be divided into half, quarter and eighth holdings.

I

Rumania

BUCOVINA

Câmpulung
(Mold.)

Suceava

MOLDAVIA

R. Seret

Jassy

R. Prut

Roman

Bacău

TRANSYLVANIA

VRANCEA

FĂLCIU

Kiegiecz

BESSARABIA

R. Dniester

TRANSYLVANIAN ALPS

Galatz

Ismail

Chilia

GORJ

Râmnic

Câmpulung
(Muscel)

Câmpina

Brăila

Sulina

R. Olt

Târgoviște

Ploești

WALLACHIA

DOBROGEA

Turnu-Severin

R. Dambovita

BUCHAREST

Fetești

Cernavoda

Constantza

Craiova

R. Danube

R. Argeș

Călărași

R. Danube

Calafat

Corabia

Turnu-
Măgurele

Zimnicea

Giurgiu

Map 3. Rumania in 1900

Rumania: Introduction

E. D. TAPPE

RESEARCH into the social and economic history of the Rumanian principalities in the Middle Ages had been until recently on a small scale. Under the Marxist régime it has been greatly extended. Yet it is perhaps too early to accept as definitely established any general view of conditions before the seventeenth century. The task of reconstructing the social and economic scene from hundreds of charters in Church Slavonic is a formidable one; there is naturally no contemporary connected account of the scene in the first three centuries of the principalities.

Although this book is concerned with the late eighteenth and nineteenth centuries, I have started with some pages of Cantemir, whose *Descriptio Moldaviae* is the earliest connected account, and whose observation of conditions in his own principality in the decades before and after 1700 is authoritative, even if his views on the previous evolution may be fanciful. Cantemir describes the social structure with three classes of nobles—boyars, courtiers and knights —a class of yeomen, and then the mass of peasants. He makes no mention of free landless men hiring themselves as labourers; but it does not follow that such a class did not exist.

Contemporary with Cantemir's account of Moldavia is the less extensive and less striking account of Wallachia by Del Chiaro. In both principalities agriculture was at a very low level, the peasants being so oppressed with taxes and, in Moldavia, harried by Tartar incursions, that they despaired of retaining any savings or possessions and did the least possible tilling. The soil being extraordinarily fertile, they were not likely to starve, however comfortless their life might otherwise be.

It was to check the flight of peasants from this frustrating and desperate plight that Constantin Mavrocordat introduced reforms into both principalities, promising free status to fugitives who should return and making provision for any serf to buy his freedom. Nevertheless it was the abuses of the fiscal system which were the chief cause of the peasants' misery.

During the century preceding the upheaval of 1821, these two vassal principalities were governed by a series of Greeks from the Phanar quarter of Constantinople, who, having risen to the top of the Turkish diplomatic service, sought the throne of one of the principalities for a period normally of three years. To obtain his throne the Phanariot prince had to distribute lavish presents to Turkish officials. He would have to continue this bribery during his term, and he would wish to make his fortune as well. He therefore descended on the principality with a suite of creditors, and set to work extorting. Under such a system no real improvement of conditions for the peasants was possible, since they alone were the taxpayers. The extent of the fiscal complications can be seen from De Bawr's account of the revenues of Wallachia. Some glimpses of agriculture, stockbreeding and industry in the Phanariot period can be caught in the extracts from Bentham, Raicevich, Wilkinson and Wyburn.

In 1821 Ipsilanti's attempt to liberate Greece with forces raised in the principalities shattered the Turks' confidence in Greek princes. They appointed native princes, and this was at a time when national consciousness was growing. In the last fifty years Western influences had reached the boyars of the principalities at second-hand through Russian officers during occupations by Russian armies, and more directly by French émigrés after the Revolution. In Golescu's book, published in 1826, we have the impressions of a boyar who, in visiting Italy and the German lands, is astonished at the contrast between the prosperity of German peasants and the misery of Wallachians.

The development of the Rumanian economy was hastened by the Russo-Turkish war. Under the treaty of Adrianople, 1829, Turkey ceased to have first claim on Rumanian supplies of corn and timber. The Danube garrison towns restored by the Turks included Brăila, which gave Wallachia a port to rival Moldavia's Galatz. Under the Russian protectorate the so-called 'Règlement Organique' was promulgated in each principality.

But although this statute improved conditions to some extent, many of its provisions were not put into practice. The boyars, especially in Wallachia, did not normally reside on their estates, and instead of being interested in improved methods of agriculture, were usually content to farm their lands to a contractor, who then extorted his utmost from the peasants. The state of industry and commerce was not healthy either. There was no native middle class of manufacturers and merchants. As these persons were mostly foreigners, under the protection of foreign consuls, especially those of Austria, their profits went out of the country. Nor was it only these profits that were drained from the principalities; there were also the revenues of vast landed estates dedicated to monasteries abroad. The Frenchman Colson gives an interesting account of the situation in the 1830s, and the picture is filled in by a Rumanian from Transylvania, Codru Drăgășanu.

By the '40s a leaven of young Rumanians who had been educated in France and Germany was working; a ferment of ideas, at once nationalist and liberal, began to change public opinion. 1848 saw attempts at revolution in both principalities, quickly suppressed by foreign intervention; there followed a Russian occupation which resulted at last in the Crimean War. The Rumanized Greek, Soutzo, and the French Consul, Poujade, are valuable authorities for the conditions of this period. In it a vast number of patents of minor nobility had been distributed among persons of small fortune. Poujade tells us that 'it is particularly in the supplementary nobility that revolutionary passions and socialist ideas have found active instruments and docile adherents'. These social climbers were called *ciocoi*. Their emergence can be traced from 1821 onwards. When, after the Crimean War, the Austrian occupation, which had succeeded the Russian, was withdrawn, the movement for uniting the principalities had its chance.

In 1859 the principalities were united *de facto* by the election of the same prince, Cuza, in each. In the same year ranks and their privileges were abolished. In 1864 the system of labour dues and tithe paid by peasant to landlord was abolished, and the peasant gained ownership of land. The vast areas belonging to monasteries were confiscated.

Cuza was deposed in 1866, but the way was clear for modernization; it came speedily under the foreign prince, Charles of Hohenzollern-Sigmaringen, who acceded to the throne of the united principalities in 1866. The first railway was opened in 1869. Beatty-Kingston describes the striking change which took place in the first decade of Charles's reign. Again, after Rumania had gained independence from Turkey as a result of the Russo-Turkish war of 1877, he found that change continued to be very swift. 'Of all the countries in Europe,' he wrote in 1888, 'Roumania has during the last decade effected the most rapid development of her internal resources and of her people's well-being.' There were, however, serious defects in the social structure. The middle class was developing, but in a lop-sided way. Trade, banking, industry, were to a very large extent in the hands of foreigners and of Jews; Jews, especially since 1830, had immigrated from the Russian Empire, and particularly into Moldavia.

The Rumanians of the middle class chose the professions and the government service, for which the educational system did not at that period supply sufficient qualified applicants. Naturally, this predominance in business of those who were not natives led to xenophobia and anti-semitism, even though the situation was largely caused by the Rumanians' distaste for such occupations.

At the end of the nineteenth century the natural resources of Rumania, its oil, its timber, were being exploited, though often wastefully and inefficiently. Rumania was exporting raw materials; manufactures were still undeveloped. Judged by the standards of North-Western Europe, the country was backward; in comparison with the principalities of fifty years before, the Kingdom of Rumania had made astonishing economic progress. But social progress had not kept pace, and in 1907 the tension between peasants and absentee landowners, having 'increased beyond measure', broke in a violent peasant revolt.

I. The Principalities of Wallachia and Moldavia

1. MOLDAVIA IN THE EARLY EIGHTEENTH CENTURY

D. Cantemir, *Descriptio Moldaviae* (Description of Moldavia) in *Operele Principelui Demetriu Cantemir* (The Works of Prince D. Cantemir), Bucharest, 1872, Tom. i, pp. 106–9 and 113–24.

(a) Ancient and Modern Revenues

THAT all Moldavia, after its foundation by Dragoş,[1] was once the property of the prince alone, is abundantly proved both by the ancient chronicles and by the diplomas of former princes. The new inhabitants of Moldavia could not choose their own possessions; according to the brilliance of each man's deserts, the prince conferred on him the honour of a barony, and villages and lands with which to maintain the dignity which he had acquired. The truth of the matter is shown by the diplomas of the old families in Moldavia, by virtue of which they possess their villages; these speak only of the gift and bounty of the prince. To throw light on this point, it is worth while to insert the deed given to our great-grandfather, Theodore Cantemir, by Stephen the Great:[2] this is roughly what it says: 'Since Theodore Cantemir, *pârcălab*[3] of Chilia and Ismail, has in defending those cities against the raids of the Turks and Tartars proved himself a faithful servant and a doughty fighter for the Cross, but has himself, inasmuch as God has permitted all those parts to be ravaged and occupied by the Turks, been forced to abandon his own ancestral estates, which his grandfathers and great-grandfathers by faithful service had obtained as a gift from our predecessors of blessed memory, We moved by Christian piety and kindness confer upon the said Theodore Cantemir three villages in the district of Fălciu and all the adjacent woods, fields, rivers and fishponds, and we appoint him warden of the whole forest of Kiegiecz and chief captain

---

[1] The reputed founder of the Moldavian State.
[2] Prince of Moldavia from 1457 to 1504.
[3] The title is said to be a corruption of the German *Burggraf*.

of the knights of Kiegiecz . . .' (who at that time, on the evidence of the historians, numbered eight thousand).

This is why practically every noble family in Moldavia draws its name from the village which its first founder had received as a gift from the prince. Thus Cantemir was later named Siliṣteanu after his village, Racoviṭa from Racova, Urechie from Urechieṣti, etc.

But when in the course of time the number of boyars increased and those donations seemed in the end likely to swallow up the whole of the prince's revenues, the princes, for the sake of the common weal, divided the revenues, which previously had been raised indiscriminately for the prince's use and for the needs of state. For the maintenance of their own court they retained all the cities and towns of Moldavia, with twelve neighbouring villages, the salt mines, the customs duties, the tithes on sheep, pigs and beehives owned by peasants and nobles of lower rank; for the boyars have always been immune from this tribute. All the rest they left to the state and the boyars, and decreed that in peacetime there should be paid for state purposes eighty aspri or one florin from each peasant household (which they call 'smokes'), but if war broke out, an imperial or 120 aspri; in times of greater need, a gold piece, which at that time was equivalent to 200 aspri.

How large a sum of money was collected in this way, can easily be conjectured by the reader, from the fact that it sufficed to pay 40,000 Moldavian soldiers, and another 14,000 foreigners, consisting of Germans, Cossacks, Serbs, Bulgars, Albanians and Greeks. Certainly the revenue of the prince alone each year surpassed 600,000 imperials; and the public records show that from Câmpulung alone 24,000 sheep were collected as tithes.

But today, alas, to such poverty and misery has Moldavia sunk, that she provides scarcely one-sixth of her former revenues! From excise and customs about 30,000 imperials are raised, from the salt mines 10,000, from the cities and towns governed by *părcălabi* 15,000, from the sheep tithes usually 10,000, and in the first year of the prince's reign, when the boyars too are bound to pay tithes, 20,000, from the tithes on beehives and pigs 25,000, from the *curteni* or nobles of lower rank 15,000; all these added together amount to a little more than 100,000 imperials. And these revenues the prince may use or abuse according to his pleasure for the convenience of himself and his court. For the public treasury the limit is set, not by the strength of the subjects, but by necessity and the greed of the Turks. Whatever they may demand, cannot be refused, nor can the prince be obliged to contribute anything from his own to the public treasury.

The management of the public treasury is wholly vested in the seven highest boyars, commonly called *boieri de sfat*;[1] they alone are allowed to enter the *vistierie*[2] (this is the room set apart for discussing the highest counsels of state). Only the Grand Treasurer has a seat with them because he is in charge of the treasury and wears the keys of the *vistierie*. So if any order is sent from the Turkish court, or if any prince thinks that some matter concerns the public interest, he bids those seven boyars by written mandate consult about the matter. They gather in the *vistierie*, and when everyone's view has been aired, they tell the prince through the Grand Treasurer what they think should be done. If the prince approves their advice, he gives orders that the matter be put into execution within so many days. Then two or three or even more if the nature of the business requires it, are sent into the provinces to collect money or corn or whatever else they have been told, and hand it over to the treasurer, from whom they obtain a written receipt. The treasurer is bound to give the seven boyars of the council an account of receipts and expenditure every three months. If times have been peaceful, about thirty or forty thousand imperials are gathered into that treasury; but if a new prince is sent, or if the old one is confirmed in his office by a new diploma, about five hundred thousand must be raised; all of which is scraped together and extorted by any means from the wretched subjects to glut the inexhaustible avarice of the Ottoman court. The number of calamities and miseries being thus daily increased, the danger of utter desolation impends.

(b) The Nobility

We know that the higher ranks of honour were granted and the political and military offices distributed by Dragoş, the founder of Moldavia, not to those who could count more titles among their ancestors, but to those who excelled in courage and loyalty. We know too that these same men planted the fields of Moldavia, devastated by Tartar invasions, with colonies of peasants brought from Poland, and either gave their names to the villages which they founded or, more probably, took the names of the villages as a sign of nobility. In the course of time, when the Serbian and Bulgarian kingdoms had been destroyed by the violence of the Turks, and the royal city of the Greeks had also come into the power of foreigners, many scions of the noblest stocks of those nations fled to Moldavia as the general place of refuge in that age, and by their faithful service won the right of naturalization and the honour of nobility. In the same way some of the nobler Tartars, having in the course of

---

[1] Boyars of the Council or Divan.   [2] *Vistierie*, from Lat. *vestiarium*.

the almost perpetual wars which were waged between the Scythians and the Moldavians, either been taken prisoner or on account of internal dissensions surrendered to the princes, adopted Christianity and were admitted to the civil and military offices of the province. Furthermore, after the lapse of a century, when princes began to be sent to Moldavia from Constantinople, many Circassians and Abazar slaves who had been bought by princes while still private residents at Constantinople proved their loyalty to their masters by long service and were promoted first to offices at court and then to noble offices, in this way acquiring the prerogative of nobility. The princes also enrolled some Poles in the ranks of the nobility, especially those who were better disposed to their reign, just as conversely several Moldavians have been taken into the Polish nobility.

When by this means the number of Moldavian nobles became too large, the princes decided to divide the whole body into three classes. The first place was given to the boyars, doubtless to those who had themselves been elevated by princes to the higher offices of state or were born of the blood of such. They are distinguished from the other nobles of lower rank in much the same way as the *boiarski rod* in the Russian empire. In the second class are the *curteni* or courtiers, who have inherited one or two villages from their ancestors, like those called *dvoriane* in Russia. In the third place come the *călăraşi*, knights, who in return for the use of the lands which princes have granted them, are always bound to follow them on their expeditions at their own expense. Last come the *răzeşi*, whom we should prefer to call free peasants rather than nobles. They correspond roughly to the *odnodvortsy* of the Russians, and have no courts of peasants, but several of them inhabit one village and till their lands themselves or by means of hired servants. . . .

There was of old a custom among the Moldavians, which by long use had almost acquired the force of law, by which youths even of the noblest family were barred from public office, unless they had given proof of their faithfulness in lesser services and had been broken in by long practice and experience of affairs. For this reason boyars of lower rank used to give their sons, as soon as they had come of age, as servants to some higher boyar; the latter, however, could only use their services to wait at table and guard their master's room. When they had spent three years learning the ways of the court and had acquired more refined manners, the same boyar later took them to the prince and by his intercession they were received among the chamberlains of the greater divan. Thence after a year they were transferred to the lesser hall of audience and thence to the armoury. There, if a man had shown signs of good disposition and honourable character, so that some hope might be conceived of him, he was co-opted among the chamberlains of the greater bedchamber. There, after a few years, at the intercession of some other boyar (for it was thought unbecoming for parents to recommend their own son to the prince) he was appointed *postelnicel* or lesser *postelnic*, twelve of whom used to be bidden to carry in the prince's presence thin white staves of the length of their own height. If he proved his faithfulness and skill in that office, he was admitted to other offices of the inner court. And having thus spent his youth, he was raised first to the third rank of boyar and finally to the first rank. But if the prince noticed outstanding ability in any man, he could in a few years raise a noble of the lowest rank to the highest offices.

Today, however, pride growing with poverty, a noble thinks that he will smirch his nobility if he serves a boyar; yet since ambition will not let him live as a private person, he tries his best by the influence of his relations to be received at one bound among the inner officials, who are called *boierinaşi* or 'little boyars'. But although this body forms as it were the nursery ground of the whole country, from which the ranks of the boyars are normally filled, it is painful to relate what sinister persons are frequently raised to the highest offices. And this is the reason why you will frequently find among boyars of the highest degree pompous, haughty and arrogant men, devoid not only of administrative experience but also of moral training, in whom you will find nothing praiseworthy except such good qualities as nature unaided by cultivation has bestowed on one or two.

(c) The Peoples: Serf and Free

We believe that hardly any other province, bounded by such narrow limits as Moldavia, contains so many diverse peoples. Besides the Moldavians, whose ancestors returned from Maramureş, a greater number of Greeks, Albanians, Serbs, Bulgars, Poles, Cossacks, Russians, Hungarians, Germans, Armenians, Jews and prolific gipsies inhabit Moldavia. The Greeks, Albanians, Serbs and Bulgarians live there freely, some of them occupied in trade, others serving the prince as mercenary soldiers. There are few Germans, Poles and Cossacks, mostly soldiers or court officials; some of the Poles (though this is rare) have actually reached the rank of boyar. The Armenians are treated as subjects, as are citizens and merchants in other cities and towns of Moldavia, and pay the same tribute to the prince as they; but they, like the adherents of the Roman religion, have sacred buildings of their own, no smaller or less elegant than the Orthodox churches, and enjoy the free practice of their own rite.

The Jews also are counted as subjects, and are bound to pay a special annual tribute, heavier than the usual one. They practise no calling other than wholesale and retail trade. They may have synagogues everywhere, but of wood, not stone. The Russians and Hungarians have attained perpetual servitude in Moldavia. The gipsies are scattered throughout the province, and there is no boyar who has not several families of gipsies subject to him. When and whence this race came to Moldavia, they neither know themselves nor do our annals record. They use that language which is customary to all gipsies in those parts and is mixed with many purely Greek and even Persian words. They have scarcely any other trade than the working of iron and copper. They have the same character and the same habits as in other regions, their ideal and their distinguishing marks being theft and laziness.

The Turks also live in Jassy and other towns for purposes of trade; but they are nowhere allowed to buy an estate or a house in any town or village, much less to build a mosque or to utter public prayers according to their own superstition, nor has the Ottoman court ever insisted that the princes of Moldavia should permit that; may it for ever remain silent!

The pure Moldavians, apart from the nobles whose classes we have reviewed above, are either citizens or peasants. By citizens we mean those who live in cities or towns, by peasants those in villages. Those in towns are subject to no one save the prince, and pay tribute to him alone. All practise crafts; the Moldavian is rarely a trader. There is inborn in the Moldavians such pride or sloth that they disdain all kinds of trade except the sale of the produce which they receive from their own lands. And that is the chief reason, I believe, why one rarely finds a wealthy citizen in Moldavia, and why our country, though it exports much more to foreign countries than it receives from them, is perpetually suffering from a lack of money. For traders of foreign origin, Turks, Jews, Armenians and Greeks, whom we commonly call *dzelepi*,[1] have by the sluggishness of our countrymen gained all the commerce of Moldavia for themselves, and having bought whole herds of cattle and sheep at a low price in Moldavia, they take them to Constantinople and other cities and sell them there for double or treble the price. But as the majority of them are not allowed to own farms or houses in Moldavia, the greater part of that money is spent outside the province; very little comes back to the Danube, and there is scarcely enough to pay the tribute due to the Turks and other public charges.

There are no purely Moldavian peasants; they are of Russian or

[1] See p. 223.

Transylvanian ('Hungarian', as we usually call it) origin. For in the
first period of the foundation of Moldavia, Dragoş, finding the new
province empty of tillers, had distributed it all to the partners in his
expedition. But since it seemed unjust that one noble should be given
to another as a labourer (for all those of Roman descent were alike
considered noble), while a race used to arms disdained agriculture,
Dragoş' successors were compelled to raid the neighbouring regions
(where serfdom had already been introduced) with the connivance
of the prince, and seizing tillers of the land, transfer them to their
own estates. The truth of this is supported by the etymology of the
word for peasant, which in Moldavian is *vecin* (*vicinus*, neighbour),
and shows that those were formerly neighbours whom the success
of Moldavian arms later compelled to work in the countryside. For
that reason, in Upper Moldavia, which first began to be cultivated
by the house of Dragoş, there are many courts of peasants, while in
Lower Moldavia, which was colonized later, there are none except
serfs whom the barons of that district bought from Upper Moldavia
and transferred to their own estates, or former *răzeşi*, who, after
selling their ancestral possessions through poverty, were compelled
by the injustice of the boyars to undergo the yoke of serfdom in
addition. That is why if in a law court a man is claimed as a serf by
a boyar, it is easy to decide his status; for if the accused proves that
his ancestors once possessed an estate, though it has been lost by
poverty or the injury of time, or that they were admitted among the
călăraşi, *curteni* or *aprozi*,[1] he will be pronounced entirely free, since
only a free man can hold those positions. Otherwise he must be
bound in subjection to some boyar.

Those who were transferred from Poland into the interior of
Moldavia have forgotten the language of their fathers and adopted
Moldavian; but those who live on the borders of Poland still talk
Ruthenian and Polish. The Hungarians, who are more tenacious
both of the Roman religion and of their native tongue, nevertheless
all know Moldavian. Of whatever race they be, they are bound to
apply themselves continually to their lords' work. No limit is set for
their working; it rests on their master's will on how many days he
wishes to set them to work. He is not allowed to take money or beasts
from them by force. Even if a peasant has acquired a very great
fortune, no part in that belongs to the lord; if he extorts any, he will
be condemned in court to restore it to the plaintiff. But if the lord
wants to act unjustly, he beats the peasant until he voluntarily
surrenders what is desired. To kill him is forbidden by law, and if
the lord causes his death in any way, he will not only be liable to

[1] From Hu. *apród* = page.

the death penalty, but he must grant freedom to the wife and children of the dead man. No private person has the right of life and death over any Moldavian, inasmuch as this is the prerogative of the prince alone. Furthermore, a boyar may sell a Moldavian subject, but not outside his native village. But if he sells a whole estate with its peasants, that sale is valid. He pays as much tribute as the prince decrees, and there is no limit laid down for that. In a word I should have declared the Moldavian peasants the most wretched farmers in the world, if the fertility of the land and crops did not, as it were, save them from poverty against their will.

They are very lazy and impatient of toil; they plough little and sow little, but reap much. They do not trouble to have what they might procure by labour, but are content to store as much in their barns as suffices to feed them for the year, or, as they say, 'until the new bread'. Consequently, if there is a barren crop or if hostile force prevents the harvest, they easily run the risk of famine. If a peasant has one or two cows, he thinks he has got enough with which to keep himself and his children. For there are cows which give forty (and at the least twenty-four) *librae* of milk a day. But if he has twenty bee-hives, with their produce he can easily pay the tribute for the whole year. Not to mention that a single hive produces seven others yearly, if the weather is as the farmer desires; each hive when cut out yields two or more measures; and one measure is sold for a thaler. Those who live in the mountains have abundance of sheep, honey and fruit; those in the plains, of crops, cattle and horses. The greatest misfortune of all these people is that they have the Tartars for neighbours. The Tartars not only steal secretly whatever they can, but sometimes, on the pretext of an expedition against Poland, since they are bound to cross Moldavia, not only plunder extensively, but even on occasions carry off all the inhabitants of villages into captivity, and sell them at Constantinople as Russians. These raids have indeed been for a long while prohibited by repeated mandates of the Sultan; but who can baulk the Tartars' cunning in this respect? More fortunate are those whom fate takes to Constantinople. There the prince's representatives can recover a Moldavian prisoner, wherever they may find him, without ransom and restore him to freedom.

What we have said above about Moldavian subjects is not to be applied to the peasants of three districts in Moldavia, who, though not nobles, are subject to no boyar. These present a certain appearance of being republics. The first is Câmpulung in the county of Suceava; it is cut off by a continuous range of very high mountains. It contains about fifteen villages, which all have laws and judges of their own. Sometimes they admit two *vornici*[1] sent by the prince, but not infrequently, if the peasants are offended with them, they drive them away, relying on the fortifications which nature herself has bestowed. They do not know how to till arable land, as they have none in their mountains; all their labour is devoted to the care of sheep. They pay an annual tribute, not what the prince demands, but what they promised to the early princes, and whenever Moldavia receives a new prince, they send representatives and renew that agreement. If the prince decides to treat them more harshly and impose new burdens, they do not spend time in negotiating, but refuse the tribute altogether and retire to the more inaccessible parts of the mountains. For this reason the princes never ask them for more than their due. Sometimes, roused by seditious persons, they have defected from the princes and paid homage to the Poles; which has given some Polish historians a pretext for claiming that Moldavia was tributary to Poland. . . .

The second lesser republic in Moldavia is Vrancea in the county of Putna near the boundary of Wallachia, surrounded on all sides by very wild mountains. It numbers twelve villages and two thousand farms, and is ignorant of cultivation, being content like Câmpulung with the grazing of sheep. Similarly the inhabitants pay a definite fixed tribute yearly to the prince, are ruled by their own laws, and utterly reject the prince's orders and his judges alike.

The third is Kiegiecz in the county of Fălciu, a forest on the borders of the Bugeac Tartars, and the strongest bulwark of all Moldavia that lies between the Siret and Bessarabia. The inhabitants pay a small tribute yearly to the prince, being all *călăraşi* or knights. Once upon a time they numbered eight thousand, but today they scarcely bring two thousand into the field. But they surpass all the other inhabitants of Moldavia in military prowess, so that it is commonly said as a proverb: 'Five Crims are stronger than ten Bugeac Tartars; five Moldavians can overcome ten Crims; but five *codreni* (foresters, for that is the name commonly given in Moldavia to the people of Kiegiecz) can put ten Moldavians to flight.'

Dimitrie Cantemir (1673–1723), son of a Prince of Moldavia, was himself Prince (1710–11) when Peter the Great moved against Turkey. After the Russian reverse at Stănileşti, Cantemir, as Peter's ally, followed him to Russia, where in 1716 he wrote his Latin *Description of Moldavia* on the suggestion of the Berlin Academy, of which he had been elected a member.

[1] Officials.

K

2. Decrees of Constantin Mavrocordat, Prince of Wallachia

Printed by A. T. Laurian and N. Bălcescu in *Magazin istoric pentru Dacia* (Historical Magazine for Dacia), Bucharest, 1846, vol. ii, pp. 280–7.

(a) *Decree of the General Assembly of Wallachia for the Liberation of such Peasants gone abroad as may return to their Homes. 1 March 1746* His Highness our enlightened and exalted Lord Io Costandin Nicolae, wishing to draw and gather all the sons of this land who are scattered from their soil, as is his duty as lord, and in accordance with the *hati-sherif* of the mighty Empire, which graciously declared and proclaimed that it is its will, desire and command, that those abroad should be gathered together, took common counsel with us, his whole nobility. It was thought good that the usual rate of tax laid upon the peasants should be lessened for those who have gone abroad, and when first they return to their country, that they may have a dwelling and the wherewithal to live, they should have respite and be free of tax for six years. And after that the rate of tax should be kept at five thalers per man per annum in four quarterly payments, and no more; and on whatever estate they settle, they should be unmolested. Only they must work six days a year for the lord of that estate, and give him a tithe of all their crops, as is shown in full in the first papers that were printed. And after this His Highness our learned Lord bethought him for some of the native peasants that have gone abroad who may be serfs[1] of monasteries or of boyars, that the yoke of servitude might hinder them from returning to their country, or that on the other hand, if they trusted to His Highness' call and came back, instead of gaining peace and quiet, they might once more fall anew under the yoke of servitude. His Highness, fearing that this sin might fall upon him since for this nothing had been said in the former papers, took counsel anew with us all, there being present at the Divan the Most Reverend the Metropolitan of Wallachia, Kir Clement. His Highness asked us, which of two things seemed to us more fitting; that some like these should be hindered from returning to their native land, or that coming they should be under the yoke of serfdom as before, for His Highness would bring this to the knowledge of all that he might not remain beneath that sin. To which His Holiness the Metropolitan replied that if they came at His Highness' call and should remain once more serfs, His Highness would have great sin, mortal sin, and in the life to come His

[1] The words translated 'serf', 'serfdom' are '*rumân*', '*rumânie*'; 'servitude' is '*robie*'.

Highness' soul would be punished, because His Highness was making himself the cause of their servitude.

And so, lest these men should remain estranged from their country, and His Highness our exalted Lord incur that sin and punishment, if they should be left once more in serfdom, first of all His Holiness the Bishop of Râmnic and we the whole body of nobles, likewise each one separately, spoke our opinion and gave counsel: that whatever serfs of monasteries or of boyars have been estranged from this soil, if they wished to return to their native soil, should settle where they wish, and be free and exempt from serfdom, without further trouble from their masters. And further, whoever wished might come to the Divan to receive a separate paper of his right upon that settlement. This decision seeming good to us all in general, it has been given in writing by this deed which has been signed by His Holiness the Metropolitan and His Holiness the Bishop of Râmnic and the Egumens and by all the nobles of the land. At our prayer His Highness our learned Lord has confirmed it with his princely signature and seal that it be unchanged, and copies of it have been made, printed and confirmed with the Prince's seal, and sent throughout the land.

(b) Decree of the General Assembly for the Liberation of all Peasants 5 August 1746

On the soil of our land we see that many of the ancient customs which have been known to be good and useful, have been thoroughly confirmed by later rulers and are preserved unchanged. But some of these old ordinances we see to be not only useless, but very harmful to the Christian soul, as has been this ancient custom of serfdom which has remained upon us from our fathers and forefathers until today. For that our brothers in Christ should be beneath the yoke of our servitude is the gravest and greatest of sins, since our Lord Jesus Christ himself in the holy Gospel teaches us, saying: 'Love thy neighbour as thyself.' But since it is right that we should be subject to this commandment and teaching, we must not put our brothers in Christ beneath the yoke of servitude. Therefore we too one and all, knowing that this holding in servitude orthodox Christians, who are of one faith with ourselves, is not a Christian thing, but very harmful to our souls, and taking thought for the serfs whom we have held till now under our lordship, they having been sold with their estates in ancient times to our forefathers, have thought it good for the relief of our souls and those of our fathers and forefathers, that wherever men are serfs with their estates to any boyar or monastery, the estates should remain under our lordship as before. But as for

the persons of the serfs apart from their estates, whosoever of us shall
be willing of his own free will to free them will do well for his own
memory; but if he will not do this good deed to his own soul, then
those serfs shall have the right to give ten thalers per head in cash
and ransom themselves, whether their lord will or no. They shall
give the money to their master, and if he will not receive it, they
shall come and make complaint to the Divan. For we have all agreed
upon this good and spiritual thing and ordained that it be preserved
and confirmed among us both by us and by all our race who shall
be left inheritors after us. . . .

Constantin Mavrocordat (1711–69) spent over twenty years as Prince of one
or other of the principalities; he was the most enlightened of the Phanariot
princes.

3. The Burden of Taxation

F. W. de Bawr, *Mémoires historiques et géographiques sur la Valachie*, Frankfurt
and Leipzig, 1778, pp. 69–87.

Of Finances in General

THE public revenues of Wallachia mostly originate in capitation
and the land tax.

The capitation has always been paid in money, and the land tax
and the tax on beasts is levied in kind by the tithe. It was originally
only a light tax, which brought in a very modest sum, but it has
been successively increased, especially in recent times. . . .

The reign of Constantin Brâncoveanu towards the end of the last
century provides the first period of increase in finances; the second
is that of Constantin Mavrocordat. This prince, making a general
change in the country in the year 1739, also changed the finances;
it is this period that is called the reform of Constantin Mavrocordat.
The arrangements which he made in the finances might have been
useful in many respects, if they had been invariably followed; but the
continual change of princes and their greed have been the cause of
all the innovations and increases which will be set forth below.

The Ancient Finances

The ancient finances may be divided into revenues of the public
treasury and revenues of the prince.

The revenue of the public treasury, or the tribute of the country
was paid twice a year under the heading of 'chief account' and
'second account', not including the Bairam present and the supplies

of meat, etc., of which we have spoken in the previous chapter,[1] any more than the detailed expenses, for the payment of which four different terms of the year had been fixed.

The prince's revenues consisted in the right of four paras per head of sheep and one para per measure of wine. The monasteries, the boyars and the *mazili*[2] only paid the former tribute once in three years, and were entirely exempt from the latter, as has been noted above.

The taxes which formed part of the revenue of the public treasury were raised by common consent of the boyars with regard to the quality and resources of each county. Those of them who were called *zapcii* or commissioners, had the task of making the detailed allotment between the different districts; the *pǎrcǎlabi* or burgraves did the same for the towns and villages. In this way the money came to the treasury without it being necessary to do more than mark the names of the villages in the archives.

As for the revenues of the prince's treasury, they were raised sometimes by tax-farmers and sometimes by commissioners.

Of the New Finances

The last period of the new finances begins, as has been said, with the reform of Constantin Mavrocordat. The ancient division into revenues of the public treasury and of the prince's treasury was no longer the same; for in 1755 the latter was confined to the salt mines and the customs. Subsequently these revenues also were removed from it, and the prince's treasury entirely abolished. But as the salt mines and the customs as well as the greater part of the other revenues are farmed out with the prince's approval, he never lacks means of recouping himself, and, arrogating for himself the right of increasing the taxes at will, he makes use of this expedient for skilfully confusing his personal needs with those of the state.

Of the Different Names of Taxes and their Administration

The *sfert* or capitation is levied by the *ispravnici*; the land tax is farmed out and only rarely levied by commissioners. Constantin Mavrocordat, wishing to put order into the finances and at the same time to make the taxes more tolerable, held a census in 1739 by *petzeder* or printed tickets. At the same time he abolished the ancient taxes, which used to be levied under various names, and fixed them at two lei per family, payable in four instalments. That is the origin of the name *sfert* which means a quarter. The first after the census of 1739 amounted to 367,500 lei in the class of peasants alone.

[1] Not included in this extract.　　　　　　[2] See p. 153.

Mihai Racoviţa imposed a fifth *sfert* in 1741, and Constantin Mavrocordat, after taking up the reins of government again, added a sixth in 1744.

Grigore Ghica secured for himself the payment, in addition to the *sferturi*, of the Bairam present and the *lipsă* or deficit of the *sferturi*; names invented to disguise this enormous increase of charges and taxes.

During the reigns of Matei Ghica, Constantin Racoviţa and Constantin Mavrocordat (the last of these was prince more than once), the sum paid for the *sferturi* kept on decreasing; on the other hand their number was so considerably increased that in the end there were as many as there were months, and sometimes these months had to be paid twice over.

In 1758 Constantin Mavrocordat, observing the enormous number of *sferturi* in one year, put them back on the old footing and called them 'general accounts'. It was then that he drew from the body of boyars commissioners for the different districts, who in conjunction with the *ispravnici* had to assess the villages. He gave them tickets on the sum payable according to the treasury lists and fixed the payment at four terms in the year.

His successor Scarlat Ghica found as a result of this measure that the *sfert* amounted to nearly 200,000 lei. He did not however follow this wise arrangement; he diminished the sum and once more multiplied the number of *sferturi*. He had them levied every month and by this means succeeded in amassing considerable sums in the years 1758 and 1759, as one can see from the list for this latter year annexed at the end of this chapter.[1]

This arrangement, so well suited to the avarice and greed of the princes, has ever since been approved, although the total of the sum paid in *sferturi* has often been diminished by the flight of the inhabitants, crushed beneath this tax.

In the year 1766, for example, the same prince Scarlat Ghica received in all from the capitation of the peasants only 849,458⅓ lei, and in 1767 the prince Alexandru Ghica only drew 785,776⅔ lei....

The Bresle

The different classes of inhabitants, other than peasants, who pay tribute to the public treasury, are called *Bresle*. Under this name are included the *mazili* or descendants of boyars, who are without employment. The *neamuri* or principal *mazili*. The *păhărnicei*[2] under the orders of their *vătafi* or chiefs of the *păhărnicei*. The clerks of the Divan, whose parents are *mazili*. Retired captains. Unemployed

---

[1] Omitted.　　　[2] Subordinates of the Grand Cupbearer (*păharnic*).

customs officers. The *alcibys* or the most distinguished among the peasants. The merchants of the twelve counties. The Craiova company, which is a representation of the merchants of that city. The Gorj company, another society of merchants from the county of that name. The *ruptaşi* or those foreigners and inhabitants with whom special agreements have been made concerning the tribute.

The *Braşoveni*, inhabitants of Cronstadt,[1] who pay tribute in virtue of an agreement. The Silistrians, the Armenians, living in the country. The Jews, the Kiprovazi and the Cabilians, residents who have come from across the Danube, all paying tribute by agreement.

The merchants and various foreigners whom we have just mentioned formerly paid their tribute to the prince's treasury; since the abolition of this treasury they pay it to the public treasury. . . .

The Spring and Autumn Provisions

These provisions, which consisted of all sorts of grain, are called *zaherele*. They were demanded for the first time in the spring of 1756. The quantity of wheat ordered is not always the same. In the spring of 1756 it was 15,000 *chile* (Brăila measure), and in the autumn of 1760 20,000 *chile*.[2] This wheat must be delivered at Brăila, whence it is transported to the storehouses of Constantinople. The *Nazir* or Sultan's town-major has the task of giving the receipts for each delivery, and the commissioner whom the princes have kept there since 1759 to prevent fraud receives various signatures from the *nazir*, who, once the quantity of wheat ordered is complete, has the whole confirmed by a general certificate. This certificate, which the commissioner only obtains with the help of presents, is then sent to Constantinople.

Furthermore, these provisions are imposed on the country in cash and levied twice a year, in spring and autumn. The wheat in kind is bought with this money in the neighbourhood of Brăila on behalf of the country by the merchants of that town, who do not fail to reap advantage from such an opportunity.

If on the one hand this arrangement suits those who are too far from the town to transport their wheat there conveniently, on the other it has its disadvantages; the purchase of a large quantity of wheat cannot fail to be expensive.

In 1766 in the reign of Scarlat Ghica this tax amounted to 60,331 lei and in 1767 in the time of Alexandru Ghica to 58,000 lei.[3]

The Oierit

The *oierit* is an ancient tithe, which was originally paid in kind and

---

[1] Braşov.   [2] See Note on Weights, Measures and Currency, p. 203.   [3] *Ibid.*

later in cash. This tax has always gone on increasing. It was at first three paras, then four and five, until finally in 1748 Constantin Mavrocordat raised it to six. This same prince in 1744, and subsequently Grigore Ghica in 1752 and Ştefan Racoviţa in 1765, took it into their heads to demand double.

What is more, the monasteries, the boyars and the mazils, who for a long time enjoyed the privilege of paying the *oierit* only every three years, were obliged to pay it every year like the other subjects. Sometimes the princes endeavoured to compensate them by granting them certificates of immunity, to each according to his rank and quality. . . .

The Salt Mines

There are some salt mines at Telega in the district of Prahova, and at Slănic in the district of Săcuieni. The great mine of the Banat[1] is in the district of Vâlcea.

Formerly the revenues from these mines were very modest; the salt was sold at a price so low that for three okes one paid only one para. At a still more distant time one only paid 20 paras for 100 okes.

Before the reform the salt mine revenues were farmed for 40,000 lei. After the reunion of the Banat of Craiova with the principality of Wallachia, the price of salt was raised by a firman, in virtue of which there was a charge in the Danube ports of the principality of 44 paras for 100 okes,[2] with a surplus of 10 per cent, and in the ports of the Banat of 50 paras, with a surplus of 15 per cent. This price has since been further raised to 50 paras for the mines of the principality, and to 60 paras for the great mine of the Banat: and when the salt is in large blocks, one is charged 67 paras for 100 okes. The first sum for farming all the mines was 90,000 lei; it has since been increased every year, until in 1766 it had risen to 150,000 lei.

The time for renewing this lease is the month of January. At each renewal the salt which is near the mines belongs to the prince, and that which is at the ports or on the road, belongs to the last farmers. The latter may not sell any of their surplus before April, the purpose of this prohibition being to favour the new farmers. The largest quantity of salt extracted from these mines was in 1755, when the total was 25,000,000 okes.[3] However they would furnish far more, if a market could be found for it. . . .

The Revenues of the Princess[4]

The gipsies who are slaves on the Hospodar's domains form part of

[1] The Banat of Craiova.
[2] See Note on Weights, Measures and Currency, p. 203.
[3] 30,000 tons.   [4] The Princess is the consort of the Hospodar (Prince).

the Princess's revenues. Some of them give gold which they fish in the rivers. An official list of Ştefan Racoviţa for the year 1764 shows that of 240 gipsies called *Rudari*,[1] 171 gave six drachms per head, 21 four and 48 three. The total amounted to 1,254 drachms, which makes 1,003 drachms of refined gold.

These same gipsies are also obliged to sell to the Grand Armaş, their chief, all the gold which they find, at two lei per drachm. He then sells it at a higher price for the benefit of the Princess. However, the quantity of gold sold in this way to the Grand Armaş does not surpass that which is given in tribute. The other gipsies, i.e. 195 called *Ursari*[2] and 473 called *Lăeişi*,[3] pay five lei per head, which makes a total of 3,340 lei.

The Princess also enjoys certain rights and monopolies, included in recent times among the customs duties, from which she receives the money due to her.

In 1763 the sum which she received from the customs amounted to   32,000 lei

the tribute from the gipsies to   3,340

        35,340 lei

This does not include the gold paid in kind.

Friedrich Wilhelm de Bawr (1735–83), a German, became a general in the Russian Army during the Russo-Turkish war of 1769.

4. FERTILE WALLACHIA

A. M. del Chiaro, *Istoria delle moderne rivoluzioni della Valachia* (History of the Recent Revolutions in Wallachia), Venice, 1718, pp. 6–8; 17.

THE country could not be more fertile or more pleasantly situated. From the Danube to Bucharest (which is in the middle of Wallachia) and from Bucharest to Târgovişte, which is fourteen hours distant from Bucharest by road, nothing is to be seen but an immense and delightful plain, in which not even a small stone is to be found. In every district one sees very fine woods (especially of oaks) laid out with such regularity and kept so clear, that from one end of a wood to the other it is easy to discover if there is anyone there. In this (as in all other kinds of exactitude) it is easy to trace the character of the incomparable Prince Constantin Brâncoveanu.[4] If we desire a clear view of the quality and extent of the country's fertility, it is enough to reflect that droves of horses, pigs and cattle are sent from Transylvania to the pastures of Wallachia. From Wallachia Venice is

[1] Woodcarvers.   [2] Bearwards.   [3] Nomads.
[4] C. Brâncoveanu, Prince of Wallachia (1688–1714).

provided with wax and steers, just as the Sultan's kitchen is provided with butter and honey in great quantities. . . .

The greater part of Transylvania is provided with excellent white and red wines, very delicate to the taste and wholesome to the stomach. The horses of Wallachia are much in demand not only from German officials in Transylvania, but also from merchants who come from Poland with orders to procure them. They turn out very well if they are given some training which they have not received in their native place, where they are apt to be skittish and full of other faults. Anyone who enjoys hunting can satisfy his desires in that country, where there is abundance of boars, chamois, stags, fallow-deer, wolves, bears, foxes, etc.; there are also great numbers of birds, both wild and domestic. . . .

Game enjoy, so to speak, a peaceful tranquillity, through the sloth of that leisure-loving nation, which scarcely troubles itself about its daily food. Not, indeed, that the Wallachians lack good qualities and courage to confront the most warlike of nations; but the continuous imposition of exorbitant taxes, which they have to pay many times in a single year, has so degraded them that of the ancient Roman virtues nothing remains but the name. . . .

These continuous oppressions have not only made them cowardly and lazy, but have even reduced them to the desperate decision of abandoning their own nest and seeking refuge, some in the parts of Turkey beyond the Danube, some in Transylvania, where I am certain that the number of Wallachians is greater than it is in Wallachia. And if anyone says to me 'How can it be so easy to leave Wallachia and enter other provinces?', I answer that it is not at all difficult for anyone who has the necessary knowledge, especially of some passes through the mountains, which lead into Transylvania, provided he keeps out of the way of the guards (called by the Wallachians *plăiaşi*), since to fall into their hands without a passport from the Prince would certainly endanger his life. . . .

As for its fertility, it is to be noted that in Wallachia they plough the land twice in the autumn, and then the corn is sown. It grows to half a span before the snow comes; then, when the snow settles on it, it sinks, and in spring continues to grow to maturity. Millet is sown in spring and reaped in July. Maize, or Turkish corn, is also sown in spring, and reaped in August. The vines are buried after the end of the vintage, and remain buried until the time comes to tie them to stakes and prune them.

Anton Maria del Chiaro, a Florentine, was from 1709 secretary to Constantin Brâncoveanu, Prince of Wallachia, and then to his two successors.

5. SHEEP FARMING

S. Raicevich, *Osservazioni storiche naturali e politiche intorno la Valachia e Moldavia* (Historical, Natural and Political Observations on Wallachia and Moldavia), Naples, 1788, pp. 67–79.

THE pastures which abound in the two principalities are suited for rearing a great number of quadrupeds; and in fact all sorts of these form their principal wealth and the most considerable branch of their commerce. The herbage of Wallachia is more suitable and fitted to small cattle, and the quantity of these, sheep and goats, amounted in 1786 to about four millions. The sheep in Wallachia are of three varieties, namely *ţigăi*, *bârsani* and *stogoşi*. The first gives fine short wool and excellent meat; the second, long coarse wool; and the third, being a hybrid, gives medium wool.

These animals always live in the open air; during the summer in the mountains, and in the winter on the banks of the Danube. The movement from the plain to the mountains takes place after St. George's Day towards the end of April; in the greatest heat they climb to the tops of the mountains, where they find excellent pasture and very cold water. In November they come down again and go to the banks of the Danube, where they are less exposed to the winds and find more temperate air, and above all, a herb which is pre-served under the snow. This the sheep eat readily, digging for it under the snow. It often happens either that the snow is too deep and its surface frozen, or that it is very scanty, and in consequence the herb does not grow. In view of these difficulties, the shepherds make stores of hay and dried grass, from which they build large, lofty piles like straw-ricks; they take the sheep there, and they eat the amount of it which they need. When furious north-east winds blow (usually with heavy falls of snow), the shepherds make the sheep keep moving round the said rick, or in the lee of a hedge or a mound of earth, frequently striking them to keep them above the snow and oblige them to move, both to prevent them remaining buried under it and also to prevent them being frozen by the great cold. The variety called *bârsan* must spend the summer in the moun-tains, because the heat would kill it in the plains. That named *ţigăi* can live on the plain, provided that there is a wood nearby to which they can retire during the day, and good water. The hybrid variety is found to be the most resistant to summer heat, and less liable to all the seasonal troubles, and its flesh is of really good flavour.

After St. George's Day the sheep are shorn. They give greater or less quantities of wool according to their varieties; the *bârsan* about four pounds, the fine variety less.

All the ewes produce one lamb a year, and few produce two; in that case the owner of the fold gives one to the shepherd. Usually both males and females are kept; the latter to propagate the flock, while the males are gelded for sale, as will be said below.

The milk is taken only when the sheep are in the mountains. It is quickly turned by the shepherds into a runny sort of cheese which they call 'white', and sell it to merchants established close by with their cheese presses, who extract the butter from it, and into a cheese called *caşcaval*, which resembles in shape and flavour that which is made in the kingdoms of Sicily. They also make a cheese of larger size and different consistency and excellent flavour, which they call 'mountain cheese', the greater part of which is consumed in Transylvania. . . .

A ewe costs about a florin and a half; a lamb from 12 to 15 carantani; a wether from 2 to $2\frac{1}{2}$ florins. They often slaughter the pregnant ewes in order to have the skin of the unborn lamb, which is black and valuable for making hats and linings of clothes. Ordinary skins serve for making leather.

In short, taking everything into consideration, it is reckoned that a flock of one thousand sheep well tended brings in per year in Wallachia a return of about a thousand florins, provided there is not unusual mortality. . . .

Oxen and cows abound in both principalities, with this difference, that in Moldavia they are much bigger and fleshier; in height they are like those of Hungary, but have shorter legs and are more corpulent. Many are exported to foreign countries, especially Silesia. A race of Moldavian gipsies called *lingurari* because of the spoons and other wooden implements which they make, rear and breed the better kind, which they sell at the rate of 60 piastres apiece to Armenians from Galicia, who rent various lands in Moldavia where they fatten the oxen and maintain the breeds of horses. . . .

Buffaloes are much used especially in Wallachia, both to draw carts and for the excellent and abundant milk which they give. However this animal demands great care, being equally inconvenienced by heat and cold. In winter it must stay in a very warm stall, and in summer it likes to stew in a swamp. Normally they are black, but there are also white ones, which are less displeasing to the sight; they are very fierce and capable of attacking a man when they are in heat.

In Moldavia there are numerous kinds of horses; every boyar keeps his own, some 100, some 200 head. The better horses are those of the above-mentioned Armenians, and everyone takes care to have their stallions.

Stefano Raicevich, a Ragusan, came to Wallachia about 1776 as a trader. He became secretary for European languages to Alexandru Ipsilanti (Prince of Wallachia, 1774–82) and tutor to his two sons.

6. VINEYARDS AND WINE

F. J. Sulzer, *Geschichte des transalpinischen Daciens* (History of Wallachia), Vienna, 1781, vol. i, pp. 127–9.

OF all the gifts of the vegetable kingdom it is the vine which has won precedence in Transalpine Dacia—and especially in Wallachia; it is one of the few products used in trade with foreign countries.

Wallachia alone, in a good year, produces over five million kegs of the best wine; a keg here, however, holds not more than 10 oca[1] or measures. This amount could be increased by half if the vineyards were properly cultivated and if all suitable ground were used for cultivation. In this almost completely flat country all the hills which form the river banks could be cultivated and would yield a rich return. This is proved by the vineyards cultivated around the country houses of the boyars in the flat country: the vineyards on the south side of the Dâmboviţa at Bucharest, and those at Graca and near Giurgiu; also at Galatz on the Danube as well as at Cotnar in the district of Hârlău, at Huşi in Fălciu, at Răcăreşti in Tecuci, and at Greţ or Greteşti in Tutova, the latter all situated in Moldavia. All this serves as proof that the flat country and the smaller hills of both these provinces are not less suitable for growing very good wine than the higher hills at the foot of the Carpathian mountains; indeed it has been said that the vine formerly cultivated around Cotnar excels all others in quality, though it is now neglected owing to the disturbances of war and for other reasons.

The same cannot be said concerning the wine of Wallachia. In general the harvest is early and of very good quality. Wine from Graca is already being retailed at Bucharest by the end of August, but it does not keep and goes flat before the following summer. Wine from the mountainous regions, on the other hand, can be kept for many years, whether it is one, two or three years old before it loses completely the small amount of acidity, and it suits those who are used to much drier wine because of its spirituous and oily ingredients.

---

[1] 1 'measure' or *oca* is rather more than 1 quart.

General von Bauer[1] has already recognized this, referring in his memoirs to the fact that there was wine from Wallachia which could compete with the Hungarian wine. However he adds that very little wine of such quality can be found because the Wallachians know neither how to make good wine nor how to keep it; this is only true of Wallachia where there are no proper cellars nor sufficient knowledge of drawing off and storing; consequently it is very difficult to get a glass of wine in summer which has not gone sour. What else can be expected where the landlord keeps the barrel out of doors behind a wooden screen in such hot weather? If one wishes to appreciate the goodness of Wallachian wine, it must be tasted at Kronstadt in Transylvania. Here one can learn the difference between Hungarian and Wallachian wine, when one sees that the people of Kronstadt ignore their local wine (which is not at all bad) and prefer the Wallachian (for which they have to pay much more).[2]

Franz Josef Sulzer, an Austrian, was brought to Bucharest in 1776 by Alexandru Ipsilanti, Prince of Wallachia, as a professor.

7. LAND AND PEASANTS IN THE EARLY NINETEENTH CENTURY

Wyburn, *Report on Wallachia*, undated (about 1820?), published by N. Iorga in *Academia Română, Memoriile Secţiei Istorice*, Seria iii, Tomul xiv, pp. 152–3.

THE ceaseless and inexhaustible fund of humidity satisfactorily accounts for the almost incredible richness of the soil of Wallachia, which resembles the black mould of an English artificial melon-bed, and in some places in summer the high roads seem composed of pounded charcoal, the pure couch of which extends in some districts to a depth of more than twenty feet and increases annually, for the richness of the soil undrained by the artificial calls of the nobler grain produces herbs and weeds, particularly hay, of such an extraordinary vigour, that, in passing through meadows near Widdin on horseback, the grass touched my elbows and the thistles left their film upon the crown of my hat.

The trifling population of Wallachia (about a million), which is not a tenth part of what the soil could easily nourish, is insufficient to consume or even *repress* this redundance of vegetation. It is left to

[1] Von Bauer = de Bawr (see Extract 2 above).
[2] I have to thank Mrs. Edith Lee-Uff for help in translation.

be scorched by the rays of an autumnal sun, drenched by the succeeding rains and rotted by a winter's congealed inundation. The
whole Dacian plain in spring displays a black swamp, as ungrateful
to the olfactory nerves as noxious to the organs of respiration and
digestion, producing agues and intermittent fevers, which abound
in these regions. In this trackless morass the horses of travellers
plunge up to their bellies, until by repeated compression they have
created a road for their light wicker waggons. The tips of verdure
which now peep through the interstices of this extensive compost are
found upon examination to be already hay three feet long, as white
as snow: they continue their elevation, nourished and supported by
this prop, until the revolution of the earth round the sun has
produced from *their* decomposition an additional superficies of compost, for the annually renewed effort of prodigal nature.

It may easily be inferred from these premises that the finest
pastures, the most certain and plentiful harvests at the least possible
expence and the most luxuriant vintages, present to the necessary
and even voluptuous desires of man all his insatiate heart could wish.
They do, and to such an extent that the (so called) necessaries of
life: meat, bread and wine are in such abundance and consequently
so cheap (from the exportation *except to Constantinople*, and even *that*
at a *maximum*, being prohibited) that this year and every year of peace
many proprietors have found themselves reduced to the necessity of
throwing away whole magazines of damaged corn, which they had
preserved for some time in hopes of a war, or such an increase of
price as would cover the expence of sending it to market.

A labouring man would find difficulty in eating a farthing's worth
of bread a day. Good wine is sold at a halfpenny a bottle, meat in
proportion. Horses eat only barley and are allowed as much as they
desire. The killow (30 lbs) [1] of barley is sold in summer for about 2/6d
English, a waggon load of hay for a shilling, and delivered and
stowed by the *seller*.

This abundance produces upon the characters of the lower classes
the necessary concomitants of gluttony, drunkenness, natural indolence and violent sensual appetites. But it renders them healthy,
strong, bold, quick of apprehension and (in the intervals of positive
corporal pain from the zabtchis) [2] proud, contented and courteous.
A Wallachian peasant (the very poorest) eats regularly four times a
day and no prince in Christendom fares more luxuriously. He may
consider the whole country at his disposition: he sows and mows hay

[1] Wilkinson, (p. 167 below) gives one English bushel (50 lb. of barley, 60 lb. of
wheat or 25 and 27 kilograms) as the equivalent of one killow. See Note, p. 203.

[2] The *zapcii* mentioned in Extracts 3 and 8.

where he pleases, merely leaving a tenth of the crop for the ground landlord, *whoever he may be*, a fact of which he does not always take the trouble of enquiring. His wife makes his clothes, and he has no other care (and consequently no other incitement *to labour*) than the repeated demands of the zabtchi (collector of taxes, an officer of the ispravnic or governor of the province). This functionary is always attended by Albanians, armed with pistols, musquets, sabres, daggers and particularly whips of an appalling consistency. The genuine Wallach scarcely ever pays a para without having previously submitted to as many blows as his posteriors can endure.

He has as natural an antipathy against the payment of taxes as the Englishman, the Scotchman or the Irishman, but, being unable to *call meetings* of his brethren, to appeal, remonstrate, menace, or rebel, he seems to have listened to and adopted Mr. Benjamin Constant's advice to Frenchmen, the doctrine of *passive resistance*, but invariably finishes as the French have done, by paying, not only the original demand, but the Albanians for administering and the zabtchi for superintending the punishment.

Practically nothing is known of Wyburn. A British officer who met him at Bucharest in 1812 mentions him as 'a Mr. Wyburn from Yorkshire . . . a very fine young man, greatly accomplished in languages, with good manners'.

8. A CLOSER VIEW OF THE PEASANTS

C. Golescu, *Insemnare a călătorii mele* (Report on my Travels), ed. N. Hodoş, Bucharest, 1910, pp. 59–60.

THESE unrighteous practices, unheard of elsewhere in the world, have brought the unhappy inhabitants to such a state, that anyone who enters the so-called villages will see neither church nor house nor fence around the house, nor cart, nor ox nor cow nor fowl nor patch sown for the family's food—in a word, nothing; only some rooms in the earth which are called '*bordeie*'. Anyone who goes in sees nothing but a hole in the earth, which will hold a man with his wife and children around the hearth, and a chimney of basket-work plastered with dung, protruding from the surface of the ground. Behind the stove is another hole, through which he must escape in haste when he perceives that someone has come to his door; for he knows that it can only be one sent to demand payment. And he having nothing to give, will either be beaten, or bound and taken away and sold, for one or two years or more, to a petty boyar or a

farmer or whoever it may be, to serve him for those years, so that
the money which is paid for those years' of service may be taken to
pay his poll-tax. (Again I say: truly, the merciful God is very
patient.)

Why should this divine creation have to live in slavery, so that he
may give to the Prince what he does not possess? And then, if one
went into those *bordeie* of theirs, it would be impossible to find on
their persons or in the house anything worth ten lei; for even the
cauldron in which they will make their porridge is not individual
property, but shared by five or six partners. And when these men,
by good fortune, got wind that a *zapciu, polcovnicu*, captain, or an
agent of the *ispravnic*[1] or of the Prince was coming to their village, they
fled with their wives and the children that were able to flee, through
forests and mountains, just like wild beasts chased by hunters with
hounds. For they knew that if they were caught, there would be a
demand for money, and as they had no money, they would receive
lashes on their backs. I do not think that the most cruelly tyrannous
master, when he sees with his own eyes this divine creation, this man
like himself, fleeing over mountains and through forests, with his
legs bare to the knee and his arms blackened and scorched to the
elbows, and his clothes mere rags, while the children are completely
unclad,—I do not think that his heart will fail to be softened, however cruel and savage he be, or that he will demand money again
from such a condition of men. But the reason is that the Princes and
we boyars never see these men; we only see those who go to use
force on them, to punish them and to distrain, men with poisoned
souls and no knowledge of their duties towards mankind.

Constantin (Dinicu) Golescu (1777–1828), a leading Wallachian boyar,
travelled as far as North Italy, Switzerland and South Germany in the years
1824–6.

9. SERFDOM AND OTHER INSTITUTIONS

I. Codru Drăgăşanu, *Peregrinul Transilvan* (The Transylvanian Pilgrim), ed.
Şerban Cioculescu, Bucharest, 1942, pp. 67–72.

FEUDALISM has never existed in Rumania. Every man is fully the
owner of his real estate; no one has any notion of chivalry, and the
past is definitely barbarian. Nevertheless feudal dues have been
introduced, according to circumstances, evidently by imitation of

---

[1] *Ispravnic*, 'prefect' of a county (*judeţ*); *zapciu*, sub-prefect; *polcovnicu*, 'colonel'
(of gendarmerie).

L

the Hungarians and Poles. Regalian rights have likewise been imi-
tated, and have been further consolidated by the Organic Law of
today.

Here small holdings are only found close to the mountains; further
off there are only estates of monstrous size, almost completely devoid
of inhabitants.

Obviously these were originally seized by boyars after the emigration of the inhabitants in consequence of the ceaseless wars with all
the barbarians, and later with the Crescent. Where there are no
peasant inhabitants, the landlords form extensive pastures, called
suhaturi, and farm them for the fattening of flocks and herds of cattle,
with which great cities, especially the imperial ones of Vienna and
Constantinople, are supplied with meat.

Serfdom here is called *clacă* and is also organized by regulation
throughout the country. The peasants call the urbarium *zămblar* (a
barbarism like 'urbarium' itself), i.e. *exemplar*, an extract from the
Organic Regulation, which covers the duties and rights of the serfs
towards the landlord of the estate, deposited in every community.

According to the *zămblar*, the serf receives nine *pogoane* [$4\frac{1}{2}$ hec-
tares] of land, including pasture, for use, since here there are no
'*commune terrenum*' and no 'urbarial forests'. For this the peasant is
bound to provide twelve working days, to take his part in serfdom
(with a different meaning from that which we have in Transylvania),
to bring a cartload of wood, and to give a tithe of all produce to the
landlord. This is on the face of things, but just look at the other
side!

The *ciocoi*[1] have transformed the working days into days' worth of
work, and the poor serf works at least three times twelve days to
complete the task allotted. Serfdom, in the Rumanian sense, is the
burden imposed on 25 peasants of keeping a servant at the manor,
like the wage-earning servants in Transylvania. The cartload of
wood is fetched very easily, when the forest is close by; but from the
empty plains, it is as if he were to be sent to fetch wood from the
Antipodes, and the poor serf, bound by his due, in order to escape a
journey to the North Pole after wood, compounds for several days of
normal work. Finally, the tithe is taken from hay as well, and even
from a bed of parsley; for it is not the landlord who takes it, it is the
rascally Greek farmer.

There is only one good thing. At the New Year, the days stipulated
in the *zămblar* can be compounded for a small sum. This year the
price of a day is fixed at 60 paras (15 silver kreutzers). The greatest
difficulty is, however, with the surplus: that is to say, if a man is not

---

[1] See p. 119 above, and p. 157 below.

satisfied with his legal allotment of land and demands extra, then for that, he bargains with the Greek, who knows how to squeeze many days' work for a small amount of land, like a Hungarian *tiszttartó*.

But what is the poor man to do? He does his days, and has as unpleasant a life as the worm in the horse-radish, since he tries to grow large crops, the prices being almost always low, and to keep plenty of cattle, for they too fetch nothing.

Gipsies

I said that here there are vagabond gipsies, that is free ones; it was so, but now the State has decided to subject them also, turning them into peasants settled upon landlords' estates. They have been promised reliefs, tax-exemption for several years, and they are bound to be regular peasants.

What has not happened from the time of the Emperor Jovian till today, will at last be accomplished in Rumania, with its culture at the chrysalis stage, where even the Rumanian, who, from having princes as his ancestors, has come to be as it were the symbol of servitude[1]—so used is he to the yoke—is forsaking the plough through terror of the farmers.

The gipsies here carry on all those small trades just as they do in Transylvania; they make, that is to say, spindles, spoons, kneading-bowls, sieves, they cast bells, patch and tin cauldrons, fish for gold and tell fortunes. But, besides these, there is a class of gipsies which, as in the Middle Ages, hunts partridges with a breed of hawk named *curoi*, which are trained young for falconry. This company of black hunters provides partridges for the tables of the Prince and almost all the great boyars.

It is gipsies too who undertake the breeding of mules, which the State buys and passes on to Turkey, making a monopoly trade, for they are not used in Rumania.

All these trades are likely to a great extent to cease in the future, as the poor gipsies, to a man, have been, or soon will be, made to toe the line; then farewell to free industry! They will have, poor fellows, to do labour services and pay tithe, rejoicing in the same lot as the Rumanian, which at present is not very enviable.

The gipsy slaves are mostly servants in the house or demesne. The knowledge that they can be sold as mere animals of itself makes them pretty miserable. Upon them the boyars exercise all feudal rights, named and unnamed, such as *ius primae noctis*.

---

[1] The name *rumân* had become the term for 'serf' (see Extract 2).

Justice

While we are on the subject of gipsies, it occurs to me to mention the prisons, for the supreme King of the gipsies is at the same time inspector-general of the prisons in the Principality, under the title of 'Vornic of the Prisons'. Detainees or convicts are otherwise treated humanely, but, of course, with strokes of the cudgel, laid down in their sentence, at intervals measured by the law, that is to say, by the opinion of the boyars of the Divan,—for here justice is mostly given by opinion, jurists being as frequent in tribunals as white crows in Europe.

Rumanian constitutionalism does not go so far as to guarantee personal liberty, but boyars exempt themselves from arrest by favours. It is a very queer sort of 'habeas corpus'.

If a criminal escapes from prison, the careless warder is imprisoned in his place, until the former is caught, or until his term is up, as the case may be. Whether this is according to the law or not, I cannot be sure, but I have witnessed such a case.

Criminal justice, though fairly partial, is European, modern, and does not admit torture or confiscation of property or even martial law.

It is defective only as regards corporal punishment, for the abolition of which the time has not yet come—according to the expression of the boyars that make the laws. Naturally the longer an evil institution is retained, the more intense is the feeling of the gap which would be left if it were abolished. From the French code has been adopted the pretty disgraceful punishment of the pillory, which consists in binding the criminal with shaven head and a ring round his neck, to a post in the middle of the market place, while above is inscribed the crime committed and the sentence pronounced, so that every one can see him. It is a sort of bloodless crucifixion, as any one can tell.

Corporal punishment does not exist; instead, by an imitation of the Russian code, criminals are condemned for a time or for life to *ocne*, that is, to forced labour in salt-mines. Many consider this punishment, like exile in Siberia, worse than death, and every one talks against it. I, with my limited knowledge, am not of this opinion. God created this world and Siberia too to be inhabited by men. Why should the criminal of another country be better than the decent people born there? If throughout Europe and in Transylvania itself free men cut salt from the mines, is it not quite humane to assign this task to criminals as a punishment instead of hanging them? Perhaps this merely hurts the feelings of the voluntary salt-miners. In any case, the criminal laws are uniform for all, unlike ours in Transylvania where the murder of a noble costs 200 florins, of a free man 40 florins and of a serf 20 florins! So you don't hear the fool saying at every turn as he does with us: 'I'll kill you, ——, and pay for you!' Anyway, criminal justice here could be a model for Transylvania: here there are not so many crimes committed, and banditry, once famous, has been completely extirpated.

Communes

The police too is to be praised in Rumania. In all communes a night watch is kept by the inhabitants, and the commune is collectively responsible for any theft or damage by violence at night. This is, of course, a measure taken in favour of the boyars and farmers, but, on the whole, it is good and deserves universal imitation.

Now that we have come to the subject of communes, it will do no harm for me to point to other communal institutions in the country, that is, in villages.

Communal life is far from being developed, but a few institutions are aiming at developing it; and this, in time, will be achieved. For the simple Rumanian is much more solid than the class of *ciocoi*, which have been assimilated in turn to Slavs, Greeks and Muscovites, and have now reached the stage of being Frenchified in ideas, language and habits. The villagers, being strangers to so-called culture, have one firm principle; they do not run after every shadow.

The communities are agricultural, ecclesiastical, scholastic and political. It is to be noted that the political commune has no definite magistrate as in Transylvania, but has a communal council, consisting of the lord of the manor or his farmer, of the local priest and of several elected representatives of the people, as well as a *logofăt* or village notary.

Besides all other attributes which everywhere fall within the sphere of the communal authority, the Council here administers the communal chest and the reserve store—two institutions unknown with us.

The communal fund is here raised in a quite peculiar way. Once in every seven years the poll tax is revised, and this is called *catagrafie*. Registers are then drawn up, according to which, until the next *catagrafie*, the whole commune must pay its quota without fail. The tax for those who die or emigrate is paid from the communal fund, while the newly-married and immigrants pay their tax into the village chest until the general registration. The growth being always greater than the decrease, the communal funds have notable surpluses.

The reserve stores are an institution introduced by the Russians,

who during the occupation of this fat land after the famous revolution of Tudor Vladimirescu, the so-called *Zavera* (literally, 'for
faith'), observed that owing to lack of foresight, when there are large
crops, everything is exported for almost nothing, and then when
there is a bad year or a war or invasion occurs, people are exposed
to famine.

Every inhabitant is bound to deposit in this communal store a
twentieth part of his annual harvest, which is renewed from time to
time, the old stores being divided up and new taken in their place.
From this store, which consists chiefly of maize, the priest receives
an annual grant; the rest is normally kept for the use—but, as experience shows, to the detriment—of the depositors. For it is robbed
by officials, spoiled by mice and the elements, and in general, like
any thing which belongs to every one, is thought of as being no one's.

Worth mentioning too is the communal seal. This consists of three
parts, which together with a ring make up a whole. One part is kept
by the lord of the manor, another by the priest, and a third by one
of the representatives. The seal contains the emblem of the county
with its motto, and the name of the division and the political community, which usually contains several agricultural communes.

It is clear that it is more difficult here to get a false certificate
stamped with the communal seal than in Transylvania, where a pint
of *rachiu* [brandy] is enough for the depressed magistrate to set his
seal, unchecked, on any paper.

Ion Codru Drăgăşanu (1818(?)–84) was a Rumanian subject of the Haps-
burg Empire. He left Transylvania in 1835 to avoid conscription, and spent
the next ten years in various parts of Europe. This gave him the material
for a travel book, which was published in 1865. It is in the form of letters
to his brother. The section reproduced here purports to have been written
from Bucharest in March 1840.

10. Privileged and Unprivileged

E. Poujade, *Chrétiens et Turcs*, Paris, 1859, pp. 442–5; 533–5; 537–42; 487–8.

The Moldavian Nobility

FORTUNES in this principality are much larger than in Wallachia.
There are several reasons for this: the first is indubitably the Moldavian boyars' excellent habit of residing on their estates and
cultivating them themselves, while in Wallachia the boyar always
lives in town and farms out his lands. It must be added that unfortunately the condition of the Moldavian peasant is much worse than

that of his Wallachian neighbour. He is bound to a greater number of working days in the service of the landlord, and this serves in no small degree to increase the incomes of the boyars. Agriculture is much more advanced in Moldavia than in Wallachia, and an estate in the former of these two principalities provides a return four times as great as that produced by an estate in Wallachia, other things being equal. These large fortunes, this life characteristic of great landlords, gives the Moldavian character something of feudal pride, and stamps it with an imprint of independence which one hardly ever sees in Wallachia. The Moldavian boyar is master on his vast domain, it is he who draws up the recruiting lists, who pays his peasants' taxes directly to the *vistierie* (Ministry of Finance), and the authorities must obtain his consent to administer justice in his district. He has not, like the Wallachian, a passion for public office, though when he does fill one, he too often shows the same lack of disinterestedness and rectitude. One does not find him assiduous at paying court to the prince, who for him is only a *primus inter pares* exalted by the will of his fellow-countrymen. Under foreign occupation the conduct of the Moldavian boyars has been much more dignified than that of the Wallachian boyars. No eager obsequiousness. The Russian agents and generals were not, as at Bucharest, the object of cringing adulation. The Moldavian salons have almost always been closed to the most brilliant general staffs, and the marriages, so frequent in Wallachia, even below the upper class, between Russian officers and the women of the country, have been extremely rare in Moldavia.

There is, one may say, in this principality an aristocracy which for a long time to come, as much and more than in Wallachia, will be the only body to give the Moldavian population the appearance of an established society. Nevertheless it is not because of its titles that the aristocracy forms a body; it is entirely because of its possessions. In both principalities the 'supplementary nobility', sometimes created by the most shameful partiality and by the rapacity of princes, conferred for services which were not more than domestic ones, or sold in many cases at a low price, has brought rank into considerable disrepute. Ion Sturdza created minor nobles for 400 piastres (about 200 francs), and there are in Moldavia almost thirty *logofeţi* (it is the highest rank of the Moldavian hierarchy), of which several have no fortune. One meets them in country towns dressed almost like peasants, wearing a beard, the distinctive sign of the great boyar, and driving little one-horse wicker carriages.

The Organic Regulation of the principalities had attempted by judicious measures to put a brake upon this cheapening of nobility.

Already the Emperor Alexander had stopped the admission of equivalence between the ranks of Moldavia and Wallachia and those of Russia, an admission made by his predecessors; but all these measures were fruitless, and, particularly under the last two princes, Wallachia has seen men risen from the ranks of domestic service or enriched by the most culpable means, advancing in the hierarchy of nobles until they took part in the council of ministers. The only remedy for this state of things seems to us to be the creation in the principalities of a national representation based solely on property.

The Wallachian Nobility

One can obtain some idea of the legal state of the principalities before the Organic Regulation by studying the reforms accomplished by this political, administrative and judicial code. But to accomplish such reforms, a combination of extraordinary circumstances was necessary; the powerful influence which the Peace of Adrianople gave Russia over the Christian populations of the Ottoman Empire; a man of outstanding intelligence and character, supported by an army of 30,000 men and wielding almost dictatorial power. We are not afraid to say that all this good could not have been achieved except at this price. Without this powerful and beneficent influence the privileged would, with a few rare exceptions, have legislated for years without ever being willing to renounce their privileges and grant their fellow-countrymen the rights for which they are indebted to the Organic Regulation. These privileged persons formed the basis of the political edifice inaugurated by the Organic Regulation, which still survives today, though profoundly altered.

It was particularly from 1843 onwards, after the fall of Prince Alexandru Ghica, that the aristocratic institutions of Wallachia underwent these alterations, which have produced the same social disorders in Moldavia. We will confine ourselves to describing the state of institutions in Wallachia when a European conference undertook to reform them. When Count Kisseleff handed back the reins of government to the two princes in 1834, and when Alexandru Ghica fell in 1842, for having wished to govern with the independence which was guaranteed to him by the privileges of the principality, the boyars properly so called were divided into three categories. Exempted in principle from all payment and invested with all rights, they by themselves formed the state. But the numbers of this class have been quintupled since 1842, and, as a result of this enormous increase, the conservative spirit no longer reigns in the privileged body of boyars, as it did at the time when the reforms were introduced into the Principalities. The new so-called 'supplementary' nobility, many times more numerous than the old, is composed of individuals who for the most part have not wealth equivalent to their rank and who lend themselves to the most disgusting abuses in the exercise of public functions, of which they have the exclusive right. Remarkably enough, it is particularly in the supplementary nobility that revolutionary passions and socialist ideas have found active instruments and docile adherents.

Other Classes

If from the nobility we pass to the other classes of the Rumanian population, we shall see that abuses and degradation have entered in, which have to a great extent destroyed the work of the Organic Regulation, and dried up the source of those benefits which the political and administrative code had led the Moldo-Wallachians to hope for, or had already conferred upon them.

Immediately after the boyars in the social scale come the *neamuri*, who should have been the nursery-ground of the nobility. The *neamuri* are held to be the descendants of ancient aristocratic families which once possessed land. They are nobles and prove their nobility by patents, but they are not boyars because they have no rank and it is rank which makes the boyar. But the ancient constitution of the county and the Organic Regulation having attached the exercise of political rights to the status of boyar, it is obvious how important it was to keep pure and gradually elevate a class from which that of the boyars is recruited.

Some measures had at first been taken to ascertain the number of families of *neamuri*, and to proceed to their moral and material betterment; but not only have these measures been abandoned, they have been systematically abolished. Thus certificates of descent were subjected to a very large fee, and titles of *neamuri* were granted to all those who were willing to pay this fee; one then saw this title, which previously inspired respect, granted to traders, clerks and domestics. This invasion of the *neamuri* class brought about an absolute revolution in the social condition of the principality; small traders above all suffered greatly from it, being unable to compete with individuals exempt from the need of a licence, because the latter had become privileged although continuing in their former business.

Below the *neamuri* come the *mazili*, who number 6,219 in Wallachia. The *mazili* pay a contribution of 45 piastres and are exempt from forced labour. Since 1842 this contribution has been increased for reasons which we shall see when we talk of licensed persons and peasants. The class of *mazili*, privileged in some respects, is almost as maltreated as that of the working peasants.

The last of the privileged classes is that of licensees. This class includes 25,514 families. Of this number only 58 are engaged in commerce or banking and have a very restricted sphere of operation; they have practically no relations with foreign countries. 309 devote themselves to small retail trade and are principally engaged in leasing land. The other licensees may be divided into residents and artisans. The licence has, since 1843, undergone the same increases as the capitation and the *mazili* tax. Except as regards forced labour, from which licensees are exempt, the licence confers no other right such as to set the licensee above the peasant. He is, like the latter, excluded from political rights, and his situation with regard to the privileged classes is the same.

The Organic Regulation had wished to favour the formation of a third estate, and to achieve this aim to which European civilization has tended, it had preserved the guilds and at the same time by establishing municipal councils had made it easy for leading members of the guilds to obtain certain rights. This impulse, given by Count Kisseleff, continued, though slowly, for several years; but soon the industrial class, the budding third estate, slipped back and fell even lower than it had been before the reforms applied by the Organic Regulation.

Three causes contributed above all to this retrograde movement. They were: (i) the ease with which peasants were admitted to the number of licensees; (ii) the profusion with which patents of nobility were granted; (iii) the decline of the municipalities. The licence was sought after, because it gave exemption from forced labour. Patents of nobility removed from the guilds their richest and most influential members. The decline of municipalities did away with this useful station in society, where the members of guilds could rest and console themselves for not attaining nobility. The consequences of this state of things were disastrous for Wallachian society; everyone who rose above the peasant class had himself enlisted in the nobility and removed from this interesting section of the community its natural defenders and supporters. Things have gone so far that the Bucharest guild of wine merchants, whose membership reaches nearly four thousand, numbers perhaps less than 500 retailers with licences. All the others have bought the right of being enrolled in the various privileged classes.

Taxation

What then is the situation of the mass of the people in the Principalities, of those who till the soil and on whom, in the last resort, falls the burden of filling the treasury and forming the militia? Let us take

Wallachia. The rural population of this principality is composed of 354,294 peasant families. These peasants pay into the treasury: (i) a tax called capitation, fixed by law at 30 piastres (about 11 francs); (ii) two tenths extra above the principal to the village funds, in order to compensate the treasury for non-payments in the interval of quinquennial assessments. . . . The peasant also pays 6 piastres (2 fr. 50) for the roads; 6 piastres for the debts caused by the Russian occupation of 1848; 3 piastres for the *dorobanţi* (county constabulary); 2 piastres for the schools; he also pays some additional centimes for the militia. All these different taxes contravene the basis fixed by the Organic Regulation. It is they which have raised capitation to the high rate which it has reached today and which have overthrown the system of uniform taxation inaugurated in 1830 by Count Kisseleff as the best remedy for the abuses of tax-collecting.

What is worse is that the services which these different supplementary taxes were supposed to help were fictitious or nearly so. For example, the sums collected amounted to 40 million piastres for the roads, $24\frac{1}{2}$ million piastres for the occupation debt, five million piastres for the schools; net result: not a road in order, only three million piastres paid for the occupation, not a school opened!

As for the relations of the peasants with the landlords, they have also been strained, and the situation of the former has been made worse and worse. It has therefore become a matter of urgency to look after the peasant class; it is in all respects the most interesting class in the Principalities. . . .

The Need for Fiscal Reform

In the thought and intentions of the authors of the Organic Regulation, capitation was an important amelioration for the peasant. In fact, before the Organic Regulation was put into effect, the personal tax was a real tyranny for the peasant. This tax was raised on the system of *liude*. The *liude* was an assembly, a group of families; five or six families formed a *liude* and had to pay 700 piastres. But this system left the way wide open for arbitrary treatment. The peasants never knew what they had to pay; extension or retraction of the *liude* depended on administrators and sub-administrators. In certain villages the peasants were crushed and ruined by the tax-collectors, who reduced them to the most frightful misery; in others they were protected by influential boyars. One of the fine estates of Wallachia, called Mogoşoaia and situated near Bucharest, only paid half a *liude* (350 piastres), when it ought to have paid perhaps ten times that sum. This system, especially from 1817 to 1830, had dried up the public revenues, caused unheard-of misery, and extinguished the taxable population. It was a matter of urgency to restore confidence, so that work could start again. Capitation had the merit of being a simple, uniform, moderate tax, and the peasant could easily tell what he had to pay. This tax was adopted; only, as this tax has the disadvantage of non-payments which occur as the result of absence or death, the legislator had created an additional tenth. This system produced the best results, and the extra tenth was not exceeded under the Russian administration or that of Alexandru Ghica; but since 1843 it has been the source of abuses which recall the bad days of the *liude*. The chief characteristics of capitation, uniformity, moderation, collection by chosen representatives of the village, disappeared; instead of one additional tenth, two, three, four and so on were levied, until the personal tax rose from 30 piastres to 100. Although this was not at all the fault of capitation, but of a bad administration, it has become a matter of urgency to apply a serious remedy to the present state of things.

Eugène Poujade was French consul-general at Bucharest from 1849 to 1856.

11. A BOYAR'S HOUSE

I. Ghica, *Convorbiri Economice* (Economic Conversations), Bucharest, 1879, pp. 592–4.

A BOYAR'S house was a veritable fortress, a state within a state. Neither the prince's police nor his justice dared to cross the threshold of a Ban or a Vornic, although such privilege could not anywhere be found in writing. At need the boyar could shut his gates and live for months on end with his family, his servants and the men of his household, eighty or a hundred souls, without having the least need of the world outside. He had maize and wheat flour in his granaries, his storehouse groaned with all sorts of groceries and pickles, and among his gipsies he had bakers, tailors, cobblers, etc. At need he could with the help of the men in his courtyard defend himself against the power of the prince, provided it was not backed by any order from Constantinople.

The part of the house around the great staircase, with four rooms to right and left of the hall spread with coverings and hangings woven and sewn in the house, with sofas and divans in the corners and cushions all around, and two or three other smaller rooms for the secretary, the coffee-boy, the pipe-boy and the footman, formed the boyar's suite. The other part of the house with the balcony, the store-room and the stairs from the garden belonged to his wife and daughters with the maids and five or six sewing-women trained from childhood, the daughters of *scutelnici* or *boiernaşi*. The male children lived in basements with the Greek schoolmaster alongside the room of the priest and choirmen, in a row with the dining-room, and the rooms of the cook, the steward and the housekeeper. At the back of the courtyard were the stables for twenty or thirty horses, coach-houses for ten or fifteen carriages, ox-wagons, carts, and coaches. At an angle with the rooms of the coachmen and grooms began another row of rooms where lived the secretary Iordache, the steward Dinu, etc. . . . when they were retired from service. As soon as their boyar took office, they one and all flew in all directions, as cashiers, clerks, tax-collectors, and returned again to the boyar's board as soon as their master went out of office; these were the celebrated *ciocoi*, who served the boyars from father to son.

At the back of these rooms were the hay and wood stores—and the garden, in which, though there were no catalpas, ailantos, begonias or fuchsias, yet you would have found in abundance cherries, apricots as big as your fist, red peaches, grapes, 'princely' apples and bergamot pears. Alongside the garden a path led to the gipsies' quarters, a yard with several rooms in which dwelt seven or eight families of domestic gipsies; farriers, harness-makers, tailors, laun-dresses, etc.

For such a population the kitchen was bound to be something grand, and in fact it was a work of architecture. In one corner of the courtyard rose a chimney like an obelisk, which opened broadening out like an upturned funnel above a vault which covered the entire edifice. In the middle, under the chimney opening, was the hearth, twelve feet long, on which whole tree-trunks were burned, as they came from the forest, uncut and unsplit; on which the ox could be spitted whole. Round about were tables, trestles and smaller hearths, a host of all sizes and all grades. Apart from the chief cooks, there were seven or eight under-cooks, each of whom cooked for the class to whom he was assigned. The boyar's table and courses were different from those of the servants, of the maids and other female servants and of the clerks.

The boyar's sons, if they had received rank or were officers of the prince's court, had each his own footman, coachman, parade stal-lion, calash and horses; each daughter had her own maid, her sewing-woman and two or three gipsy girls to help her at the embroidery-frames and at breeding silk-worms; each clerk had his own gipsy who dressed him, gave him water to wash, swept his room and made his fire.

For biographical note see p. 190.

12. THE MIDDLE CLASS

J. W. Ozanne, *Three Years in Roumania*, London, 1878, pp. 39–41.

THE middle class in the towns is composed, as I have already said, almost exclusively of the foreign element, of French and Germans and Jews—Polish, Austrian and Spanish. But there is also a small proportion of the native population which may come under this head, and it is with this, as in duty bound, that I shall deal first. The general run of the doctors, lawyers, officers of the line, and civil servants belong to this class. Of the two former professions only a very small average may be ranked with the boyars, and these are for the most part persons who have arrived from abroad, and whose position and talents have at once secured for them a high place in the estimation of their fellow-citizens. Neither the medical men nor the lawyers can, as a rule, pretend to much distinction. Some of them have been brought up at home, others in France and Germany. A few of them make tolerable incomes, but the mass lead a struggling and shabby existence.

The majority of the officers of the line are not much to boast of. They perform the ordinary routine of service, and then repair to the café, where they take their meals and pass their leisure time. Not over well paid, they just contrive to jog along without getting into debt. The civil servants are usually men of much the same stamp. They are divided into various departments; but the Post-office and the Telegraph officials are the most numerous class.

The younger men are not much considered, and the common people have bestowed on them the nickname of *Cinces*, or Fivers, because they are currently believed to be in receipt of exactly five napoleons per month. They are accused, with what truth I know not, of sacrificing everything to appearance, and are said often to dispense with their meagre dinners, in order to have a little spare cash to pay for their seat at the play. One fine day, while I was at Bucharest, the Government suddenly ordered that they should all turn out in uniform, and soon the *Cinces* were to be seen swaggering about the streets in all the bravery of lace and swords, much to the disgust of their military *confrères*, who had hitherto had all the admiration to themselves. Poor fellows! Sadly do they sometimes complain of the penury to which they are reduced; but how their salaries are to be raised I know not, as Roumania is, *par excellence*, the land of officialism, and, small country that it is, possesses more civil servants than either France or Prussia. The people naturally grudge the expense, for they are not particularly wealthy; hence their sneers at the unfortunate Fivers. But I believe that both officers and civilians are good fellows enough. They pull very well together, and are altogether most friendly. This is the class which supports the Republican party.

J.W. Ozanne was an Englishman who worked in Rumania from 1870 to 1873.

13. THE JEWS

E. Poujade, *Chrétiens et Turcs*, Paris, 1859, pp. 445–7.

THE environs of Jassy are picturesque; one can see charming country houses and monasteries of which each has its legend. The town is defaced by the Jewish quarter, where more than thirty thousand Israelites swarm in hideous hovels, surrounded sometimes by filthy mud and sometimes by thick dust. When one arrives from Galatz on the hills of Socola, Jassy offers a striking prospect, but one whose harmony is destroyed by this mass of miserable shacks through which one must pass to reach the city.

Furthermore, Moldavia is literally invaded by Jews, who flock there from Russian Poland and Galicia. It was the government before that of Prince Grigore Ghica which opened the Moldavian frontiers to the Jews, and they have rushed there to escape military service and heavy taxes, and to enjoy a milder administration. The prince found profit in this, seeing that the Jews were compelled to pay an exceptional and arbitrary tax. What is more, from time to time a rumour was spread of their impending expulsion. Then they would gather together and bring to the foot of the Moldavian throne their supplications, which, being supported by irresistible arguments, were received with paternal condescension. These *avanias*[1] were more than outweighed by the immense advantages offered by residence in Moldavia. Little by little they became masters of all the business, penetrated into every house, and today every boyar has his

[1] Exactions (Tk.).

Jew, just as a great house has or had a steward, a tutor or a chaplain. They have, with the unwise and culpable assent of the landlords, covered the countryside with taverns, where they sell a fruit brandy which takes from the peasant almost all that he earns, and dries up the very source of his prosperity, the vigour of his muscles. Finally, the Jew is a ladies' dressmaker, and sometimes makes corsages and waists which the best workshops in Paris would not disown.

The Jews now people some country towns and villages, as in Galicia; some have even taken leases of estates as in Poland, where everything is given over to them, including the village churches, which in their hands have become stores for agricultural implements or for cereals. In general they are hard on the peasants. Hitherto, they have not been allowed to acquire land; the exceptions which exist in favour of Christian foreigners do not apply to them. Even naturalization does not give them this right. I have known some very enlightened and humane Moldavians; if they are to be believed, it would have been a real misfortune to allow the Jews to acquire landed property. The Moldavians are convinced that the Jews, with such authorization, would within twenty years, by their usury and their excessive business ability, be owners of half the principality. It is certain that this is serious, and that a sentiment so universally and deeply rooted ceases to be mere prejudice and deserves to receive the attention of statesmen. One must add that the Israelites in Poland, Bucovina and Moldavia live outside society because of their customs, their costume and their attachment to old Talmudic habits. The more they become assimilated to Christian society, the more right they will have to equality before the law. In Wallachia they are not at all numerous, the authorities having always created difficulties for them; but those who are established there, and notably the bankers, who have important businesses, have entered European society in their customs and way of life. In both principalities they have freedom to practise their religion.

14. POPULATION BY OCCUPATION AND RELIGION (MOLDAVIA), 1849

N. Soutzo, *Notions Statistiques sur la Moldavie*, Jassy, 1849, pp. 66–8.

IN respect of occupation the population can be divided thus:

193,640 agricultural households, namely

Privileged persons	2,746
Slujbaşi [Servants of Landlords]	15,053
Gipsies of monasteries and private owners	3,018
Mazili and *ruptaşi*[1]	21,077
Peasants paying tax	140,818
Persons without domicile	2,919
Privileged emigrants	4,509
Gipsies of the State	3,500
	193,640

27,698 merchants and artisans practising all sorts of trades, namely

Gipsies of monasteries and private owners	2,000
Merchants and artisans	10,695
Jews	11,056
Foreigners engaged in trade	3,284
Gipsies of the State	663
	27,698

71,083 employed persons and other classes who are not engaged in any sort of industry, such as

Boyars and sons of boyars	3,750
Employed persons	515
Clergy	8,948
Teachers and doctors	104
Foreigners	3,000
Stewards and domestics	16,010
Gipsies of monasteries and private owners	3,017
Soldiers	1,138
Slujitori [Militia]	2,125
Invalids and widows	32,478
	71,083

In respect of the principal religions the total figure of the population can be divided as follows:

Christians of the Greek rite	1,356,908
Catholics	44,317
Armenians	5,600
Jews	55,280

[1] See pp. 135 and 153 above.

M

The Catholics have 73 churches in the country: two cathedrals, at Jassy and Bacău, 17 parish churches and 54 chapels of ease. The head of these churches, which are divided into four districts, is a visiting bishop; each district has a vicar, each chapel of ease a priest-in-charge.

The Armenians have eight churches in Moldavia.

Nicolas Soutzo (1799–1871), son of a Prince, had a political career in Moldavia.

15. Ships on the Danube

(a) A Caravel

R. G. Boscovich, *Giornale di un viaggio da Constantinopoli in Polonia* (Diary of a Journey from Constantinople to Poland), Bassano, 1784, pp. 98–101.

At the extremity of the city [Galatz] is the port, to which one must descend, as it is situated in what was obviously once the bed of a river. On this former bed of the Prut there is, on the shore of the Danube itself, a very large space, which is flat and but little higher than the surface of the water. To the shore of this river come the saicks, even the largest three-masters, to load and discharge their cargoes, and at a considerable distance from the river are warehouses, with an ample flat space between them and the water.

On this site we found an enormous ship of the kind which the Turks call Caravels, already almost finished. It was being built there for Isac Aga, the chief customs officer of Constantinople, who owns several other ships and is engaged in trade, and who intends to use it for traffic with Alexandria. It was a terrifying contraption to behold. Several of our company climbed to the top of it, and pacing out its dimensions, found that its interior was 70 paces long and 17 wide; this is a much greater length than that of the ship of St. Carlo of Venice, on which I had travelled with the Venetian Ambassador to Constantinople as far as Tenedos, although the latter ship had 84 cannon, all bronze. Seventy paces are equivalent to much more than 140 feet. My leg was steadily growing worse, so that when, limping, I had dragged myself so far, I contented myself with looking at the ship from below. Its design seemed very bad to me, and also bad and very clumsy were some carvings on its poop, intended for decoration. Worst of all, as the man who was superintending its building told us, it had all been constructed, as their custom is, with wood which had been freshly cut in the forests a short time before; and as this shrinks in drying, it makes the ship gape at the seams, so that it does not last long and has little solidity. It costs very little to build ships in these countries, but very frequently much of the expense is in vain; often it is all in vain. Thus, of three warships which the Gran Signore had had built not long before my arrival in Constantinople, one, I was told, which had just been launched in the sea, sank to the bottom. It is unbelievable what disorder and profound ignorance exist now in the Turkish navy, both in building ships and in navigating them. In the latter respect, I myself have seen incredible things during the 23 days I spent going with the Ambassador I have mentioned from Tenedos to Constantinople on a Turkish galley. Besides, the superintendent of the construction of that caravel told me that every year in the Black Sea many hundreds of vessels perish. As soon as the weather threatens and grows heavy, they all rush towards the shores to break up the vessels and save their own lives, because their boats are most wretched both in design and in construction.

On the same site I saw several small boats, each hollowed out of a single tree trunk, like the American canoes, but one of these was of considerable size, and could hold many people; I found it 30 Parisian feet long, and 4 feet wide inside. I was told there that the mouth of the Danube is 50 hours' journey away, and that in the good season one can go there in two or three days. . . .[1]

Ruggiero Giuseppe Boscovich (1711–87), a Ragusan, was an eminent mathematician and a scientist of very wide interests. In 1762 he travelled from Constantinople to Poland in the company of the British Ambassador, James Porter.

(b) River Boats

W. Wittman, *Travels in Turkey* . . . , London, 1803, pp. 471–2.

AT Silistria we had received on board three Turks as guards; our number, therefore, was now augmented to twenty-five individuals, consisting of Greeks, Germans, Italians, English, Turks, and Wallachians. The latter, twelve in number, composed the crew; and, as the vessel was unprovided with sails, had a very laborious employment in rowing and steering her when under way. The construction of these vessels, which navigate the Danube with passengers and merchandize, is somewhat singular. They are in length about an hundred and twenty feet, and in breadth eighteen, with a roof of

[1] I have to thank Miss Beatrice Corrigan of Toronto University for help in translation.

planks, about fifty feet in length, in the centre, which resembles the ridge of a house, and beneath which the most valuable merchandize and the passengers are placed. Under this roof the traveller fancies himself rather in a house, or booth, than in a vessel: over it there is a kind of terrace, about seven feet square, which may be considered as a species of kiosque, and which, as it commands a fine view of the scenery on each side of the river, affords a pleasing retirement in the evening. These vessels, which are so deeply laden that they sink as low in the water as our heavy barges, come from Vienna with goods of every description for Galatz and Jassy in Moldavia. They are provided, in the fore part, with twelve oars of a moderate size; two very large ones, which appeared to me to be from forty to fifty feet in length, at the bows; and two others of the same description at the stern, to answer the purpose of a helm, in regulating the direction of the vessel. Being destitute of masts and rigging to steady them, they are constantly anchored near the shore when it blows fresh, as well as in the night-time.

William Wittman, a doctor attached to the British Military Mission co-operating with the Turkish army against the French in Egypt, returned to England by way of Rumania in 1803.

16. CRAFTS OF EIGHTEENTH-CENTURY BUCHAREST

(a) Textiles

I. Ghica, *Convorbiri Economice* (Economic Conversations), Bucharest, 1879, pp. 575–8.

THE water from the fountain of Filaret was a source both of health and of wealth.[1] In summer the plain was covered with working women; girls and matrons, with the status of masters, journeymen and apprentices. They rinsed *testemeluri* in the spring, after first fixing the living colours by soaking them in alum; then they spread them on the grass in the sunshine, singing our beautiful *doine*. The *testemel* was the head dress of the Rumanian princesses and ladies. A reel of cotton worth ten paras turned between the fingers of the Bucharest working women into a muslin thin as the spider's web; and with two or three limewood printing blocks and several vegetable dyes, log-wood, saffron, madder, and sumach, a genuine polychrome process,

[1] The period with which this extract is concerned is the last quarter of the eighteenth century.

the resulting product sold for a hundred times the original value. The Rumanian spinners, weavers and dyers were generously repaid for their toil and trouble by the sale of the *testemeluri* which emerged from their hands.

The *testemeluri* made in Bucharest were not inferior to those of Constantinople, and this industry, if well conducted and encouraged, would easily have come to rival the finest muslins. At a gala ball at the Hôtel de Ville in Paris nine years ago, the Marquise de Lavalette, the wife of the Minister of the Interior and former ambassador at Constantinople, wore a dress of *testemeluri* which won the admiration of all well-dressed women.

This industry has completely vanished from Rumania; it has given way to the hats and caps *à la Livezeanca*, made in Paris and Vienna, for fools (à l'usage des Principautés et de l'Amérique du Sud) as the milliners of Paris say.

On the verandahs in summer, beneath the shade of the eaves, were spread thousands of embroidery frames of all sizes. The girls sewed in relief on muslin, on merino, on satin and on velvet with silks, wool, cotton, chenille, thread, braid and sequins. The Rumanian needlework of those days did not shrink from comparison with that of Switzerland or of Aleppo and Damascus. Handkerchiefs, scarves and lace worked by the women of Bucharest were sought by the ladies of the greatest harems in Constantinople.

The needlework done in the boyars' houses was the pride of our ladies. . . .

In spring, as soon as the leaves came, the women gave up their apartments to silk worms. Amid the feasts of mulberry leaves the women planted some stakes in the garden and wove the yarn which had been spun during the winter by the light of the fire on the hearth. . . . In June the open spaces on the bank of the river were full of women gathered in groups around the pans in which they drew the silk off the cocoons; and after reeling off the silk thread, they got down into the pit, where with four wooden posts hewn with the axe and with an extremely primitive reed and shuttle, they rigged up a sort of loom, on which they succeeded in making all sorts of two- and three-ply textiles. The spinning wheel, that powerful instrument of civilization and enrichment in the West, had begun to be introduced in Bucharest and had dethroned the distaff and spindle. Today this beneficial apparatus is only seen on the stage in the hands of Mr. Franchetti's Marguerites and Desdemonas.

When the south wind blew, a sour, offensive smell came from the direction of Broșteni; a crowd of tanners had settled below Radu-Vodă. Not only did they supply the needs of internal consumption;

skins tanned in Bucharest were sought after in Germany and Turkey and had become the object of an important export trade. It is enough to mention that the population employed in this industry was up to the days of Prince Cuza numerous enough to inspire fear and respect in the court and among the boyars.

Besides the tanning of hides there had also arisen another industry in which our city held the first place in Europe. The furrier's art, which had attained real perfection, was a work of patience and good taste; the tiny pieces of fur pieced together and sewn with an artistic skill and delicacy formed a mosaic worthy of admiration. Sables, lynx, ermine, marten, black fox, the most beautiful and costly furs of Russia were worked upon there. The warden of the furriers' guild in Bucharest was in daily correspondence with the Sultan's seraglio. Closely connected with this trade was that of hat-making; the handling of the greyish-white sheepskins and the various shapes of *işlic* was a work of art far surpassing the manufacture of silk hats and felt ones. Braiding employed a large number of masters and journeymen.

Of all these important and profitable industries nothing now is left except the name written on the boards at street corners; names which today have no relation to what actually exists. . . .

For biographical note, see p. 190.

(b) *Leather and Glass*

J. Bentham, from a largely unpublished travel diary, reproduced in part by E. D. Tappe, 'Bentham in Wallachia and Moldavia', *Slavonic and East European Review*, vol. xxix, no. 72, December 1950.

WHILE at Bucharest, where different necessities obliged me to spend eight days, I bought two skins, one red, the other yellow, both good, but the red in particular excellent; it was of a rough grain, such as I have seen employed in a few instances for the richest bindings for books in England; I was told it was goat skin manufac-tured at Russchuk[1] on the Danube. The red I was asked four piasters for (a piaster is about 3/6 or 4/6). They took 2½ owing to the good offices of a faithful conductor I had with me; for the yellow they asked, I think it was, two piasters, and took 70 paras (the value of a para is about an English half penny). I passed through Russchuk, but did not know of this manufacture till afterwards. At Bucharest also there is a house or two houses together, where I saw them

[1] Ruse.

manufacturing red leather; but the specimens I saw of it at the shops were very different from the other, and much inferior; and I found the manufacture there was in so little account, that but few persons, out of many I questioned, knew of its existence. . . .

Besides its leather manufactory, Bucharest has its glasshouse, which affords a tolerable Crown-glass, still cheaper than the cheap Bohemian glass which abounds there. Firewood almost for nothing; building in brick proportionately cheap, notwithstanding the immense quantity of materials employed in waste. What a situation for hot-houses! and yet hot-houses are as little known as ice-houses in Arabia.

Jeremy Bentham, English philosopher and jurist, founded the Utilitarian school of philosophy in his main work *Principles of Morals and Legislation* (1789). In 1785 he set out to visit his brother, a naval officer in Russia, travelling by way of Constantinople, the Balkans and Rumania.

17. EXPORT RESTRICTIONS AND TRIBUTE, 1820

W. Wilkinson, *An Account of the Principalities of Wallachia and Moldavia*, London, 1820, pp. 74–85.

THE trade of Wallachia and Moldavia, notwithstanding that it labours under a variety of restrictions and partial prohibitions, is one of their most important sources of opulence. Its details are little known, and less noticed beyond the neighbouring countries, although they are by no means deserving of inattention.

Of the common productions of the soil, the most abundant is wheat, of which the two principalities are supposed to give an annual return of ten millions of killows[1] although hardly one-sixth part of their extensive and fertile plains is cultivated, and that a certain space of this is sown by Indian corn, barley, and hemp.

The other productions, proportionably important in a commercial point of view, are the bees-wax, honey, butter, cheese, hides, timber, staves, and ship-masts of all sizes and descriptions; and an annual supply of five hundred thousand hare-skins, six hundred thousand okes[2] of yellow-berries, and forty thousand kintals[3] of sheep's wool.

The three last-mentioned articles are alone perfectly free of exportation; the remainder are kept at the disposal of the Turkish government; and it is only in times of abundance, after the usual supplies

[1] A killow (Constantinople measurement) is equal to an English bushel (*Author*).
[2] One oke is equal to 2⅘ lb. English (*Author*).
[3] The kintal weighs 44 okes (*Author*).

have been fixed upon for the granaries and arsenal of Constantinople, that leave can be obtained to employ in foreign trade any portion of them. The exportation of wheat alone is considered as under a permanent prohibition; it is not in the power of the Hospodars to suffer any of it to be taken out of the country on private speculation; they must be authorized so to do by Ferman, a permit which is never granted to Rayahs,[1] and very seldom to other Europeans, as the foreign ministers accredited at the Porte, aware of the difficulty of obtaining it, and the value that the Ottoman government would set in the gift of it, prefer abstaining altogether from applications on the subject, more especially as their success would only be profitable to some individuals, without being productive of any permanent good to the trade at large.

The quality of the Wallachian wheat is inferior, but it is far from being bad; that of Moldavia is better, and not differing much from the Polish wheat. Their ordinary price stands between 2 and $2\frac{1}{2}$ piasters[2] per killow. As an article of general trade, the charges upon it from the Danube to Constantinople would hardly amount to one piaster more. The Turkish government send their own ships every year to transport their share of it, which is each time fixed at 1,500,000 killows, as well as the other articles necessary to their use, the quantity of which is not fixed, though generally very considerable.

The Moldavian timber is far better than that of Wallachia; it is of the finest oak, and perfectly well calculated for the construction of vessels. A great number of ships in the Turkish fleet are built of it, and fitted out with masts and ropes of Moldavian growth and origin. In the two provinces, these articles are sold at the lowest possible prices, and indeed the same thing may be said of all the prohibited articles; which, restricted as they are, from the monopoly arrogated by the Porte, have but little demand, except for the local consumption.

The hare-skins commonly stand at 35[3] paras each, in large purchases, and the yellow-berries may be had at 40 or 45 paras per oke. The usual method of securing any quantity of these two articles at the lowest prices, is by bespeaking them at the different villages, and paying something in advance; the villagers engaged in such contracts never fail to fulfil them in proper time.

The hare-skins are of the first quality, but the yellow-berries are inferior to those of Smyrna, and only demanded when the crops in Asia Minor have proved deficient.

[1] Christian subjects of the Turkish Empire.   [2] See p. 166 above.
[3] 40 paras make a piaster (*Author*).

The sheep's wool is considered to be very good: cleaned and washed, it is sold at about 60 paras per oke, or 66 piasters per kintal; when in its original state, it is offered at 35 to 40 paras.

The principalities abound also in cattle and poultry of all descriptions. Every year they supply Constantinople with 250,000 sheep, and 3,000 horses. They send, besides, a great number of these, and oxen, into the surrounding provinces, where they are usually sold at great profit.

All the productions and commodities that are employed for the exigencies of the Ottoman capital, are bought by the local government for about one-fourth of the prices current in the market, and one-sixth of their value in Turkey. They are paid for by a deduction from the common tribute, and, sometimes, by an extraordinary imposition of an amount equal to their cost. . . .

Galatz is the great market for the produce of the two principalities, and the only landing-place for some principal articles of importation. Having all the resources of a seaport, it is apparently a very flourishing town. Its market is always well stocked with the productions of the interior. The timber, masts, and staves are conveyed to it along the small rivers, that come from various parts of the country, and fall into the Danube nearest to it. There are public granaries for the wheat, and a great number of large warehouses, belonging to private merchants, for all articles. It is chiefly inhabited by commercial men, who, notwithstanding the rigour of the prohibitive measures, often find the means of exporting some quantity of wheat, and other contraband articles; but their principal trade is that of importation. The town and its dependencies are governed by two deputies of the Prince of Moldavia, called *Percalabi*. The number of the fixed inhabitants does not exceed seven thousand, but the great concourse of people occasioned every year by commercial pursuits, gives it the appearance of being very populous, and all the bustle of a place of great trade. The presence, in particular, of a great number of commercial vessels, increases considerably that appearance. . . .

The general system of this import trade is ill contrived, and it is subject to many inconveniencies. The purchasers have recourse to the markets of Smyrna and Constantinople, where, of course, they buy at high prices. The goods, which have already paid custom-house duty in Turkey, are taxed with a new duty of the same kind, of three per cent, on being landed or brought into the principalities, as well as with other charges of an arbitrary nature, which amount to as much more. The latter are not, indeed, established by the local governments, but merely exacted by their officers, and as they are tolerated, they become unavoidable, unless the proprietors of the goods happen to be subjects of European courts, and as such, receive protection and assistance from the consuls residing in the country.

Wallachia and Moldavia are at present supplied by Germany with all kinds of cotton and woollen manufactures and hardware, either by land or by the Danube. The plain and printed calicoes, the chintz, glass and earthenware, brought to their markets, are, without exception, German; but they are called English, and as such sold at higher prices than they would fetch were their origin made known.

William Wilkinson was British consul at Bucharest from 1814 to 1818.

18. MERCHANTS AND TRADE AFTER 1829

F. Colson, *De l'état présent et de l'avenir des Principautés de Moldavie et de Valachie*, Paris, 1839, pp. 210–11; 213–18; 221; 225–8.

Import Trade. The import trade is one of the causes of disaster for Wallachia. Ill-advised consumption, export of coin, upkeep of unbridled luxury; such is the harm done in the first place; it rarely offers any advantages. But before I tell you what the imports consist of and what is the benefit of them, I must speak of the merchants engaged in it, of their manner of operating and of the losses which they suffer.

Bucharest is the central depot of this branch of commerce. All the other towns of Wallachia draw from it the objects needed for their consumption. The forty fairs established in the country only offer articles of inferior quality. Foreigners, known under the name of *Lipscani* because they go for supplies to Leipzig, keep all the articles of luxury and of French, English, Austrian and Saxon manufacture at Bucharest. Others, called *Marchitani*, sell the products of Russian industry and commerce. The former are Germans and Armenians, under the protection of Austria; the latter, Russians or Greeks. The third set of imports is Turkish goods. This trade is in the hands of the Armenians. The fourth set is goods from Braşov (Kronstadt) in Transylvania. In Moldavia, trade is not concentrated in the capital. In every county town one finds shops as well stocked as in Jassy. Imports are the same for Moldavia as for Wallachia; but, with the exception of some foreigners, the masters there are the Jews. . . .

The *Lipscani* are generally found to have everything concerned with the toilet of men and women, including the products of the goldsmith and the perfumer; foreign wines, more especially champagne, porcelain, glass, silver, earthenware, lustres, Vienna carriages and harness, mirrors and furniture from Pest. These latter articles have a considerable sale since European habits have caught on.

The *Marchitani*, who bring their wares from Russia, always make a profit of 25 per cent, although the competition is very great. These wares are wrought copper, porcelain, leather trunks, furs, hides for saddlery and shoemaking, furniture, military equipment, tea, iron bars and locksmith's goods. Next come Turkish wares, some bought in the stores of Constantinople, others real produce of Turkish soil and Turkish industry, colonial products, coffee, sugar, rum, incense, etc., comestibles such as oil, rice, olives, lemons, citrons, grapes, dry Smyrna figs, salt fish, caviare, etc. Textiles and things to wear, Indian silks, plain, striped, figured in gold and silver; Indian cottons, muslins, prints, cambrics, madras, cashmere shawls and materials, print handkerchiefs called testemetz and bajamaz; spun Indian cotton, soap from Candia and Adrianople, Turkish boots and shoes, metal worked or unworked, tin, copper, colours for dyeing.

Then the wares from Kronstadt in Transylvania; sham hand-wrought iron padlocks, all sorts of nails, common cloths, felt garments for peasants, common blankets, imitation lace, ropes.

This way of doing trade is full of defects. It will not grow up; its practitioners are mere pedlars. It is just because these merchants do not take the produce of the country in return for their imports, because the export trade is in other hands, because no exchange takes place, that their business is in such a bad way. Foreigners, who understand trade much better than the Germans, have tried and are still trying to create an exchange trade. If they supply the principalities by sea, if they take no more ducats, which are a foreign commodity in the country and very dear, but rather the products of the boyars' estates, if they can avoid the great expense of the Leipzig journey and the fiscal vexations of transit through Austria, will they succeed? That is something which I cannot affirm; for Austria which exports to the value of over ten millions to this principality, will be against it on the one hand; and on the other, the administration, which uses quarantines to ruin traders, and the uncertain position of the Moldo-Wallachian government, are here all the more sorely felt because politically this nation is under the yoke. Its industry is only beginning, and in this respect it is completely dependent on Austria. . . .

It would be worth while paying more for the products of a country which might take an interest in our political situation rather than supporting the monopoly of Austria, who makes us pay for her products, and never gives us anything in return for the profits which she draws. Why, for example, continue her privilege of pasturing 500,000 sheep on our territory at the rate of eight sous per head? Since pasture is scarce in Austria, would it not be better to export on our own account the beasts which we have reared? This power has nearly always 30,000 subjects in Wallachia and Moldavia, and, although they are foreigners, raises more than 40,000 ducats in taxes on them. Why should her subjects pay her, and not pay a tax to the country which provides their living? If famine breaks out in Transylvania, which is very common, Austria authorizes emigration into Wallachia. Austria's trade is ruinous. It is therefore important to discover with which power Wallachia has most interest in trading. We shall try to show that this power is England; and we are not suggesting rivalry between Austria and England. By means of English trade, a revolution could be brought about in the material interests of the two principalities. This would involve not only a direct trade treaty, based on reciprocal rights, but also influence on the institutions and well-being of the inhabitants. Let 3,800,000 be the figure for the population of the two principalities.

The wealthy or propertied classes can satisfy their needs, but only at great expense. The goods imported by foreigners are too highly priced. The poor cannot yet attempt to buy them. So far no one has seriously thought of changing the condition of the poor and enabling them to enjoy the benefits of civilization. The workers in the fields are practically without clothing. The gipsies usually go about naked. None of the necessities of life are to be found in the homes of the poor.

The present régime, imposed by the Russians, has not rescued them from the slough of misery into which the Phanariot régime had plunged them; on the contrary, it has only served to make them more wretched. You will never find in their dwellings a single article of foreign manufacture or importation. In any case the traders who have the import trade in their grip only keep luxury articles for the use of the upper classes. It would therefore be an immense service to this country to send it ordinary agricultural implements, cheap cotton fabrics, strong cloths and common household utensils. If colonial products are sent direct by sea, they can be offered at a lower price, and in the same way one could offer certain things to sweeten the life of these poor people, whose drink is at present limited to a few glasses of wine or plum brandy, and their food to maize porridge, fruit, and a little meat and milk products. They are clothed in sheep skins; their wives make their own cloth and spin their own linen. Their houses, their reed mats, their shoes, their ploughs, their carts are of their own rough workmanship. Their cattle are born and feed on the ground. Thus in Wallachia and Moldavia the majority lack the products of industry; the inhabitants dress like the Dacians and feed like the first men.

The import of simple, solid goods is becoming necessary to the two principalities. The only power capable of supplying this demand, and supplying it cheaply, is England.

Export Trade and Ports. Moldo-Wallachia is a new country for exports. Before the treaty of Adrianople,[1] the two principalities, by the terms of the convention of Akerman, enjoyed freedom of trade for all the products of their soil and industry, apart from the restrictions imposed on the one hand by the supplies due to the Turks, and on the other by the needs of the country. But in fact this liberty did not and could not exist. There was only one port, Galatz, where traffic took place. But since the treaty of Adrianople the Moldo-Wallachians have been exempted from supplying corn, ships' timber, beasts and other produce, as well as workmen for the fortresses and all other sorts of forced labour. Finally the restitution of the pashaliks and demolition of the fortresses, Turnu,[2] Giurgiu and Brăila, where the Turks had fortresses and garrisons, enabled Wallachia to turn Brăila into a port and to found a city which will soon be the finest and richest in the principality. . . .

All the export trade of Wallachia, which amounts in the average to 16,000,000 francs, is directed on three points: Transylvania, the right bank of the Danube, and Brăila; that of Moldavia on Austria, Wallachia, the left bank of the Danube, and Galatz. Austria and Transylvania take in particular the produce of the neighbouring districts, and in addition wines, beasts, wax and wool. Turkey takes victuals and objects of Moldo-Wallachian manufacture. Brăila and Galatz may be considered as the centre of all this export trade. These ports are free, and goods declared as in transit are not subjected to customs duty. Brăila, a new port, is not yet a depot for goods, the land route not yet having been adopted. Its export trade, on the other hand, is more considerable than that of Moldavia. It has a large number of good warehouses well placed and built on the banks of the Danube.

Galatz, two leagues from Brăila, is in entire control of the seaborne import trade of the two principalities. This is easily understood; for in 1837 there was not a single banking house in the Wallachian port. It was impossible to negotiate a bill of exchange there; the only possibility was with the bankers of Galatz and Bucharest. . . .

[1] 1829.   [2] Turnu-Măgurele.

Trade in these ports is carried on by Greek brokers, most of whom inspire no confidence. In 1837 449 ships entered Brăila. Imports amounted to 280,747 francs; exports to 2,782,501. The chief articles of export from this port are: wheat, wool, barley, tallow, beans, cheese; in smaller quantities, wax, maize, tobacco, soda, oak, linseed and hemp.

In 1837 528 ships entered Galatz. Imports amounted to 3,753,950 francs; exports to 2,830,029. The chief articles of export from this port are: hard wheat, soft wheat, maize. The quality of the soft wheat is not so good as that of Odessa wheat; but the culture of cereals is improving every day. The maize is of very good quality. Barley and rye are exported in smaller quantities: for, to get the rye distilled in Moldavia, a duty of four Bucharest piastres per kilo or 15 per cent is collected on exportation. Moldo-Wallachian tobacco might be exported, inferior as it is in quality to that of Turkey; but there is no demand for it.

The trade of Moldavia is subject to far more prohibitions than that of Wallachia. Tobacco, common wine, brandy and salt are prohibited as imports, because Moldavia is glutted with all these products. Its distilleries are very harmful to the people, especially since they have increased excessively; there are now ten times as many as in 1832. . . .

The powers which have established relations with these ports for the import trade are as follows. England sends manufactured articles, spun cotton, grey cotton cloth and a very few Indian prints. Turkey and Greece: oil, olives, dried fruits, tobacco, a little raw cotton. France: refined sugar. Russia: caviare and rope. Sardinia: a very small quantity of furniture. As the sea-borne import trade is still only in its infancy, all these goods come, at least in part, from Constantinople.

As for exports, the maize makes for Trieste; the wheat for Genoa, Trieste and the Archipelago; the tallow for Constantinople and England; wool for France, Belgium, England and Trieste; wine for Odessa; staves and spars for Constantinople and Egypt. But England and Marseilles complain of the high cost of freight. The beans go to Genoa and Trieste; the linseed goes to Genoa and England; butter and cheese to Turkey and Greece; soda to Constantinople; silk to Trieste.

Félix Colson was secretary to the French consulate at Bucharest about 1835–40.

19. Obstacles to Industrial Development

F. Colson, *De l'état présent et de l'avenir des Principautés de Moldavie et de Valachie*, Paris, 1839, pp. 232–8.

Manufacturing industry, still in its infancy in Moldo-Wallachia, is of two kinds; either it works on materials of native origin, or it is confined to working imported materials. The internal trade in Moldo-Wallachian products is quite large and lucrative; it covers all the products of agricultural industry in general and those of manufacturing industry, chiefly coarse cloths, pottery, hats, common linen, striped fabrics, glassware, and the work of wheelwrights, goldsmiths and saddlers.

Wallachia is less populated than Moldavia; but does it follow that colonization would give a new impulse to trade and industry? I think not; at least, not in the sense generally meant. People have spread the view that Wallachia would not be slow to prosper if she had more population, and have proposed to introduce Swiss colonists. First of all, the laws of the state would not allow them any more than other foreigners to possess land; a ridiculous law among a people which shares in the European legal system. Next, would these agricultural colonists, or rather tenants increase the number of consumers? Will they accumulate capital on land which will not belong to them? Thus a colonization by foreigners of peasant status would be useless; it is in fact impossible. It is first necessary to reform the legislation, and to encourage able and intelligent foreigners, the owners of a certain amount of savings or capital. They will soon perfect the agricultural industry, divert part of the population from being inevitably farm-labourers, open the mines, establish manufacturing industry and produce goods exchangeable for agricultural produce. Under the present system the agricultural population, which is not obliged to buy any of these products, whether of the land or of foreign or native industry, is and must be self-sufficient. Only two outlets remain; the towns which must be fed, and the markets to which exports must be made. The number of the inhabitants of towns and villages will determine the quantity of Moldo-Wallachian products exchanged or sold in the country, and will rouse a feeling of the need to encourage export or to create a new class of productive consumers. The accumulation of all sorts of agricultural produce in those parts of the country far from Brăila and Galatz shows better than any reasoning the imperative necessity of making good roads and canalizing the main rivers which, normally, are not navigable. . . .

The interest on money is very high, the rate being severe in proportion to the uncertainty of the return. The annual drain of tribute money and monastery revenues neutralizes capital and the agricultural and manufacturing industries; these monasteries of foreign monks own one-quarter of the land in the two principalities. Then the fiscal authority, which has an export duty on raw materials, is careful not to encourage manufacturing industry, which might turn them into products for the use of consumers, since it levies a fresh duty when they re-enter after being manufactured. For example, on wax, and on wool which goes to Transylvania and re-enters as very coarse cloth for the people. The princes are at fault in this; they ought, in accordance with the legislation, to give bonuses to encourage manufacturers, but they do not. It is a matter of urgency to found national banks; foreigners, for the most part under the protection of Austria, have practised this calling hitherto. But the many successive bankruptcies of the last twenty years, by means of which Austria has carried off the capital of the boyars, and so rendered them tributary to her industry and commerce, forbid individual fortunes to be left any longer in the hands of faithless businessmen, and prudence requires such creations.

In Moldo-Wallachia monopolies no longer exist. The most perfect freedom of trade and industry flourishes. In the two countries there are nearly 5,000 factories, including plum distilleries.

Moldavia. In Moldavia most of the interior trade is done by Jews. The peasant only trades in plums, maize, wine, leather, pitch, wheel-wright's wares, brandy, peasant clothes, hemp, flax, rope, wooden troughs, chests, hay, barley, game and fish, bricks, shingles, pipes, wooden saddles, common rugs, mats, thread, salted goods, coarse linen, honey, fruit.

On the other hand, in the towns it is the Jews who carry on all the retail trade; more particularly they deal in brandy, butcher's and baker's stuff, pitch, lambskins, hare skins, common furs, tanned hides, rope, prunes, and saddles for horses.

Although the Moldavian landlords are much richer than those of Wallachia, I do not believe that they are more orderly or economical; on the contrary, the condition of the peasant exhibits a greater degree of servitude; for, once we admit that it is only the forced labour of the poor which makes the great profits of the rich boyars, the possessors of landed property, is it not obvious that if the Moldavian boyar draws from an equal number of peasants ten times the revenue which the Wallachian landlord draws, the Moldavian peasants are nine times more burdened? This overburdening strikes one when one has crossed the frontier. They have not the nonchalant air of the Wallachian; they are thin and emaciated, humble, submissive and ready to endure anything. Their hollow eyes, which they dare not raise, proclaim their slavery and absence of well-being.

The manufactures, says Prince N. Soutzo in his *Aperçu sur les besoins industriels de la Moldavie*, which promise a sure profit and may be a benefit to society, are those of certain raw materials which are at present exported from the country and re-imported in a finished state. Besides the fact that most of these manufactures do not require expensive processes, the producer can rest assured that he can rise above competition from the importer. The foreign merchant, apart from his profit, must cover the cost of transport and import duty, as well as the risks and damage en route, expenses which the native producer is spared. This will be to the profit, first of the pioneer manufacturer, and subsequently of society, when the number of manufacturers forces them to lower the price of the product to the level of the production costs.

Raw wax, wool and oleaginous seeds are in this position. Glass and pottery works might also be established with advantage; fuel, which plays a great part in factories of that sort, can be obtained at small expense. Forests which are yielding nothing could be used in that way. The culture of silkworms and the breeding of merino sheep might also be extended; these two activities prosper in the neighbouring countries, and there is no reason why they should not do so in Moldavia.

The upkeep of stud and the improvement of the strain of cattle might also be very usefully extended; the product would amply recompense the care devoted to it, since the horses and cattle coming from this country are much sought after for their qualities, pasture being plentiful there and little used. Some of the land should be devoted to these purposes, and agriculture would gain in all respects.

There is no need then for colonization to increase the labour force, but rather for bringing in men who are owners of industry and capital. A population becomes numerous once it possesses the means of easy subsistence. Large sums of capital may be met with; great industries may flower wherever the spirit of commerce is favoured by habits and institutions. The Moldo-Wallachians pride themselves that they will soon enter on this path. Already the young men sent to Vienna at the state's expense are back in their homes. You can see at Bucharest the industrial establishment, imperfect as it is, of Dr. Sucker. It is hoped that the one which is going up at Câmpina will be superior to it and may become a real 'Conservatoire des Arts et Métiers'. Such at least is the idea of its founders.

N

II. United Rumania

20. THE AGRARIAN REFORM LAW OF 1864

V. Boerescu, *Codicele Romane* (The Rumanian Codes), Bucharest, 1865, Appendix, pp. 133–40.

Act to regulate the distribution of rural property

CHAPTER I

Of the property rights of the peasant who holds
land by personal service, and of the redemption
of his dues to the owner of the land

Art. 1. The peasant who holds land by personal service has and retains the full rights of property in land which he holds (whether as possessor or owner), as those rights are defined by existing laws.[1] This area (excluding the plots occupied by the peasants in the village itself for their houses and gardens) comprises:

(*a*) In the districts this side of the Milcov (Wallachia)
  1. For a peasant possessing 4 oxen and 1 cow, 11 *pogoane*[2]
  2. For a peasant possessing 2 oxen and 1 cow, 7 *pogoane* 19 *prăjini*[2]
  3. For a peasant possessing 1 cow, or for a forester, 4 *pogoane* 15 *prăjini*

(*b*) In the districts beyond the Milcov (Moldavia)
  1. For a peasant who has 4 oxen and 1 cow, 5 *fălci*[2] 40 *prăjini*
  2. For a peasant who has 2 oxen and 1 cow, 4 *fălci*
  3. For a peasant who has 1 cow, or for a labourer, 2 *fălci* 40 *prăjini*

(*c*) In the districts beyond the Prut (Bessarabia)
  1. For a peasant who has 4 oxen and 1 cow, 6 *fălci* 30 *prăjini*
  2. For a peasant who has 2 oxen and 1 cow, 4 *fălci* 30 *prăjini*

---

[1] i.e. the Organic Regulations of 1830–1 which defined serf rights and duties, and the Supplementary Legislation of 1851.

[2] See Note on Weights, Measures and Currency, p. 203.

3. For a peasant who has 1 cow, or for a labourer, 2 *fălci* 70 *prăjini*

Art. II. Those living on rural property who are not in possession of the extent of land to which the preceding article gives them right, will receive it in accordance with the law.

Art. III. In no case shall more than two-thirds of the property of a landlord pass into the ownership of the peasants. In computing the entitlement of peasant and landlord no account shall be taken of forest land.

Art. IV. Childless widows, invalids, and peasants not engaged in agriculture and who therefore do not hold land to their own use as cultivators in exchange for labour service, but possess only their houses and an enclosure, become proprietors only of the areas fixed by the law for their house and garden, i.e.:

In Wallachia, 400 square *stânjeni* in the plain and 300 in the mountains (the measure is the Wallachian *stânjen*)

In Moldavia, 10 Moldavian *prăjini*

In Bessarabia, 10 Moldavian *prăjini* for a labourer, 11 for the peasant who has two oxen, and 12 for the peasant who has four oxen.

Minor children of a peasant will be granted the quantity of land possessed by their father at the moment of his death, if his widow undertakes to pay the compensation stipulated by this law.

Art. V. The inhabitants of any village who, by special agreement with the owner of the land, held only a house and garden in the village without giving labour service, and who therefore had no right to land as cultivators, are not entitled to claim the land which in accordance with Art. I of this decree is granted to those holding land by labour service.

Such peasants have, however, right (if they choose to exercise it) to receive land on the State domains.[1]

Art. VI. The right to move to the nearest State domains belongs to:

(*a*) peasants to whom the area of land laid down in this law cannot be given without taking from the owner more than two-thirds of his land

(*b*) newly married men who are not in possession of the extent of land fixed by existing laws.

Both classes, on transferring to State domains, have the right to sell the houses and plantations which they have made on the

---

[1] These were the former monastery estates, taken over by the State in 1863; they represented about one-fifth of the total arable area. Settlement of these properties was not undertaken till after 1876.

property which they are leaving, and the commune has the right of pre-emption.

Art. VII. For a period of 30 years starting from the day of the promulgation of this law, no peasant nor any of his heirs shall alienate or mortgage his property, either by testament or by legal act during his lifetime, except to the commune or to another peasant.

After the period of 30 years he may dispose of his property according to the rules of common law, reserving, in case of sale, the right of pre-emption by the commune.

Art. VIII. If a peasant dies intestate or without legitimate heirs, his allotment of land will be taken by the commune, with the obligation to pay on his behalf the compensation due under Art. XXII for loss of labour service.

The property of any peasant who, by the time of liquidation, cannot for whatever reason pay the compensation due to the owner and who declares that he does not wish to keep his property, shall likewise pass to the commune.

Art. IX. The rights over forest land which were assigned to peasants on Moldavian estates by Art. 44 of the law of the mountain region (i.e. the districts of Putna, Bacău, Neamţ and Suceava) and to those on Wallachian estates by Art. 140 § 4 of the law of 23 April 1851, will remain in force now and in the future. But after 15 years the proprietors shall have the legal right to demand that their forests be freed from this liability, either by private agreement or by decision of the court.

This right shall likewise be exercised by the communes, the public establishments and the State.

Art. x. The following are for ever abolished throughout Rumania: labour service, tithe, free transport, repair work, transport of firewood, and all similar charges or dues owed to landowners, whether in kind or in cash and whether established by laws, charters, or agreements, whether permanent or temporary.

Art. XI. In place of labour service, tithe and other dues abolished by this decree, the landowners shall be awarded, once and for all, a single payment of compensation, the amount of which will be calculated by the rules given in Chapter III.

Art. XII. Labour service is no longer permitted. Newly married men shall make only temporary agreements with landowners.

Landowners and peasants are free to make such agreements; but when a peasant binds himself by agreement to render service in person to the landowner, the agreement can only be made for a period of five years.

The agreements at present in existence for land in excess of the amount fixed by the law and for a limited time are not annulled; provided that they were not made for a period of more than five years, and that the landowner has not made with the peasant an agreement which covers both the area determined by law, and that in excess of it.

Art. xiii. The peasants have the right to receive as part of their legal allotment the orchards of which they are in possession today.

Any other orchards which the peasant has over and above his legal allotment are secured to his use, either in accordance with existing agreements or by present local custom.

Art. xiv. The lands for pasture, tillage and haymaking, which by special laws landowners are bound to grant to the priests of village churches, are in no way affected by this law. In the future as in the past these lands shall continue to serve for the upkeep of the clergy in the communes in question.

Art. xv. The pastures, hayfields and arable land which become the property of peasants in virtue of this decree shall be surveyed and the boundaries marked with stones. Sufficient land surveyors, appointed and paid by the State, shall be appointed to each district to direct and expedite this work.

Art. xvi. In cases where the lands mentioned in the preceding article are scattered in many directions, they shall as far as possible be consolidated. This work shall be the object of an *ad-hoc* commission, composed of two members, chosen one by the landowner in question and the other by the communal authority. In case of disagreement between the members of the commission, an arbitrator shall be drawn by lot from among the members of the permanent committee of the district.

In the process of consolidation the peasant shall as far as is possible, be given land of the same extent and quality.

CHAPTER II

Of land held within the village

Art. xvii. Land held within the village shall be surveyed and delimited as shown in Art. xv.

Art. xviii. The landowners shall retain as their own property all the buildings, plantations, workshops and enclosures, as well as the ponds and mills, which they have in the village area.

Art. xix. As to the ponds mentioned in the preceding article, the peasants shall in future retain the right of watering their beasts, provided always that they contribute with the landowner to the upkeep of their watering-places, as far as is necessary for the purpose of watering.

Art. xx. All the lands and buildings comprised in the village itself which, in virtue of the above article no longer belong either to the peasants or to the landowner, such as churches, cemeteries, communal houses, schools, presbyteries and their gardens, squares, streets, reserve stores, and other communal establishments in existence today, become the absolute property of the rural communes without compensation.

Art. xxi. All monopolies, such as butchery, bakery, drink, etc., in the village itself are abolished.

The landowners shall retain the right to carry on in taverns, inns and other such buildings (which, under Art. xviii, remain their property) any lawful business, provided that they take full responsibility for their conduct of the business, both to the State and to the commune.

Chapter III

Of the assessment of compensation to be paid for
labour service and other dues

Art. xxii. As compensation for labour service, tithe and other dues abolished by this decree, the peasants shall pay for interest and amortization yearly, for not more than 15 years, and in cash at the Treasury rate, in accordance with the table annexed hereto:

Those who have 4 oxen and 1 cow, 133 *lei*[1]
Those who have 2 oxen and 1 cow, 100 *lei* 24 paras
Labourers with 1 cow, 71 *lei* 20 paras

Peasants from the mountain villages in Moldavia will pay yearly

Those who have 4 oxen and 1 cow, 94 *lei* 10 paras
Those who have 2 oxen and 1 cow, 73 *lei* 2 paras
Labourers with 1 cow, 51 *lei* 36 paras

[1] See Note on Weights, Measures and Currency, p. 203.

These sums must be paid at one time and within the same period as the taxes.

Art. xxiii. The sum due as compensation is taken as the value of the peasant's labour service and of the tithe, with legal interest at 10 per cent. On this basis, the landowner shall receive as full compensation:

(a) for the dues of the peasant who has land for
    4 oxen and 1 cow, 1,521 *lei* 10 paras
(b) for those of the peasant who has
    2 oxen and 1 cow, 1,148 *lei* 20 paras
(c) for those of the labourer with 1 cow, 816 *lei*.

For peasants from the mountain villages in Moldavia:

(a) for the dues of the peasant with
    4 oxen and 1 cow, 1,076 *lei*
    2 oxen and 1 cow, 834 *lei* 1½ paras
    for those of the labourer with 1 cow, 592 *lei* 2 paras.

Art. xxiv. For the purpose of establishing the number of peasants on each estate liable for labour service, their different categories, and the sum due to the landowner as compensation under Art. xxiii, there shall be set up in each sub-district a commission composed of one delegate chosen by all the landowners of the sub-district, one delegate chosen by the communal councils of the villages inhabited by peasants liable to labour service, and one delegate of the Exchequer.

These commissions shall be bound to finish their work within eight months from the day of their formation.

Art. xxv. The commission shall establish, for each village, the items of information required under Art. xxiv, as they were on the date on which the decree was issued.

Art. xxvi. The findings of the aforesaid committees shall, if the interested parties are dissatisfied, be submitted on appeal to the district councils or the permanent committees.

Art. xxvii. In case of appeals against the decisions of district councils or permanent committees, the Council of State pronounces in the final instance.

Art. xxviii. The amount of compensation due to each landowner being assessed in the manner prescribed above, the commission mentioned in Art. xxiv shall issue to the landowner in the name of the commune a certificate showing the sum due to him as compensation.

These certificates, after being verified and authenticated by the permanent committee or the district council, shall be presented to the central committee at Bucharest to be exchanged for bonds in the name of each commune.

Art. xxix. When disputes arise over the work of the commission, the certificate issued by it and attacked before the inferior administrative courts in the manner prescribed above, shall, if they are invalid, have their defects made good by the final administrative decision of the court to which the appeal is carried.

Art. xxx. The period fixed for appeal to the district council or permanent committee shall be 10 days from the issue of the certificate mentioned in Art. xxviii.

The period fixed for appeal to the Council of State against the decisions of district councils or permanent committees shall be two months from the date of these decisions.

Art. xxxi. The district councils or permanent committees shall not be able to verify or authenticate certificates issued by the sub-district commissions until 10 days after the issue of these certificates.

Art. xxxii. The central committee shall not be able to exchange the certificates or final administrative decisions for bonds until three months after the date of these decisions.

Art. xxxiii. As regards the compensation due to landlords in respect of the land occupied by the houses and enclosures, which in virtue of Art. iv of this law, remain the absolute property of invalids, peasants not engaged in agriculture, and widows not liable to labour service, this compensation is valued at the sum of one ducat[1] or corresponding currency, which shall be paid direct into the hands of the land-owner, one half-ducat every six months after the promulgation of this decree.

Art. xxxiv. As soon as the landowners, with the help of the subvention granted by the State in virtue of Art. l, shall have received the compensation due to them for the abolition of labour service and other dues, the payment which the peasants are bound to make in virtue of Art. xxii shall cease.

CHAPTER IV

Of the compensation fund [OMITTED]

[1] 1 ducat (or *galben*) = 11·75 lei.

Chapter V

Of the sale of lands which form part of the State domains

Art. LIV. To meet the cost of the obligations laid upon rural communes the government is authorized to sell lands which form part of the State domains to newly married men and to peasants coming under the provisions of Art. V and VI.

Not more than 12 *pogoane* may be sold to any one family.

Art. LV. On each of the State domains that portion in which pieces of land will be sold shall be determined as soon as possible by a ruling of public administration. In so determining, a suitable place shall be chosen for the formation of a village.

Art. LVI. The price of one *pogon* on these domains shall be five ducats. Payment shall be made over 15 years in instalments of one-fifteenth at the beginning of each year, without interest. After the period of 15 years the government shall be able to raise the price per *pogon* to future buyers.

The fixing of the new price must first be sanctioned by a law.

Art. LVII. The peasants who have bought lands on the State domains shall not be able, within a period of 30 years, to alienate their land except to other families of peasants.

In the latter case, the land which passes to the new purchaser shall pass encumbered with the charges laid down in Art. LVI.

Art. LVIII. The sale of lands to the peasants shall take place under the direction and control of the Ministry of Finance. Every peasant who shall have enclosed the land bought and have effected the final payment of the purchase price, shall receive a definitive deed of ownership showing the boundaries and area of the land. This deed shall be signed by the Minister of Finance, but it shall not be authenticated till after the completion of payments and according to the rules of common law.

Art. LIX. Each year the Ministry shall present to the legislature a table of the sales made during the year and of the sums received. The accounts for this shall be presented to the Court of Accounts.

Art. LX. In the manner and on the conditions prescribed above, the government is authorized to sell from the State domains called 'colonies', all the land which is not occupied today by these colonies.

Art. LXI. The government shall have the power, in the course of three years from the application of this decree, to come to the aid of the liquidation fund by selling from the State domains plots of 100 to 500 *pogoane*. The amount of plots put up for sale, as well as the form of the sale, shall be fixed by a later administrative regulation. Bonds issued to landowners under this law may be accepted instead of cash in payment for these plots when sold.

Art. LXII. This decree shall come into force from 23 April 1865. Till then the government shall hasten on the preparatory work of enquiry and demarcation provided for in this law.

CHAPTER VI

Various provisions

Art. LXIII. The farmers of State domains, who do not wish to take advantage (in consequence of the application of the new agrarian law) of the option of cancellation granted them in their contract, shall, as compensation for the abolition of labour and other dues of the peasants established on these domains, receive a rebate on their rent proportionate to the labour and other dues abolished, as laid down in Art. XXII of this law, and that according to the number and category of the peasants.

Art. LXIV. As regards the parcels of land which, in virtue of Chapter V of this decree, must be sold to the peasants, the farmers, if they do not cancel the contract, have the right of compensation for the area taken from them, of half a ducat per *pogon*, and that each year until the expiry of their contract.[1]

Given at Bucharest, 14 August 1864
ALEXANDRU ION[2]

21. AGRARIAN REFORM

J. Green, Extract from an unpublished report to the Foreign Office 'on the present state and future prospects of Moldo-Wallachia' (F.O. 78/1811), Bucharest, 31 December 1864.

. . . THE Wallachian peasant, according to the law of 1851 which slightly modified the 'Règlement Organique', had to labour for the

[1] I have to thank Mr. R. G. H. Whitworth for help with legal phraseology throughout this extract.

[2] A. I. Cuza (1820–73), Prince of the United Principalities of Wallachia and Moldavia, 1859–66. See p. 119 above.

proprietor with his oxen for twenty-two days in the year; and had to give him one-fifth of the hay and one-tenth of all other produce of the land he held. In return for this, besides his house and enclosures, each peasant with four oxen and a cow was put in possession of about 14 acres; each peasant having two oxen had about 10 acres; and those having no oxen, about 6 acres. Every male peasant on coming to manhood was entitled to be put in possession of land on these terms, holding it for life, if he did not choose to remove from the estate, which he was at liberty to do. For any surplus land the proprietor wished to cultivate beyond the quantity he could so cultivate by the 22 days labour of the peasants on his estate, he had to enter into mutual agreements with the peasants.

The late decree[1] stipulates that the service of labour and tithe, hitherto paid by the peasant to the proprietor as rent of the land he cultivated or made use of as pasturage, is abolished; that the peasant becomes the unlimited and unreserved owner of his house and inclosures, and of all the land he possesses or might possess, in virtue of the existing laws. In return for this the peasant is to pay the government annually for fifteen years: those who have four oxen and a cow, 133 piastres (£2); those who have two oxen and a cow, 100.24 p. (£1.9.0.); and the remainder 71.20 p. (£1.1.0.). In compensation for the loss of his land and the labour and tithe of produce hitherto due by the peasant, the proprietor is to receive Treasury Bonds calculated as follows. For each peasant with four oxen, 1,521 p. (£22.8.0.); for each peasant with two oxen, 1,148 p. (£16.18.0.); and for the other, 816 p. (£12.0.0.) each. The bonds are to bear interest at the rate of 10 per cent, and are to be extinguished by annual drawings by lot within the period of 15 years.

Prince Couza declares with perfect truth up to the present time, that to the praise of the agricultural classes, in no country could so important a social reform have been carried out as easily as in the Principalities. 'The landowner and the peasants', he says, 'have vied with each other in zeal and concord in the application of the new law. Everywhere the most perfect order has prevailed and continues to prevail, and I can assure you that from the 23 April next, the new rural law will be applied to its full extent.'[2]

---

[1] Of 1864: see preceding extract.
[2] For the implementation of the law, see H. L. Roberts, *Rumania: Political Problems of an Agrarian State*, Yale and Oxford, 1951, pp. 10–13. According to K. Grünberg (see Y 25, p. 387), *Die Bauernbefreiung in Rumänien, Handwörterbuch der Staatswissenschaften*, 3rd edition, Jena, 1909, the law of 1864 granted freehold ownership to 402,900 families who received 1,726,000 hectares, and left between 53,000 and 150,000 families without land. Although, as Grünberg emphasizes, the official figures are unreliable, it appears that the majority of families received a

'My Government', he goes on to say, 'has already taken and will continue to take the most energetic measures to insure the regular payment to the proprietors of the indemnity prescribed by law. This is a national debt; it is placed under the guarantee of the honour of the Government and the Nation.'

It requires to have some knowledge of the upper classes of this country to account for the resignation and apathy they have exhibited under the process of being deprived of what on an average may be looked upon as half their fortunes. With hardly an exception I am convinced that they have been studying the question of the indemnity, and how they can convert the bonds into cash, with far more attention than they have given to the other bearings of the law. Owing to the proverbial extravagance and prodigality of the boyards, there is hardly an estate in the country which has been for three generations in one family; the largest fortunes are squandered as a matter of course in a few years. To such men an arrangement putting them in possession of treasury bonds which may be sold to the Jews, and which in some instances will amount to very large sums, has an agreeable side; and I have observed that any prediction that the indemnity clause will be thrown overboard, and that the Government will not enforce it, is always received very badly. My own opinion is that the annual aggregate sum due by the peasants will prove so large that they will be unable to pay it, especially as there seems a probability from what has already occurred this autumn, not one-tenth part of the usual cultivation having taken place, that being no longer compelled to work, they will do much less than usual, and that for some time there may be a considerable falling off in production.

John Green succeeded Colquhoun as Agent and Consul-General at Bucharest in 1859.

22. UNCONSIDERED EARTH

I. Ghica, *Convorbiri Economice* (Economic Conversations), Bucharest, 1879, pp. 348–9.

WHEN foreigners visit our country and in summer time cross the plains golden with wheat which stretch the whole length of Rumania between the Danube and the foothills of the Carpathians, they are

holding. The scope of the law was thus much wider than that of the law of serf emancipation in Hungary, where the half a million urbarial peasants who received land were a minority of the total number of peasant households.

startled by the wealth of the country. Here are the calculations of Edgeworth (nephew of the famous Richard Lovell), an Englishman with whom I found myself last summer in the train from Brăila to Ploeşti. 'What a wealthy country!' he said, watching how the wind played with the shadows of the clouds over the ripening ears. 'Have you any idea, sir, of the number of hectares under crops?' When I told him that according to the latest information of the Bureau of Statistics we had between twelve and thirteen million *pogoane* (about six and a half million hectares) sown with different crops, he closed his eyes, moved his lips and exclaimed: 'That makes the agricultural income alone over five milliards of francs! If we add another two milliards for the industrial production, the gross income of the country amounts to seven milliards. A wealthy country indeed!'

As an English agriculturist, our foreigner was reckoning 40 hecto-litres (six *chile*) per hectare (three *chile* per *pogon*) and 20 francs as the price of a hectolitre (133 new *lei* per *chilă*). How surprised he was when I told him that our agricultural production does not rise above 400 million francs a year, that the backward state of agriculture and the lack of means for making the loans needed for the land do not allow us, on an average, to count on more than two killows[1] per hectare (one *chilă* per *pogon*) and that if we take into account the inferior quality of our agricultural produce, the average price can only be reckoned at $10\frac{1}{2}$ francs a hectolitre (72 new *lei* or six *galbeni* per *chilă*).

As for industrial production, his surprise was still greater when he found that it does not even amount to 50 million francs a year. The reality of the figures reduced his estimates only too perceptibly and confronted him with a wealth sixteen times smaller than he had supposed. Yet the truth is that a balancing of the state finances and the giving of good guidance to agriculture and industry could in a few years bring us near to the Englishman's figure, without any need of German colonists. It has been proved today in agriculture, that abundance of production depends more on the perfecting of cultiva-tion and on capital than on the labour force. The greatest production is found where the agricultural population is not very numerous. In the following table in which I have shown the relation in the different states of Europe between the agricultural population, the production of wheat per hectare, the head of cattle per thousand inhabitants and the area of land, we can see that the greatest production corre-sponds on the one hand to the smallest proportion of agricultural population and on the other to abundance of cattle. Although the

[1] The Rumanian killow was equivalent to 12 bushels, being twelve times as great as the Constantinople killow (see N. Soutzo, *op. cit.*, p. 132).

number of cattle per inhabitant is larger in our country than anywhere else in Europe, that figure of 2,222 or more than two cattle per inhabitant means on the whole small cattle; for of 10 million head only three million are large cattle. . . .

	% relation of agricultural population to total population	Average production of 1 hectare in hectolitres of wheat	Head of livestock per 1,000 inhabitants	Head of livestock per 100 hectares
Rumania	62	7	2,222	41
England	12	40·8	515	478

Ion Ghica (1817–97), son of a Wallachian boyar, studied engineering and political economy at the Sorbonne. He not only had an academic and literary career, but was also Prime Minister and later Rumanian ambassador in London.

23. THE NEED FOR EDUCATION

I. Ghica, *Convorbiri Economice* (Economic Conversations), Bucharest, 1879, pp. 399–400; 402–3.

THE sum of money earmarked for our primary education is in fact very small, and the government's concern has, unfortunately, been still smaller. . . . In no country in Europe does the education of a child in primary schools cost as much as in Rumania, where the expenditure reaches on an average 40.77 fr., if we accept the official figure for the number of children. But if we take the real figure, which cannot be half or even a third of that which appears in the minister's speeches, a child costs over 100 fr. a year. In Prussia the cost is no more than 9.33 fr., and we know that there children do learn. According to our official statistics the number of children who attend primary schools is 17 per thousand inhabitants: but in reality it does not exceed seven or eight. The proof is that the number of youths who emerge from their primary schools knowing how to read and write is so small in comparison with the needs and requirements of our services, that they all leave agriculture, and if one does stay in the village, he becomes a notary, clerk or secretary at the headman's office, that is to say, the administrator of the commune, a position in which he finds an easy and profitable living. Abusing the ignorance of those whom he administrates, he robs them, persecutes them and oppresses them without fear of responsibility or punishment; it is enough that he should be a useful tool at election time and persistent to the point of cruelty in the exaction of taxes. But the great majority hasten to the towns, seize upon the numerous jobs in national and county administration paid for by the taxpayers, and increase the number of place-seekers. . . .

It is owing to the lack of schools that our carpenters, builders, cobblers and tailors are today just what they were a hundred years ago. To this very day the carpenter joins the roof-frame with bolts, the builder has no idea of the properties of the various sorts of lime, the tanner has not the least notion of the improvements which the tanning industry has made. Yet there are people who seem to think that only a law or decree of protectionist or prohibitive character is needed for us to see Rumanian industry flourishing. We have shoe-makers, joiners, blacksmiths and upholsterers who stand up to foreign competition, who make enough profit and have even grown rich; but we must admit that they are nearly all Frenchmen or Germans, who have acquired the knowledge necessary to the craft which they ply in the schools of their own country and have worked in work-shops under the direction of skilled masters. The European workman is no longer what he was, a muscular force; he is today what God meant him to be, an intelligent force. He is passing from the state of artisan to that of artist. What do we do, what has the government done for the Rumanian workman except to parade him on Sundays and holidays and to tax him during the week?

24. Social Progress after Independence

W. Beatty-Kingston, *A Wanderer's Notes*, London, 1888, vol. ii, pp. 58–62.

In Cusa's birthplace, as in all the larger Roumanian towns, with the exception of Bucharest, the Jews transacted all the retail trade of the city. There was but one shop of any real importance in all Galatz kept by a Christian Moldavian. The export grain business was chiefly carried on by Greeks; the import trade, ship-broking, ship-chandlery, etc., by Englishmen, Greeks, and other foreigners; the native Moldavian was, if a boyar, a seller of natural products, or a house-owner; if a proletary, a hewer of wood and drawer of water. Before the war of 1877 it really seemed as if any means of bread-earning not immediately connected with his native soil and its agronomic produce had been invincibly repugnant to the true-bred Roumanian. He was *fruges consumere natus*, and apt to manipulate that fruitful earth from which he drew wealth for his masters and susten-ance for himself; but he appeared incapable of learning any other avocation than that which exacted from him the minimum of intellectual and the maximum of physical effort. He earned less, and contributed more, in proportion to the gross amount of his income, to the public treasury, than any other class of his fellow-subjects. He was the milch-cow of the State, as well as of the boyar; and I am bound to say that neither the one nor the other did much for him in return for his patient productiveness. The Jews in Moldo-Wallachia, unquestionably, had special, definite, and serious griev-ances, which cried aloud for prompt remedy; but it seemed to me that the Roumanian peasant's life was one long grievance, and that, by reason of his being utterly inarticulate, in the Carlylian sense of the word, the chances of justice being done to him were lamentably small. His condition would have been an insufferable one to any less enduring, amiable, and humble-minded being than himself.

Ignorance, of course, was the root of his many evils; and it behoved his 'pastors and masters' to dig it up and destroy it for him, those being tasks he was not constituted by nature for executing *proprio motu*. He was as superstitious as a Red Indian, and as im-provident as an Australian savage. He let his children, his own and his under-populated country's main hope, die for want of the com-monest cares that one might fancy instinct would have dictated. When he himself lay ill, he would see no doctor and take no medicine, unless it were *raki*, or some devil's broth brewed for him by a village sorceress; he laid him down to die, with much of the Turkish fatalism lurking at the bottom of his conviction that nothing could avail to help him through his illness.

The Roumanian peasant woman was as hard-working as she was prolific; but she rarely reared her children, whose lives she sacrificed to the performance of her daily avocations. She was the servant, not the equal or companion, of her husband. The staple of both their food was *mamaliga*, or maize-flour, moistened with water into a sort of porridge, and eaten with a little salt. They but rarely ate meat, and were consequently unable to resist illness or even severe fatigue. Children succumbed in hosts to maladies that prove in Western Europe by no means necessarily fatal to the infantine population. In a village between Ruginoasa and Roman, belonging to a friend of mine, who maintained a medical man at his own expense for the benefit of his peasants, out of sixty children under seven years of age, fifty-seven died in 1874 of diphtheria. The parents would not let the doctor into their houses, nor even prevent their neighbours' children from clustering round the pallets of the little sufferers. The most they would do was to hire a professional witch to mutter a charm or pronounce an incantation from time to time. Whilst the Roumanian

Jew—I do not speak of the Polish or Russian Israelite immigrant, who was too frequently as ignorant and superstitious as the Christian native of the soil—eagerly availed himself of the discoveries and resources of medical science, the Wallachian or Moldavian utterly and obstinately rejected them.

In other respects, the contrast between the races was as striking as in that relating to sanitary conditions. The Roumanian would not mend a window, tile a roof, nor make a pair of breeches. All these trades, and a legion of others of the plainer, more merely mechanical sort, were exercised by the Jew and the German. The Roumanian worked hard, from childhood to the tomb; his sole pleasure or amusements were the *hora*,[1] or the raki-flask; his theatre, lecture-room, picture-gallery, museum, and club was the roadside *krisma*,[2] kept by the Jew who was his confidant, adviser, news-purveyor, agent, tradesman, money-lender, matchmaker, and, in a word, sole manager of his affairs and arbiter of his fate. He was, I verily believe, the hardest-used, as he was the easiest-going man in Christendom. Everybody else in the country, Boyar, Jew, priest, and foreigner, lived upon him. Others danced, and he paid the music. Not that he was a fool; on the contrary, his natural gifts were by no means despicable, but they had never been cultivated, and indifference to his fate had become an integral part of his character.

With the achievement of Roumanian Independence, however, the *terranu*'s[3] lot changed for the better, morally, intellectually and physically. Enforced military service and compulsory education worked wonders in the way of raising his standard of self-respect and opening his eyes to the expediency of improving the conditions of his existence. From a mere drudge of the glebe he has, in many thousands of instances, become a skilled handicraftsman, operative, journeyman, and even petty tradesman.

In the towns, sanitary science has done much to render life possible, if not enjoyable, to the poorer classes of Dacians, whilst railways and village-schools have carried with them a certain measure of civilization into the vast majority of the country districts. Of all the countries in Europe, Roumania has during the last decade effected the most rapid development of her internal resources and of her people's well-being. Along the highroad of progress she has shown the way, not only to her petty neighbours, Servia and Bulgaria, whose political emancipation is coeval with her own, but to great Russia, who lags far behind her in all the essentials of material advancement. Roumania's chief provincial towns, to a few of which particular reference has been made in this chapter, are now better

---

[1] *horă* = round dance.   [2] *Crâşmă* = tavern.   [3] *ţăran* = peasant.

O

paved, lightened, drained and administered than are St. Petersburg
and Moscow; her peasantry are better taught, clothed and fed than
are the Russian *moujiks*; her army, as far as its discipline, equipments,
mobility and military spirit are concerned, is infinitely superior to
that of Muscovy, with the sole exception of the Guard-Corps, the
high efficiency of which is due to the personal supervision of Czar
Alexander Alexandreivich.

William Beatty-Kingston (1837–1900) was on the staff of the *Daily Telegraph* and visited Rumania several times.

25. Economic Progress

G. Benger, *Rumania in 1900*, London, 1900, pp. 106–11; 121–4; 138–9;
152–3.

(a) The Petroleum Industry and Foreign Capital

Before the middle of the nineteenth century, the Rumanian
petroleum industry was limited to a few wells, which were worked in
a small way, the product being used for lubricating the country
carts.

This particular use of petroleum was already known ages ago, as
indicated by the names of many villages, such as Păcureţi, from
păcură, raw petroleum or cart-grease. Not till 1858 were there any
signs of a somewhat more developed exploitation.

Hitherto the naphtha industry of Rumania had had to suffer from
the above-mentioned lack of local capital and the unsatisfactory
state of the communications. Owing to the want of capital the
workings could not be taken in hand systematically in accordance
with the requirements of modern times. But what foreign capitalists
suffered most from was the fraudulent way in which the workings
were conducted. Thus borings 30 metres deep, which could not have
cost more than £1,200, were not unfrequently debited four or five
times that amount to the company. Various companies—French,
English, Austrian, German—which had tried to establish themselves in the seventies, have again suspended operations. The first
decisive result was obtained by the 'Steaua Română',[1] which, in
association with the 'Buda-Pest International Naphtha Company',
laid out £400,000 on its successful borings at Buştenari. It erected a
refinery capable of treating 21,000 cartloads of petroleum, and large
reservoirs at Constantza, from which the petroleum is drawn off
directly to the tanks one and a half kilometres distant.

The oil-bearing region of Rumania is very extensive. Almost

[1] German-financed.

everywhere where persistent search has been made positive results have been obtained. At present the centres of activity are the districts of Prahova, Dâmboviţa, Buzău, and Bacău. . . .

Most of the oil-fields, and these the most productive—Câmpina and surroundings—are owned by the above-mentioned Steaua Română joint-stock company. Numerous pits are also owned by an English company, three Dutch—with capitals of £40,000, £80,000, and £120,000 respectively—and an Austrian, on the lands of the communes of Câmpina, Buştenari, Doftanetz, and Băicoi-Zintea, which have an average daily production of from one to two cartloads of raw petroleum. Those producers who have wells on their own lands but far from any railway station, and work them in a primitive fashion, often suffer great losses in bad weather, the conveyance to the nearest collecting railway stations over the bad country roads being very difficult and attended by considerable cost. An important turning-point was reached in 1898 by the deep and wide borings undertaken by the Steaua Română Company, and resulting in an increase of the annual production from 12,000 cartloads in the year 1897 to 30,000 in 1899. The Galician output is thus already exceeded, while a yield of even 100,000 cartloads is anticipated in a not very distant future. This vast development has attracted the attention of English, Dutch, and Belgian capitalists and company-promoters to the Rumanian oil-fields. English companies are taking steps to open up more especially the Egyptian and Sudanese markets for the supplies of oil which lie nearest to hand, while the petroleum associations have been much restricted in their operations by the Russian industrial law of 1897. The value of the new works opened in the two last years is estimated at £640,000, and the total number of borings undertaken by these new agencies at about thirty.

As regards the quality, according to the analyses of several chemists the Rumanian petroleum contains more pure, clear oil than the Galician, American, and Caucasian.

The yearly production, which in 1862 was only 30, and in 1873 not more than 139,000 double quintals,[1] shows a steady increase during the last decade—from 74,000 in 1886 to 234,000 in 1896. In 1897–8 the total yield was 1,341,000 double quintals valued at £260,000, and in 1899 there was a further increase of 25 per cent.

[1] 'Double quintals' is a mistranslation of 'Doppelzenten' (quintals). One quintal equals 100 kilograms or one-tenth of a metric ton. But there appear to be errors in the figures, which should show a continuous increase. In an earlier work (*Rümanien, ein Land der Zukunft*, Stuttgart, 1896) Benger gives the following figures, in quintals: 1862, 30,000; 1872, 140,000; 1882, 350,000; 1894, 670,000. These are in accordance with official statistics. Output of crude petroleum rose to 1·8 million tons in 1913 and reached its maximum of 9 million tons in 1936.

The production might be considerably increased were its local consumption not so greatly shackled in many towns by municipal charges. Thanks to these imposts, petroleum is dearer in Rumania than in the countries to which it is exported. . . .

Of refineries there are 73, of which, however, only about one-ninth are distilleries in the strict sense of the word; the others give unsatisfactory returns. The most important are owned by the Steaua Română Company of Câmpina, and the Bucharest Company. The latter has special appliances for the preparation of paraffin and the heavier oils.

Of these establishments only ten are conducted in a systematic way, all the rest being in a very primitive state. Three-fourths of the raw material, and seven-eighths of the refined oil, are in the hands of the Steaua Română, which, with its joint-stock capital of £800,000, besides £200,000 5 per cent scrip, commands the largest capital of any Rumanian company. In the year 1898–9 it realized a profit of £880,000, which, after setting aside £440,000 for redemption and transference to the special reserve, left a net profit of over £40,000, and a dividend of 7½ per cent for the bond-holders.

The competing power of the Rumanian petroleum industry depends on the proximity and low rates of the railways, combined with the general cheapness of labour on the spot. The three oil-yielding districts are encircled by a network of railways, which are easily accessible on all sides. This is also true of the riverside ports, especially those of Galatz, Brăila, and Constantza for Russia and the West, Giurgiu for the Balkan States, Turnu-Severin and Vercerova for Austria-Hungary and South Germany.

The exports, which ranged from 16,000 tons to 20,000 tons in the years 1891–7, rose in 1898 to 40,000 tons. This trade lies almost exclusively in the hands of the Steaua Română, which began the sea-borne traffic at first in drums forwarded to Genoa, and is now already introducing tank-steamers in order to supply the Scandinavian, Greek, Egyptian and Levant markets.

When the refining of Rumanian petroleum is carried to greater perfection, it will be able successfully to compete with the American petroleum ring in Germany by utilizing the Danube route. The Steaua Română has already had large reservoirs constructed at Ratisbon, and has the oil forwarded thither by tank-steamers. In 1897 the government occupied itself with this project, which might be equivalent to a monopolizing of the petroleum business. Recently, however, a disposition has been shown to leave the export trade to private enterprise.

(b) Forest Spoliation

. . . Rumania is distinguished from the neighbouring states by the considerable extent of land still under forest. This amounts at present to from about 1½ to 1¾ million hectares, or one-sixth of the superficial area of the kingdom. . . .

Wherever the woodman's axe has not yet penetrated, the mountain ranges are still clothed with primaeval forest. Access to the uplands is at times obstructed by blown-down timber strewing gigantic and already partly decayed stems amid the tall firs. Higher up, stretches of bare rock alternate with stunted growths and dwarf juniper. Here are also situated the extensive upland pastures, which have continually encroached more and more on the pine-forests, whereby the aftergrowths get seriously injured. . . .

Everywhere in East and South Europe the forests are exploited in the most reckless manner. Such was also long the case in Rumania, where wood had in fact no market value.

But a change was brought about by two innovations—the secularization of the monastic lands in the year 1863, by which the State acquired over a million hectares of forests; and the development of railway enterprise and of the lumber industry. Thereby timber gradually became more valuable, while more system was applied to the management of the forests. At first academically trained officials were secured for the Crown lands; then the State forests were provided with the necessary hands educated for the purpose, while the private woods were brought under some control. By these means, followed in 1886 by the introduction of government regulations in effecting clearances, an attempt was made to put an end to the hitherto prevailing wastefulness.

But there is still much to be done. Between 1882 and 1891, eighty-two of the private forests, comprising 98,836 hectares, and fifty-three belonging to the State, comprising 75,558 hectares, or presumably some 10 per cent of the whole area under timber, had been brought under economic management. . . .

In fact, the forests of the Rumanian Carpathians present far too tempting a field for speculating capitalists, who, thanks to the impecuniosity of private owners, have an easy game to play. A systematic management of the woods is also often hindered by ignorance of forestry, a lack of practical and trained foresters, their bad treatment and poor pay, and the defective inspection of the private woods by the government officials. Thus, during the last decade, a frightful extent of woodlands has been cleared. Where, till quite recently, magnificent timber was still standing, nothing is now to be seen except worthless herbage, poor unproductive arable ground, or else plantations so badly managed that they can scarcely any longer be regarded as such. At present there are scarcely ten of the private owners who have their estates systematically managed while hundreds allow their woods to be wasted by reckless lumber-dealers or ignorant officials.

(c) Railways

Only a few decades ago, traffic was still carried on in Rumania on utterly neglected tracks by means of rude ox-wagons. Nothing was done for the highways because, as for instance also in many German districts, people feared they would prove more harmful if found practicable by hostile forces. The first roads were taken in hand by the government over seventy years ago, and at the beginning of the sixties they had a total length of 775 kilometres. But a new and unknown factor was, so to say, sprung upon the land by the sudden appearance of the locomotive.

On 1 November 1869, the first Rumanian railway was opened, between Bucharest and Giurgiu, a distance of seventy kilometres. This was followed by the Itzcani-Roman line (102 kilometres); and the network advanced from 936 kilometres in 1872 to 1,514 in 1883. . . . Of the Danubian ports the following have railway connections: Turnu-Severin, Calafat, Corabia, Turnu-Măgurele, Zimnicea, Giurgiu, Călăraşi, Feteşti, Cernavoda, Brăila, and Galatz.

In 1879 the government began the nationalization of the railways, and since 1888 all the lines have been State property. . . . Of the railways, which have at present a total length of 3,140 kilometres, 1,270 kilometres were constructed by concessionaires at an expenditure of £18,672,000, and 1,870 by the State for £11,108,000, making a total of 3,140 kilometres and an outlay of £29,380,000. . . .

(d) Danube Shipping

The efforts made by Rumania to achieve her economic independence have nowhere met with so many difficulties as in the attempt to secure a controlling influence over the passenger and goods carrying-trade beyond the kingdom itself. Only a few years ago she was in this respect still entirely dependent on foreign countries, and especially on Austria-Hungary, which controlled this traffic on the one hand by the Danube Steamship Company, and by the Austria-Hungarian Lloyd's on the other.

The first inducement to establish a Rumanian steam service on the Danube was occasioned by the Directors of the State Monopoly

Department undertaking the export of salt to Servia, whereby great difficulties arose out of the transport question. Rumania was driven to provide ships of her own, and the Directors were commissioned to procure the necessary materials for building them, a total credit of £200,000 being placed at their disposal for this purpose in the years 1890–2. With this sum not only were the required vessels provided, but the wharves constructed by the Austrian Steamship Company at Turnu-Severin were bought up.

This carrying business was so rapidly developed that it was soon able to enter into friendly reciprocal relations with the South German (Bavarian) Danube Steamship Company.

A great influence was exercised on the progress of navigation and of the local transport service by the 'European Danubian Commission', which was appointed in 1856 independently of the Rumanian government, and in which are represented the seven Powers who took part in the Paris Congress of 30 March 1856, and since 1885 Rumania itself. The Administration, which has its seat at Galatz, is intrusted with the execution of such works as are necessary for the maintenance of the navigation of the Danube, consequently with the regulation of the river, the removal of all obstructions in the Sulina branch and at its mouth, as well as the steady improvement of the waterway, for which purpose large workshops are maintained.

The operations begun by the Danube Commission in 1857, and comprising the section of the river from Brăila-Galatz to the Sulina mouth, are in every respect amongst the most imposing and successful of such fluvial regulations. They aimed on the one hand at deepening the channel, on the other at the construction of a seaport at Sulina. The first object was achieved by cutting through twenty-three sharp and dangerous windings in the Sulina branch, and thus creating a straight channel which is 22¾ kilometres shorter than the old river-bed.

The growth of trade through the Sulina branch and the Sulina mouth during the last decades is shown in the following table:

	Total	Sailing Vessels	Steamers
1857			
Ships	1,938	1,800	140
tons, in thousands	335	288	47
1887			
Ships	1,678	607	1,071
tons, in thousands	1,203	104	1,099
1898			
Ships	1,419	327	1,092
tons, in thousands	1,476	69	1,406

It thus appears that the steam traffic, which is, moreover, estimated to have a carrying capacity three times greater than that of sailing vessels, has increased thirtyfold since 1857.

Benger visited Rumania in 1892 and was later Rumanian consul-general at Stuttgart.

26. CAUSES OF THE PEASANT REVOLT, 1907

I. L. Caragiale, *Opere* (Works), vol. v, ed. Şerban Cioculescu, Bucharest, 1938, pp. 167–71.

. . . THE recent uprisings of the peasant masses, which assumed the proportions of a definite terrorist revolution, almost of a ruthless civil war, were bound to cause excitement and astonishment in Europe. But anyone who is, as we are, closely acquainted with the organs of this state and their working, is surprised, not at what is happening, but—granted that there was all that energy in those masses (which he was justified in no longer supposing)—why this colossal public upheaval did not erupt much earlier. As a matter of fact, there is perhaps in no state, at least in Europe, such a vast discrepancy between appearance and reality, between the creature and the mask.

Rumania is an almost entirely agricultural country; a few industrial beginnings, scandalously protected by the state, and even the beginnings of the exploitation of petroleum provide a proportion of the produce of national resources which is tiny and almost negligible in comparison with that of agriculture. The soil of the country is owned:

1. By *the great landlords*: of these the largest is the state; then the Crown with its royal domains; philanthropic foundations, like the Hospitals Board; cultural foundations, like the Academy, etc.; and the great private landlords.

2. By *the medium landlords*, and

3. By *the small landlords*, the enormous mass of peasants, who became landlords after 1864 and 1888.

All the peasants are ploughmen; they cultivate their own small properties and the great and medium properties. These small landlords (almost five millions out of a total population of about six) cannot subsist upon the produce of their own properties; for, on the one hand, the necessities of life and the taxes have grown and are continually growing, while on the other, their lands have shrunk and keep on shrinking, as they pass in fragments to children by inheritance under the common law (though alienation is forbidden by law and exchange is only allowed in compensation between peasants) and become in the end broken up into such small pieces that they would only be useful for high-grade intensive cultivation—a type of work which is impossible here owing to longstanding habits, lack of special intelligence and patience, ignorance of the methods needed for scientific cultivation, and lack of capital and credit.

On the other hand, the great and medium properties have no means for their extensive cultivation except the arms of the peasants. The latter demand pieces of ground for working and producing as much as possible according to their powers. They pay for the pieces rented, either in money and service, as in Moldavia, according to local custom, or in kind, as in Wallachia. In the latter case, the peasant works the land and shares the produce with the great landlord, as laid down in a contract confirmed by the authorities of the commune. The peasant is also bound to this contract by the fact that a small property has no pasture at all for his cattle; pasture is exclusively owned by the great landlord. Agricultural contracts, although civil obligations, are enforced at need by the authorities *manu militari*, like the so-called 'hard labour' of the penal law. (Corporal constraint was abolished in 1881 by a law modifying the previous barbarous law. In law it no longer exists; in fact it continues to be applied. This is a truth which no one could deny, just as no peasant would dare to take advantage of the legal abolition of corporal constraint, because he knows well that he would then expose himself to corporal punishments which were abolished still earlier, by the Constitution of 1866.)

This is a general truth. . . . There is unfortunately, however, something else which is generally true. Of the great and even of the medium landlords very few cultivate their estates themselves. The majority, a large majority, lease them as a whole to the highest bidder. Private persons do the leasing by private contract; but the state and the foundations do it by public auction, in accordance with the law of state accountability. Only the Crown estates are administered directly without the intervention of tenants. With a certain amount of capital and indeed with moderate credit, anyone may bid for the renting of great and medium estates. In Moldavia more is needed, because, by local custom, lands are subleased to peasants for money and service, and the chief tenant needs cattle, carts, machines, etc. In Wallachia less is needed; if you have rented an estate, you pay an instalment of the rent, you have some money for seed and for advances on loan to needy peasants; after that, you sublet it almost all in portions to the peasants. The latter work from spring till autumn, from crack of dawn till the rising of the stars; and in autumn, according to the agreement, the peasant first carts the tenant's share to the granary or the station, and only after that may remove the share which belongs to himself.

Let us not forget to say that needy peasants, in wintertime when they have no work and can usually produce nothing, raise loans at a more or less infamous rate of interest from these same tenants, being left to settle the account the following autumn. Often the peasants, after working for more than eight months, find themselves left in debt for the following year. And again there comes a hard winter upon their sad and lowly hearths, and again there are requests, hat in hand for a new loan. . . . And so on. . . .

The competition of tenants has raised and continues to raise the price of rents, which suits the landlords; and from this, naturally, results the growing oppressiveness for the majority of ploughmen of the conditions of subtenancy. Thus we have the following strict formula: the tension of reckless competition on the part of the chief tenants increases in proportion to the submissiveness of the small tenants, the ploughmen, to contracts.

Well, here is the root of the trouble; here lurks the cause of the present state of affairs—the tension has increased beyond measure. And the trouble has other roots too, as we shall presently show.

Let us note in passing that the large majority of the tenants consists of foreigners—in Moldavia, Jews; in Wallachia, Greeks, Bulgars, Albanians and a few Rumanians from Transylvania who are Hungarian subjects. As a rule, apart from rare and honourable exceptions, they are men of low origin, hard where profit is concerned, and lacking in human feelings and any elementary education. The harshness of interest, common everywhere, is here aggravated by a lack of national solidarity, by indifference to tradition and public opinion, by audacity encouraged by the corruptibility of the public administration on the one hand, and by the protection of a foreign flag or some powerful universal Alliance on the other, and by an open brutal contempt for the uneducated, downtrodden and longsuffering peasant.

What has resulted from this system? The following:

1. The ruin of so many great landlords, who have increased their expenditure as their rents rose, plunging into increasing extravagance and luxury in the hope of a continuous rise in their incomes;

2. The phenomenal prosperity of the class of great tenants, and in

addition, the prodigious increase in banks and institutions of credit utterly out of proportion in an agricultural country;

3. The misery of the peasants.

It is bound to be so. The pressure on the latter's resources has given rise to the reckless luxury of the landlords, the boundless enrichment of the tenants, the enormous profits of the banks, the bribery of the public administration, and, what is more, the continuous growth of the state revenues.

Ion Luca Caragiale (1852–1912), the greatest prose-writer and playwright of Rumania in the nineteenth century, wrote the article from which this extract is taken for the Vienna newspaper *Die Zeit* in 1907.

Note on Weights, Measures and Currency

1. *Weights*

1 oke (*oca*) = 1·28 kg. = 2⅘ lb.

2. *Capacity*

1 oke (*oca*) in Moldavia = 1·28 litres = 2⅕ pints.
1 oke (*oca*) in Wallachia = 1·52 litres = 2½ pints.
Liquids: 1 *vadră* (keg) = 10 okes.
Cereals: 1 *chilă* (killow) in Constantinople = 1 bushel.
　　　　 1 *chilă* (killow) in Moldavia = 12 bushels.

3. *Area*

1 *pogon* = ½ hectare = 1¼ acres.
1 *fălciu* = 1·42 hectares = 3½ acres.
1 *părjină* (in Moldavia) = 26·76 sq. m. = 1 perch.
1 [square] *stânjen* (in Wallachia) = 3·88 sq. m.

4. *Currency*

The old *leu*, like the piastre, was equal to 40 paras. In the middle of the nineteenth century the rate of exchange was about 35 lei for 1 Austrian ducat. In 1867 the new *leu* was introduced, equivalent to the French franc and divided into 100 *bani*.

Bulgaria

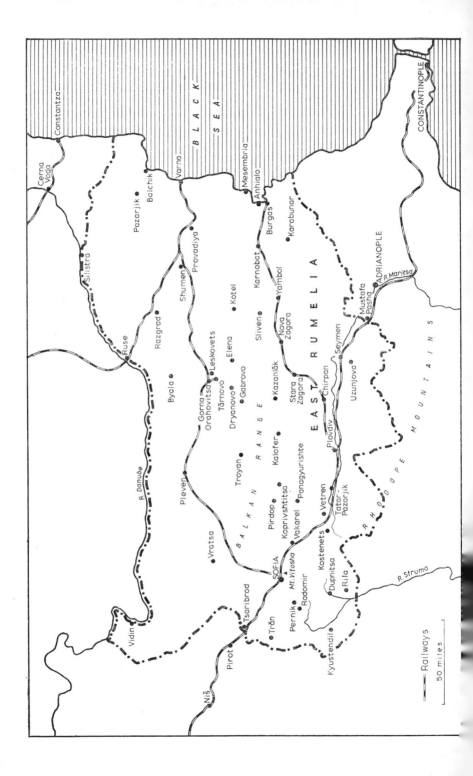

Bulgaria : Introduction

V. de S. PINTO

BULGARIAN commerce on any notable scale dates from the beginning of the eighth century when, following the treaty of Prince Tervel with Justinian II in 705, Bulgarians visiting Constantinople became aware of the possibilities of import and export. This was, however, but a beginning, for the Bulgaria of Tervel's reign was still far from being the centre of commerce it was to become in the tenth century, when almost all raw materials for Byzantium from the west and north were imported via Bulgaria. This transit trade was extended during the Second Bulgarian Empire to include dealings with the Ragusans, Venetians and Genoese.[1]

Thus Bulgaria had already become an important centre of east European commerce when the Turkish armies advanced into the Balkans in the latter part of the fourteenth century. Even Lala Shakhin, the Turkish army commander, reporting back to Sultan Murad I in 1384 on the Bulgarian territories he was conquering, appears to have been favourably impressed:

> The Sofia basin is extremely affluent in agriculture and cattle-farming. It could support an enormous army for a lengthy period. . . . Industrial institutions and workshops exist in Sofia in considerable number, and woollen and cotton materials, both thick and thin, are worked there and used to clothe both infidel troops and the numerous resident population. Commerce in the town is quite advanced, because on all sides are to be seen organized roads constantly traversed by travelling merchants and their caravan trains of various goods and wares which are worked in Sofia and then distributed in all directions throughout Rumelia and beyond.[2]

[1] These commercial relations continued under the Turks, who confirmed them by further treaties. The extent of trade undertaken by the Ragusan colony in Sofia, for instance, is indicated by the entries in Benedetto Restić's ledgers kept there continuously from 1590 to 1605.

[2] D. Ikchiev, 'Materiali za istoriyata ni pod turskoto robstvo' (Materials on our History under Turkish Servitude) in *Yubileen sbornik I. N. Denkoglu* (Jubilee Collection for I. N. Denkoglu), Sofia, 1907, pp. 51 ff.

The period of Bulgarian history which ensued 'under the Turkish yoke'[1] has commonly been represented as the Bulgarian 'Dark Ages', an epoch of unmitigated misery, poverty and servitude. It was the dark side of life under alien rule—dark it undeniably was at times[2]— which patriot writers of the nineteenth century *Văzrazhdanë* (Bulgarian renascence) and since have understandably stressed in their efforts to arouse and sharpen consciousness of Bulgarian nationhood. In fact, however, replacement of the frequently unstable and unsettling Bulgarian imperial rule by a Turkish administration meant the exchange of an old for a new, if alien, autocracy. For the Bulgarian urban and artisan population it had (as secret Turkish government archives[3] now reveal) certain compensations. It meant a degree of stability, order and at times even prosperity,[4] once the rout of Christian armies in the Balkans had been assured by the victory of Murad II at Varna (1444) and the capture of Constantinople by Muhammad II (1453). It meant, too, not only an assured duty-free market for Bulgarian artisan industry within the extensive territories of the Turkish Empire stretching from Transylvania to Egypt and Tripoli, but also, even more important, Turkish patronage of such industry in its functions of maintaining Turkish strategic centres and communications and also of supplying goods and services to the Turkish armies in campaign or on garrison along the north Balkan and Danubian frontiers. As early as 1566, for instance, a thousand sets of horseshoes were ordered from the Samokov smiths, followed in 1571 by consignments, likewise from Bulgarian workshops, of anchors, nails and timber assemblies for shipbuilding delivered to the Turkish naval arsenal at Anhialo. By firman of the

[1] Title of the Bulgarian 'national novel' by Ivan Vazov, *Pod igoto* (Under the Yoke), which is concerned with the concluding years of Turkish rule. First translated into English by Edmund Gosse, London, 1912.
[2] Especially during the internal disorders of the eighteenth century. See below, p. 211.
[3] See *Turski dokumenti za izuchavane na bălgarskata istoriya* (Turkish Documents for the Study of Bulgarian History), transl. P. Dorev and Prof. P. Mutafchiev, Bulg. Acad. Sciences, Sofia, 1941. Also Prof. Ahmed Refik's collection of such archives in *Bălgariya pod tursko upravlenie, 1565–1841* (Bulgaria under Turkish Rule), Sofia University, 1938.
[4] This improvement is already reflected in Vladislav Gramatik's *Prenasyane na moshtite na sv. Ivan Rilski ot Tărnovo v Rilskiya monastir* (The Conveyance of St. John Rilski's Remains from Tărnovo to the Rila Monastery), written at Rila in 1479 and appended to Patriarch Evtimy's famous *Zhitie na sv. Ivana Rilski* (Life of St. John of Rila) of the previous century. The gifts presented to monasteries during this period, i.e. the late fifteenth century, also reflect a certain degree of urban prosperity.

Sultan dated 8 July 1572, the Turkish *cadi* (magistrate-in-charge) at Plovdiv was charged to ensure that all local artisans, tradesmen and grocers concerned with work for the Turkish army 'be in no way hindered but receive fullest co-operation and respect for their existing practices', while the smiths of Samokov, Kostenets and Raduil on state contracts were to work full time on these, accepting no local orders. Muhammad IV's firman of 1684 to the Sofia and Pirot district authorities details the dispatch to the Hungarian front of privileged *bulderi*, i.e. *raya*[1] master-builders, and experts in siege and defence works, specifying a wage of 80 grosh payable from the state coffer, 40 in advance and the remainder payable on St. Demetrius' Day.[2]

Such was usual official policy (though not necessarily local practice) during the long Turkish occupation until, in the nineteenth century, we find Bulgarian clothiers from Koprivshtitsa and neighbouring towns working whole quasi-military factories in Constantinople, e.g. the Khambar barracks, exclusively for the Turkish army. Turkish patronage carried privileges as well as pay. Some twenty-five categories were specified as key trades on account of their value to the Turkish army or because they provided essential public services such as building and maintenance of barracks, bridges and clocks and municipal plumbing, including waterworks, fountains and thermal baths. Such skilled workers were given every facility to execute their contracts and were also accorded privileges such as exemption from labour conscription, military levies and other special *ad hoc* taxes. Bulgarians responded by working alongside Greeks, Jews, Armenians and Turks, and became numerically dominant in many trades and crafts[3] and likewise in the network of *esnafi*, the professional guilds through which these were organized.

With these developments went a steady growth and extension of the small urban economy, not only in the older Bulgarian towns,

---

[1] Turkish term for infidel or Christian population under the Moslem theocracy.

[2] 26 October, the traditional day for making annual labour contracts, especially the hiring and pricing of farm labourers. See also pp. 266 and 296 below.

[3] Of the 60 trades practised in Sofia and enumerated in the Turkish registers of 1604, 1671 and 1685, Bulgarians dominated half and were well represented in most of the others, only 7 or 8 (e.g. the barbers, saddlers, tobacco dealers and café-keepers) being wholly in Turkish hands. Again, the sixteenth- and seventeenth-century guild records (*kondika*) of the Plovdiv clothiers show a marked preponderance of Bulgarian masters and apprentices. See Professor A. Ishirkov, *Grad Sofia prez XVII vek* (The City of Sofia during the Seventeenth Century), Sofia, 1912. It should however, be realized that there was little, if any, attempt to organize and direct Bulgarian influence corporatively in this field until after Sultan Mustafa III's firman of 1772, which legally established the traditional Bulgarian trade guilds, and granted them rights of guild autonomy and administration.

P

but also in new urban centres which grew up round Turkish garrisons and other strategic points, e.g. Tatar Pazarjik, Ruschuk (Ruse)
and Mustafa Pasha (Svilengrad), and also in the original highland
refuges from the Turkish invasion (e.g. Gabrovo, Sliven and Kalofer)
which remained always less accessible to Turkish administration and
marauders alike. In this growth of the urban economy lay the
material and social context for a national awakening and the leadership essential to it.[1] By contrast, the Turks played a declining part in
urban economic life, owing to their preoccupation with the civil
bureaucracy and military service, and to their casualties in war and
the recurrent epidemics which they accepted fatalistically as the will
of Allah. They seemed content—as their wills and other documents
testify—to leave all but a few trades increasingly to the *raya*.

These contrasting yet complementary roles of Turk and *raya* in
the economy of the Balkan province explain some apparent contra-
dictions in travellers' accounts, which range from admiration for
local prosperity to commiseration with the oppressed *raya*. The Turks
were, of course, by right of conquest, the landowners, and their
interest lay in agriculture, cattle-farming and the exploitation of
their estates; in this sector of the economy accordingly the peasants
bore the full and often calamitous brunt of the Turkish yoke. For
the Bulgarian villager the Turkish conquest meant serfdom under an
oriental feudalism even more oppressive than before. A few villages,
mostly in the highlands and so less accessible, were compelled by the
Sultan to guard passes or provide skilled workers, for instance,
miners and bridge-builders, or guard conscripts. In return they
received various privileges, such as exemption from tax (even from
the livestock tithe, up to one hundred sheep); legal hereditary
ownership of their land (without right to sell it); the prohibition of
Turkish immigration; and, for the 'military' villages, the right to
carry arms and wear vivid garments. For the rest, however, the
boyars of the Bulgarian Empire were replaced by the spahis, i.e.
Turkish cavalry guards of the Sultan, who held their estates as
hereditary fiefs; these comprised all the good valley lands, together
with the *raya* on them. Though they could not be bought or sold,
these serfs became *de facto* the spahi's own property, and were thus
bound (on pain of grave reprisal for any attempt to migrate) to work

---

[1] Even so, the response to Paisy's call to nationhood in 1762 proved strangely
slow. Its full significance appears to have been first fully appreciated by Professor
M. Drinov, in his article 'Otets Paisy, negovoto vreme, negovata istoriya' (Father
Paisy, his Time, his History) in *Periodichesko spisanie*, Year I, Bk. IV, Brăila, 1871,
pp. 3–26. Prior to this, the *Văzrazhdanë* was generally considered to date from the
1830s.

their land to meet such heavy liabilities as the tithe on all agricultural produce and livestock, a head tax on all male *raya* over 15
years old,[1] a chimney tax on each dwelling, free bed and board for
Moslem travellers and, most oppressive of all, the *angariya*[2] (forced
unpaid labour). Such multiple feudal liabilities could, and often did,
mean a desperate struggle for bare existence, exacerbated in the
eighteenth century by wholesale banditry and the civil strife consequent on local separatist régimes such as that of Pazvantoglu Pasha
in Vidin. Many peasants moved to the towns (or to other places
granted rights of fortification) both for security and to escape the
Turkish landlords' ruthless and desperate efforts to preserve the old
feudal structure, as it crumbled before the new monetary economy
which, with the opening of the Aegean, Black Sea and Danubian
waterways for commerce, was rapidly replacing the old rural
economy of barter and payment in kind.

The nineteenth century brought improvement in the condition of
the *raya* and notable prosperity for the tradesmen and merchants.
Banditry and other disorders were brought under some control, and
in 1826 Mahmud II disbanded that ancient and often unruly
institution, the corps of Janissaries, replacing it by the *nizam* (regular
army), which proved a specially good customer for Bulgarian
merchandise. There followed a series of reforms, collectively known
as the *Tanzimat* or Reorganization, notably Sultan Abd-al-Mejid's
Noble Rescript of the Rose Chamber (3 November 1839) and the
Imperial Rescript of 1856, designed to liberalize the Turkish Empire
by ending feudal practices and granting equal rights to all subjects
irrespective of race or creed.[3] Though the reforms bred confidence,
encouraged local industry and commerce and led in due course to
a movement for Bulgarian religious autonomy and national independence, they meant much less to the peasants, whose Turkish
masters were quick to get their feudal rights replaced by legal
documents of hereditary ownership. So the spahis ceased to exist,
but in their place the beys and estate-owners held sway and in some
districts (e.g. Vidin and Kyustendil) even continued to enforce the
tithe and *angariya*. In the words of M. Majarov's memoirs of his
childhood:

> I pointed out to my father this rich countryside which was
> indeed our native land. I pointed to the barns piled high with

[1] See below 1 (*a*) for S. Gerlach's account of these liabilities and their oppressive
application.
[2] See below 8 (*a*), also the account in Tsani Ginchev's *Gancho Koserkata*, first
printed in 1890 in his periodical *Trud* (Labour), Tărnovo, 1887–93.
[3] See Bernard Lewis, *The Emergence of Modern Turkey*, London, 1961, pp. 75–125.

bales and mountains of corn, and he told me of these people's arduous life. 'All you see is not theirs. The tithe will deprive them of 20–25 per cent of the corn, though only 10 per cent is laid down as due to the state. The hens and chickens will go mostly into the bellies of Turkish gendarmes and Turkish guests: the peasant's home is not inviolable, as are the houses of Koprivshtitsa. Here any Turk may enter and commit any outrage he please. If one day Bulgaria is set free, it will be freed for the peasants, not for us. We already are free. We are injured only by the bandits who hinder our free transport and our trade. Apart from this I doubt whether other countries enjoy greater freedom than we do in Koprivshtitsa.'[1]

Majarov goes on to contrast the poverty and decrepit shacks of the Bulgarian villages he had toured with the luxuries of an average two-storey house in Koprivshtitsa, furnished with silk hangings and covers from Constantinople and Egypt.

Though the Bulgarian peasants had acquired the legal right to purchase and possess land through the Turkish reforms, in practice they could rarely find the money, so that *de facto* their situation remained generally unchanged until after the Liberation. The Turkish landowners were, moreover, soon joined by the native notables from the ranks of the wealthy Bulgarian cattle-dealers and tax-contractors.[2] In amassing their estates, often of considerable size and predominantly in Eastern Bulgaria, these merchants commonly increased their capital by high interest usury, for which an almost insatiable market was offered by their poorer countrymen, who in a universal and long pent-up hunger for land of their own were fatally gullible, and so often reduced through indebtedness to economic serfdom.

With the Liberation (1878) and the ensuing exodus of Turkish landowners to their homeland, the chiflik system rapidly disappeared. By the *Law for Improving the Condition of Agricultural Population on Chifliks* (1880), those working on any land continuously for ten years were given possession (articles 4 and 6). The remaining large estates were heavily taxed and soon put up for sale, to be bought often with money borrowed at exorbitant rates of interest. The great estates won from the boyars of the Old Bulgarian Empire by the Turks and held by them for nearly five centuries were at last broken up. The distribution of land and the achievement of political independence

---

[1] M. Majarov's memoirs of a journey from Thrace to Koprivshtitsa in the 1860s, published in the journal *Turtsiya* (Turkey), 1872.

[2] See below, 6 (a), (b) and (c).

proved, however, no solution to the gravest economic problems of the time, notably a peasantry burdened by usury and lack of capital and the ruin of an extensive small-scale industry specializing in textiles. This had been prosperous under the Turkish Empire, but was quite unable to compete with European mass-produced factory goods, which became readily and cheaply available as a result of the low tariff and the improvements in rail and water communications made in the last decades of Turkish rule. Such was the economic legacy inherited by the independent Bulgarian state.

I. Under Turkish Rule

1. OPPRESSION

(a) In the Sixteenth Century

Stephan Gerlach, *Stephan Gerlach des älteren Tage-Buch der . . . an die ottoman-ische Pforte zu Constantinopel abgefertigten und durch David Ungnad vollbrachten Gesandtschaft*, Frankfurt am Main, 1674, p. 517.

THOSE Christians who live far from Constantinople are in pitiable plight because their judges, beys, spahis, janissaries and other Turkish officials residing in their villages are able with impunity to seize from them their corn, wine and other things—all that they want. Those living nearer to Constantinople live better because they can lodge complaints, though not of course without bakshish. Every adult man has to pay an annual tax of one gold piece and in addition a levy on houses, gardens, vineyards, meadows and other real estate.

Direst abuses are committed by the spahis who have their tributary districts among the villages and receive from them a tithe in payment for military service but, instead of a tenth part, take a seventh and even a fifth. They fleece these unfortunate folk till they hardly have any bread left to eat. No spahi permits his peasant ever to eat a fowl. Fowls, vegetables, money—everything they take from them; the spahis living far from Constantinople besides this rape their women and children, and the poor peasants have to accept it in silence.

The Turkish feast of little Bairam starts on the first of March and lasts three days. One or two days before, the Bulgarian shepherds bring here several thousand sheep and all who have the least bit of money buy one to sacrifice, i.e. to slay and share out among the poor. This sacrifice is called *kurban*.

According to a Hungarian from Segedin,[1] the Albanians and Bulgarians marry off their sons at an age of eight or nine years old, solely to release them from the Turkish tithe of children, because married persons are exempt. But apparently some parents are so godless in these circumstances that they gladly give over one or two of their sons so that they themselves may be released from war service.

[1] Szeged.

They are thereby exempt from military service; otherwise they must go with the Sultan to serve in the wars in all fortification works, and take part in preliminary assaults on the enemy and to be exposed to the fire of enemy guns. . . .

These are slave people who do nothing unless first struck or beaten; then they run and do what you wish and so the Turks and their bailiffs beat them much. When they know they could surely earn a *para*[1] or two, they come out to foreigners bringing for sale bread, cream, cheese, sour milk, sometimes even pork, as they keep many pigs. Here in Vetren we ate strawberries for the first time, as in Constantinople there were none, except in the royal gardens.

Gerlach was a Lutheran priest, presumably of German origin, and accompanied David Ungnad on his mission in 1572–3 from Vienna to Constantinople. His correspondence and verse upon life in Turkey and the state of the Greek language were published by Martin Crusius of Tübingen (his professor?) in *Germano-Graeciae Libri Sex* and *Turco-Graeciae Libri Octo*, both published at Basle in 1584. Gerlach is also described elsewhere as having been Ungnad's secretary. Crusius refers to him as 'doctus et pius iuvenis'.

(b) In the Eighteenth Century

Albert Maurice Blanc de la Nante, Comte d'Hauterive, 'Journal inédit d'un voyage de Constantinople à Jassi, capitale de la Moldavie, dans l'hiver de 1785', in *Revue de géographie*, Paris, 1877, vol. ii, pp. 120–31; 274–87.

AFTER the Turkish village Eski-polos comes Kodja-Torla, the first Christian Bulgarian hamlet on our route, property of the Sultan's senior musket-bearer, who annually torments his unhappy vassals in a thousand ways to extract from them 150 piastres a household. Last year the inhabitants in their desperation and inability to pay this sum decided with one voice to run away and leave their fields and houses to the Turks. But soon men were sent after them to fetch them back with a few shots and a good many blows of the club to return them back under the yoke. Their houses are of reed and most original. A chimney like a beehive, very wide at the bottom, occupies a corner and illuminates the whole room, there being no other windows. Rain and snow fall into the house through this chimney and through it come also the daylight and the moonlight. A second room is hidden in the depths of the house, having no other exit but a small door which links it with the first. This is where 30 creatures sleep, men, women, children, cows, oxen, sheep, ducks, goats, etc. The interior is not however so poor as may be thought. Couches and

---

[1] A small coin, in the eighteenth century equivalent to about one English half-penny.

hangings are ranged round the room and are loaded with domestic accoutrements and necessities. Bulgarian clothes are rough without being too simple. In each house there are two looms, one for cloth and one for linen. The men make the clothes while the women sew the shirts and embroider them with threads of different colours in quite good taste. The women's only ornaments are bracelets on their arms and perforated coins which are hung round their heads falling from the temples to the toes. . . . I met one who was loaded with so many *para* threaded one above the other that they formed a solid surface. She was wearing more than 10,000 pieces, if one included those on her head and tresses.

2. ROSES AND OTHER SPECIAL CROPS

M. Blanqui, *Voyage en Bulgarie pendant l'année 1841*, Paris, 1843, pp. 230–2.

BULGARIA is destined to become rich one day from the cultivation of certain crops which I shall call industrial, such as rice, flax, tobacco, madder, sesame, cotton and roses. In the region of Eski-Zaar and Kazanlǎk are to be found these fields of rose-bushes . . . the production is considerable and the demand comes entirely from the East, where it will always be as large as the producers can satisfy. . . . Tobacco is another such crop which yields considerable revenues, flourishing particularly in the low fertile lands, and I must admit that Turkish tobacco is much superior to all others. . . . Sesame cultivation has in recent times been enormously extended. . . . Rice, the cultivation of which centres on the great plain of Philipopolis,[1] is farmed under the administration. . . .

But the fortunes of Bulgarian agriculture will rest above all on stock-raising, numbers being already very great in the country, especially oxen, buffaloes, sheep and unfortunately also goats, to be reckoned by the hundred thousand, but without any serious commercial value. A pair of working oxen fetches less than 80 francs, a sheep five and two goats are sold for the price of a sheep. Poultry of all sorts, chiefly chickens and turkeys, are so abundant that they are to be bought for 25 or 50 centimes a piece. . . .

When Bulgaria enjoys a régime of security, the immense regions which today are left to the ravages of goats and poor pasturage will be put under cultivation. Then the country will be able to sustain a population three or perhaps five times as great as the present. The

[1] Plovdiv.

silkworm, of which southern Turkey has hitherto held the monopoly, would add its profits to those of other branches of industrial agriculture.

3. FARMING AND FORESTRY

A. P. Vretos, *La Bulgarie ancienne et moderne*, St. Petersburg, 1856, pp. 156–68.

WITH the growth of a more liberal administration in Bulgaria, cereal cultivation has likewise greatly increased, for of all peoples— at least in the Orient—the Bulgarians devote most care to their fields; only the methods of work remain just what they were in ancient times. The earth is only worked to a small depth and with ploughshares so imperfect that they barely scratch it. . . .

The farmer is free to choose from the vast plains of his country the field most suitable for sowing. These lands, with certain exceptions, belong to the government, which grants their use to whoever wants to sow them on the sole tacit condition of tithe payment. Such facilities should have put the farming class in a comfortable and happy position, were it not exposed to the various pesterings of government agents who abuse their simplicity and timidity to extort money from them on every sort of pretext.

The Ottoman farmers are held to ransom in an even more revolting way by the purchasers of their wheat in the maritime towns of the Black Sea, Varna and Balchik, where they go to sell it and where reside the alleged wheat merchants who are usually only agents of the great trading houses in Constantinople. These despicable creatures employ for their enrichment every illicit means condemned by morals and religion. Woe betide the Consul who should venture to repress these iniquities. Slander and sometimes destitution would be his reward for not having been able to close his eyes and ears.

The numerous and extremely dense and vast forests one sees in Bulgaria could afford trade an article of great importance and the state a very considerable revenue, if care were taken of the woods and forests. Oak, beech, ash, elm and mulberry exist there in great abundance. But the government draws no profit from all these woods, though it is the sole owner of them, because it has not yet found a practical way to administer them. Not a single forest guard is to be met with, and the incredible carelessness of the charcoal-burners who go about their job in the actual forests makes it a real miracle if fires do not take place frequently. . . . Cutting takes place continuously without selection of trees and at the first comer's whim. Indeed, for their home use the peasants choose the finest and most mature trees suitable for ship-building. Most act thus with the culpable object of forestalling forced labour, should the government wish them transported to some roadstead and used for the navy. Others cut wood to sell it and in fear of being denounced to the government, try to obtain its permission for wood-cutting by a vizir's firman. Once obtained, be it for even a very small amount of wood, the firman is used to cover a long term of cutting controlled by no inspector. Should by chance some remonstrance come from the local authorities or customs officer of the place into which the cut wood is brought, they reply with unruffled assurance that they have cut only a tiny part of their firman concession. Export of wood abroad is done by contraband in the Fonduceli roadstead (a few miles from Varna) and at Mesembria. Export of wood for building and burning is permitted only to Ottoman subjects but in practice is never forbidden to foreigners. Permission is always obtained by a firman issued from Constantinople. . . .

Bulgaria with its excellent pasturages does not contain the great variety of horned cattle herds which it could support, because the herdsmen are subjected to the same irritations as the farmers at the hands of the government's agents. The pasturages abound with buffaloes, oxen, goats, sheep and horses. Mules, donkeys and pigs exist in very small quantity. The consumption of these last is very limited; pork is eaten by Bulgarian Christians only in the last days of the carnival (before Lent). Little use is made of mules and donkeys, everyone preferring to ride horses like their ancestors. The horses are mostly small but very strong and agile. Buffalo herds outnumber those of oxen, because their strength makes them more useful for goods transport and the milk they give in plenty is one of the chief articles of consumption. Buffaloes are estimated at two million and oxen at one million, of which several thousand are yearly exported to Hungary. Export of wool-bearing animals is also quite considerable.

The wool of sheep and ewes is bought, even before shearing, by government agents for their factories at Selimno.[1] They buy more than they need, to sell the excess secretly to Adrianople[2] merchants with whom they have connived in advance. Thus everywhere abuse takes place at the expense of the poor Bulgarians. All the rest of the wool is sold to cloth manufacturers at Schoumla[3] and Tărnovo. . . .

A type of cheese called Katzicavalli[4] and made from milk of ewe and goat is exported in large quantities to Constantinople, as are also

[1] Sliven.   [2] Edirne.   [3] Shumen.   [4] Kashkaval.

buffalo butter and ox fat. The skins of these beasts untanned and with the horns still attached—a curious practice—are exported to Constantinople and so abroad. Those destined for Hungary are sent up the Danube by the Ruschuk[1] route.

In the lakes of Bulgaria and on the banks of the Danube fish of various sizes and excellent quality are caught in great quantity. The fishing of both these and leeches is unrestricted. Leeches, now become rare in Europe because of the great use made of them nowadays by medical science, still abound in Bulgaria. They are caught in numerous lakes and other marshy places. They may be exported only by the dealer who has bought the monopoly direct from the Ministry of the Sublime Porte, though the government does not forbid anyone to catch and use them, but if they are to be sold they must be given up to the dealer.

The dealers buy the right to export this article so necessary to humanity to all regions of the Ottoman Empire and subsequently sell to others their right in one or more provinces. A total of 70 to 80 quintals[2] of leeches is exported each year from Bulgaria to Constantinople, where the general depot of the chief dealer, Mr. D. Sakellarides, a Greek subject, is situated. The dues paid by him to the Sublime Porte amount to 15,000 francs a year.

In general the people of Bulgaria are not subject to heavy taxes and easily pay the direct and indirect taxes which are imposed on them. Each parish pays a tax proportional to its financial means, spread by the local authority among each family and varying from 15 to 100 fr. according to the value of its patrimony and means. This tax is fixed for the *raya* by their respective elders, the Chorbajis.[3] These latter are elected by universal suffrage of their fellow citizens, and it is from them that the local authority chooses the mayor of the parish (*Cogiabassi*) who defends its interests before the authorities and participates in sessions of the *Soura*.

The Cogiabassi, with his colleague Chorbajis, is responsible for the taxes imposed on the population. He thereby exercises a certain juridical influence on them and, likewise assisted by the Chorbajis, acts among his co-religionaries as a justice of the peace or magistrate sending the parties at dispute before the local authorities if he cannot settle their dispute amicably.

The *raya* are also subjected to the personal tax of the *kharaj*[4] (capitation) which is 7 fr. 50 for owners of livestock and 3 fr. 50 for other individuals who have attained legal age. Women alone are exempt as they are throughout the Orient. The collection of this tax, by an ordnance of the reigning Sultan promulgated in 1851,

[1] Ruse.   [2] 1 quintal = 0·1 metric tons.   [3] See pp. 225-7.   [4] See p. 295 below.

must be effected by the bishops of the Christian subjects and the chiefs of the Judaic cult, that their co-religionaries might no longer be troubled by abuses of government agents, sometimes even rousing the *raya* to revolt, as happened in Bulgaria in 1841 in the chief towns of Niš, Sofia and Vidin.

With regard to indirect taxes, besides the tithe which the government levies on agricultural products, the Bulgarian must pay 2½ per cent of the sum that his animals fetch at the market. Owners of oxen, buffaloes and horses pay a fixed licence fee of 1½ fr. per head. Owners of goats and sheep, in addition to the tithe they must pay for their grazing rights in the government's valley, must also pay a tax called *chubuk parasi* of 20 para (five French sous) per head. Shepherds who are itinerant or stay only one year in these pasturages are exempt from this tax. This causes endless disputes between these shepherds and the tax agents called Beylixides,[1] charged with collecting this tax, as well as the tithe calculated on the number of goats and sheep in each flock. These tax agents are required to give the shepherds a receipt certifying the number of animals taxed, but the dishonesty with which they do this counting causes disputes and endless troubles for the poor shepherds. The law requires the tithe to be paid in money and not in kind, yet the tax agents, in greed and abuse of their office, insist in being paid in kind, and choose the fattest animals to sell them afterwards and earn the excess on the tax. Confident of their rights, the shepherds resist these agents, whereat the latter depart refusing to give them their receipts—lucky is he who escapes being wounded by these agents, armed as they are from head to foot.

4. THE PEASANT STANDARD OF LIVING

(a) In the 1820s

R. Walsh, *Narrative of a Journey from Constantinople to England*, London, 3rd edition, 1829, pp. 199–202.

THE great body of them is altogether pastoral, and live in small hamlets, forming clusters of houses, which have neither the regularity nor deserve the name of towns. They have a few, however, where they are engaged in commerce and carry on manufactures. The town of Selymnia,[2] on the south side of the Balkan, contains nearly 20,000 inhabitants, the large majority of whom are Bulgarians. Here they fabricate, to a great extent, several manufactured articles,

----

[1] i.e. *beglikchii*. See p. 225 below.   [2] Sliven.

which are famous in Turkey; one is a coarse woollen cloth and another, rifle gun garrels, which are held in high esteem. But that which is most congenial to their rural habits is the preparation of the essential oil, called otto or attar of roses. A large district, in the neighbourhood of Selymnia, is laid out in gardens for this purpose; and the abundance of rose trees adds another feature to this beautiful country. A great part of the produce is brought to England; and we are indebted to these simple peasants for the most exquisite and elegant perfume in nature.

Of all the peasantry I have ever met with, the Bulgarians seem the most simple, kind and affectionate; forming a striking contrast with the rude and brutal Turks, who are mixed among them, but distinguished by the strongest traits of character. On the roads we frequently met groups of both, always separate, but employed in the same avocations; the Turks were known by turbans, sashes, pistols and yatigans, but still more by a ferocity of aspect, a rude assumption of demeanour and a careless kind of contempt, that at once repulsed and disgusted us. . . . The Bulgarians were distinguished by caps of brown sheepskin; jackets of cloth, made of the wool, undyed, of dark brown sheep, which their wives spin and weave; white cloth trousers and sandals of raw leather, drawn under the sole and laced with thongs over the instep. . . . The Bulgarian women are exceedingly industrious and are never for a moment without their spindle and distaff; they frequently asked for needles. . . . Their villages generally consist of forty or fifty houses, scattered without order or regularity. Their houses are built of wickerwork, plastered, and are clean and comfortable in the inside; where we were neither annoyed by smoke, or fleas, or bugs, or bad smells, or any of the torments which beset the rich in the houses of the poor; and one end is generally filled with bags of wool, or bales of cloth or carpet. They seem to possess all the necessaries of life in abundance; a mild climate, a fertile soil, a beautiful country, cattle, corn, wine, wood and water, in profusion.

Robert Walsh, LL.D., Rector of Finglass, Ireland, Chaplain to Lord Strangford, British Ambassador in Constantinople. Author of works on Dublin, Constantinople, Brazil and the history of the early Christians, published 1818–39.

(b) In the 1860s

Henry C. Barkley, *Between the Danube and the Black Sea*, London, 1876, pp. ix–xi.

THE Bulgar villager produces by his individual industry almost everything he requires in the world. The clothes of both men and women are entirely home made. The men wear a sheep-skin cap, either black or white, a short rough jacket of good home-spun cloth over a waistcoat of the same, loose baggy knickerbockers, cloth gaiters, and cow-skin moccasins. Their underclothes consist of a linen shirt and drawers made from home-grown flax. The women, in summer, wear a handkerchief twisted into their long hair, a linen jacket gathered in at the waist, and a home-spun woollen petticoat reaching just below the knee, their feet and ankles left bare. In winter, both men and women wear sheep-skin jackets, the wool turned inside, and the exterior prettily embroidered.

The houses are well and substantially built of either timber, stone, or 'wattle and dab'; the dwelling-rooms are generally over a large stable, in which the cattle are housed at night. To economize warmth, of which a Bulgar never has too much, they leave a hole about as big as a man's head open through the floor of the rooms into the stable, through which ascends the heat generated by the cattle, and with it a smell you may almost see! This is rather trying for fastidious Europeans; but with this exception the rooms are comfortable, dry, clean and warm. Furniture there is next to none, for all squat on mats on the ground, after the manner of Turks. In the sleeping-room are always found piles of coverlids and woollen rugs, all made by the women, and also in most houses some home-made linen sheets. The coverlids are quilted, either with fine combed wool or the down off the bulrush, and all are warm and comfortable on a winter's night, and in summer form a soft bed to lie on. . . .

If only absolute security for person and property could be obtained, I believe Bulgaria would be one of the most prosperous countries in Europe; and even as it is, I should be glad to think that the labouring poor of England and Ireland were as well off, well clothed and well housed, as the Bulgars.

For biographical note see p. 243.

5. Merchants and Peasants

Henry C. Barkley, *Bulgaria before the War*, London, 1877, pp. 163–4.

THERE is no such thing in Turkey as commercial morality, and anyone who indulged in such a Quixotic notion would be thought a fool, and when one hears of a good merchant or trader, one at once understands he is a cunning, successful cheat. They are so proficient in the art of cheating, that they can seldom over-reach one another, so they all prey on the villager, both Turk and Christian, and consider they have done badly if they do not do him out of ten to fifteen per cent on every bargain they make.

When the corn is coming up from the villages, the merchants' touts may be seen far away on the road trying to make a bargain. 'The price of corn has suddenly gone down. No ships are in the harbour. The governor is buying up the corn in the town, at a nominal price, for the Government.' In this way the peasant is induced to make a bad bargain before he reaches the town. Then his corn is measured out of his bullock-carts with false measures, and when the number of measures is mounting up, and there is a biggish row of notches on the tally-stick, one may constantly hear a dispute going on. The teller has dropped suddenly from calling 510 to 410. The peasant corrects him, and is at once shown the stick with its notches; a dispute is carried on for an hour or more, but as perhaps a dozen different peasants are all discharging into one magazine, and it was perhaps half full of corn previously stored, nothing can be done. Then, the bland, oily merchant arrives on the scene. He hates disputes, would rather lose his money than quarrel with friends, etc., and so 'we will split the difference, and go on counting from 460. Ah! you won't have it so? Then come before the governor, and we will ask him if a consul is likely to swindle. Come along!'

For biographical note see p. 243.

6. Commercial and Economic Groups

S. S. Bobchev, *Novi prinosi i osvetleniya za bălgarskoto văzrazhdanĕ* (New Contributions and Light on the Bulgarian Renascence), Sofia, 1937, pp. 67–72; 74–5; 42–4; 75–7.

(a) Cattle-dealers

THE *djelepi* were formerly a class or category of the *raya*, whose names were recorded in special registers with the obligation of supplying the state with large and small[1] livestock in prescribed numbers. This was in the early times of Osman rule, in the sixteenth to eighteenth centuries, and perhaps even up to the *Tanzimat* reforms (1839–40).[2] At the close of the eighteenth and especially at the beginning of the nineteenth century, however, after the reforms of Selim III and Mahmud II, this type of *djelepin* ceased to exist. Since, however, suppliers of cattle were urgently needed either for the army

[1] i.e. goats and sheep as well as horned cattle. [2] See p. 250 below, footnote 3.

in time of campaign or at Edirne and Constantinople, the profession was readily adopted by voluntary *djelepi*. Hence the definition of 'dealers in cattle (large and small stock)' to be found in all stories, chronicles and dictionaries, as, for example, in Sami Bey's well-known Turkish dictionary: 'Merchant-dealer in cattle (large and small stock) for raising and re-sale. Both dealing and raising is done by experienced assistants. *Djeleplik* is the occupation of the owner of a *djelep*. . . .'

I have been told how on their arrival in Kotel these dealers used to attract attention by their picturesque and elegant clothing. Clad in clothes covered with filigree work with (as overdress) a *chepken* (a short sleeveless cloak likewise finished in filigree), they bristled with arms in their broad sashes (pistols and knives) and, as they rode on their fine roan-black horses, attracted the attention of their countrymen, inspiring pride in their lordly state and the great influence they enjoyed with the local Turkish *subashi*[1] and *kadiyi*.[2] From my inquiries of elderly inhabitants of Koprivshtitsa and Kotel, it can be concluded that the richest, most notable *djelepi* in our past came from Panagyurishte and Koprivshtitsa. The top people and men of substance from these towns devoted themselves to buying and raising cattle which they drove to Edirne and Constantinople to sell wholesale. On arrival in Constantinople, the wealthy Koprivshtitsa *djelepi*, whose herds and flocks were driven by special herdsmen, were met and received by local wholesale buyers, and a price per oka was agreed for the cattle on the hoof. To estimate the cattle's value without calculating difference in weight, the buyer selected the feeblest beast and the *djelepin* the fattest; then each was weighed separately and the sum of their weights divided by two, this average being taken as the weight per head.

Almost all this is confirmed by those experts in this work, the men of Kotel, with houses and stockyards in Dobrudja, who raise great numbers of cattle, often several together in partnership. Some of them bought large and small stock like the Koprivshtitsa men, drove them to Edirne and Constantinople for wholesale dealing, and so became *djelepi*.

These dealers were influential people in the districts where they bought and raised cattle, and also in Edirne, and especially in Constantinople with the pashas, vizirs and the Sultan himself, to whom they presented the pick of their cattle either for Bairam sacrifice or for other occasions. Their intercessions to the dignitaries, officials and Sultan himself were often respected (all the more as they were on the spot) when made on behalf of someone unjustly thrown into

---

[1] Police officers.   [2] Magistrates.

prison or exiled to Diar-Bekir in Asia Minor. What distinguished them far more, however, was the sacrifices they made in their home districts to support schools, churches and above all monasteries, especially the Rila monastery, which is adorned with the names of Koprivshtitsa and Panagyurishte *djelepi*, whose houses in Plovdiv often became a refuge for the persecuted and oppressed.

(b) Tax-contractors

The word *beglik* (Tk. *beylik*) has several meanings: it may denote a coffer, a treasure, or the state treasury, something appertaining to institutions or the state; but it may also mean the tax gathered as a tithe of sheep and goats on behalf of the treasury. The tax is fixed in advance and sold by public auction, the buyer having the right as *beglikchiya* to collect it, within the limits, of course, of traditional law and custom.

Beglikchii of this sort existed throughout Bulgaria. As men of substance who paid in advance a sum equivalent to the *beglik* for a whole district, often for a whole province, they, like the *djelepi*, attracted the attention of the Turkish officials, who treated such rich men with a certain respect, making them various concessions, hearing their petitions, releasing prisoners on their appeal, or putting in a word to the magistrate for the repair of old dilapidated churches and sometimes even for the building of new ones. . . .

In the words of K. Jireček, speaking of the rich Plovdiv *beglikchii* whom he graces with the title of 'patrician': 'These notables were mainly *beglikchii*, men who leased from the government the collection of the *beglik* or tithe of cattle which grazed in great herds and flocks on the mountains and plains of the whole of European Turkey; they were mostly natives of Koprivshtitsa. . . . Some of them were also in the Turkish service and were treated with great respect in Constantinople.'[1]

(c) Notables

A critical examination shows that the institution of *chorbajiya*, despite certain ugly aspects, was an important factor in our national renascence. It was virtually a spontaneous Bulgarian phenomenon. In other Balkan countries its appearance was sporadic, occurring only in some places and never playing the great role which characterizes it in Bulgaria.

The term *chorbajiya* comes from the Turkish or, rightly speaking,

[1] K. Jireček, *Cesty po Bulharsku* (Travels in Bulgaria), Prague, 1888, i, 4, p. 104; see p. 255 below.

Q

Arabic word *chorba* (broth). *Chorba* was the staple diet of the Corps of Janissaries. The *chorbajiya* there was its cook, and everywhere where there were janissary cookhouses, there were head-*chorbajii* in charge of catering.

As the more well-to-do householders in Bulgaria entertained their Turkish rulers as visitors to their houses, such householders were for these rulers *chorbajii*. The word assumed the wider meaning of heads of households and of the various local institutions and organizations to do with commerce, crafts, etc. Finally, a *chorbajiya* came to mean every well-off, more or less substantial and therefore influential Bulgarian.

The *chorbajiya* idea well suited the Turkish administrative authorities as an auxiliary institution and intermediary class to facilitate and expedite their duties. It was particularly convenient for the many scattered little police-sergeant posts. In every small town where there was a *subash* (police-officer), and especially where there was no population other than Bulgarian, the *subash* was surrounded by the most influential notables or elders. On all questions of local government: roads, communications, forced labour, stamp duties and licences, disputes, etc., the *subash* would turn by tradition to these leading people of the district for counsel, though he was under no legal obligation to do so.

Small disputes, such as quarrels, assault or damage to farmland, the *subash* would usually settle in conjunction with the elders, but often, without any formalities, he would remand the disputing parties to the notables themselves, who had their own council and would decide the issue according to their conscience; should the opponents not agree among themselves to carry out the decision, then the *subash* would impose it on them. In this way the *chorbajii* became an important institution, and for this reason the authorities themselves turned to these notables, great and small, and offered them various government offices: tax-gatherers, liaisons with Turkish officials and the like.

In conformity with this policy, the local regional authorities (voyvodas, pashas, etc.) for their own convenience and by way of providing parish autonomy for the population, recognized the elected mayor as a *bash-chorbajiya* (i.e. senior elder) and sometimes even as a *memleket-chorbajiya* (county elder). To make manifest the relations of the authorities to these notables the governor would call the elected person to the local centre and in token of investiture hand him a club, saying: 'Be henceforth *chorbajiya* of such and such a place.'

Through these notables relations between the authorities and population were greatly facilitated. Not everywhere, however, did they enjoy the full confidence of their electors and taxpayers. The latter often became discontented and rebellious.

Together with complaints against the people's oppressors (i.e. the Turks) there also came complaints against the notables to the regional authorities and even to the central government in Constantinople itself. In 1857 a decree was issued to regulate the position and legal standing of *chorbajii*; it recognized the *chorbajiya* as an institution, defined its function, services, pay in election time, rendering of accounts, etc.

Here it must be stressed that the notables, whether they were simply men of influence, not in service, or were in service and so able to help the population, or were self-made men who had raised themselves above others by their intelligence and talents—all took part in national activities such as the church and school committees and guild associations; in many places they even built churches and bridges, protected the people, opened their eyes, upheld in them the spirit of self-confidence, and in their direst misfortunes gave them to understand that their slavery was approaching its end and that the most important instrument in this was education, i.e. the Bulgarian school, language and book.

Thus the notables acted not only as men of influence with the government and participators in the *subash* councils, but also as intermediaries between the people and the authorities in administrative and police matters, channels through which they could very effectively help the people in their private affairs; they were the church governors, monastery patrons and protectors of those old school teachers who were persecuted by the Greek bishops and others.

In the ranks of the leading merchants, guild grandmasters, *djelepi* and such like, they were the chief initiators and builders of the various positions essential to the renascence.

There is no town, large or small, or village of any size in Bulgaria which cannot point to some such notable, who distinguished himself by his influence, resources, counsel and defence of the poor.

(d) The Guilds

The guilds (*esnafi*)[1] are trade corporations which appeared in our land very early in the period of Osman rule, originating from Turkey, (more strictly, from Anatolia) or from the Western guild system. It is a fact that an extraordinary number of Turkish names and terms

[1] See pp. 268–9 below.

refer to the structure of the guilds, their functions and outer forms. This circumstance led the great Slavonic philologist and authority on guilds, Professor B. Tsonev, to insist on the idea that our guilds were of Turkish origin.

Being a universal factor in local economic life, and one of interest to the administration and society in general, the guilds in many places occupied a notable place in the hierarchy of social activity. All trades had their guild organization, but some of these guilds had superior standing, wide geographical range, strong management and boundless influence. Such for instance was the tanners' guild.

Each guild was headed by a council who chose a grandmaster (*protomaystor*) as its president (*ustabashiya*, in Sofia *iit-bashiya*). His associate was a *chaush* (executive officer) who carried out the council's arrangements and the president's orders.

Apart from this council there was a great assembly of guilds called the *londja* (Italian *loggia*). This great assembly represented a kind of parliament, the decisions of which were binding for all guilds and all craftsmen—in a word, it legislated. Its sphere of legislation was wide, including: the relations between masters and apprentices in the period of service during which the *chirak* (apprentice) became a *kalfa* (journeyman), and often even a *maystor*; the *maystors'* methods of production, their duties and rights and those of the guilds in general, the relations of the guilds to the authorities, infringements of the guilds' statutes or accepted rules; punishments which the *maystor*, guild council and the highest body (*londja*) had the right to impose. These punishments were very varied: fines, giving wax for candles, beating, temporary closing of establishment or total deprivation of the right to practise a certain profession, which was the equivalent of the death sentence in respect of membership of the guild and so of a craftsman's activity. This was called *kyustyah* (from the Persian *kyustakh*). This last penalty could only be imposed by the supreme assembly (*londja*).

In many towns the guilds (grocers', furriers', tailors', cloth-dealers', etc.) had quite well-organized funds which helped in the maintenance of local schools and churches, and undertook the construction and opening of the same. According to official data, in Sofia there were 63 guilds, of which 20 were exclusively Bulgarian while the others, in which Bulgarians also participated, included Turkish, Jewish and Armenian members.

It is hardly necessary to add that, thanks to the legal position of the guilds and their recognition by the authorities and to the fact that some guilds included not only Bulgarians but also Turks, their influence was extremely great, and they were able to protect churches, schools and all who were assailed by the Grecomanes, Greek bishops and other unscrupulous sources.

Stefan Savov Bobchev (1853–1940), Professor of Law in Sofia University, was the author of numerous studies in Bulgarian law, history and folk-lore.

7. REFORMS OF MIDHAT PASHA (AFTER 1857)

N. T. Obretenov, *Spomeni za bălgarskite văzstaniya* (Reminiscences of the Bulgarian Risings), Sofia, 1942, pp. 28–31; 70–4.

WITH the coming of Midhat Pasha[1] as governor in Ruse, great changes took place in the life of the Bulgarians who till then had been in a very pitiful condition. His assumption of power was at once felt by Turks and Bulgarians alike. He was a highly educated man with a strong will and great tact. His ambition was to restore the health of the Ottoman Empire in which various companies of Circassians, together with bashi-bazouks and other brigand bands roamed like locusts ravaging and robbing the defenceless Bulgarian population. This calamitous situation directly provoked the Bulgarian rebellions of 1841 (Niš), 1850 (Western Bulgaria) and 1856 (*Dyado* Nikolov's). To meet the indignation which had spread rapidly among the Bulgarians, immediate measures had to be taken and something had to be done to improve conditions. Midhat Pasha as a great reformer sought to pacify the land at a single sweep. In a short time he managed to quell the brigandage for which the immigrant Circassians had been mainly responsible, and thereby rendered secure the property and estate of the Bulgarian population in the villages. Simultaneously, he worked at increasing the prosperity of his province.

He used state lands to create the model farm estate near Ruse called 'Model Chiflik'[2] [which today houses the Agricultural School]. By its creation he sought to further improvements in agriculture and here for the first time modern agriculture was demonstrated with

---

[1] The Turkish statesman Midhat Pasha (1822–84) was the chief protagonist of reform in the Empire in the third quarter of the nineteenth century. After undertaking the reforms in Bulgaria described above, he became Governor of Niš in 1860 and there carried out similar reforms. In 1866 as Governor of Baghdad he reformed the administration, though with less success. He was twice Grand Vizier, but was finally defeated by his enemies and in 1879 was dismissed, tried and condemned to death, the sentence being commuted to banishment on the intercession of the British Government. He died in exile in Arabia.

[2] From Tk. *chiftlik*, estate.

the ploughs, harvesters and threshers he obtained [but unfortunately these were soon abandoned to rust for lack of repairs]. To advance viticulture new varieties of vine cuttings were brought from Asia. Midhat likewise did a great deal to encourage artisan crafts and commerce. Most important of all, with his coming the Bulgarians found a 'shield'. Under him many Bulgarians were appointed to senior official posts. In Ruse especially he made great changes and reforms which did not, however, greatly please his compatriots because he gave 'surat' (priority) to the giaours (Christians). Midhat thereby earned himself the nickname of Giaour-pasha. Actually Midhat was a great and far-seeing Turk who worked ardently at restoring the health of the Turkish state. . . .

On taking over the province, Midhat Pasha obtained and installed a press to inaugurate his cultural and educational work. He arranged for the publication of the government paper 'Dunav'. The press employed about ten to fifteen young Bulgarians, seven to eight young Turks, a couple of foreigners and some twenty to thirty prisoners to do the chores. This press had great services to its credit in training typesetters both for the emigrant presses started in Bucharest and for some of the Constantinople papers, as well as those of our State Press (founded in 1881). This work of Midhat's was indeed a great cultural achievement for European Turkey (as it was then) and played a constructive role for us Bulgarians too. Here were printed many Bulgarian books which were avidly read by the people.

In a few years there was a noticeable advance in the prosperity of the population. Bulgarians could engage in commerce and trades. With the establishment of this equality of Christians and Mohammedans before the provincial authorities, many Bulgarians began to come down from the Balkan mountains and settle in Ruse.

Among these settlers was a cooper named Gatyu. When he began to practise his trade of barrel-making, the Turkish coopers complained about him to the pasha. Gatyu was summoned by the pasha to be informed that the coopers' guild did not permit him to make barrels, to which he replied: 'Pasha effendi! I will make a barrel without hoops and will bring it to you, rolling it along the street without its breaking apart. Let those in the guild make one like that too, and let the maystor of whichever turns out the stronger have the right to ply his trade.' A few days later Gatyu brought his barrel to the *konak*, but the Turks refused to make one. The pasha then gave him permission to ply his trade. Gatyu was the first Bulgarian cooper in Ruse. Till then the coopers had been Turks and at the vintage the Bulgarian vineyard-keepers had had great difficulty in

persuading them to visit their houses and clamp up the wine
barrels. . . .

Midhat Pasha opened a school-hostel for poor children and waifs
and strays, called 'Islyahane'. In it were collected all the waifs and
strays regardless of faith and nationality. These children learned
reading and writing, and also various trades such as iron-work,
carriage-making, saddlery, printing, cobbling, carpentry, fishing,
etc. The young Bulgars, who were the more intelligent of the children, studied type-setting in the press of the paper 'Dunav'. In
Islyahane there were Bulgarian teachers for the Bulgarian children
to study the Bulgarian language. The teacher-maystors for the trades
were foreigners. The young gipsies learned fishing. The aim was that
all pupils leaving the school-hostel should know some trade, in order
to be able to earn their livelihood.

Midhat Pasha collected the pupils who had completed their
course to make carriages, covered outside with leather and furnished
inside with red cloth, mirrors, little windows with coloured window-
panes, bells and other embellishments. Some worked the iron part
of the carriage, others the wooden parts and others the leather.
These carriages were very beautiful and were called 'Sherket
arabasa'. The company which made them was called 'Sherket'; even
the street in which they made these carriages was known until two
or three years ago as Sherket Street. For the making of these carriages and later of phaetons, Ruse held first place not only in
Bulgaria but even abroad; thus, for instance, people came from
Bucharest to buy phaetons from Ruse. . . .

It was said that Midhat Pasha was disgusted at the exorbitant
interest which some Bulgarian chorbajiyas[1] charged. . . . For this
reason, he arranged for agricultural savings clubs to be formed to
supply the population with cheap credit. To achieve this aim every
cultivator (peasant or townsman) had to give yearly from the
threshing floor one *shinik* of corn for every pair of beasts of burden;
and this corn was sold to provide capital for the fund.

The most solid achievement of Midhat Pasha was the linking of
towns by high-roads and bridges, then called 'king's roads'. Thus
the town of Ruse was linked by a high-road with Niš via Byala,
Pleven, Orhanie, Araba-Konak, Sofia. The road forked at Byala for
Tărnovo. A special ceremony inaugurated work on these roads. The
governor invited the councils of each faith to the place where the
Tărnovo road was to begin; here every nationality made a public
prayer of supplication according to the rites of its faith. After finishing the prayer and before beginning the excavation of the road,

[1] See pp. 225-7.

first Midhat Pasha broke the soil with a pickaxe, after him—the Turkish Council, then the Bulgarian, and after it the leaders of the other faiths. The road to Varna was begun at Sara-bair, going through Razgrad, Shumen and Provadiya. All these roads were constructed by the forced labour of Bulgarians; saplings were planted along both sides and encircled with stakes which were cross-woven with canes. The purpose of planting these saplings was not only to improve the climate but also to make the road easily recognizable when buried under snow in winter.

With the organization of the roads, postal communications were also improved. Previously, letters were carried by couriers who were always neatly dressed in sandals; they had a bag over the shoulder for letters, and bells on their feet so that they could be recognized and immediately given right of way. Subsequently, the post was carried by Tartars who rode horses with leather pouches on them to hold the letters. This post used to go from Odrin[1] via Shumen and Razgrad. On coming to Sara-bair, the Tartars began to shout: 'Hu-u-u! Hu-u-u!' till they reached the place arranged for their halt in the town. Everyone who expected a letter had himself to go to where the post stopped to get his letter, written perhaps a month before. Should anyone be angry that his letter had not arrived sooner, he was told: 'You've got it now, what more do you want?' After the completion of the high-road, the post was brought in 'Sherket-arabasa' which later started taking in travellers also. There were stations along the high-road where fresh horses were always kept; here the tired ones were changed and others harnessed to continue the journey.

After the Crimean War, the Circassians were expelled from Russia and settled in Turkey. Midhat Pasha wanted to settle some in Bulgaria and with that object a commission was formed called 'the Circassian Commission'; it had the task of collecting help for settling Circassians in Bulgaria. This commission imposed on the population a new tax which was gathered by the collectors like the other taxes. The proceeds went towards the construction of a thermal bath above the Customs house, the hotel 'Islyahane' where the town council is housed today, the building of the former 'Palat' where the commissioner for the railway from Ruse to Varna then lived, a steam mill, two iron-works by the Danube, the fine hotel 'Gyulshen' which after our liberation became an arsenal and then a joinery school which was finally demolished when the quay was built.

In addition, Midhat Pasha built a hospital in every town of the whole Danube province; buildings were also constructed for the

[1] Adrianople, Edirne.

administration, everywhere built on one and the same plan. These were known by the name 'konak'.

After our liberation, a special envoy was sent from Constantinople to seek out the properties built by the Circassian Commission, but Petko Karavelov, then minister, apparently told him that the state could not interfere in these matters as they were the private concern of the Ruse municipality. When asked, the municipality in Ruse replied that these places were municipal and that no rent or tax had been paid for them. On hearing this, the official returned to Constantinople and these properties are to this day administered by the Ruse municipality.

Nikola T. Obretenov (1849–1939), a leading Bulgarian revolutionary, was imprisoned by the Turks for his part in the abortive rebellion of May 1875, led by Hristo Botev, whose death he witnessed. Released in 1878, he held the posts of district prefect in Tutrakan and county governor in Ruse and Sofia, and was elected to Parliament. The work quoted above was edited by Professor M. Arnaudov and published posthumously.

8. Changes in Pirdop District (1860s and 70s)

T. G. Vlaykov, *Prezhivyanoto* (Experiences), Sofia, vol. i (1934), vol. ii (1939), vol. iii (1942). Vol. ii, p. 257; 262–7; vol. i, pp. 77–8.

(a) An End to Forced Labour

At that time the women and children of our village used to go every summer to the rice fields—they were forcibly rounded up and driven off to the Pazarjik region to reap the rice crops of the beys there under forced labour (*angariya*). This work, it seems, was arduous and agonizing, and a great storm of complaint was raised each summer against this cursed 'rice labour'. One year *haji* Yovan, driving his livestock to Constantinople, met there a certain Bulgarian, an inner official in the Saray.[1] Through him he passed a petition to the Sultan himself, complaining that in his village women and children were driven by force to the rice *angariya* when the *angariya* was forbidden by firman. This petition of his was granted, and a royal order issued to the authorities in our township to abolish the rice *angariya*. The order was handed to *haji* Yovan himself for him to deliver it personally to the deputy-prefect. On his return to the village *haji* Yovan found that a company of women and girls had just been

[1] Sultan's Court.

rounded up to be sent to the rice labour in Pazarjik. *Haji* Yovan
went straight to the town hall where the company had been concentrated, threw open the gates, exclaiming: 'Come along, all of you,
off you go home! From now on there is to be no rice labour!' (The
royal order was duly obeyed and, though *haji* Yovan was abducted
by Turks and never seen again, an end was finally put to this rice
angariya. . . .)

(b) Turks and Bulgarians

The greatest owners of property among all the Turks in our village,
the Chekrovtsi, . . . always had two or three Bulgarian labourers each
and in summer, when work in the fields began, the women of the
whole village quarter went to hoe, reap and thresh for them. And
all the women made much of how their Turkish mistresses looked
after them so well, and attended to their needs.

[Apart from such rich people] the other Turks were all people of
average standing. They had courtyards with flowing streams, large
fountains and fruit trees. They lived by carting and farming; each
had his pair of oxen with which he would cultivate his own land and
most of them worked their oxen on other people's jobs as well. They
came to plough and cart waste, hay and sheaves for the Bulgarians
who rarely had a cart and oxen. They worked conscientiously too
and were much in demand by the Bulgarians. Their wives took in
wool for spinning from our braid-makers and cloth-makers (as Bulgarian women did likewise), receiving a few *grosh* per *oka* for this
work.

Turks and Bulgarians got on well together. The women of a village
quarter bordering on Turkish houses mixed with the Turkish women
in a neighbourly way, while the children played with the little Turks
as with their own playmates. The Turkish women and children
spoke Bulgarian quite well and the Bulgarians, like their children,
managed to get by in Turkish, the result being a sort of mixed *patois*.

Those Turks who worked at Bulgarian houses were accepted there
as close friends. . . . My playmates would argue with me which of
the [two] Turks [Uncle Musa and Uncle Bambala, who came to
work for our families] was the better.

We were used to the Turks. We Bulgarians lived our own life, to
be sure, we had our own dress, our own customs and stuck to our
own faith, while they lived in another way, had other customs and
other costume, their faith too was different. But all this we took as
being in the order of things. In the order of things also was the
wearing of hats by our older people and of turbans by the Turks, of
a *sukman* (gown) and headcloth by our women, while the Turkish

women wore their *feredje* (cloak) and covered their faces with a white veil. We would go to school, the Turks went to worship in the mosque. The clappers of our church were beaten morning and evening, while from the call-tower of the mosque the *hoja* would call five times each day and by that we knew throughout the day what time it was: when it was noon, when it was mid-afternoon and when it was late evening. We would celebrate Christmas and Easter, the Turks—Bairam. We Bulgarians went to school in our school building and the Turkish children to the Turkish school which was at the mosque. Each lived his own life. So it was appointed and so it went. . . .

Compared with the life of the Turks, our life was patently on a higher level. Take livelihoods. For the Bulgarians these were so varied—there were indeed hardly any trades, hardly any manufactures or fields of commerce in which they did not deal. As for the Turks, their agriculture was all they knew. And our leading people, our merchants and *chorbajii*—how much higher they stood in alertness of spirit, in national consciousness as well as in monetary wealth than the Turkish leading folk. Or again the schools: how did ours and the Turkish ones stand? . . . My father once took me to the Turkish school to buy from the *hoja* a reed for pens to write Turkish characters (for we were then learning Turkish too and Turkish is written with pens of brown reed such as were to be got only from the *hoja*). It was then that I saw the Turkish school: a little dilapidated room with an earth floor covered with rush matting. Not a bench, table or chair in it. Along the wall a score of boys squatting Turkish-wise, each holding an open book in his hand and all spelling aloud in unison. On one side the *hoja*, likewise squatting on the ground Turkish fashion, held an open book in his hand and corrected the pupils if they went wrong. Before him lay a long rod with which he gave a tap when some lad showed slackness. . . . When I compare this low, half-dark and bare room with our large, tall school with its fine front loggias, its wide bright rooms with glazed windows where there were so many pupils sitting on the benches, when I compare too that old and rather naïve little *hoja* with our young, enlightened teachers who taught us with such acumen and skill, I feel a kind of pride and a spiritual satisfaction in what we Bulgarians had. . . .

Yet for all this, we Bulgarians felt a sub-conscious fear of the Turks. Of our close acquaintances we were of course not afraid, for we looked on them as on our own and did not consider them as Turks. This feeling of fear we experienced towards those we did not know, towards the Turks in general: . . . thus coming back from church our people would walk in groups chatting freely, but no sooner did they reach the market square where Reshid's Turkish café was and where there were always Turks sitting outside, smoking their long chibuks and drinking coffee, than everyone would fall silent and pass by with bowed head. . . . Fear of the Turks was even more strongly felt among us children, . . . a fear which was unconsciously transferred even into our attitude to young Turkish children . . . thus when the little Turks would come out of their school at the mosque, we would dart off quickly up the hill so as not to meet them.

The fear of all our folk for the Turks arose from the fact that, although we lived in the village unoppressed by them, we felt nevertheless that they were the masters: the governor in the *konak* was a Turk; the bailiffs were Turks, the watchmen in summertime were Turks too. Then, the prefect and the judge in the citadel also were Turks. Turkish was the whole power. Turkish was the kingdom. And we Bulgarians were their subjects, we were their *raya*. . . .

(c) A Voluntary Health Service

On the subject of healing and an *ekimin* (doctor), I recall another episode from those times. . . . A Greek, Atanas the *ekimin*, as he was called, then acted as a kind of doctor in our village. The better-off people were always after him for treatment. But father never called him when there was someone ill in the house. Then one day there came to the village another doctor, a Koprivshtitsa man. They called him Sergiya. Why did a second doctor come when one was there already? Later I got to understand this matter. Some of the more go-ahead among the leading people would not have Atanas, it appeared, because he was a Greek. They wanted a Bulgarian doctor, and so they found this Koprivshtitsa man. But for him to agree to come, they had to fulfil a preliminary condition: at least forty persons had to bind themselves to pay 50 *grosh* each annually for doctoring their families throughout the year—something which in the language of today would be termed a subscription. My father was one of those who agreed to take on this obligation, and although our position was then pretty penurious, he found the means somehow to pay the required sum to ensure the permanent services of a Bulgarian doctor for our home.

Todor Genchof Vlaykov (1865–1942), author, social and educational reformer, and politician, was the leading figure of the Bulgarian *narodnik* movement of the eighteen-nineties and subsequently became a leader of the Bulgarian Radical Party and editor of its periodical, *Demokraticheski pregled*

(Democratic Review) (1905–25). He came from Pirdop, the district and inhabitants of which form the favourite setting of his *Razkazi i povesti* (Tales and Stories), stories written in his youth and retirement, and collected in his *Săchineniya* (Works), vol. i, Sofia, 1925; vol. ii, Pleven, 1926; vol. iii, Sofia, 1928). His writings on political, social, co-operative and agrarian problems comprise the remaining three volumes. He also wrote a literary self-analysis, *Zavoi* (Turning Points) (Sofia, 1935) and an autobiographical trilogy, *Prezhivyanoto* (Experiences), in which he recounts his *Childhood Years* (vol. i, Sofia, 1934), *Boyhood* (vol. ii, Sofia, 1939) and *School Years in Sofia* (vol. iii, Sofia, 1942). This work, in addition to being a valuable personal memoir, gives an illuminating picture of local Bulgarian life in the eighteen-seventies.

9. Competitive Crafts: Uzunjova Fair

M. Blanqui, *Voyage en Bulgarie pendant l'année 1841*, Paris, 1843, pp. 250–7.

INDUSTRY in Bulgaria has not the character it assumes in civilized Europe, and yet it is not unworthy of economists' attention. It is simple, individual, patriarchal and manual. There are no steam machines in Turkey, no mechanical spinning or weaving, no civil engineers, trained or experienced builders or clockmakers. The native people have, however, a very great aptitude for imitating processes better than their own, and one could make excellent cloth manufacturers out of the crude Balkan weavers. Their fulling and corn mills, their wheelwright shops and tanneries are certainly very backward, but their saddlery, braid and trimming, and embroidery could compete with the products of London or Vienna. . . . All trades are organized into corporations, governed by a kind of elected syndicate, which metes out justice and represents its members before the authorities. . . .

Commerce inevitably reflects the feeble state of the industries. The Turks seem more suited to it than the Bulgarians, and trade lies almost entirely in their hands. One can judge what it must be like in a country where a bill of change is almost unknown, where the currency has from century to century been repeatedly altered, where the average rate of interest is 20 per cent, and where the difficulties resulting from the diversity of written and spoken dialects complicate all relations. The absence of communications gives rise daily to the queerest contrasts of dearth and abundance. Thus, while wood for fuel abounds in the Balkan mountain forests and forage in the plains, these two articles fetch such a high price in Constantinople that they are sold by the pound like bread. Any merchandise which cannot, like cattle, transport itself, or is not of small volume like certain precious objects, can only be marketed within a very narrow region. Apart from the bazaars of the larger towns, internal commerce is reduced to the supplying of small shops carrying a little stock. One could not understand how the producers in European Turkey could place their products, had they not the aid of certain large fairs where within a few days is concentrated all the activity brought to a standstill during the rest of the year.

Uzunjova is a town of two thousand inhabitants, the situation of which, almost exactly halfway between the Black Sea, the Danube and the Mediterranean, would not seem at first sight to justify the preference accorded to it as the site for the great fair which takes place there every year in September. But as the internal meeting-point of all the European provinces of the Empire, this municipality seems well chosen by reason of its central position. Its streets and environs had already been invaded by countless wooden booths similar to those improvised by our own merchants at Beaucaire and Guibray. Open-air theatres, jugglers, tooth-extractors, menagery-managers took up a part of the site, devoting themselves to the same exercises as ours, and yet the appearance of the fair differed in more than one respect from its counterpart in our civilized countries. No police or public force, as far as could be seen, presided at this enormous reunion of more than fifty thousand men, wherein the most perfect order never failed to reign. Greeks and Bulgarians, Moldavians and Wallachians, Turks and Persians, Austrians and Russians, Jews and Christians were present at this reunion, and lived in perfect harmony, with no other object than to do some good business and earn money. The consuls of the various European powers had arrived to watch over the interests of their nationals; ours was conspicuous by his absence.

I was particularly struck by the splendour of certain of the merchants who figured at this important fair. One of them, from Wallachia, we were told, displayed a shop full of furs superior in their high quality and variety to those of the finest houses in Paris and London. His wares were folded in huge leather wallets covered like portfolios. . . . Not far from him, Persian traders were displaying their cashmere cloths, long, chequered and of a thousand brilliant shades; the manufacturers of Asia Minor spread out their velvet carpets of all sizes, and there were as many as twenty merchants of precious stones to be counted, all finding buyers. Colonial produce, drugs for dyeing, iron in bars, rice, leather, coarse and fine cloths, and cotton materials were in great demand. Glassware, porcelain, wools and silks were exchanged in considerable quantities. It was easy to see that all the buyers were stocking themselves for a whole year, and it is this which explained the almost delirious movements of such a conglomeration of men. The means of exchange at this fair consisted of ingots of silver and gold, which everyone could check by the touchstone.

The way in which these merchants contrived to live for a fort-night within such a restricted space was really remarkable. Only Orientals are capable of such *tours de force*. Their sobriety and the simplicity of their habits can alone explain how famine had not dissolved an assembly of such numbers within forty-eight hours. Those who had come in carriages used them as their dwellings, while others pitched their tents on the plain, spread their carpets and covered them with cushions, and could thus take up a house residence as though in their own native town. A few coffee-pots and kettles sufficed for the mobile kitchen, always very simple in the Orient, and reduced during travel to its bare minimum. Butchers killed the beasts in the fields; from a neighbouring forest wood was fetched for roasting the meats and fountains supplied the water. These various encampments were remarkable for their mutual tolerance and the general order which reigned everywhere. There were not even bad smells to be experienced, such was the care which each took in maintaining the cleanness of his surroundings from fear of averting prospective buyers by disagreeable impressions.

10. DOMESTIC INDUSTRIES

A. P. Vretos, *La Bulgarie Ancienne et Moderne*, St. Petersburg, 1856, pp. 165–6.

TĂRNOVO and Schoumla manufacture that cloth known locally as *souchno* or *aba*, fairly coarse and used by peasants and the poor of Bulgaria and even by those of Rumelia.[1] In the second of these towns carpets are also made, of rather inferior quality, but strong and of quite a good standard in blending of dyes and design. They sell on a large scale in Constantinople itself, where oriental luxury reigns. At Schoumla there is also a tannery for buffalo and ox leather to supply the inhabitants, and a factory for copper goods. At Gabrovo knives and other iron household utensils are made, which, as one might well imagine, are pretty rough.

Goldsmiths are not lacking in the towns and larger villages. Wheelwrights and blacksmiths are to be found in considerable

[1] See map and p. 244 below, footnote 1.

numbers in both the large and small towns and likewise in the villages, the smiths being mostly gipsies.

Finally, throughout Bulgaria the people, men and women, busy themselves with the making of mats of varying workmanship which are used to carpet rooms, even in the poorest huts. The heavy cloths manufactured at Tărnovo and Schoumla, together with the carpets of this town, are taken to the four important fairs which take place yearly, in April at Bazarjik, in May at Giouma, in June at Schoumla and in July at Carassou. The most important is that of Giouma, a town situated in the neighbourhood of Razgrad, a few hours from Ruschuk. As certain honourable merchants assured us, the value of merchandise sold at the Giouma fair of 1849 may be reckoned at two million francs. At these fairs there is a great sale of cloths, colonial goods, cotton and thread materials, dye products, groceries, iron strips, arms, steel ware, fabrics of gold and silver, furs, horses, and horned beasts. German merchants swarm there by the Ruschuk route.

11. MERCHANTS AND HAND-LOOM WEAVERS IN PIRDOP

T. G. Vlaykov, *Prezhivyanoto* (Experiences), Sofia, 1939, vol. ii, pp. 258–61.

AFTER the old *chorbajii*[1] come a series of other leading people in the village, younger than them, yet quite elderly. These are the merchants—merchants of cloth (*aba*) and heavy braid (*gaytan*). These merchants buy up loads of wool, distribute it to be spun, and their looms then weave it into this heavy cloth. The same merchants also buy up the braid. In the autumn, when they make these cloths and braids up into bales, they take off this merchandise to various lands, some to Serbia—these being very numerous—some to Rumania, and others to Macedonia and Albania. When they have sold out their goods, the merchants return in winter with much money. They all go about finely dressed in braided trousers and jackets of velvet cloth with multicoloured belts, tasselled fez and greatcoats lined with fine furs. Their women likewise always go finely dressed in gowns of costly colours, silk waistcoats and silk headdresses, gilded belt clasps, great strings of coins, and, in wintertime, velvet cloth coats with fox-fur lining. They all have fine houses, stucco-rendered outside and colourfully decorated inside with windows of

[1] See pp. 225-7 above.

glass panes and loggias extending on the sides. These merchants are many in number . . . all are forthright, lively people and held in great respect, for they give work and bread to many people in the village.

There are also several merchants who deal in another product—the manufacture of bath towels and napkins. In their houses and in special premises they have installed numerous looms where these towels and napkins are woven. Manufactured in large quantities, these products are taken off by these merchants each spring and autumn to Plovdiv and Zagora and to the fairs. Two of mother's brothers took up this manufacture and, together with Uncle Nedko's three sons, formed a kind of combine. Though in a more modest way than the other merchants, they too commanded respect in that they likewise provided work for many people.

Next, a set of publicans and innkeepers, grocers and tradesmen were considered as being among the leading people of the village. . . . Among the last were a fair number of pedlars who every autumn and spring took off a consignment of napkins, threads, needles and other such trifles to the highland districts and thence brought wool. . . . Along by the village river . . . were many rooms with bobbins which revolved and rattled all day and night. Under the eyes of the girls the braid was woven there, later to be bought up by the merchants. A lot of people kept bobbins in their rooms and earned their living from braid-making.

Scattered through the village were a fair number of people of various trades: bobbin-makers who made new ones and repaired old; tailors who worked in their own houses where they sewed men's and women's clothes; a number of cobblers, too, and slipper-makers and several shoe-makers; also dyers, who dyed the yarn and the braid, furcoat-makers, goldsmiths and coopers; and also many carpenters.

But most numerous of all were the weavers, for almost the whole range of merchandise exported from Pirdop—cloth and rugs, towels, napkins and kerchieves—was all worked on looms, so that in the lower village quarter (*mahala*) one would come across a loom in nearly every other house; still more numerous were the spinstresses—all the widows and quite a few of the married women too, earning their living by the spinning-wheel. All day long until late in the evenings, the village was filled with the continuous sound of spinning-wheels whirring, looms banging, cogs rattling and mallets tapping.

In summertime the world of Pirdop lay scattered across the fields and meadows and the whole landscape was filled with the noise of hoes, the ringing of scythes and sickles and the creaking of carts. . . .

R

So all through the year there was a ceaseless bustle of life in the village and over the fields—everyone busy at work and a livelihood for each.

For biographical note see pp. 236–7.

12. COMMUNICATIONS

(a) Roads and the River

A. P. Vretos, *La Bulgarie Ancienne et Moderne*, St. Petersburg, 1856, p. 169.

NEITHER government nor parishes have so far turned to opening up communication routes, whether public or special. Everywhere there reigns a state of nature. The roads are however good enough in summer and can even be covered in a carriage thanks to the good quality of the soil, which is in large part clayey, and thanks also to the vast plains. But in winter they are everywhere bad, and in some places even impassable. Commerce is thus suspended for five months of the year, to the great disadvantage of the inhabitants and trade relationships with the interior and abroad. . . .

We must point out too that since the periods of freezing and thaw of the Danube at the Black Sea end are uncertain, and no one can predict the rare mild winters in which the great river continues navigable, it often happens that several vessels with cargoes of perishable goods are caught by the ice and are immobilized for long periods without being able to reach their destinations . . . consequently many prudent captains and traders dare not risk their persons and goods in speculation which could have a perilous outcome. That is why commerce on the Danube water-route flags during winter or gets by only with great losses. . . .

(b) The First Railways

Henry C. Barkley, *Bulgaria before the War*, London, 1877, pp. 1–3.

DURING the five years that I was employed on the Kustendjie[1] railway, reports had constantly reached us that the line from Varna to Rustchuck[2] was about to be commenced—first by one company and then by another; but somehow these reports one after the other came to nothing, and the Kustendjie line continued the sole representative of railway engineering in Turkey in Europe until the spring of 1864. . . .

[1] Kyustenja, now Constantza, ceded to Rumania in 1878.   [2] Ruse.

There could be no doubt as to the great advantage that would accrue to the country [from the new line], for it was to start from the seaport of Varna and then run inland up the great valley past the maiden fortress of Shumla, to the fortified town of Rustchuck, and would enable the government at Constantinople to transport troops and materials of war from thence to the front in twenty hours. Yes, to the front, for Rustchuck was, and is, one of the eyes of Turkey that is constantly on the strain looking out for the hostile forces of the great Czar. Then it must be remembered that up to the time the Varna and Rustchuck railway was made there was no such thing as a road in all Bulgaria, and that the only way of transporting material, in or out of the country, was to drag it over the muddy tracks in bullock carts, and that even these could not be collected in sufficient numbers when any great emergency arose, such as a threatened attack from over the Danube.

Besides the advantages to be derived from the line in a military point of view, there were those that always should, under a good government, follow from the opening up of a rich country—such as offering to the agriculturist and the merchant an easy access to the best markets, both foreign and local, for his products and merchandise. Any how, after years wasted over various schemes to get this line made, the Turkish government at last offered sufficiently enticing terms to induce an English Company to take the affair in hand, and my elder brother (and former chief) had the management of all the works. . . .

Henry Barkley, civil engineer, aged 20, arrived in Varna in 1857, and lived in Bulgaria for 12 years, in which he learnt to like and admire the Bulgarians. The three brothers Barkley built the first railway line from Kyustenja (now Constantza) to Cerna Voda on the Danube (completed in 1860) and the second from Varna to Ruse (completed 1867). The former line now lies in Rumanian territory and was reconstructed between the World Wars. (See further pp. 269 and 279-80.)

II. Independent Bulgaria

13. PEASANTS AFTER LIBERATION

K. J. Jireček, *Cesty po Bulharsku* (Travels in Bulgaria), Prague, 1888, pp. 127–9; 129–32; 406–12.

(a) Bulgarians Buy Land

SINCE the Russo-Turkish war agricultural conditions in the Principality and Rumelia[1] have been in a state of transition. On both sides of the Balkan range the whole Bulgarian population is dominated by an insatiable desire to acquire land. They plough up the pastures in the precincts of their villages, and buy land as much as they can, and often more than they can cultivate. To get money to buy, they first of all sell cattle, and then plunge into debt, which with the present high interest rate is a great evil, and pay their taxes quite irregularly, so that there are large deficits in all parts of Rumelia and the Principality.

Sales of land since the war have amounted to a large sum. In the department of Stara Zagora, according to A. T. Iliev,[2] total purchases of land from the end of the war to 1885 amounted to about $50\frac{1}{2}$ million grosh (one gold lira of 100 grosh = 22 francs 70 centimes), of which 40 million were purchases by Bulgarians from Turks. The annual turnover in this department is estimated to average six million grosh. One consequence of these purchases is a considerable flow of gold coin out of the country, for four-fifths of the vendors are Turks who are emigrating from Rumelia.

According to official reports on land sales in all Eastern Rumelia, the total sum for the $4\frac{1}{2}$ years from the beginning of Rumelian

---

[1] Bulgaria at the time was divided into the Principality of Bulgaria and the province of Eastern Rumelia. The Treaty of San Stefano (March 1878), dictated by Russia, set up a large autonomous principality of Bulgaria, which was reduced in size by the Treaty of Berlin (July 1878) to the territory between the Balkans and the Danube, while the territory between the Balkans and Rhodope became the autonomous province of Eastern Rumelia. In 1885 Eastern Rumelia united with the Principality of Bulgaria.

[2] *Staro-Zagorski okrăg v narodo-ikonomichesko otnoshenie* (Economic Conditions in the Stara Zagora District), Stara Zagora, 1885 (*Author*).

administration in the spring of 1879 to 1 November 1883[1] amounted to 102 million grosh, of which 72 million grosh represented sales by Moslems to Christians, 0·4 million sales by Christians to Moslems, 24·8 million sales by Christians to Christians, and 4·8 million sales from Moslems to Moslems.

The price of land depends on local conditions. In the departments from which we have quoted examples, the dearest lands are in Chirpan, where one *uvrat*[2] of the best black earth soil fetches up to 500 grosh, and in Kazanlǎk, where good land is scarce; the cheapest lands are in the sparsely populated region of Seymen, where an *uvrat* of arable land sells for 40–75 grosh. In the last years of Turkish rule, land in Stara Zagora was dearer by 40 to 50 per cent, in Kazanlǎk by 25 per cent. The fall in the price of land was caused not only by the enormous volume of sales, but also by the fall in the price of agricultural produce, which began after the first years of Rumelian administration. Immediately after the war the price of crops rose steeply, for the harvest of the war year 1877 was destroyed and the harvests of 1878 and 1879 were poor, so that there was a great shortage of grain in the country.[3] But from the year 1883 prices fell sharply. . . .[4]

This desire to acquire land, together with the emigration of the Turks, has had a further consequence: the former Turkish estates have to a large extent been bought up by whole village communities and parcelled out into small pieces for individual members of the community. Under the Turks the land was divided among a smaller number of proprietors who ruled large estates; now it is divided among a larger number of farmers who on the average acquire small plots.

In the surroundings of Stara Zagora and Nova Zagora the biggest peasant farm is reckoned at something like 300 *uvrat*, worked by two to three pairs of oxen; the smallest property has from 10 to 40 *uvrat*, worked by one pair, in Nova Zagora even with a single ox, so that neighbours must agree to help each other with their various teams.

---

[1] From the Plovdiv newspaper '*Narodni Glas*' (National Voice) no. 456, 21 December 1883 (*Author*).

[2] See Note on Weights and Measures, p. 280.

[3] In Kazanlǎk, which was a battlefield, the harvest of 1877 was not even gathered, and in 1878 only a small quantity of summer crops could be sown; in 1879 there was total famine in many regions and in the Principality, as for example in the Kyustendil region (*Author*).

[4] A. T. Iliev, *op. cit.*, p. 36, gives a table of grain prices at Karabunar station for the years 1876–84. A kilo of wheat in 1876 was 50 grosh, in 1879 85, 1882 72, 1884 only 46; maize in 1876 22, 1879 56, 1882 37, 1884 25 grosh (*Author*). See Note on Weights and Measures, p. 280.

In the Chirpan plain farms up to 600 *uvrat* exist, while in the uplands of Kazanlǎk you will find tiny properties up to five *uvrat*. In Seymen, nine out of ten former farm labourers who worked on Turkish estates are today proprietors of their own land. In Stara Zagora about one-fifth of the former workers are now peasants with land of their own.

The Turkish estates themselves were often quite small, and in extent and management cannot be compared with the great estates of other countries; usually they were cultivated by only three to six ploughs. Some still exist in the district of Stara Zagora (45 per cent), but in other parts of the department they have shrunk to insignificant relics, and even these are coming to an end. In 1886 there were nine in Nova Zagora district, five in Chirpan, four in Seymen, and one in Kazanlǎk.

(b) Share-croppers and Farm Labourers

The estates were worked in the past, the remainder still are, in one of two ways which are the same throughout Bulgaria. Either the land is rented to neighbouring peasants in return for half (or some other share) of the produce, a method which is known in its principal form by the Bulgarian term *izpolitsa*; or the proprietor of the land farms it with hired labourers, who have no land themselves and are called *ratayi, argati*; in Kyustendil, Dupnitsa, and Radomir they are also known as *momtsi*.

The rent is fixed in various ways. When farming is on a genuine half-share basis, the owner deducts the seed for sowing if it was provided by him. In Zagora the crops are divided between the master and the share-cropper while still standing in the sheaf, in Kyustendil after the threshing. This type of share-farming has dominated southern Europe from the Middle Ages to the present day, and is familiar in the Ionian islands, in Dalmatia, Istria, Italy, southern France, and the southern regions of Spain. Bulgarians learnt it from the Byzantines back in the time of the Old Empire, for the terms *izpoli, izpolnik* occur even in medieval chronicles.[1] In the Zagora plain, genuine half-sharing exists alongside tripartite division, whereby the owner takes one-third of the crop and the tenant two-thirds. Sometimes the division takes the form of deducting one-tenth or simply the amount of the tax. The last method is used where the land is poor, and where it might remain uncultivated if

[1] In the translation of Byzantine agrarian laws, printed by Huba, *O znaczeniu prawa rzymskiego i rzymsko-byzantyńskiego u narodów słowiańskich* (The Meaning of Roman and Roman-Byzantine Law among the Slavonic Peoples), Warsaw, 1868 (*Author*).

a tenant could not be found. These factors led to a modification of the old half-share custom in the uplands of the Balkan Peninsula (for example in Greece and Epirus) and the Western Empire. Moreover, a recent practice has spread of letting land in return for a fixed rent per *uvrat* in grain. . . .

The conditions of agricultural labour are very diverse. The contract depends on whether the worker is married, old or young; in accordance with the various local customs he is paid wages in money and board, or in money with the sowing rights of an allotted piece of land, or exclusively in produce or money. Sometimes the labourer lives in his own cottage near the estate, but more usually he lives in a hut assigned to him by the farmer. Furthermore, payment in cash is a novelty. Before the war, labourers had always been paid in grain or general farm produce in Western Bulgaria, Radomir and Kyustendil. The plot of land allocated to the labourer for sowing is called *paraspor*, hence villagers living entirely on other people's land are known as *parasporjiyi*. The labourer is hired by the year or half-year; the working period begins either on St. George's Day in spring or on St. Demetrius' Day in autumn.

I will give a few details. In the villages round Stara Zagora the labourer receives 300–500 grosh in money, 15 to 18 kilos (44 *oka*)[1] of grain, as food, and seed to sow the allotment of 2–3 *uvrat*, part in maize, part in wheat or barley; he is also given salt and shoes (sandals). In some villages the allotment is determined by allowing the labourer to plough for two days on his own behalf, working on the master's land. What he ploughs becomes his allotment. On this he uses the owner's implements; on some lands the straw from the allotment remains the property of the master, and the grain goes to the worker. . . . Such workers are not only Bulgarians, but also gipsies and Turks. Many spend their lives migrating with their families from one estate to another.[2]

In the plains of Rumelia the labour shortage is now widely felt. The inhabitants cannot even harvest the crops without outside help. The reapers, both men and women, come to work from the mountains of Vetren and as far as Mesembria, where the grain ripens later. . . . In the year 1884 I happened to be touring the southern side of the Balkan range from Vitosha to the Black Sea, and back along the northern side from Varna to Sofia in the harvest season,

---

[1] See Note on Weights and Measures, p. 280.

[2] A. T. Iliev, *op. cit.*, pp. 40–2; K. Jireček and M. Sarafov, *Raport ot komisiyata izpratena v Kyustendilski okrăg da izuchi polozhenieto na bezzemelnite seleni* (Report of the Commission sent to investigate the condition of landless peasants in Kyustendil district), Sofia, 1880 (*Author*).

and saw this wholesale movement of mountain-dwelling harvesters as they went gaily from field to field, singing and playing their bagpipes. In Stara Zagora and Chirpan reapers also come from the neighbouring Sredna Gora, where the crops ripen later. Only the Kazanlǎk district can dispense with outside workers. There is nothing like this in the Principality; the population to the north of the Balkan range is denser and the inhabitants can harvest the crops themselves. In the somewhat backward farming conditions of Rumelia, a great change occurred in the same year, which I was able to see for myself. The reapers had been continually raising their wage demands, when suddenly they observed something unheard of in the Thracian plains, viz. machines. Through the efforts of the Rumelian government and the local officials, a quantity of agricultural machinery was purchased, and this was turned to immediate account. In 1884 38 horse-reapers were at work for the first time in the department of Stara Zagora, 17 in Plovdiv and 13 in Burgas. In consequence, wages for harvest work fell by half.

(c) The Land Reform Problem in Kyustendil

Agrarian conditions in Kyustendil give rise to a special local problem which needs to be dealt with in some detail.

The old Turkish state in its heyday recognized four chief categories of land: *mulk* or private property, *has* or property of the Crown, *vakuf* or property dedicated to a religious or charitable purpose, and *timar* or property in fief. Other types of ownership were insignificant in extent, such as the *bashtina*[1] of soldiers, falconers and *muselimi*.[2] Most important were the lands held in fief tenure. Up to 1839 the old Turkey was a feudal state.[3]

Rule over the occupied territory was maintained by the settlement of soldiers who were supported by tribute from the Christian and Moslem peasantry, and in time of war could rapidly concentrate at stated points to form emergency bands of trained cavalry. The fief-holding soldier was known as spahi, and his fief as the spahilik. The fief was granted only for life; a personal title was granted by the Sultan to each spahi on taking possession. The few so-called 'temporary fiefs' by which one man was bound to perform intermittent military service were only rarely heritable, and then only through

[1] Hereditary properties (from Bulg. *bashta*, father) in medieval Serbia and Bulgaria, also in the Turkish period.

[2] The *müsellem* (Tk.) was a soldier bound to provide services for armies in transit, in return for which he was exempt from taxation and held land in hereditary ownership.

[3] See p. 211 above and p. 250 below, footnote 3.

the female line. The spahi could be deprived of his fief for dis-
obedience or cowardice, but for good service he could be promoted
to a more profitable estate.

Fief holdings were divided into two classes. The large estates, the
holders of which went into the field of battle with a retinue of about
twenty men, were called *ziamet* (and their holder the *zaim*); the
smaller ones were called *timar*, of which the holder (*timarliya*) took
the field alone or with only one to four horsemen. Originally the
spahis were bound to reside on their holdings in their *kula* (Tk.
walled property) or chiflik (estate). In practice, however, they mostly
lived in towns that were the centres of local or provincial juris-
dictions. As income they took a tithe of the crops of Moslem and
Christian peasants, and from the Christians they took an additional
tribute in cattle, vegetables, fruit, honey and so on.

In the sixteenth century the fief system was still in being, the
grants and titles being renewed and controlled from time to time,
but from the beginning of the seventeenth century onward the whole
system fell into such chaos that renewed land registration was no
longer possible. On the one hand the beglerbegs, who had the right
of allocating the smaller fiefs, began to distribute them to their
favourites and protégés instead of to deserving veterans. In this they
followed the example of the central government as a matter of
course, since it, too, had ignored the old principles and had granted
the majority of the fiefs to court officials or other persons who neither
undertook military service themselves nor provided others to serve
in their stead. The spahis themselves continually sub-divided their
estates and in this way gradually acquired the fiefs as their hereditary
property. According to accounts, even in the sixteenth century not a
single fief had remained intact, and at the beginning of the present
century many spahis did not even own as much as one-tenth of a
peasant household.[1] The ranks of the soldier spahis were thinned and
the fief-holdings lost their usefulness, while at the same time the
smaller the spahilik was, the more harshly did the spahis exact
tribute from their subject tenants.

Finally the Turkish government recognized that the finances, the
army and the economy of the Empire were falling into ruin through
the continuance of this feudal system. The huge revenues of the
Sultan's lands (mostly in corn tithes) were accruing not to the State
Treasury, which had long been wrestling with a permanent deficit,
but to the spahis. The spahis themselves, as is clear from the

---

[1] In 1858 Hahn (*Reise von Belgrad nach Saloniki*, second edition, p. 103) found the
village of Charadzin near Skoplje divided among 18 spahis, although it included
only 25 Bulgarian households (*Author*).

examples quoted by Hahn from Albania, had converted the crop tithe into a fixed payment known as the *kesim*, levied either in money or in kind.[1] The word *kesim*, in previous Turkish legislation, is recalled as the sum paid in certain sanjaks of Asia Minor as rent for market-gardens, i.e. a kind of special supplement to the tithe on produce.[2] Finally, after the suppression of the Corps of Janissaries (1826) and the bitter experiences of the Serbian and Greek revolutions and the war with Russia (1829), Sultan Mahmud II (1808–39) decided to abolish the surviving feudal institutions and to confiscate the majority of the fiefs. The change was announced by his son, the Sultan Abd-al-Mejid, in the 'hatisherif Gülhane' of 1839, also known as the *tanzimat*.[3] The spahis were deprived of their estates, and the tithe, which they had hitherto received as army-pay, was levied as a state tax. A regular army, mainly infantry, raised from among the Moslem population on West European lines, took the place of the janissary infantry, the spahi cavalry and other old formations. At the same time the administration was reformed; in place of the spahi-chieftains, subashis, alaybegs and ayans, whom the local Turkish nobility had latterly been selecting for themselves (not without bitterness and bloodshed), officials, 'Stambolijis' nominated by the Sultan himself, were now appointed in the provincial towns. By centralization, the Ottoman Empire gained greater unity and strength, and was enabled to survive even in the new conditions of the present century. Life pensions were granted to the spahis deprived of their fiefs; even today a few old people are still receiving compensation for their expropriated estates in this way.

The abolition of the spahi system and the introduction of the new order led to great conflicts in the western provinces of European Turkey, and particularly in Albania and Bosnia. Reformed Turkey was neither strong enough nor able enough to wipe out the old institutions.

They were soon forgotten in the Danube plain and Thrace, but lingered into the thirties in the mountain regions of the central

---

[1] Hahn, Alban. Studien, I, 132, *Reise durch die Gebiete des Drin und Wardar*, p. 331. For example a village in the Lower Mati paid as *kesim* two horse-cart loads of maize for each pair of oxen (*Author*).

[2] Hammer, *Osmanische Staatsverfassung*, i, 270, 271, 277 (*Author*).

[3] The *Tanzimat* (Reorganization) refers to a series of reforms, of which the Noble Rescript of the Rose Chamber (the Khatt-i Sherif of Gülkhane) was the first and most important, proclaiming the security of the subject, the abolition of tax-farming, fair and public trial of persons accused of crimes, and equality of persons of all religions in the application of these laws. The abolition of tenure-in-fief, to which Jireček here refers, was proclaimed by Mahmud II in 1831. See Bernard Lewis, *The Emergence of Modern Turkey*, London, 1961, pp. 89–90 and 104–5.

peninsula, in the Serbian and Montenegrin borderlands. An agreement was discussed for regulating the duties of peasants to spahis and landlords in the Niš pashalik in 1835. This was due to the proximity of Serbia, for after the new frontier was drawn in 1833 the population living in Turkish frontier territory began to riot and was pacified only by the mediation of Prince Miloš.[1] Spahis and peasants were still negotiating in 1858 when Hahn was touring the area. This writer found a great deal of unrest in Niš after the return of a delegation sent from seventy of its villagers to Constantinople.[2] After the Russo-Turkish war, the Bulgarian government found a considerable residue of spahi estates in Kyustendil, as also did the Serbian government in Vranska, Leskovac and the Niš region. The number of spahis was particularly large in the upper reaches of the Struma and Morava. . . .

In Kyustendil (which together with Krayishte included 159 villages), about one-third of the cultivated land was in Turkish hands in the last years of Turkish rule. The osmanli population itself amounted to only about 700 households in the town of Kyustendil and eight small neighbouring hamlets with mixed population. Similar conditions were widespread in the adjacent plain of Radomir and in some places round Dupnitsa. The peasants in these villages worked on Turkish estates and were divided by Turkish law into three classes, ispoljiyi, momtsi and kesimjiyi (i.e. share-croppers, labourers and 'serf peasants').[3]

We have already mentioned share-croppers and labourers in our sketch of Bulgarian agriculture above. The serf peasants in Krayishte, in ten hamlets in the Kyustendil basin, and four villages round Dupnitsa,[4] are a local speciality. While the last two classes had some land of their own, and worked for the aga on agreed terms, the serf peasants inhabited whole villages, which collectively, not individually, paid to the landowner (spahi, as they still called him) a fixed produce-levy or kesim (from Tk. kesmek, to cut), that is a fixed number of kotel (of 20 oka each) per year. Besides this, they had to

[1] See an interesting letter about this mediation from Avram Petronijević, who directed foreign affairs for Miloš, dated July 1835 from Jagodina, in Miličević, Kraljevina Srbija (The Kingdom of Serbia), p. 45. There has recently appeared an important study on the history of feudalism and landownership in Serbia by Stoyan Novaković, Proniyari i bashtinitsi (spahija i chitluk-sahibija) XIII–XIX veka (Conditional and Absolute Property (spahi tenure and estate-ownership) from the thirteenth to the nineteenth century), Belgrade (first number of series issued by the Royal Serbian Academy), 1887 (Author).

[2] Reise von Belgrad nach Saloniki, 2nd edition, p. 136 (Author).

[3] 'Serf peasants' appears an appropriate translation of kesimjiyi, since Jireček contrasts them with free peasants.

[4] Author's footnote listing villages and hamlets omitted.

work off a certain number of days per year by forced labour, mowing, reaping, threshing, hoeing vines, picking grapes and so on, often far below the mountains of Krayishte in the plains of Kyustendil; and in addition were obliged to deliver fixed amounts of cheese, butter, wood, charcoal, stakes for fencing, lambs for the feast of Bairam and so on. True, the house of the peasant was his own, but the spahi could sell the estate or could sell the income from the property, consisting of the said produce, rents and labour services, to another spahi. State taxes were paid by the dependent peasants.

As the villages increased in size, the serf peasants took over larger and larger pieces of land for cultivation, and the agas continually increased the produce levy. . . . Some of the richer villages have commuted their obligations by money payments and so bought themselves free in recent years.[1]

A most peculiar feature is that among the enserfed villages there are also numerous free villages, and even in the enserfed villages there are some free households. This recalls the Macedonian villages of medieval times, among which, as can be seen from the fourteenth-century estate rolls of Hilandar estate, there existed side by side church serfs, lords' serfs, and independent *eleftheri* or, in Slavonic, *svobodniki*.[2]

After the war the position of the agas and peasants of Kyustendil attracted the attention of the Bulgarian government, all the more because of an outbreak of famine in Krayishte in 1879 in the first winter of Bulgarian administration. The Turks of Kyustendil, who had fled before the Russians, returned, but remained in the towns and did not venture into the villages. Yet they claimed their incomes and referred the matter not only to the Bulgarian government, but also to the Porte and the representatives of the Great Powers in Sofia. The peasants, however, rejected the old conditions and prepared to welcome their masters in a none too friendly way.

In August 1880 the Bulgarian government decided to send out a commission to investigate the confused problem of the 'landless peasants' on the spot. Mr. Mihail Sarafov and the author of this book were appointed members of this commission. For the first few days we were accompanied by Mr. P. Karavelov, then Minister of Finance. We worked for twelve days. We took evidence both from the representatives of the villages, summoned to Kyustendil, and the Turkish landowners themselves (about twenty of them), who, impoverished by the war, appeared rather depressed.

[1] Author's footnote listing villages omitted.
[2] Th. Uspensky, *Materialy dlya istorii zemlevladeniya v XIV veke* (Materials for the History of Agriculture in the Fourteenth Century), Odessa, 1883 (*Author*).

All the agas were Turkish types with aquiline noses, except for one with a snub-nosed Tartar face. Some were dressed in the old style, in long fur-embroidered kaftans, blue in colour, with white turbans on their heads; others had modern blue or black coats of uniform cut and wore the red fez of the 'New Turks'. Only one displayed any kind of official or military bearing, and he kept on his elastic-sided boots, while the rest, in accordance with Turkish etiquette, took off their slippers at the door and came into the room in stockings. The discipline of a ruling class was evident in their clear-cut questions and well-considered answers. All spoke Bulgarian with perfect fluency.

The peasants were all original highland characters, in coarse brown clothes with red belts and big sheepskin caps, some with their hair cut, others wearing their hair long; some were astute types with ready logic and trenchant phrases, but there were also withdrawn suspicious types, who were almost savages.

Our official report was published and distributed among the deputies in the Assembly.[1] The share-croppers and labourers were not discussed, for most of them had their own land, and moreover farmers all over Radomir had been buying up Turkish properties and dividing them among themselves. Thus attention was mainly focused on the kesim-paying peasants.

In our report we had pointed out that the institution of *kesimji* had arisen chiefly through the failure to reform the old-style feudal spahilik. The spahis in these remote territories had appropriated feudal rights and had endeavoured to appear as hereditary owners. The best proof of this is that the peasants continue to call the present landowners by the name of spahi, and the tithe, now levied by the government, by the name of spahilik.

The Turkish agas were naturally not much impressed by our argument. (Moreover, comparison with the rights of the *chitluk-sahibs*, as they continued to exist in Serbia, judging by Vuk Karadžić's description of them,[2] makes it clear that something of those institutions derived from personal ownership as well, and not merely from the spahilik.) Owing to the absence of written documents it is of course difficult to make investigations even about recent affairs. The evidence of the Turks and peasants had revealed that these conditions had in some cases arisen through the indebtedness of the peasants, or were intensified by it; the agas made good the

[1] M. Sarafov and K. Jireček, *op. cit.*, *Report of the Commission of Enquiry on the condition of landless peasants in Kyustendil district*, Sofia, 1880, 39 pp. (Reprint from Official Gazette) (*Author*).

[2] For this description, see p. 295 below.

tax deficits for the villages, and the peasants as debtors of the land-owners were forced to consent to various permanent payments and recognize the aga as landowners. Moreover, in some places the existing villages had evidently grown out of settlements of workers on Turkish estates. The villagers of course asserted almost unanimously that all these burdens had been imposed on them in recent times, especially in the great repression after the Serbian rising, and they related in detail how this or that powerful Turk of two or three generations earlier had seized such and such a village. Furthermore, it was clear that the right to collect produce-levies and forced labour was continually being dealt in by the Turks, so that the present owners were not the descendants of the former proprietors, but had either purchased the rights themselves, or such rights had been acquired by their fathers.

We proposed that the kesim-paying villages should be valued on the basis of the produce-levy, to be estimated by fixing the quota of grain to be handed over to the landowners, and by stating average prices per *kotel* at the earliest sales from the various villages. On this basis compensation would be paid to the Turks by the government, and the population would reimburse the State Treasury for the outlay by annual instalments. The Turks quickly assented to our proposal, for their chief aim was to emigrate as soon as possible with the cash.

(d) *The Law of 1880*

The National Assembly then passed the 'Law for Improving the Lot of the Farm Population on "State Lands" and Chifliks' proposed by Minister Karavelov.[1] 'State Lands' meant the lands of the kesim-paying peasants, which the law decreed should become the property of those who cultivated them. Similar provisions were laid down for the share-croppers and farm-labourers, to the effect that whoever had cultivated a piece of land on any estate without interruption for ten years should become the owner of both the land and the cottage if he had lived in it for ten years or more. Compensation for this expropriation should be paid to the landlords of these estates, who of course retained the remainder of the land.

Several years have passed, and the land problem in Kyustendil is still what it was. Other commissions came to examine land areas and values in detail, and these sat at Kyustendil for a whole month. Their records were however destroyed in a fire at a wooden building of the National Assembly in Sofia and the work had to begin anew. The affair dragged on from year to year with no result. The Turks,

[1] *Law of 10 December, 1880,* Official Gazette, ii, no. 93 (*Author*).

weary and embittered, sold their rights one by one to various local business men—Bulgarians or Spanish Jews—and emigrated. The government began to force some villages to pay the levy in grain as before until the whole matter was settled, but in doing so they met with strong opposition. Meanwhile the price of land steadily rose, and the once favourable conditions deteriorated. In September 1885 I read in the Bulgarian press that the agrarian question in Kyustendil had been finally settled, and that all the landowners' rights were to be bought up by the government for 800,000 francs. Five years earlier the total purchase price was estimated at a much lower figure. But a few days later the Plovdiv rising broke out, and so far as I know the matter has been settled only on paper.[1]

Konstantin Josef Jireček (1854–1918), son of the eminent Czech scholar Josef Jireček (1825–88), ranks as the leading nineteenth-century historian of the South Slavs. In 1878 he was invited by the Bulgarian Government to organize education in the principality, and worked in Bulgaria from 1879 to 1884 in various official capacities, including that of Minister of Education (1881–2). After the East Rumelian rising of 1884, he returned to Prague, where he became Professor of History at the Czech University. In 1893 he became Professor of Slavonic Philology and History at Vienna University. His major works on Bulgaria are *Geschichte der Bulgaren* (History of the Bulgars) (Vienna, 1876), *Cesty po Bulharsku* (Prague, 1888) and *Das Fürstenthum Bulgarien* (The Principality of Bulgaria) (Vienna, 1896). The two last were republished in Bulgarian as *Knyazhestvo Bălgariya*: part i, *Bălgarska dărzhava*, and part ii, *Pătuvaniya po Bălgariya*, Plovdiv, 1899. His classic *Geschichte der Serben* (History of the Serbs), *vol. i, to 1371* (Gotha, 1911) and *vol. ii, 1371–1528* (Gotha, 1918) remained unfinished at his death.

14. SOCIAL EQUALITY

(a) A Slav View

K. J. Jireček, *Cesty po Bulharsku* (Travels in Bulgaria), Prague, 1888, p. 35.

I T should be emphasized that Bulgaria is a land of peasant farmers, without a nobility, where by the standards of other countries there are neither rich nor poor. The faint beginnings of a merchant plutocracy are barely discernible. People are more or less equal, and even the educated classes address each other as 'thee' and 'thou'.

---

[1] The question was settled in 1887, by the payment of one million levs by the state as compensation to the landowners; the kesim-peasants acquired the land as their free property. (I. Sakázov, *Bulgarische Wirtschaftsgeschichte*, Berlin, 1929, p. 193).

Even so, the old order is seen to survive in odd ways, recalling the phraseology of medieval Slavonic, as for instance the simple but courtly formulas used in the Dubrovnik correspondence of the fourteenth and fifteenth centuries. To these survivals belongs *vasha milost* [your honour, your excellency]. *Gospodin* (Greek δεσπότης) was reserved until quite recently for addressing bishops, and it was also a personal name in the feminine form, like the Greek Despina. Town and country notables a generation ago were addressed as *Kir* (κύριος), a married lady as *Kira* (κυρά) and an unmarried lady as *Kiratsa* (κυράτσα), a Byzantine word I myself have heard among old Sofia people as a sort of survival from the past. In the towns today it is all *gospodin, gospozha,* and *gospozhitsa*.[1]

(b) —and the English Attitude

The Marquis of Bath, *Observations on Bulgarian Affairs*, London, 1880, pp. 4–9.

THE Bulgarians may be described as a population of landowners, holding tenaciously to long-established customs and laws, and to social institutions more democratic than those which prevail in any of the older-established European countries. They have been accustomed to a large amount of local self-government; for whatever may have been the oppression of the Porte, it contemptuously allowed them, by communal and municipal institutions of their own, to settle their own affairs among themselves. They are without an aristocracy, without a landlord class, or any upper class living on realized property and able to devote itself, according to the taste of its members, to amusement, to art and literature, or to the affairs of state. Their language has no expression to mark the acknowledgement of a superior rank; for the titles assumed by the Turkish authorities were borrowed from the Turkish language, and will not be adopted by the free Bulgarians in their intercourse with one another.

The country has no tradition of feudalism and none of the bitter memories this engenders. It is free from that antagonism of classes, and that bitter hostility between parties which constitute the present weakness and threaten the destruction of more prosperous and older established States. Conditions so unusual render the progress of a people under them a matter of interest, even to those who do not look on them as affording any guarantee of ultimate success.

---

[1] These terms for Mr., Mrs., and Miss persisted up to the communist period.

15. THE ZADRUGA

(a) Its Communist Principle

I. E. Geshov, 'Zadrugata v zapadna Bălgariya' (The Zadruga in Western Bulgaria) in *Periodichesko spisanie*, Sofia, 1887, year v, vols. xxi–xxii, pp. 426–49.

MACEDONIANS assure me that the zadruga is to be met in present-day Macedonia, not only in the villages but even in towns. In the absence of direct information on this ill-starred part of our land, it is possible to get comparable data from that part of Western Bulgaria that has entered the principality. From Tsaribrod to Kyustendil, in the Sofia valley, in Grahovo (Radomir and Breznitsa districts), in Znepole (Trăn and Tsaribrod districts), in Burel (Breznitsa and Tsaribrod districts), in Plakariya (Samokov district), in the Radomir area, the zadruga is to be found throughout in almost every other village with features which, according to Macedonians, strongly resemble those of the Macedonian zadruga. So, if we cannot speak positively of the communal family in Macedonia, we can describe it as it exists in the counties of Sofia, Trăn and Kyustendil, especially in the first two, and so give an approximate conception of this family institution in the whole of Western Bulgaria. . . .

The headman of the zadruga is called the *domakin* and he is chosen not for his age but ability, and can be changed within his lifetime. Morally he is a kind of father of the whole family, while economically he is a kind of elected director of a company which holds a common undivided property, and to which all its members are obliged to contribute all they earn. The domestic housework is managed by a *domakinya*, who is usually the *domakin*'s wife, unless he has an old mother or mother-in-law; in such case the old woman assumes this role, provided she is not ailing.

Generally, the male members of the zadruga are related by blood. But there are cases in which outsiders are also accepted as zadruga members. This usually happens when the zadruga has many girls and few youths. Then, instead of all the girls marrying outside the zadruga as usually happens, they bring into the family group a son-in-law or two who, by such act of introduction, gain the rights and shoulder the duties of their new zadruga. The headman is usually married or a widower, though he may be a bachelor, while it is even possible for a woman to be head of the zadruga. Common custom, however, demands he be a man and very naturally he must, as the headman, not only run the zadruga but represent it before the

S

outside world. He directs it, keeps its accounts; sells, buys, weighs and answers before the courts. The zadruga as a whole decides and he executes. Without consulting it he can purchase only some minor household requisites; and he is allowed to sell nothing on his own. Buying and selling are done through him or by his arrangement through some zadruga member. The distribution of duties among the men is done by the zadruga itself, but the headman has the right to give orders in the execution of these duties. They owe him respect and obedience, while he owes them advice and protection. To him are entrusted the property and honour of the whole family; if he fails to defend them, if he turns out incapable, negligent, or dishonest, he is given to understand he is unworthy of his position; if he does not accept this, he is deposed, and in extreme cases even expelled from the zadruga.

The headwoman (*domakinya*) is a married woman or widow. In exceptional cases when there are no married women, or if they are invalids, the headwoman can also be a girl. Usually the headwoman is either the wife of the last headman, i.e. when she is the eldest in the household, or the wife of the new headman; thus, with his election the headwoman is also elected. When he has no wife, the oldest in the house becomes headwoman: the age and experience she has to offer and the reverence she inspires are accounted by our Bulgarians more necessary for a headwoman than her ability. The headwoman must have authority to impose on women fellow zadruga-members, the more so in that their duties are not so strictly ordained by the zadruga as are those of the male members, and their time is not so exclusively devoted to the zadruga's interest as is the men's time. It is the headwoman who arranges the order in which the female members are to bake and cook for the whole zadruga; it is she who must judge when free time must be left to Mariya or Petkana to care for the household matters of her own particular family—to watch her newborn child, to attend her sick husband, to knit and weave, to do a little sewing and laundry for herself and her own. The headwoman is directly responsible for the food and drink of the whole zadruga, and indirectly also for the clothes of each individual family, as she by her words and example must inspire the other members to orderliness and love of work. In a word she has the duty of watching over the domestic order of the whole zadruga; if this order is upset by any woman, the headwoman has the right to call her to task and if need be report her to her husband or her father if the latter is in the zadruga. . . .

The rights and duties of male members can be summarized in the communist principle: from each according to his strength and to each according to his needs. And in truth, if a member be sound in limb or unsound, ill or well, he is bound to hand in all he can earn according to his strength to the zadruga; and on the other hand, be he married or unmarried, childless or with a whole dozen children, the zadruga has to provide him with house, food and clothing according to his family's needs. As his children grow up, they too are obliged to help; if, however, his child goes to the town *gimnaziya* (secondary school), the zadruga maintains him just as it also maintains his children should he happen to be taken for conscription. . . .

Once married, members already gain a vote in the running of the zadruga. In fulfilling their duties, they have the right to demand of the headman and other members the fulfilment of their rights. If anyone of the members is not satisfied with the way the zadruga affairs are going, he has the right to withdraw from it, as the zadruga also has the right to expel any member with whom it is not pleased. In such a case the member leaving is given the share due to him, his clothes and nothing else. What else could he take, seeing that of what he has earned, nothing was left to him as his private property, as his *peculium*?

The girls take nothing, either when they leave the zadruga to marry, or when their father and mother dies or the zadruga is dissolved. They have the right only of dowry, consisting exclusively of clothes and bedding and in return for which the zadruga receives (of course into the communal chest) the so-called *prid* (bride money), a sum of money proportionate to the dowry, from the son-in-law. . . . When a girl is taken into the zadruga from outside, she likewise brings a dowry against which the agreed *prid* is naturally paid from the zadruga chest. This dowry is not however regarded as zadruga property but as the bride's private possession. It can be said to be the sole *peculium* in the zadruga. That and clothes. These are made by the women and belong to those for whom they are made. . . .

The labourers do not form part of the zadruga family.

Such in general lines is the *Rechtsorganismus* of the Bulgarian zadruga, inspiring confidence in members and outsiders, thanks to the care taken in preserving the old customs on which they rest, to the extent that our Bulgarians, otherwise so distrustful in many respects, make loans to the headman against zadruga property, buy and sell from him and to him in the account and name of the zadruga, despite the fact that there is no law in our land obliging members to recognize the acts of the *domakin*.

For biographical note see p. 264.

(b) Why It is Vanishing

K. J. Jireček, *Cesty po Bulharsku* (Travels in Bulgaria), Prague, 1888, p. 370.

THE districts of Trăn and Breznitsa, the uplands of Radomir (excluding the valley itself or the so-called 'fields'), and certain regions round Vitosha are the only parts of Bulgaria where large related groups of families still live together. Such a group, known as a *rod*, numbers from 30 to 50 persons, the head of which is known as the *stareyshina*, who may be a woman. This primitive way of life still obtains here because of the above-mentioned emigration of the men to other districts for work during the summer. Their long periods of absence necessitate stronger family ties. Naturally enough these groups are breaking up everywhere under the pressure of individualism.[1] It is interesting to note that the large families in these mountain regions were not missed by at least one old traveller: Gerhard Cornelius van der Driesch described them in 1719 as a characteristic of the rural population round Pirot.

16. MIGRANT MARKET-GARDENERS[2]

I. E. Geshov, 'Nashite gradinarski druzhestva' (Our Market-gardeners' Associations) in *Periodichesko spisanie*, Sofia, 1888, vol. xxvii, pp. 328–41.

(a) Origin and Growth

THE gardening trade was brought to Leskovets from Constantinople 150–60 years or more ago.[3] At that time in Northern Bulgaria there did not exist a single gardener in the proper sense of the word. Some Leskovets men, encouraged by the patronage of Hrustem Bey's descendants (of whom Leskovets was a *vakuf*[4]), began going to Constantinople some years before 1720 and worked at the so-called *beglik* ovens baking bread and bakery products for the army. Their example was followed by other Leskovets folk. Soon their number

---

[1] I asked many people about this family institution, but people did not like talking about it; the reason became clear to me in Breznitsa. Miličević in *Godišnjici* (Yearbooks), 4, p. 266, mentions in the village of Crvenka Jabuka, on Serbian soil to the south-west of Ruja, a zadruga of 66 persons, among them 17 'married heads' (*Author*).

[2] Much of the following information I. E. Geshov obtained from the Leskovets writer Tsane Ginchev, whose grandfather, Tsane Bradvichkata, had been one of the pioneer Bulgarian market gardeners. See also T. Ginchev's study of the subject in volumes xvii–xxi of the Tărnovo periodical *Trud*.

[3] Date of writing: 1888.   [4] Tributary possession.

increased till there was no longer room for everyone at the ovens. Some had to seek another livelihood, and so turned to the Constantinople gardeners, and began to hire themselves to them and work at the Vlanga gardens and at other Greek gardens in and around Constantinople.

Once trained in gardening, the Leskovets men sought to open their own gardens in Constantinople. But the suspicious Greeks took fright at this new Bulgarian invasion and the Constantinople gardeners' guild refused the Leskovets men permission to open gardens, so they had to spend the summer working for the Greeks and return each winter to Leskovets. One winter in Tărnovo they met a Tărnovo merchant who travelled in silk to Braşov. The Leskovets men told him their complaints against the Constantinople Greeks and, when he extolled Braşov to them, the young gardeners resolved to try their fortune in this Hungarian town hitherto unknown to them. Next spring they went to Braşov, earned good money, returned, went again—and so began the migratory Bulgarian gardening which continues up to the present day.

After Braşov the gardeners began to go also to Jassy, and even to Bucharest, and so gradually the whole of Rumania was covered by these peaceful invaders who, however, knew how to replace hoe by gun in time of need. . . .[1]

Simultaneously with their dispersion through Rumania, these Leskovets men also began to open gardens in some Bulgarian towns: in Shumen, Varna, Ruse, Vidin, and Silistra, places where the Turkish army was quartered and vegetables fetched a price. Soon the gardens multiplied to such extent that they were forced to take on more partners and assistants. . . .

The liberation of Serbia opened a new field of activity for the enterprising men of Leskovets. The three brothers who had been the apostles of this gardening were the first to take the step of going to Belgrade. They selected a place in Topchi-dere and asked Miloš for it. Prince Miloš was surprised at the idea of making a garden out of such a thorn thicket. The gardeners assured him that they could do this, and he agreed to concede it to them gratis for a few years. Bulgarian persistence overcame the Belgrade thorns and thickets and there soon appeared in Topchi-dere the first garden,[2] and then more, and not only in Belgrade but also in other Serbian towns.

[1] Ginchev recounts how they took part not only in Bulgarian risings but also in others, such as the Ypsilante rising, when they fought the Turkish janissaries and spahis from the Nyamtsuluy monastery, firing their coins from their guns when their bullets were exhausted (*Author*).

[2] Topchider, near Belgrade, later became the site of a royal palace, park and model state farm. See p. 312 below.

Serbia is near Croatia and thence entry to Austria is easy. Our gardeners made use of this route and started going north of the river Sava. Their gardens so multiplied that they could not find enough helpers in the villages of the plains but had to get lads from the Balkan (i.e. highlands), notably from Elena district. They grew rich; some also took up other branches of commerce, while others acquired higher education. . . . Those who remained gardeners took to visiting not only Russia but also Germany and France . . . , while now one of the Ruse brothers, who has gardens in Tulcha, Crimea and the Caucasus, is apparently thinking of going to America this year to see whether there might not be some small place for Bulgarian enterprise in that great Anglo-Saxon republic.

(b) Co-operative Organization

The unit of the gardening association is the gardener-workman. Once he has worked for some time in a garden and has proved a good workman, he can enter an association even if he has no money. Capital, as we shall see, is not a necessary condition for entering a gardeners' association.

How is such an association formed? When the end of the winter-break comes, one or two of the more experienced or enterprising gardeners take the initiative of forming such an association, company or *tayfa* (as it is termed in gardeners' speech) and so the *tayfa* comes into being. It varies in strength according to the garden it is to cultivate or the town in which it is to sell its products. Thus, our Bulgarian towns being small, the gardeners' *tayfa* operating in them is likewise small, usually 6–12 persons, whereas abroad, in the great towns like Bucharest, a company might have 40–50 members. I am informed that gardener Pano, who, with his brother Ruse, runs gardens in Tulcha and Odessa, Crimea and the Caucasus, has a *tayfa* of 60 in Novocherkask (Don region) this year.

The *tayfa* has two types of member, the *ortak* and the *chirak*. The former are partners, to whom is allotted a share in the company, the latter those who receive a fixed annual wage from it. The great majority in the company are partners; the wage-earners are very few. A company of 6–12 partners rarely has more than one wage-earner, while a large company of 30–50 persons will have at most 5–6 wage-earners. . . .

Most partners on entering a company contribute capital, each as he is able, of 200, 300 or 500 levs. However, not all are obliged to contribute, a very characteristic feature, showing that the gardener's true stake, for which he gets his share, is his working experience, capital being a secondary factor, absence of which does not deprive him of the right to a share. . . .

All are bound to work to their capacity. Even the chief must work in the garden when free from his other obligations, i.e. managing (after the preliminary council of the company), keeping accounts and catering for the whole company, for which he buys flour and other supplies. One of the members bakes bread for all, another cooks, again for all. All members, both partners and wage-earners, partake of the same bread and the same meals. The garden is a kind of self-constituted and spontaneous phalanstery held under God's open sky, in God's fresh air. All in it is for the associates as long as they work in it. . . .

I think I would not be far wrong in reckoning the total number of our migratory gardeners from Central Bulgaria at 12,000 persons.[1] The gardeners themselves account themselves as more but, in my view, without solid basis. If we suppose that each one of these 12,000 persons sends or brings to Bulgaria each autumn an average of 300 levs apiece, we shall find that annually the gardeners bring into Central Bulgaria about 3,000,000 levs, a figure higher than that earned in Central and Southern Bulgaria by the products of our two main industries—braid (*gaytan*) and rose oil.

A profit of 300 levs a head is considered generally by the gardeners themselves as very mediocre. They are hardworking, frugal and temperate. They earn a profit in the face of all the high rents paid for gardens and shops which often surprises the Hungarian and Rumanian landlords. . . . Some of them, like the Statelovs, Geshovs, and Bumbalovs of Leskovets, have amassed quite considerable amounts of capital from gardening and trade. Others have introduced new methods, new plants and new machines from the advanced countries visited by them into the backward areas in which they were born. They brought to Tărnovo county the idea of ploughing with horses and sowing land with lucerne and clover; they also introduced threshing-machines. These last our smiths are already starting to make, and today in many Tărnovo villages the threshing of corn is done not by flail but by such machines. Thus the gardeners not only themselves profit materially and scientifically from their work in foreign lands, but also benefit their homeland.

---

[1] For those reading this year's Finance Ministry report *Svedeniya po ikonomicheskoto săstoyanie na Bălgariya* (Information on the Economic Condition of Bulgaria) the figure 12,000 may seem small, for on p. 47 thereof it is said that 'as good as half the population of the districts of Tărnovo, Orehovo, and Elena are gardeners'. Half the total male population of these three districts would amount to 35,862 persons (*Author*).

Ivan Evstratiev Geshov (1849–1924), economist and statesman, studied under Jevons in Manchester, where his family's Plovdiv textile firm had established a branch. After his return to Plovdiv, he was condemned to death by the Turks, but released on British and American intervention. In the 1880s he became director of the National Bank, and held other official positions. In 1901 he succeeded K. Stoilov as leader of the National Party. He was Premier in the coalition Cabinet of March 1911–May 1913, resigning at the successful conclusion of the war against Turkey to campaign for arbitration to avoid the 'Criminal Madness' (as he entitled his pamphlet) of the Second Balkan War against Serbia and Greece. A collection of his articles on financial, economic and political subjects was published by the Academy of Sciences under the title *Dumi i dela* (Words and Deeds) together with a memorial biographical volume, *Spomeni i studii* (Memoirs and Studies), Sofia, 1928.

17. CO-OPERATIVES IN MANY FIELDS

I. E. Geshov, 'Zadruzhno vladenie i rabotenie v Bălgariya' (Co-operative Ownership and Labour in Bulgaria) in *Periodichesko spisanie*, Year VI, vols. xxviii–xxx, Sofia, 1889, pp. 539–49.

THESE are the chief trades in which co-operative forms of work are most often to be found:

(1) Ram and sheep-keeping.
(2) Harvest work, trade of the so-called *zagortsi*, the reapers—men and women—who each summer go from Central Bulgaria to 'Romanya' (Thrace) for the harvest.
(3) Carpentry, found either in Central Bulgaria or in the Debăr, Planina and other districts of Macedonia.
(4) Baking, especially by the Macedonians.
(5) Carting, especially by the Gabrovo cottagers, who bring wool, honey and other products to Gabrovo and take away Gabrovo manufactures.
(6) Slaughterhouse work, especially in Gorna Orehovitsa, Dryanovo, Pleven, Vratsa and other places.
(7) Kettle-making, in Central Bulgaria.
(8) Soap-making, likewise throughout Central Bulgaria where salesmen distribute soap round the villages, trading it for chickens or cash.
(9) Pottery, especially of the Troyan, Trăn and Pirot master-craftsmen, who have a distinctive secret jargon. . . .[1]
(10) Halva[2]-making, especially by the Macedonians.

[1] See Dr. Jireček in *Archiv für Slavische Philologie*, 1884 *(Author)*.
[2] A Turkish sweet.

Having enumerated these trades, I will proceed to give a few details of the distinctive features of the co-operative forms of work in the first few of these trades, beginning with the Panagyurets ram and sheep-keepers. As all Sofians know, before the 1877 war the once wealthy cattle-dealers of Panagyurets would buy tens of thousands of sheep in Western Bulgaria and the Pirot and Niš districts, and sell them in Constantinople. Few of them have stayed on to follow their fathers' trade. Their number has decreased, but their mode of work has not altered. Even today the Panagyurets sheep-farmers give their shepherds not a fixed wage but a part of the profit. The sheep bought are usually divided into flocks, large and small—the large consisting of 800–850 sheep each and the small of 600–650. Four shepherds are allocated to a large flock to accompany and tend it till it is sold, and three to a small one. All expenses of shepherds, sheep and horses, for food, pasturage or dues, are borne exclusively by the cattle-dealer. But the greater part, if not the whole, of these expenses are covered by the production of wool, as the Panagyurets men usually buy their sheep before shearing. When the sheep are sold and the money collected, the accounts are settled; any clear profit remaining after deduction of expenses remains in kind (i.e. sheep). Of this remainder, the first shepherd then receives as his share a net profit of 70 to 80 sheep, the under-shepherd about 60, the third some 40–45, and the fourth, who performs mainly a servant's tasks, about 35. The rest of the profit goes to the cattle-dealer who has supplied the whole capital, as the shepherds do not contribute any principal. Net profit per sheep can be as high as six levs but is usually three to four levs. . . .

Next come the *zagortsi* (highlanders), the men and women reapers who go each summer from Tărnovo county to reap in Romanya (the name which our ancestors gave to Thrace from the earliest times). They work in teams.

Insufficiency of work in the north Balkan (highland) districts and lack of labour in the Thracian plains attract these reapers from Northern to Southern Bulgaria. This summer invasion of the highlanders was on a large scale in Turkish times. Then, as is known, there were great Turkish estates in the Stara Zagora district, and their owners, not finding enough working hands in Thrace, sent their bailiffs, especially at harvest-time, to bring them reapers from Northern Bulgaria. There is a tradition that at first only gipsies came to reap, but soon the Bulgarians began to come too, as they still do today. No longer do they come in such numbers as in Turkish times, as most of the Turkish estates have been bought up in small holdings by Bulgarian farmers who do not need many reapers. But today the teams of highlanders still go to reap for the larger farmers in the districts of Stara Zagora, Karnobat, Burgas and others. . . .

How is the profit divided between the members of the team? By sex and age. It is generally estimated that during the harvest a man can reap six kilos,[1] a woman four and a boy or girl two. Supposing that the whole team has reaped 1,000 kilos which have been marketed at eight levs a kilo, then the team will have made 8,000 levs in all. Supposing again it numbers 225 persons comprising 100 men, 75 women and 50 boys and girls. Each man then takes for his six kilos 48 levs, each woman for her four kilos 32 levs, and each boy and girl for their two kilos 16 levs. . . .

Still more interesting from the economic viewpoint are, I think, our carpenters' associations. I have no precise information on the carpenters of Central Bulgaria. But the Macedonian carpenters' associations greatly resemble those of the Leskovets gardeners.[2] Their companies or teams also consist of 10, 15 or 20 persons. Their chiefs too are called by the title *maystor* and they migrate like the gardeners, as they visit not only all the Macedonian towns but also many places in Bulgaria, Serbia and even Rumania. Finally and most important of all, their maystor likewise takes two shares while the rest take $1\frac{3}{4}$ or $\frac{1}{2}$ a share each; the share rarely amounts to less than half. . . .

At the beginning of October the team is formed and sets off for its destination. Here it starts inquiries about buildings to be erected, selects one and enters into negotiations about its construction. Sometimes it hires itself out to build large structures like bridges. For instance, a large company of 25 Debăr men, with 30 shares, made a bridge over the Struma at Gorna Djumaya (North Macedonia). Once agreement is reached, the team begins work. It lives and eats together. One bakes the bread, another cooks for all. When they are to build a private house in a town, it is usual for its owner to offer them free hospitality. Other expenses come out of the advances which the team receives from the house-owner and are recorded by the maystor. When the work is finished, the company receives the cost of the building, settles up and deducts expenses; the net profit is then divided according to shares. Often there falls to each share a net profit of 300 levs. Each takes his share and goes home to rest for the summer. Besides company members, many of these teams also have apprentices who get a fixed wage for the whole building and the whole time from St. Demetrius' Day (26 October) to St. George's Day (23 April).

[1] See Note on Weights and Measures, p. 280.
[2] See pp. 260-3 above.

The Macedonians find this company system very satisfactory in having these two real advantages:

(1) All the workmen take care to work as well as possible, else the building might not be accepted by its owners and in such event all, not only the maystor, would suffer and

(2) nothing is stolen or lost, but there are in general great economies in the use of materials.

The Debăr carpenters living in Sofia, however, no longer work in this co-operative manner. The draught of an ill-comprehended individualism seems to have blown on them too. But the men of Palanka are taking on work as company undertakings not only in Sofia but also in Rumania. A team of 60 men from there worked last year as such a company on the newly constructed railway line from Tsaribrod to Sofia and Vakarel.

For biographical note, see p. 264 above.

18. INDUSTRIAL PROBLEMS

K. Bobchev, *Promishlena politika* (Industrial Policy), Sofia, 1932, pp. 37–40; 140–6.

(a) Crisis in Crafts

UNDER Turkish rule, especially during the eighteenth and first half of the nineteenth century, artisan crafts in Bulgaria achieved considerable prosperity. Being both more receptive and more active commercially than his Turkish master, the Bulgarian had all the conditions for creating and developing a flourishing craft industry. Apart from the skill and receptiveness of the Bulgarian people, the conditions for this development at that time must be sought in the extensive market for craft products represented by the Turkish Empire, in the benevolent attitude of the Turkish authorities to the guilds and in the development of the towns, especially those along the Balkan mountains, where agriculture could not afford a livelihood for the whole population. The main centres of our artisan crafts at that time were the larger towns (in the first place Constantinople), especially those which were the seat of a garrison (Sofia, Shumen, Yambol, Plovdiv) and finally a series of towns and smaller towns in or near the Balkan range, in which, in addition to artisan crafts, home industry flourished in its three forms of finishing work, crafts and industry.

The artisan crafts in Bulgaria and especially in Turkey were organized at that time in tight corporations—the guilds (*esnafi*). The creator of these Turkish artisan organizations—which existed even in the Seljuk period—is considered to be Ali Evran-Beli (thirteenth–fourteenth century).

In the seventeenth century these Turkish organizations had already spread into European Turkey. Some consider that our artisan organizations were of indigenous origin, and were marked by a spirit of greater tolerance than the West European guilds, but then fell under the influence of the Turkish organization in Constantinople where there were many Bulgarian artisans. According to others, our guilds during a certain period (the fifteenth–seventeenth century) developed under Western influence, diffused through the inhabitants of Dubrovnik, who, as merchants, enjoyed privileges in Bulgaria even before the coming of the Turks. An indication of this is to be found in some of the words of Italian origin borrowed by our artisans, e.g. maystor, londja (loggia), regula, kondika, etc.

It is certain that by the eighteenth century our artisan organization had come under Turkish influence. This is shown in particular by the firman of Sultan Mustafa III in 1772, on the organization of Bulgarian guilds, on whose insistent request it was issued. It did not create new status or rights, but rather confirmed and legalized such as were already established by custom and common law. It confirmed the right of Bulgarian artisans to organize themselves in guilds; granted these a monopoly position, in that no one might practise a craft in a given place unless he joined the guild; and conferred the right of self-government: the guild must formulate its own constitution, which according to the firman must be in writing, decide on the admission of new members and administer the guild courts of settlement.

The Bulgarian guilds at this time set themselves primarily the following tasks: (a) defence of common corporative interests, (b) distribution of loans and help in money or kind to needy artisans, (c) general marketing and supply of raw materials, (d) selling of wares at prices defined by the guild, (e) determining the relations between masters and apprentices, by regulating the period or term of work for these two latter, the payment of journeymen, length of the day's work, sometimes too the maximum number of assistants whom one master had the right to keep. As can be seen, there were many points of resemblance between the guilds in Bulgaria and the medieval guilds in Western Europe. Thus, no one could practise a craft unless he entered a guild, and the guild was a closed organization, entry into which could take place only in certain conditions.

The feature which seems to distinguish our Bulgarian guilds from the medieval guilds of Western Europe is that they were never so closed, and the conditions for entry were never so rigid as in the west. The chief conditions were: to spend a certain probationary term first as apprentice and then as journeyman, and to pay a fee. Travelling, taking an examination or preparing a master's work were not required conditions. In more recent times we find instances of even more liberal conditions in the omission of the probationary requirement. . . .

Even before the Liberation the decline of Bulgarian artisan crafts had already become noticeable. This is explained by the progressive association of Turkey with the European economy. The first factors in this process were the establishment of Danube navigation after the Crimean War and then the construction of the first railroads in European Turkey: Cerna Voda–Kyustenja (1860), Ruse–Varna (1867), and Constantinople–Sarambey with branches to Yambol and Dedeagach (1872). The competition of European goods superior to the products of our craftsmen in elegance and cheapness, if not in quality, began to dominate not only Turkish, but also Bulgarian habits of consumption.

Parallel with this, there was a noticeable weakening of the guild organizations, starting with the administrative reforms of Sultan Abd-al-Mejid known as the 'tanzimat' (1839).[1]

After the Liberation, the position of craftsmen continued to deteriorate for several reasons. These were: the closer commercial relations with Europe, coupled with the restriction of Bulgaria's import tariff to a level of 8 per cent *ad valorem*; a considerable contraction of the market, as Bulgaria became a separate political entity; and the mass emigration of the Turkish population, changing tastes and the urge towards Europeanization; and finally the growth of local industry.

With the fall of the Turkish régime, the guild organizations were deprived of any sort of legal basis whatsoever and the majority disintegrated. Those that remained in existence lingered rather as a tradition and then only in some of the smaller and more remote artisan centres.

The position of Bulgarian craftsmen at the time was aggravated because for many years after the Liberation governing circles, absorbed as they were in purely political questions and in the military and administrative organization of the state, showed little interest in artisan crafts and took no measures to regulate and organize them. And so, unaided by the state and without organization, the artisans

[1] See pp. 211 and 250 above, footnote 3.

experienced years of grave crisis in their crafts, years also of general economic crisis in the country.

(b) Slow Growth of Tariff Protection

Long after the industrialization of Western, and later Central Europe, after the emergence there of factories working raw materials with machines driven by mechanical power, Bulgaria still remained industrially only at the level of small-scale production and artisan trades. Thus at the Liberation of Bulgaria there were only about 20 larger scale industrial undertakings of which many, measured by present standards, could hardly be called industrial. The capital invested in them was primarily foreign, mainly French.

After the Liberation, certain conditions undoubtedly favoured the creation of a primarily industrial agriculture: raw materials, and a diligent, energetic population. But many other conditions for this were still lacking: there was insufficient local capital and the political and economic position of the country did not yet offer sufficient inducement for foreign capital; there were no coal mines under exploitation; rail and road communications were poorly developed; towns were small, while the villages and even most of the towns had not yet become fully integrated into the commercial economy, and in general the internal market for industrial goods was very limited. Moreover, the competition of an advanced foreign industry kept increasing and proved a great obstacle to creating local industry.

Finally, there was no independent, systematic protective policy for industry. This is not hard to explain. On the one hand, concentration on the political and administrative organization of the young principality, and also on the various political struggles and controversies so absorbed statesmen that they had little chance of paying much attention to problems of economy or economic policy. Secondly, there were very few persons trained or competent to direct a sound consistent economic policy, nor were there the requisite organs and services for this purpose. Finally, Bulgaria was not fully independent. Apart from the Capitulations,[1] which involved a series of privileges for foreigners, Bulgaria was burdened by the obligation imposed by the Treaty of Berlin not to raise its import tariff on

[1] Privileges granted by the Ottoman Empire under treaty with other states, giving their nationals exemption from taxation, including customs and excise duties. As Bulgaria remained nominally a part of the Turkish Empire under the Treaty of Berlin, these privileges continued in force after independence. According to Dicey (*The Peasant State*, p. 91) they 'bar the way to any equitable redistribution of Bulgarian taxation . . . the whole system has become a barbarous anomaly'.

Western European goods for a specific period above 8 per cent of the value—a protection entirely inadequate for an industry in its early growth.

However, the state did not remain indifferent to the fate of industry even during the first years after the Liberation. From the date of the Liberation till the end of 1894 (when the first law for the encouragement of local industry was passed) a series of measures were contemplated or undertaken by governments or the National Parliament. Most of these, it is true, lack the necessary forethought and deliberation, but nevertheless they display the great desire of statesmen and public servants to assist the advancement of national industry.

One of the first measures of Bulgarian industrial policy was the granting of concessions. Thus in 1881 a concession was granted for a spirits factory in Knyazhevo. By 1883 industrial policy became noticeably more active. In that year for the first time measures were taken for the advancement of Bulgarian industry by a special law for the development of national industry, which obliged policeman, commissionaires and soldiers to wear clothes and footwear produced by local industry. In the same year the policy of granting state interest-free loans to industrialists began, a policy which continued up to 1894. In 1884 a special law reduced the import duty on un-worked pelts—with the object of encouraging the leather industry. Likewise in 1884 it was decreed that in the supply of clothes and footwear to soldiers, local tenders should be preferred to foreign, even if the price difference was as much as 15 per cent. In 1887 discussions took place in Parliament on the proposal of deputy Dyukmejiev for the advancement of Bulgarian industry and commerce. This proposal fell through, however, as it contained almost nothing more than had been envisaged in the law of 1883 for the development of national industry. At the beginning of 1892, another special law widened the scope of the 1884 decrees concerning local supplies for the army. In the same year the government organized in Plovdiv the first Bulgarian agricultural industrial exhibition which was extraordinarily successful and aroused wide interest in Bulgarian economic policy. At the end of the year the Minister of Finance, G. Nachovich, introduced a bill for encouraging local industry which envisaged systematic encouragement of larger scale industry in Bulgaria; since the Minister resigned, this bill did not become law. At this time also the first law on commercial and industrial trade-marks was passed. . . .

The year 1894 is a landmark not only in Bulgarian industrial policy but also in the general political and economic situation. At the beginning of that year the seven-year régime of S. Stambolov fell, and there ensued a political calm in the country which re-established foreign confidence in Bulgaria, enabled statesmen to pay greater attention to the advancement of the economy, and likewise aroused the population's interest and energy in tackling new econo-mic undertakings.

In Dr. K. Stoilov's new government the posts of Minister of Finance, and also of Agriculture and Trade were taken by I. E. Geshov,[1] author of the declarations of the agricultural-industrial congress in Plovdiv and a man fully acquainted with the needs of the economy. Immediately, in the winter of 1894, Geshov introduced a bill for the encouragement of local industry, showing a notable im-provement on G. Nachovich's bill of 1892. In January 1895 this bill became law, and with it began an enduring, consistent and effective policy for the creation of a large-scale modern Bulgarian industry, by means of a series of benefits, such as duty-free import of raw materials and machines, transport by Bulgarian State Railways at reduced rates, concessions, abolition or reduction of taxes, the release by the state of sites and materials free of charge and prefer-ence in public contracts. Just at that time Bulgaria managed to shake off the Treaty of Berlin restrictions which did not allow her to increase the import tariff above 8 per cent *ad valorem*, and from 1 January 1895 the import tariff was raised to $10\frac{1}{2}$ per cent. This tariff, however, was still too low to rank as protectionist—it was rather of a fiscal character. Shortly after, also in 1895, a special law instituted Chambers of Commerce and Industry at Sofia, Plovdiv, Ruse and Varna whereby the state acquired valuable counsellors and colleagues in the field of economic and industrial policy. In this and the following years a strong public movement was created in the country in favour of a national protectionist industrial policy which the government did much to facilitate by its measures.

At the beginning of 1897 Bulgaria raised its import tariff to 14 per cent *ad valorem* and during the year concluded its first trade treaties with a number of countries, as a result of which treaties the duties were fixed at rates between 8 per cent and 25 per cent *ad valorem*. From this point it can be seen that the government used tariff duties in its policy of industrial development. In 1897 also, the law for encouraging local industry was widened and a law was passed for the compulsory wearing of local clothes and footwear by all state, borough and municipal officials and by national deputies— during the fulfilment of their duties. At the end of the same year the

1 See biographical note, p. 264.

first commercial and industrial museum in the country was established.

Konstantin Nikolov Bobchev, economist, wrote *Wertbegriff und Ertragsgedanke* (The Concept of Value and Theory of Profits), Sofia, 1927, and other works.

19. WELFARE AND DEVELOPMENT

Sir Edward Dicey, *The Peasant State*, London, 1894, pp. 37–9; 40–4; 185–211 (selected).

(a) *The Peasant Standard of Living in the 1890s*

OF the existing population [of three and a half million] five-sevenths (or two and a half million) are engaged in agricultural pursuits, and the overwhelming majority are small landed proprietors. The proportion of labourers, who work on other men's lands, is extremely limited. At harvest time, a certain number of foreigners, chiefly Macedonians, come into Bulgaria to seek employment; and the poorer peasant farmers of the country, when their own crops are gathered in, are ready to work for wages on the lands of their wealthier neighbours. But it may safely be asserted that, throughout the rural districts, there is no important section of the community depending for its means of livelihood on any other source of income than the produce of its own lands. There is as yet no *cadastre* in Bulgaria, though one is shortly to be undertaken. Nor is there, so far, any very satisfactory system of agricultural statistics. It is not, therefore, easy to say what are the average holdings of the present proprietors. According to the estimate of residents well acquainted with the country, the average is about six acres, taken all round, though in many instances the holdings are very small, only amounting to a single acre or even less. According to the law, which is still mainly based on the old Turkish legislation, the father of a family has only a qualified liberty of testamentary disposal. If he has only one child, he is obliged to leave that child not less than one-half his property; if he has two or more children, he can only alienate one-third; and, in default of children, his other relatives, including his parents, if still living at the time of his death, have a legal claim to a certain share in his estate. Of course, this system tends to promote the indefinite subdivision of landed property, though, in the case of very small farms, this tendency is modified by voluntary arrangements between the different heirs to the property, in virtue of which one of them is allowed to keep the farm for himself in consideration of his buying

T

out the other claimants, either by paying cash down, or by assigning them a charge on the profits of the farm. There are obvious disadvantages to the State in this continued mutiplication of small farms; and there has been some talk of legislation, with the view of checking the further subdivision of estates. The passion, however, for owning land, and the preference for agricultural labour, are so universal amidst the people, that, no matter what legislation may attempt, Bulgaria, for many generations to come, will remain a land of small proprietors. . . .

In Turkish days the tithe was mainly paid in kind; during the last few years, various, more or less successful, attempts have been made to substitute payment in cash for payment in kind. But these reforms have not made so much progress as might have been expected. Owing to the intense conservative characteristic of peasant communities, and to their profound distrust of any innovation, even if it can be shown to be conducive to their own advantage, payment in cash is viewed with scanty favour by the mass of the population. The tithe system tends to check improvement in agriculture or the employment of money in the development of the land. . . . In consequence, the Government are anxious to do away with the present mode of estimating the land-tax in proportion to the produce of each particular year, and to substitute for it a fixed rental, payable in coin, irrespective of the rise and fall in the amount of the year's production. In other words, if the proposed changes should be carried out, the tenant will become a freehold owner, subject only to the payment of a yearly land-tax to the State in virtue of a perpetual settlement.

The communes hold their lands, which are not of very large extent, under a different tenure. Each commune owns a certain amount of pasture land and woodland, which is held in perpetuity, and for which no rent is paid either in cash or kind. Every member of the commune has the right of grazing his cattle on the parish pasture grounds, and of cutting fuel from the parish woods. As the population increases, and as the land becomes more valuable, the commune tenure will probably have to be altered. For the present, the system works fairly well, and is popular with the country.

The condition of the peasantry has also been improved by the establishment of the *Caisses Agricoles*, which owe their origin to Turkish rule, and which have been largely developed under the recent administration. When poor Midhat Pasha—a sort of oriental Hamlet, born in an evil hour for himself, to try and set right a world that was out of joint—lived at Rustchuk, as Governor-General of the vilayet of the Danube one of his many measures of reform was the establishment in Bulgaria of Mutual Assurance Associations for the development of local industries. . . .[1] When Bulgaria was declared independent, the native government found these institutions in working order, and has since largely increased their number. There are now not far from a hundred of these Caisses to be found in the country, possessing an aggregate capital of £600,000 and having power to borrow loans from the National Bank. None of these institutions have ever actually failed to meet their liabilities, though naturally enough several of them have invested portions of their funds unwisely, have made bad debts, and have thereby diminished their available resources. Still, on the whole, they have done good work, they have enabled farmers in many instances to tide over bad times without resorting to the native usurers, who charge exorbitant rates of interest, and they have acquired the confidence of the general public. As a proof of this, I may mention that the Sobranje has recently passed a law authorizing the guardians of children under age to invest the trust funds at their disposal in the Caisses Agricoles. . . .

Each village is administered by a Mayor, assisted by a council of two or more members, in proportion to the population. The Mayor and the Councillors are elected by the direct suffrage of their fellow-villagers, and hold office for three years. In Bulgaria, as in most countries composed of peasant proprietors, there is a standing prejudice against centralization, and a strong preference for local self-government; this sentiment manifests itself constantly in the Parliament, which, in the main, is a chamber of peasant land-owners.

Take it altogether, I should say the lot of the Bulgarian peasants was a happy one. They live very roughly, very thriftily, and, one might almost say, very sordidly; but they have sufficient to eat, they are warmly, if coarsely, clad, and they enjoy generally a certain amount of rude comfort. They work hard, but they work for themselves, and they are now, even more than in the old days, free to live out their own life after their own fashion. Poverty, in our sense of the word, does not exist. In the towns there are individual cases of destitution owing to drink or misconduct, but these are few and insignificant. There is, as yet, no need to make any public provision for the relief of the poor; there is no question of the conflicting interests of workmen and employers; strikes and trades unions are alike unknown. For all these things the Bulgarians have ground to thank the causes which have made them what they are, a nation of peasants.

[1] See p. 231 above.

(b) Obstacles to Industrial Growth

The agent of a number of English mercantile firms complained to me recently that he found it impossible to push business in the Principality. When asked for the reason of his failure, his explanation was that the great mass of the people had absolutely no wants which they could not satisfy for themselves. The Bulgarian peasant needs extremely little, and that little he provides from the produce of his own land. The average cost of a peasant's daily sustenance does not exceed twopence. Their food, during the greater part of the year, consists solely of bread and garlic. Their only beverage is water; not that they have any objection to beer or spirits, but because they object to paying for them. Sheepskins, provided in most cases from their own flocks, form the universal dress of the peasantry. The clothes, both of men and women, are generally home-made. Commonly, they only possess one suit, and they sleep at night in the same clothes as those which they wear during the day. Their beds are mattresses laid on the mud floors of the rooms where they have their meals. On these mattresses the whole family lie huddled together. Even in the towns separate bedrooms are almost unknown. The servants sleep on rugs in the kitchen, and their masters and mistresses are lodged in a way any English artisan, earning good wages, would regard as intolerable. . . .

[The peasant's] one dominant passion is the hunger for land, and if he sees his way to add an acre or two to his patrimony, he will part with his savings for the purpose. Indeed, the greed for land is one of the causes which are tending to alter the conditions of Bulgarian existence. When the Pomaks[1] quitted the country, their lands were left vacant. A very large portion of these vacated lands was bought up by the peasants in the neighbourhood, and, in order to complete the purchase money, they had to borrow. Having got the lands, they found they had to borrow more. The result is that a large number of the peasant farmers are nowadays burdened with loans on which the interest runs at the rate of 12 per cent per annum; and, in order to meet their liabilities, they are finding it necessary to increase the yield of their lands. Still, there is as yet no very general indebtedness, as the great mass of the peasantry live well within their means. They are satisfied if their crops yield sufficient

[1] Pomak = Bulgarian who has accepted Islam (originally under duress, subsequently by heritage). Dicey is here mistaken; the vacant lands were former Turkish property. The Pomaks did not leave Bulgaria with the Turks, at least not in significant numbers; they still inhabit areas in the Rhodope mountains. See M. Macdermott, *A History of Bulgaria, 1393–1885*, London, 1962, pp. 45–6.

to supply food for themselves and their families. Supposing there is any surplus left, they are willing to sell this surplus, but only at their own price; and if that price is above the market rates, they would sooner store the grain and let it rot than sell it at what they consider to be a sacrifice.

No capital, therefore, for the development of the lands can be got from the agricultural class; there is not much more to be got from the trading class. Owing partly to their exemption from direct taxation under the Capitulations, and still more to their superior experience and aptitude, the wholesale trade of the country is very largely in the hands of foreigners, especially of Greeks, Austrians and Rumanians. The retail consists mainly in the sale of articles of very simple description, almost all of which could be produced in the country at much cheaper rates than those at which they can be imported. There is, therefore, a growing agitation in favour of raising the import duties on all articles which could be manufactured at home. Indeed, I fail to see how a country, situated as Bulgaria is now, can ever develop native industries without some form of protection. But even a protective system cannot create manufactures unless the capital required for their installation is forthcoming; and, for the present, capital cannot be obtained from native sources.

The Government has made various efforts of late to promote the development of native industries. For instance, advances have been made by the state to private manufacturers with the view of re-establishing the local silk trade. Silkworms were kept formerly in almost every peasant's house. A few years ago, however, there was a sort of epidemic among the grubs; the stock perished, the peasants were unable to procure fresh supplies, and the trade died away. Owing to the assistance of the Government who advanced money for the purchase of eggs, the house-to-house culture of silkworms has largely revived, and last year some £80,000 worth of silk skeins were exported from Bulgaria. In the same way, great exertions are now being made to revive the cultivation of the vine, which was almost killed for a time by the ravages of phylloxera. The native wine, which is largely drunk here, is a coarse, wholesome drink, a good deal resembling the inferior brands of Burgundy. . . .

The state has no large funds at its disposal for the promotion of industrial enterprise; and, even if it had the requisite funds, the subventioning of private undertakings on any important scale would not be in accordance with the frugal and almost parsimonious policy of the Sobranje. The obvious remedy for this state of things would be the development of local industries by the aid of foreign capital.

But there are certain difficulties in the way, though rather on the part of the people than of the Government. There is a general conviction in Bulgaria that the railways ought to be the property of the state; I doubt whether any foreign company would nowadays obtain a concession to construct a railway on Bulgarian soil. This determination, however, to keep the railways national property is due far more to the unsatisfactory experience of the lines which have hitherto been constructed and owned by foreign companies in Bulgaria, than to any abstract preference for the principle of state ownership. . . . All minerals belong by law to the state, and two or three coal mines are now worked by the Government in order to secure there always being a sufficient supply of coal available for the public service. But the Government are ready to grant concessions to any person, native or foreign, who wishes to work the public mines at his own expense and risk, and for his own profit. Quite recently they have given permission to a private company to work a coal mine adjacent to the state collieries at Pernik.

For the present, the only native bodies which have any considerable means at their disposal are the municipalities of the large towns; that is, they are the only corporate bodies who are in a position to raise any substantial amount on the security of their revenues. Unfortunately, they have availed themselves of this power to nearly the full extent of their credit, and the money thus raised has been mainly employed in local improvements, which are expected ultimately to pay a good interest on the outlay, but which can yield no immediate return. The municipality of the capital succeeded, some years ago, in effecting a loan in London to the amount, I believe, of £80,000. The interest on this loan has hitherto been regularly repaid. . . .

The following statistics have recently been published, giving, I believe, an accurate account of the various industrial enterprises as yet established in Bulgaria. There are already:

54 woollen factories,	28 cotton mills,	3 pottery works,
36 printing offices,	8 soap works,	1,206 cord and string
8 distilleries,	1 silk factory,	works,
2 ink manufactures,	17 breweries,	66 steam and
2 dyeing works,	2 paste	water mills,
1 basket factory,	manufactures	2 powder mills,
92 cigar and cigarette	23 wool-carding	23 saw mills,
factories,	works,	55 tanneries,
	16 flax works,	2 snuff factories.

Thus in a country of over 3,500,000 inhabitants there are only

1,647 factories or works of any kind important enough to deserve recording, even in a list published in the official organ of the Government, and intended to demonstrate the great industrial progress which has been made of late years. It may be added that of these 1,647 factories, 1,206 are small rope-walks, so that there are only 441 factories which in our use of the word would be deemed worthy of being so described. . . .

The coal from the state colliery at Pernik is sold in Sofia at about 10 francs a ton. It is of inferior quality, and is more like slag than English coal; still, it throws out great heat, and has completely driven out the use of wood fires in the capital. In those parts of the country, however, which are not close to a railway, the cost of coal, owing to the difficulty of transport, is so great that it is very little used. As the country is opened by the various railroads now in the course of construction, the freight of coal from the seaports must obviously become cheaper. . . .

At present Bulgaria is traversed by two main lines of railway, both going from east to west and having no connection with each other. The first and oldest is the Varna–Rustchuk Railroad, which was built some 25 years ago by an English company, and was constructed to provide direct and rapid access to Constantinople from Western Europe, not with much idea of developing the then almost dormant resources of the country which it traversed. The line in question did not prove a financial success, and there were any number of disputes between the English company and the Porte. By the Treaty of Berlin, Bulgaria was compelled to take over all the liabilities contracted by the Ottoman Government in respect of this unfortunate railway. After protracted negotiations the Varna–Rustchuk line became the property of the state at a cost of £1,876,000 which was raised by a 6 per cent state loan; so that, taking into account the price at which the bonds given in exchange for the loan were issued and the cost of commission, the purchase must have cost Bulgaria not far short of £2,000,000. As the line is only 140 miles in length, it follows that it was bought at the average price of £14,000 a mile; not a bad price for a line which up to then had barely paid its working expenses. . . .

By the railway Convention, concluded in Vienna in 1888, between Turkey, Austria, Servia and Bulgaria, the last-named state agreed to construct the Tsaribrod–Vakarel railway, which formed the final connecting link in the direct line between Constantinople and Vienna. This line was completed in 1889, at a cost of £1,200,000 which was provided for by a fresh loan of like amount. Unlike the Varna–Rustchuk, the last-named line was of immense service to

Bulgaria, as it placed her in direct communication with Western Europe and above all with Austria.

For the present, the great railway need of Bulgaria is direct communication between the north and south of the country. As between east and west communication is fairly well provided by the Oriental railway and the Rustchuk–Varna line. Between these two lines, however, there is no railway connection of any kind.[1] If you want to go from Sofia to Rustchuk, a distance, as the crow flies, of not over 150 miles, you must either go to Constantinople or Bourgas by rail, proceed thence by steamer to Varna, and re-cross Bulgaria by rail to Rustchuk; or, if you prefer to go entirely by land, you have to make an enormous détour by Belgrade, Zegedin,[2] Orsova, and Bucharest to Giurjevo,[3] a town just opposite to Rustchuk on the northern bank of the Danube.

Edward Dicey (1832–1911) was editor of the *Observer* 1870–89, and the author of many books on foreign affairs, of which the most important were *England and Egypt* (1884); *The Egypt of the Future* (1907); and *The Peasant State*, quoted above.

[1] The connection was made by the completion of the line from Sofia to Shumen in 1899.

[2] Szeged.   [3] Giurgiu.

Note on Weights and Measures

The *kilọ*, the measure of capacity, varied with locality, with considerable differences between the *kilọ* of Constantinople, of Varna, and of the Danube. The Bulgarian *kilọ*, standardized in 1889 = 1 hectolitre of grain (approximately = 45 kg. of wheat).

The *šinik*, standardized in 1889 = 20 litres.

The *oka*, a measure of weight, standardized in 1889 = 0·78 kg.

The *uvrat*, or Turkish *donum*, the measure of area, standardized in 1889 = 1,600 square metres or 0·16 hectares, equivalent to almost half an acre.

Yugoslavia

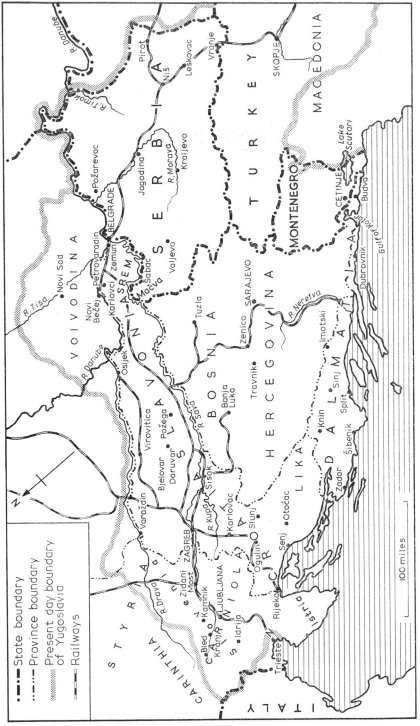

Map 5. The Territories of Yugoslavia in 1900

Legend:
- ·—·—· State boundary
- ·····— Province boundary
- Present day boundary of Yugoslavia
- Railways

100 miles

CARINTHIA
STYRIA
R. Drava
R. Drava
Bled · Kamnik
Kranj · LJUBLJANA
Idrija
Zidani Most
Trieste
Istria
Rijeka
ITALY
Senj
Otočac
LIKA
Ogulin · Slunj
Karlovac
R. Kupa · Sisak
CROATIA
Daruvar · Požega
Bjelovar
Virovitica
SLAVONIA
Varaždin
ZAGREB
Zadar
Šibenik
Split
Sinj · Imotski
Knin
DALMATIA
HERCEGOVINA
R. Neretva
Travnik
Banja Luka
R. Sava
BOSNIA
Zenica · SARAJEVO
Tuzla
Dubrovnik
Gulf of
Kotor
Budva
Lake Scutari
CETINJE
MONTENEGRO
ALBANIA
TURKEY
MACEDONIA
SKOPJE
Vranje
Leskovac
Niš
Pirot
R. Timok
R. Danube
SERBIA
Jagodina
Kraljevo
R. Morava
Požarevac
BELGRADE
Petrovaradin
Zemun
Karlovci
SREM
Mačva · Šabac
Valjevo
Novi Bečej
Novi Sad
VOIVODINA
R. Tisa
R. Danube
Osijek

N

Yugoslavia: Introduction

PHYLLIS AUTY

BEFORE Yugoslavia became an independent state in 1918, the greater part of the country had been for centuries under foreign rule. Serbia had gained its independence from the Turks in the nineteenth century; Montenegro, a tiny principality, had preserved home rule since the Middle Ages. The remainder of the country had belonged to three different states, Austria, Hungary and Turkey. Croatia had been included in Hungary as a vassal state since 1102, though in 1868 it had gained a fairly high degree of autonomy. The Slovenes had come under Austrian rule in the Middle Ages, and in the nineteenth century inhabited Carniola and adjacent provinces. Dalmatia had been Austrian since 1797, when with Venice it had been absorbed by the Monarchy; it was administered as a separate province, and like other Austrian provinces received a provincial diet in 1861. Bosnia-Hercegovina, under a Turkish governorate until 1878, was then occupied and governed under a special Austrian administration until 1908, when Austria annexed the provinces and established a provincial diet. The territory now known as the Federal Republic of Macedonia was under Turkish rule until 1913, when it was ceded to Serbia after the Balkan wars.

Since the economic and social history of Yugoslavia is involved—in some regions completely identified—with that of the several states and provinces into which the country was formerly divided, the following documents and extracts have been arranged in sections corresponding to the political boundaries of the nineteenth century. For reasons of length, it was clearly impossible to include extracts illustrating the history of all the component parts of the country; yet at the same time it was necessary to make the selection regionally broad, in order to illustrate the contrast between the more and less developed regions, an outstanding feature of Yugoslavia's economic life. To resolve this dilemma, we have chosen extracts to illustrate the sequence of major changes in the position of the peasantry in Serbia, Croatia and Slovenia, the more advanced regions, while for some of the other regions—Dalmatia, Montenegro and Bosnia-Hercegovina—we have selected one or two extracts only, to illustrate the nature of their economic and social life—a method which, though inevitably inadequate, serves to reveal some long-term factors in their backwardness. Macedonia has not been included, except in so far as the international impact of the Cincars has been briefly noted; and with the exception of a brief reference to the grain trade, nor has the Voivodina, where economic life and social institutions were almost completely identified with those of Hungary in the second half of the nineteenth century. A few extracts have been included to illustrate some of the more important trade and transport connections which crossed the national boundaries.

As there was no political unity during the nineteenth century, it is not surprising that progress in different parts of the country was very uneven. In the central regions social changes were profound, and along the main river routes trade expanded, while in the outlying regions the oppressive old Turkish institutions outlasted the century, and the economy more or less vegetated. The century witnessed a great increase in economic disparities between regions, for the obvious reason that the growth of railway transport, the beginnings of the industrial revolution and improvements in agriculture affected some regions more than others. But it would be a mistake to regard the contrasts between regions simply as the outcome of different rates of growth prevailing in the different political units during this period. On the contrary, they go back much earlier in time, having their origins in the physical as well as in the political divisions of the country.

Even in the Middle Ages, contrasts in economic and social levels were strongly in evidence. The fourteenth-century Serbian Empire of Tsar Dušan, which extended to parts of Bosnia, Dalmatia and Macedonia, incorporated as living organisms some tribal institutions which were then archaic by comparison with contemporary Western Europe; it was an embryonic feudal society emerging from tribalism, with a money economy rather advanced for its time, with foreign workers in its mines and foreign merchants in its towns. To reconcile conflicts between ancient and modern—shepherds and farmers, lords and bondsmen, foreign merchants attracting workers to the towns and landowners striving to tie them to the land—was the object of the Code of Dušan of 1349.[1] In this aim the Code failed, since the Empire fell into disintegration before the Turkish conquest.

---

[1] For a translation of the Code, see Malcolm Burr, 'The Code of Stephan Dušan', *Slavonic and East European Review*, vol. xxviii, pp. 198, 516; and for its relation to the history of social institutions in Eastern Europe, see D. Warriner, 'Controversial Issues in the History of Agrarian Europe', *Slavonic and East European Review*, vol. xxxii, p. 198.

Such tensions have been constant elements in Yugoslavia's history, because they are rooted in the natural environment. Tribal and clan institutions survived in the mountain fastnesses; the settlement of the best agricultural land was hindered for centuries by chronic warfare against invaders; the mines, whose silver gave fourteenth-century Serbia a key position in the economy of medieval Europe, have always attracted foreign interests whenever these were powerful enough to gain access.

Geographical diversity has thus tended to preserve differences throughout the history of the country. Two-fifths of the territory of Yugoslavia is poor or barren land, lying in the Dinaric chain which separates the ports of Dalmatia from the fertile plains and mineral resources of the interior. This great barrier and other mountain ranges, while hindering economic development, yet at the same time provided a refuge conserving traditions and institutions, so that the population has long been distributed in relation to social security rather than economic resources.

The agriculturally richest lands of Yugoslavia lie in the north of the country, in the south of the Danubian (or Pannonian) plain. They comprise Slavonia: the territory between the Drava and the Sava, from 1745 to 1918 included in the Kingdom of Croatia, Slavonia and Dalmatia; and the Voivodina (the Duchy): the territory north of the Drava and Danube and in the basin of the Lower Tisa, which from 1849 to 1860 was a separate Austrian province, known as the Duchy of Serbia, and thereafter part of the Hungarian counties of Bácska and Baranya and the region of the Banat. After the Turkish occupation of Hungary (1526–1718)[1] these regions were depopulated, leaving a no-man's-land which was systematically resettled during the eighteenth century, partly under the Military Frontier administration, partly in large estates owned by Hungarian magnates and peasant farms colonized by Germans, Magyars, Croats, Serbs, Slovenes, Rumanians, and even Bulgarians.

As a result of this resettlement and land reclamation, there was a great increase in agricultural production and exports during the eighteenth century. At the same time, peace brought growth of trade between the Turkish Empire and Austria-Hungary. Austrian government policy strengthened these trends through the construction of the great highways to the ports, while merchant enterprise came in to develop trade. In all probability, economic progress in these regions was faster in the eighteenth than the nineteenth century, although it cannot be argued that the eighteenth-century

[1] In these regions, the Turkish occupation lasted till this date.

advance made good the immense loss caused by two centuries of devastation. At the beginning of the nineteenth century, these rich lands were still sparsely peopled and under-cultivated, with an insufficient degree of urbanization even by the standards of the time. The poorest lands, such as the Lika district of Croatia, Montenegro, and much of Slovenia, were by comparison rather densely settled.

Thus in the early nineteenth century there were already great contrasts in the position of the peasants in different parts of Yugoslavia's territory. To obtain a conspectus, we may compare the first extracts in each of the three main sections, on Serbia, Croatia-Slavonia and Slovenia.

Serbian peasants, as depicted by Vuk Karadžić, the great ethnographer and linguist, led a robust patriarchal life in an ample pastoral habitat. Turkish land-grabbing and terror in the last years of Ottoman rule are described in the first extract, and also the life of the peasants in the zadruga, the extended family institution, then still firmly rooted in most of the South Slav lands. 'There are no members of the Serbian nation but peasants' is a theme continued in later extracts. In spite of oppression, these peasants were clearly well-fed, with a high animal protein intake, which doubtless gave them energy to revolt and strength to retain what they had won.

In Croatia, by contrast, the peasants in the western districts of the Military Frontier were living on the verge of starvation, as is shown in the account given by the officer statistician Demian (extract 7). As a physiocrat and statistician, Demian well emphasizes the diseconomy of over-population in the barren regions and sparse population in the fertile lands; but confronted with the vicious circle of inertia, low production and irregular consumption, this censorious observer blames it mainly on the laziness of the peasants and their ignorance of good German farming, particularly on the absence of the manure pit, that eighteenth-century dynamic.

In Slovenia in the 1780s, the humane Hacquet, who had, as he said, spent most of his life 'amongst those whom the *literati* call semi-barbarians', was puzzled by the starving peasants' attachment to their stony land, and condemns not their laziness, but the waste of resources entailed in excessive church-building (16). These two authorities, so utterly different in outlook, are interesting not only for their acute observations, but also because they are concerned to interpret rural poverty, or as we should now say, under-development, in the terms of their enlightened time.

Turning from these contrasts in the agricultural background, we may now consider the social history of the regions, which in the greater part of the country was concerned with the struggle for peasant ownership of land.

In Serbia, as in Bulgaria, peasant ownership was attained at the same time as national independence. Serbia indeed came into existence as a peasant state, not, as historians sometimes seem to suggest, through spontaneous combustion, but as an act of deliberate policy. During the risings of 1804–13 and 1815, the Turkish landowners were driven out of the pashalik of Belgrade, and in 1830 a decree abolished the institution of spahi tenure and the payment of tribute to landowners. The land then reverted to the ownership of the state, and was declared to be the property of the peasants who occupied it— in which decision Prince Miloš overrode strong pressures to create a new feudality among the leaders of the revolt. The type of Turkish landownership described by Karadžić continued to exist for half a century longer in the parts of Serbia which were united with the independent state in 1878. Although the institution of spahi tenure was abolished in 1831 throughout the Ottoman Empire the landowners in these remote regions continued to exact tribute and labour until the agrarian reform laws of 1880–2 transferred the land to the peasants.

The simple agrarian reform of 1830 took place in exceptional conditions, since land redistribution is rarely undertaken when there is land to spare. At that time the population of Serbia was still very small, and there was much uncultivated land, ownership of which could be acquired by occupation and cultivation or the clearing of forest land. Miloš ordered the inhabitants of villages where there was free land to allow landless men to establish themselves there and build farms. In this way every Serb could become a peasant proprietor, and in consequence there was no landless proletariat throughout the nineteenth century (except in so far as labour immigrated from Montenegro and Hercegovina).

The second extract, from a report by the first British consul in Belgrade, illustrates the importance of the pig trade in the Serbian economy. Prosperity had been based on pigs long before independence, because livestock, unlike field crops, was not subject to produce-levies from the Turkish landowners, and markets had been expanding since the Austrian-Turkish trade agreement, after the peace of Požarevac in 1718. In 1793, the Porte had granted to Serbia the privilege of exporting pigs to Austria. By 1837, as this extract shows, the country was exporting 225,000 pigs to Vienna per annum—on foot and over the river—an enormous total for a small country at that time, as can be appreciated from the fact that a hundred years later the total exported from Yugoslavia as a whole was no greater. (Another 200,000 were exported from Slavonia.)

Pigs, grazed on acorns in the vast oak forests and fattened on the maize of the fertile river valleys, were to remain the mainstay of trade and diet throughout the century. This constant factor explains the stability of the oddly egalitarian social life of Serbia, described in 1851 by an anonymous author, who found that its conditions contrasted favourably with the pauperism of the working class in Western Europe (3). But by the end of the century, the balance had shifted from country to town, and social inequality had grown to the extent that an educated town middle class had taken over political leadership. Economic equality by and large endured, though it did not prevent chronic political instability in the second half of the century, and may indeed have contributed to it, because the emerging middle class found politics more rewarding than economic enterprise. The arteries hardened, perhaps because the peasants were in their own eyes affluent enough, perhaps because absorption in party conflicts strangled economic progress. For whatever reason, farming methods in 1900 were still in the main primitive, although, as extract 4 shows, the growth of population required the development of a more intensive agriculture. In Serbia, as in the greater part of the territory of Yugoslavia, the agricultural development of the nineteenth century consisted chiefly in the extension of the cultivated area, and a gradual shift from pastoral to arable farming, in which the most important step forward was the increase in maize and potato cultivation.

The next two extracts link the economy of land-locked Serbia with Croatia-Slavonia and the main channels of international trade, and explain something of the commercial situation in the central regions in the early nineteenth century. Zemun in the preceding century had become a great entrepot for east-west trade, most of which was in the hands of the Greeks and the Hellenized Cincars from Macedonia, whose activities ranged along the main trade routes from Vienna and Trieste to Constantinople and Salonika (5 and 6).

In Croatia-Slavonia, the social turning-point of the century was the emancipation of the serfs in 1848. By contrast with Serbia, the social structure of civil Croatia and Slavonia was rigidly stratified. The peasants were either true serfs, bound to the land, or semi-serfs, holding land on condition of labour service and other dues; in Croatia there were also local concentrations of peasant-nobles or 'sandalled noblemen' (see above, p. 58). Nobles were numerous in Croatia, as compared with Slavonia, and estates with some exceptions were not large, while in Slavonia they were enormous. Most of

these large estates were the property of Austrian or Magyar landowners; in the late seventeenth century a conspiracy among the
Croatian nobility had led the Habsburgs to confiscate about two-
thirds of their land which was then granted mainly to alien families.
The duties and rights of the peasants were regulated in theory by the
urbarial laws, the agrarian reform legislation of Maria Theresa and
Joseph II, but in practice, as Tkalac emphasizes, landowners exceeded their legal rights and the law offered little protection except
in so far as it determined the area of land in serf holdings, as in
Hungary (p. 30 above). Two other passages from Tkalac illustrate
the transition from subsistence to money economy, and the degenera-
tion of the feudal estates through over-spending and absenteeism
(9). Desprez, in a celebrated passage, observes the visible extremes
of wealth and poverty (10).

   In the Military Frontier districts of Croatia and Slavonia, which
included nearly half the total population, there were no feudal
institutions; the peasants held the land in large family holdings, on
condition that all males, with the exception of the head of the family,
should perform military service as frontier guards from the age of
16 to that of 60. Since they were not subject to exactions from
landowners, these peasants should have been in a better position
than the serfs of the civil provinces, but as extract 7 shows, there
was much poverty in the district of the Lika, though in military
Slavonia the peasants were evidently better-off, in spite of their
ignorance of good farming (8).

   On the emancipation itself, we have selected two standard documents, the celebrated manifesto of Jelačić, traditionally regarded as
the liberator of the serfs, and the text of the Croatian law of July
1848 (11). Out of their intricate context these can be misleading, as
is shown in extract 12, from the concluding section of an article by
R. Bićanić. After emancipation, the future of the zadruga divided
opinion (13). This old institution, however, gradually broke up, in
spite of legislation designed to preserve it, as it did at the same time
in Serbia and Bulgaria (see pp. 308 and 260). In the remoter parts
of Yugoslavia, however, it survived into the inter-war period, as
Olive Lodge and Ruth Trouton have shown.

   Following serf emancipation in the civil provinces, the status of the
farmers in the military districts was improved by a series of reforms,
reducing the period of military service and improving tenure conditions. In 1873 the separate administration of the Military Frontier
was abolished, and with it the military service obligation; in 1881 the
civil and military provinces of Croatia and Slavonia were reunited.
The old structure left its mark in that farmers in the former military

U

districts of North-West Croatia and Slavonia were among the most prosperous peasants in Yugoslavia territory, as they had largish farms on good land, while those in the Lika remained among the poorest. The differences in population density observed by Demian have persisted, basic to the contrast between rich and poor regions, until the present day.

How far this social change in the position of the peasantry was a condition of economic development is a controversial question; for Marxist periodizers are obliged to regard the formal termination of feudalism as representing the beginning of capitalism, and so convey an impression of economic change and growth which the facts may not vindicate. A. Blanc, in *La Croatie Occidentale* (Paris, Institut des Études Slaves, 1957), emphasizes the stagnation of the rural economy in the second half of the nineteenth century, in which agricultural production did not keep pace with the growth of population, and convincingly argues that technical advances in a few modern enterprises do not constitute an industrial revolution if the volume of industrial employment remains small. At the end of the century, both Croatia and Slavonia were still profoundly rural, with only a very small proportion of the total population employed in industry.

However, in export trade and transport there was certainly development, indicated by extracts 14 and 15; the former discusses the arguments for the construction of the railway line from the river port of Sisak to Zidani Most, which in 1862 linked the Danube region with Trieste and Rijeka, while the latter describes the expansion of the timber trade in Slavonia in the seventies, a consequence of lower transport costs. Agricultural industries relying on export markets expanded in the Voivodina and Slavonia, benefiting in the first instance the owners of the vast estates which still prevailed in these regions, and who had obtained large sums from the serf redemption payments.

To Slovene peasants, however, the opening of the Südbahn, which connected Vienna with Ljubljana and Trieste in 1857, brought disaster, at any rate in its immediate impact. It destroyed the carrying trade, which Hacquet had observed to be the main occupation of people precariously poised on the subsistence margin (16). At mid-century the fragmented small holdings were unable to support their population, and paternalistic government circles were concerned with the need for finding substitutes for the lost earnings (17 and 18). Ljubljana in the eighteen-fifties, indeed, was about a century ahead of its time, canvassing and applying many of the remedies now proposed for under-developed countries, measures to

check fragmentation, vocational training in crafts, travelling agricultural teachers—all that is now called community development,
including one genuine Simmental bull. Some policies were futile,
others effective. The recommendations of Dr. Bleiweiss, for example,
are obviously inadequate if considered as solutions for the immediate problem, yet perfectly sound considered as a long-term
policy of agricultural improvement (18).

Under-employment was an acute problem for a generation and
more after the coming of the railway; and yet rural poverty was to
a certain extent overcome through a multiplicity of policies and
processes. The long-sustained official efforts to encourage better
farming did in time bear fruit, in the expansion of maize, dairy and
livestock farming and generally more intensive cultivation. At the
same time there was sufficient industrial development to draw some
labour off the land and some emigration, while the domestic industries offered off-season employment (19). Feudal relations were not a
central issue, and the abolition of serfdom in 1848 had no great
significance, for most of the agricultural land was already in
peasant hands; peasant-landowner conflicts arose only in a muted
form over such questions as forest rights and the use of the Alpine
pastures as chamois preserves (20). The Catholic clergy, arraigned
by Hacquet a century earlier for encouraging extravagance, now
encouraged thrift through co-operative organization, which reached
an extremely high level. In the nineties the peasants of Carniola,
like farmers everywhere, were suffering from agricultural depression (20). But thanks to all these influences, and above all to their
higher level of education, the Slovenes at the end of the century
were by far the most advanced farmers among the Southern Slavs.

Dalmatia was cut off from the interior of the country, and its
economy—vineyards, fishing, shipping and emigration—was tied to
the Mediterranean, while its land tenure, a form of métayage known
as the *kolonat*, resembled that of the Mediterranean lands. Wilkinson's classical account (21) condemns Austria for its neglect of
agriculture, though, as the following extract shows, there was an
improvement in peasant living standards towards the end of the
century, chiefly through the increase of tobacco cultivation.

Montenegro, a primitive community of shepherds and farmers,
was over-populated even in the 1840s, as Wilkinson observed (23),
and isolated both from the interior and the ports.

Bosnia-Hercegovina was isolated by political frontiers, though the
trade route from the Danube basin crossed its territory via Sarajevo
to Dubrovnik and Zadar, and there was some export of livestock. In
the early nineteenth century the iron mines at Zenica were still

worked, and in Sarajevo and other towns there were the crafts and domestic industries, such as tanning and cotton-weaving, typical of the Turkish provinces at this period. But, as the anonymous author of extract 24 shows, the land was little cultivated and the economy was mainly pastoral, like that of Serbia. While Serbian peasants fought their way to farm ownership and the serfs of Croatia rid themselves of feudal burdens, the peasants of Bosnia remained under the oppression of a degenerate form of the old Turkish land system, paying tribute to landowners, who, though habitually described as Turks, were in part the descendants of Bosnian landowners who had accepted Islam in the fifteenth century, in part descendants of Bosnian or Turkish spahis.

In 1878, the Austrian occupation found a small oligarchy in power, nominally under the rule of a vizier appointed by Constantinople, but actually going its own way; the Turkish land reforms had not been carried through. The Austrian occupation brought much improvement in roads and railways, and rapid development of the iron industry. But although the occupation had been undertaken with the express purpose of reforming the land system and so pacifying the turbulent provinces, no real agrarian reform was undertaken, and the system remained in essentials unchanged until the Yugoslav land reform law of 1919 abolished the '*kmet* relationship'. The last extract, on this unsolved land tenure problem, is taken from Grünberg's authoritative work which shows so remarkably modern an appreciation of the economic effects of a bad land system, and also throws light on the attitude of the peasants in the years before Sarajevo.

As a result of this diverse social history, the new state of Yugoslavia in 1918 inherited a variety of agrarian structures: peasant farms in Serbia and Slovenia; semi-serf tenures in Bosnia-Hercegovina and Macedonia, métayage in Dalmatia; and much inequality of ownership between large estates and dwarf holdings in the territories of the Pannonian plain, formerly included in Hungary, where there was a large agricultural proletariat. The land reform laws of the inter-war period to a large extent removed these anomalies by quickly giving the ownership of the freehold of their land to the peasants in Bosnia-Hercegovina, Dalmatia and Macedonia, and slowly and hesitantly dividing up much of the land held in large estates in the northern Pannonian regions. When the reform was complete, there still remained much variety in types of farming and rural levels of living, but peasant proprietorship was established as the main form of tenure throughout the country.

The other heritage of the past, widely divergent levels of economic development, was recognized as constituting an economic problem in the inter-war years, and explains some of the political tensions of that period. Political independence, however, did not succeed in drawing together the interests of the nationalities composing the new state, nor did it diminish the contrasts between rich and poor regions. On the contrary, during the economic depression of the nineteen-thirties, the position of the food deficit areas (then known as the 'passive regions') grew much worse, reducing their peasants to stark poverty. But in Yugoslavia at that time the existence of depressed areas was taken for granted. Today, however, the distinction between advanced and under-developed regions plays a great part in state planning policy, and is the most contentious political issue. Because of this present concern with the problems of regional under-development, the question of how and why such great disparities arose assumes a new interest. Some background for the answer is provided in the following texts.[1]

[1] Extracts 1, 6, 9, 11, 12 and 13 have been translated by Dr. S. Bićanić, and extracts 4, 7, 8, 16, 19 and 25 by the editor.

I. Serbia

1. THE LIBERATION

Vuk Karadžić, *Geografičesko-statističesko opisanije Srbije* (Geographical-Statistical Description of Serbia), *Danica* (The Morning Star), Vienna, 1827, vol. ii, pp. 79–83, 99–105; also *Istorijska čitanka, odabrani tekstovi za istoriju srpskog naroda* (Historical Reader, Selected Texts from the History of the Serbian People), Belgrade, 1948, pp. 81–3; 83–6.

(a) Turkish Landowners

THE spahis[1] do not have either houses or bailiffs in the villages, nor is it customary for the peasants to work for them. When in the autumn the spahi comes, or, if he lives a long way away, sends someone else to collect the poll-taxes and tithes, the people are bound to carry these to the house in which he is, unless he has sold them back to the peasants or someone else. The spahis take poll-tax only from married men, but it is not everywhere the same amount, nor is the amount regulated in any way, for sometimes it includes various kinds of tithes, for example wine or beehives. Many spahis, especially those who live a long way away, come to an agreement with the peasants, and married men pay a certain amount yearly to cover everything; for example, I know certain villages which up to 1804 paid about 10 grosh a year to the spahi (a grosh then being worth 6 florins and 40 krajcer, though it would now be barely two silver florins)[2] per married man, and nothing more. As a spahi does not have his own house in the village, he rides on arrival to the house he knows to be the best in the village, and all the peasants must feed him while he is there. Spahis are bound to protect their peasants from all want and injustice, and this they gladly do everywhere, especially those who are better off. The Rašković family, who were Serbs, had a spahiluk[3] in Stari Vlah until 1805 when they gave it as security to a Turk; perhaps there, and in Hercegovina,

---

[1] Landowners who in law held their estates in fief from the Sultan, with the right of exacting tithes from the peasants. For the origins and history of spahi tenure, see the extract from Jireček quoted on pp. 248-50 above.

[2] See Note on Weights, Measures and Currency, p. 387.   [3] Estate.

one might still find here and there families who had kept their houses from olden times; but in the pashaluk of Belgrade there is not a single Serb who is a spahi today, nor can a Christian become a spahi in Turkey.

The spahis today in Serbia have a good reputation; but in some villages there is another evil, i.e. the chitluk-sahibs,[1] who take a ninth. In those villages which have only a spahi the peasants say the land is theirs, and the spahi's only a tenth of what they produce; but where there are chitluk-sahibs they say that the land is his, for not only does he take a ninth part of all that they produce, but in addition they must work for him (formerly only on Sunday, but recently on other days too if he wants something done). Sometimes the chitluk-sahibs build houses in the villages, or, to people's annoyance, do not move away from the village. Probably some villages had to submit to the chitluk-sahib system a long time ago, God knows because of what unhappy events; but since the recent Turkish-Austrian war[2] the bashis have forced the chitluk-sahib system on almost the whole of Serbia. Sometimes the chitluk-sahibs have imposed themselves upon the peasants without any kind of payment or agreement, simply by saying: I am your chitluk-sahib. Some who wanted to do it in a legal way as a guarantee for the future bound and beat the peasants to force them to sell their land (because they—the Turks—wanted it). It is easy to understand that the spahis hate the chitluk-sahibs, who are considered even by the imperial court as unjust masters. Now (in particular since 1815) in the Belgrade pashalik not one chitluk-sahib dares to show himself.

Both under the spahis and under the chitluk-sahibs any man can move from one village (or district) to another whenever he wishes, without informing the spahi from whom he has moved, or to whom he is going. He can sell his old land or house or pull his house down, and can return to his old land to gather the fruit from his orchards and vineyard and give the spahi a tenth; and in the place to which he moves he can build a house on empty land and clear fields and meadows, and plant vineyards and orchards wherever he wants.

Besides the spahis' tithes and the poll-tax, the serf must pay the Turks the Emperor's *harach*[3] (the imperial poll-tax) and taxes. In Serbia and Bosnia the *harach* is 112 para,[4] and, with all kinds of expenses, amounts to three grosh[5] per every male head from seven

---

[1] Landowners who had no legal feudal rights or obligations, i.e. land-grabbers. (Tk. *chiftlik* = estate.)

[2] 1787–91.   [3] Tk. *kharaj*, a poll-tax levied on non-Moslems.

[4] The *para* was a small silver coin, equal to one-quarter of a piastre, or about ½d.

[5] About 12s. at the rate of two florins to one grosh quoted on p. 294 above.

years up to old age. Taxes are usually paid twice yearly, that is, on St. George's Day and on St. Demetrius' Day; they include the tax for pastures and all other expenses for the district, such as payments to the village headmen and to the local police, and the cost of entertaining a pasha or some other important traveller. For this reason taxes are not always the same, like the *harach*, but sometimes smaller, sometimes larger. In addition a tax of one or two para per head must be paid for sheep or goats. Those growing tobacco must pay customs duties on it. All these dues when collected together come to less than in some European countries.

But there are some other evils of which European countries do not have even a trace, i.e. fines. If someone kills a man little effort is made to find the murderer, but blood-money is demanded (at least 1,000 grosh); nor is blood-money paid only for murder, but also if a man falls from a tree or a horse and kills himself, or if he drowns or dies of cold or if for any reason he is found dead.[1] A man who dies in this way cannot be buried until the Turks have seen him and made a *chesh*[2] which must be paid for separately. Blood-money according to old custom is paid only by the village where the blood is spilt or in the area in which the body is found, but in recent times (to bring in more) it has been levied on all surrounding villages and is called *djivar*. If a man commits a murder he runs away to another district or somewhere nearer, but after the blood-money has been paid and the murder forgotten he seeks reconciliation with the relations of the murdered man and is then free to return home. No less than blood-money is the fine that an unmarried girl must pay if she bears a child, which luckily seldom happens (the origin of this fine is most likely because children of this kind are usually found dead; and later no one asks whether they were dead or alive). These are common and general fines, but additional ones on the accusation of individuals (i.e. that someone has said something against the Turks) are innumerable, especially for those who are known to have money.

(b) The Peasant Nation

In Serbia the largest villages have about 100 houses; some have not even 20, but mostly they are between 40 to 60, so that one could say that by and large villages consist of about 50 houses. In the plains, particularly in the district of Požarevac and Mačva, the houses in the villages are close to each other; but in the mountains the houses

---

[1] The object of exacting blood-money in cases of accidental death was to prevent Serbs from murdering Turks or their collaborators under the guise of accident.
[2] Inspection.

are so far away that some villages of 40 houses cover an area larger than Vienna; the houses are spread as far as the village land extends. In such a way one can have a neighbour from another village closer than one from one's own. The houses in the plains, and particularly in barren localities, are mainly covered with bark; but in the mountainous settlements the houses are good; they are built of durable materials; many of them have stone foundations and most are roofed with shingles; in some houses there are no separate sleeping-premises and people keep warm round the hearth in winter; and there is not one single peasant who has two rooms for sleeping in one house.

The Serbs live mainly in zadrugas:[1] in some houses there are four to five families and one-family households are few. There are as many huts round the house as there are married couples in the household. They eat together in the house, but only old women and men sleep there; the others sleep in their huts with their wives and children without fire summer and winter alike. Round some rich houses there are huts and other buildings (for instance barns, corn-racks, sheds) making it like a little settlement. Each house has a headman (*starešina*) who manages the house and the whole property: he gives orders to adults and young people where to go and what to do; he communicates with the Turks and takes part in the village and district meetings and talks; he sells what has to be sold and buys what has to be bought in agreement with the members of the household; he keeps the money-bag and pays the *harach*, taxes and other dues; he starts and ends at prayers; when there are guests in the house (and in a large house there is hardly a day without them) he talks to them and has meals with them (in larger houses where there are many members food is served first to the headman and the guests at one table, to the adult men and young men who work on the fields at another; after that the women and children have their meal). The headman is not always the oldest in the house; when the father grows old he hands over the function of headman to the cleverest son (or brother or nephew) even be he the youngest; but if it happens that a headman does not manage the house well, the members of the household elect another. In zadruga households every woman spins, weaves and makes shirts for herself, and for her own husband and children; the women prepare food in turns a week at a time. A woman when it is her turn is said to be the *redar* or *reduša* in charge. The *stanarica*[2] is appointed for the whole summer and is usually the *starešina*'s wife.

[1] For this institution in Bosnia, see p. 376 below; in Bulgaria, pp. 257-60 above; in Croatia, pp. 320 and 341-5 below.
[2] Store-keeper, in charge of food preparation for the winter.

There are no members of the Serbian nation but peasants. The small number of Serbs who live in towns as traders (practically only shopkeepers) and craftsmen (mainly furriers, tailors, bakers, gunsmiths and coppersmiths) are called townsmen. They wear Turkish costumes and live according to the Turkish way of life; during rebellions and wars they shut themselves up with the Turks in the towns, or run away to Germany with their money; for this reason they are not called Serbs by the people and are indeed despised by them. The Serbs, as peasants, live only from land and livestock. True, among them there are some traders who buy pigs and other livestock, game, beeswax, honey, and other trifles, but they live in houses like other peasants. Among the peasants there are smiths (who forge and sharpen axes, hoes and ploughshares; cauldrons and other small things are mended by the Turkish gipsies in the towns), bakers, tailors and furriers, coopers, wheelwrights, carpenters, rope-makers and in some places potters. Every carpenter is also a mason, and every furrier a tailor. Tailors, coopers and carpenters do not work in their own houses, but in those of the family for whom they are doing a job. Even in towns and market-towns the peasants build houses and other buildings. Practically every Serb can do joinery, though not everyone has the tools to make new barrels or carts, for example; and a master craftsman is seldom needed for putting the metal rim round a wheel or for repairing a mill. In the same way the Serbs cut timber, build houses and other buildings (particularly the poorer ones). Every Serb makes his own sandals. The gipsies wandering round the country make spoons, water dippers and troughs which they sell or exchange for flour or other things. The Serbian women sew, prepare, spin and dye flax and hemp, spin wool, weave cotton material and cloth, embroider, knit stockings and gloves. Besides this woman's work they also work with the men in the fields, scything, digging, gathering hay and plums, picking maize and grapes, etc.

Throughout Serbia bread made of maize is mostly eaten; it is true that wheat, barley and rye can be grown in the whole of Serbia, but these grains are not much cultivated except by those who grow them more for sale than for their own consumption. An exception here is Mačva where people eat wheat bread every day. Potatoes have recently been introduced, and are cultivated more as a rarity than as a necessity although they could be of great value. Besides maize bread the usual Serbian food is beans and onions during fasts, and at other times in winter sauerkraut and fat bacon and in summer milk, cheese and eggs. The usual drink is water. Wine is mainly drunk at festivities and that by richer people; and otherwise plum brandy is commonly drunk with food, and luckily is not very strong and so is harmless. The greatest treat in summer is roast lamb, and in winter roast pig and with it unleavened bread, plum brandy with honey, pastries and cheese pastries; on Fridays the greatest treat is fish (i.e. when fish is eaten because it is not always allowed during fasts) and beans with oil.

Throughout Serbia, except the plains and the marshes of Mačva, wine can be grown as good as any in Hungary; but nowadays people seldom plant vineyards to sell wine, only a small number of vines for their own needs. Many empty spaces, old and new, show how many vineyards there used to be, and it is likely that they were neglected during the wars. Serbia has many good apples, pears, cherries, sour cherries, and peaches, and above all plums which are cultivated for plum brandy. Walnuts grow wild and in certain places also chestnuts and service berries.[1] Some money can be got from the sale of wine and plum brandy and also from other crops, but this is nothing compared to cattle and pigs. Oxen and cows are sold every spring to the Bosnians and Hercegovinians who resell them on the coast; goats and sheep are bought by the Turks, and pigs are regularly exported to Germany. It is pigs that are of the greatest and best use to the people because it is easy to fatten them in the forests and because they can be sold at all times of the year.

Vuk Stefanović Karadžić (1787–1864), the father of modern Serbian literature, took part in the Serbian revolution of 1804–13 as reader and writer of letters to its leaders; after its collapse he went to Vienna, where in 1814 he published his first book, a collection of Serbian songs and heroic ballads. His literary work followed parallel lines: collecting and publishing songs, proverbs and folk-tales to show the wealth of the Serbian heritage; and laying the scientific foundation for the adoption of the Serbian vernacular as the literary language, in his Serbian grammar (Vienna, 1814) and his great work the Serbian Dictionary, *Lexicon Serbico-Germanico-Latinum* (Vienna, 1818). From 1826 to 1834 he published an annual, *Danica* (The Morning Star), containing contributions to Serbian ethnography and history. During the reign of Alexander (1842–59), against strong opposition from the Orthodox church, he carried through epoch-making linguistic reforms: the adoption of a new Cyrillic orthography, and the translation of the New Testament into Serbian.

---

[1] Small elongated fruit of a European tree, rare in England, with leaves resembling those of the mountain ash.

2. The Commerce in Swine

Colonel G. Lloyd Hodges (first British Consul in Belgrade), *Report to Viscount Palmerston*, 14 December 1837. Public Record Office, London, F.O. 78/312, Consular 14.

Servia is very fertile and is capable of producing all sorts of grain and flour. The peasantry however until within the last few years cultivated exclusively the Indian corn[1] of which enormous quantities were sown, but of which there is still cultivated *one-third* more than any other grain. In consequence therefore of the almost exclusive consumption of the Indian corn by the peasantry, barely sufficient wheat was sown for the use of the large towns and Turkish garrisons, and the towns situated on the Danube procured the grain and flour of Banat which forms the Austrian frontier. Within the last few years however a much greater quantity of wheat has been sown, for the peasantry begin to perceive that they were in error to suppose it an economy to cultivate the Indian corn exclusively. And at the present period wheaten bread is consumed almost universally.

Servia has therefore no further occasion to procure the corn of Banat, but on the contrary, had she the means of transport, a considerable quantity might be exported. The districts of Servia most productive in wheat are those of Shabatz[2] and Jagodina.

Wheat is seldom sold by the farmer in wholesale until converted into flour, in which state it is sold in the districts situated on the Danube and Sava, at from 40–50 piastres the 100 ochas or 10 shillings 11½d. the Winchester quarter of eight bushels.[3] In the interior as far as Kragujevac it is cheaper, and in districts bordering upon Roumelia[4] flour is sold at half the above price. . . . Only a sufficient quantity of barley is sown for the consumption of horses and frequently it is imported from Banat, though in small quantities. The price of barley is one-third cheaper than flour.

Oats are very little cultivated in Servia, barley being found preferable for horses. The price of oats is the same as barley. Rice is not cultivated, but it is imported from Roumelia and is sold at 150

---

[1] Maize.   [2] Šabac.

[3] *Author's General Note*
    Florin of Austria = 2 shillings.
    10½ piastres (Turkish) = 2 shillings 2¼d.
    Ocha (dry measure) = 2½ lb. English.
    Quintal = 110 lb.
    Ocha (wine measure) = 3 pints.
[4] The region between the Balkans and Rhodope.

piastres the 100 ochas or £1.16.9 the quarter. Servia has no duties on grain or flour.

Servia produces always a sufficient quantity of wine for home consumption. The Servians in general make little use of wine, but in those years in which much is produced, much is consumed and at a cheap rate; on the other hand when it is scarce, the Servians do not regard the want of it, making use of slivovitz (a spirit distilled from plums). . . .

The tobacco cultivated in Servia is hardly sufficient for the consumption of this article by the inhabitants. It is in general of a bad quality. In the district of Shabatz however the tobacco is very good; it is also good in some districts of Valievo. 75,000 ochas or 187,000 lb. (English) of tobacco are yearly imported into Servia from various parts of the Turkish dominions for the use of the large towns. No duty is charged on foreign or other tobacco. A duty of 3 per cent on the value is charged on snuff imported into Servia.

The commerce in swine is by far the most considerable and important in Servia and it is the chief object of domestic economy. The poorest peasant is the owner of some of these animals upon which he devotes much of his time and attention to the great detriment of all other agricultural pursuits. The sheep and oxen are even deprived of all nourishment during the winter months, all herbage or other food being appropriated to the vast herds of swine that overspread the country.

The Servian government in consequence endeavoured to establish a law limiting each family to a certain number of pigs, but it was not carried into effect, so great is the prejudice in favour of the superior profits to be derived in this trade, that the Servian peasantry persist in continuing it and it is feared that an attempt to enforce such a law might produce a revolt.

The trade in pigs is carried on exclusively with Austrian dealers who come to Servia in the spring of each year for that purpose. The sale takes place at this season when the pigs are in lean condition, each animal weighing 80–100 lb. (English), and after much cavilling a purchase is effected from the Servian dealer. The price usually agreed on is from 70–80 piastres the pair, or from 13/1½ to 15/– the pair. Payment is made by the Austrian merchant drawing bills on Vienna or Pesth at two months after date, but they are rarely paid when due and frequently not at all.

The number of swine imported from the various points of Servia into Austria is annually 225,000. The export duty on swine produces the principal revenue derived from commerce in Servia. The duty which is paid by the seller is 10 piastres 20 paras or 2/– per pair.

There is also a tax levied of 3 piastres or 6¾d. on the boat each voyage which transports them; these boats are capable of containing from 80 to 100 animals.

The duty paid in Austria on importation is 33 piastres or 6/2d. per pair, besides the fees of the visiting customs house officials. These duties are paid by the buyer. . . .

Ten million ochas of rock salt (or 11,160 tons) are imported annually into Servia from Wallachia at the rate of £7.13.3 per ton. Much of this salt is afterwards smuggled into Austria. The salt mines in Wallachia from which the salt is procured are chiefly contracted for and worked by the Prince of Servia. The import duty paid in Servia on salt is 9s. 3¼d. per ton.

665 tons (English) of iron are imported annually from Bosnia at the rate of £14 per ton. . . .

Groceries of all kinds are imported into Servia from Trieste amongst which is a considerable amount of sugar. Every article of hardware requisite for the use of the Servians is imported from Austria; firearms and other weapons are however procured from Russia and from the province of Bosnia. . . .

Abstract of the Import and Export Trade of Servia

Articles Imported	Whence	Articles Exported	Where to
Tobacco	Turkey	Swine (225,000 head)	Austria
Snuff	Pesth	Leeches (9,700 lb.)	Do.
Iron	Bosnia	Wool (550,000 lb.)	Do.
Salt	Wallachia	Tallow (500 cwt.)	Do.
Groceries	Trieste	Beeswax (880,000 lb.)	Do.
Oils	Do. and Albania	Valonia[1] (22,320 lb.)	Do.
Woollen Manufactures	Austria	Honey (440,000 lb.)	Do.
Linen	Do.	Skins (all sorts) (760,000)	Do.
Hardware	Austria and Russia	Horn (300 cwt.)	Do.
Rice	Roumelia	Silk (7,000 lb.)	Do.

3. SOCIAL EQUALITY

Anon., *Betrachtungen über das Fürstenthum Serbien* (Reflections on the Principality of Serbia), Vienna, 1851, pp. 7–17.

BESIDES many defects, the Principality of Serbia also displays many

[1] Acorn-cups of the valonia oak, used for tanning.

merits, some which it has in common with the most civilized states of Europe, and others which are peculiar to itself. In these peculiar characteristics it should take just pride, and more powerful countries might rightly envy them.

It has no nobility; this I consider to be one of these special merits. All the inhabitants have the same rights and duties, are equal before the law and the courts, and are taxed equally. Here I cannot discuss the question of whether the existence of a nobility in old countries is valuable for the community and serves the state; but in young and newly-created countries I am convinced that the absence of an aristocracy and the refusal to establish one can only be advantageous. The general opinion concerning hereditary nobility in Serbia is that what is natural must be right, and since it is unnatural to punish the son for the sins of his father, it is equally unnatural to reward him by honours and privileges for services performed by his ancestors. Personal nobility they understand to mean that physical, financial, intellectual and moral pre-eminence should be recognized, valued and rewarded.

Let us compare the position of Serbia with that of Wallachia, where among the mass of the people there is sloth, mental indolence, defencelessness—not to say cowardice—and indigence. In Serbia, by contrast, the dominant qualities are physical and mental alertness, valour and courage, and prosperity—or at any rate a fair standard of comfort—among the mass of the people. Yet Wallachia has long been governed by its own princes and laws, has no Turks in the country, stands nearer to the Protector—through whose power and grace Wallachia was freed from Ottoman rule by no effort of its own—possesses a fertile land, better frontiers, access to the sea, and so on, and should in consequence be better off. But it has over 600 boyar families, who monopolize income, office, power, honour and right, and consider themselves to be the real nation; the rest of the people are *misera contribuens plebs*, fit to work the boyars' inherited or purchased estates, but unworthy to enjoy the same rights as these do-nothings. That is why 'the present reigning prince found a deficit or debt in the treasury of 20 million piastres (probably at the current rate of 32 piastres per ducat) ascertained by a commission of enquiry at the beginning of his reign', according to a not ill-informed article in *Indépendence Belge* (no. 346, 1850).

In the remote past Serbia also had feudal institutions. Perhaps Turkish rule did one good thing for Serbia, by destroying them before it was itself destroyed. Under Kara-George[1] and also under

[1] See Ranke's *Serbische Revolution*, 2nd edition, p. 162 (*Author*).

Miloš[1,2] some voivodes and princes wished to make their titles heritable, and had they succeeded an hereditary nobility would no doubt have come into existence. This Kara-George might have had to accept, for the voivodes were too strong for him, but Miloš opposed the hereditary principle, and although it is alleged that his motives were selfish, the decision was probably to his own detriment and certainly to the benefit of his people. L. de S. Bystronowski puts this point well in his little work *La Serbie* (Paris, 1843, p. 76): 'Prince Miloš wisely utilized the political situation in Europe to found his country. But the powerful men who had helped him to liberate it hoped to win privileges exactly like those enjoyed by the boyars of Wallachia or the magnates of Hungary. They meant to replace the Turkish spahis whom they had expelled, and succeed to their feudal rights as *timars* and *ziamets*. They even began to exact from the people the old payments of tribute and forced labour. But Prince Miloš suppressed these abuses, proclaimed all Serbs free and equal subjects under the same law, and abolished all the privileges and prerogatives which were in process of being established. Thus Prince Miloš, though loved by the people, became a despot or Christian Pasha to the powerful men in his own country. Thus there came into existence the opposition which was based, in spite of its liberal exterior, entirely on wounded amour-propre and frustrated feudal ambitions.'

Next, as the opposite, if not the corollary, of the absence of a nobility, the Principality of Serbia has another peculiar merit: it has no proletariat. It knows no pauperism—that general problem and advancing scourge of all European society. Of course I understand that the sparsity of the population—about 1,000 to the square mile[3]—helps to produce this result, together with fertile soil and modest needs. But whatever the cause may be, the fact is undeniable.

Really rich people are not to be found in Serbia, for property is more equally distributed and there is less poverty and more general comfort than in the rest of Europe. Only the lame and the blind are beggars, and a few work-shy foreign refugees. Cripples are kept by their relations, or by the parish. The blind are often bards, who sing heroic ballads to the music of the *gusle*, to entertain, instruct and

[1] *Ibid.*, pp. 343, 344 *(Author)*.

[2] Karageorge ('Black George') (*c.* 1766–1817) led the Serbian revolt of 1804 and founded the Karageorgević dynasty. Miloš Obrenović I (1780–1860), founder of the rival Obrenović dynasty, was first a leader of the 1804 revolt under Karageorge, but later became his enemy. He led the revolt of 1815; in 1830 was recognized as hereditary Prince of Serbia by Imperial decree, and reigned till 1839 when he was deposed, to be recalled in 1859, shortly before his death.

[3] See Note on Weights, Measures and Currency, p. 387.

inspire their attentive audience, in this honourable way earning
their keep by alms willingly given. O ancient, mighty, wealthy,
learned, ambitious Europe, look with respect on this little country
whose people you call half-savages!

In most European countries wealth, intelligence, prestige and
power are unequally distributed between town and country, with
the towns receiving the lion's share. It is, of course, the capitals
which have grasped this pre-eminence, and nowhere does this un-
balance appear more striking than in France, where Paris claims to
represent the whole country and to some extent actually does so. . . .
In little Serbia the position is quite different: here it is the country,
not the town, which preponderates. The capital has not more than
20,000 inhabitants, who are less militant and, in the opinion of the
peasants, less patriotic than the inhabitants of the countryside. None
of the provincial towns has a population of over 5,000, and they are
therefore without significance. Up to the present, every important
event has started from the country, never from one of these towns.
The prestige and influence of the townspeople is probably diminished
because they include many foreigners and immigrants,[1] and are
mostly shopkeepers or tradespeople, collectively known by the rather
derogatory names of *čifle* (old-clothes men) or *čivitari* (reddlemen).

It may be objected that the absence or rather insignificance of the
third estate is no merit, but rather a disadvantage. Yet I believe
that the country benefits by neither needing nor desiring to have
ranks, castes, bourgeois grades and classes. Where there is no first
class, there can be no third. He who works more, has more; who has
more, pays more; and who pays more carries more weight. The
peasants in Serbia have most, pay most and do most for the country;
and so they carry most weight. Such is the convincing logic of the
state!

To some people it will no doubt seem paradoxical when I assert
that there is no state in Europe where the people are more lightly
and justly taxed than in Serbia. Yet it is quite true. Direct taxes now
amount to about five thalers[2] per person liable to taxation. At present
there are about 150,000 such persons, who together pay 750,000
thalers in two half-yearly instalments. The district N., for example,
has one hundred taxpayers, and so its tax liability is 500 thalers per
year; but as they are not all equally well off, the village elder

[1] These were the *prečani*, 'those from the other side', Serbs settled in the eighteenth
century in Southern Hungary or the Military Frontier districts (see 7 and 8 (*b*)
below), who returned to the new state and as an embryonic middle class played a
part in the development of Serbian trade and industry.

[2] At the current exchange rate, 1 thaler = 4 English shillings, so that tax
liability per head = £1.

X

divides up the total between three tax-classes, of which the highest pays 10 to 12, the middle four to five, and the lowest two to three thalers per head.

There are a few landowners who pay as much as 20, 40, or 60 thalers per head, but always on the principle that he who has more pays more. What the tax reformers in France have so long vainly advocated—direct proportional taxation—the Serbs have achieved, in the simple belief that it is the only fair way to set about it.—As to indirect taxes, Serbia has only those recognized as equitable and retained even in the freest states of Europe, namely 3 per cent duties on exports and imports. . . .

Under paragraph 45 of his *Ustav* (constitution), every Serb enjoys freedom to practise any trade or occupation. So there are no monopolies, either private or public—a significant fact. Before the enactment of the *Ustav* in 1838, some royal monopolies existed, in salt, fishing, river-ferries, and so on; but since then they have all been abolished.

In spite of the fact that Serbia is so lightly taxed and has no monopolies, there is no state debt. Expert financiers will of course say that there is no credit against which debts could be created. To that the Serbs would reply with simple common sense that it is better to dispense with credit than to accumulate debts, and that there are many nations who are rich in debt and also poor in credit.

But this country, which—apart from Sweden—is the only debt-free state in Europe, is not so poor in money as many may perhaps believe. The money in internal circulation is almost exclusively Austrian gold and silver. Taxes are paid in this coinage, evidence that trade must be active. Turkish money is now used only as token coinage in small private dealings, for the danger of depreciation inherent in the circulation of Turkish money was foreseen long ago. . . .

Even the jewellery of the fair sex—apart from pearls and corals—consists only of coined gold and silver. Every woman has her dowry —silver for the poorer, gold for the richer—and wears it on breast, neck and head. Of the total population of half a million females, at least 300,000 wear such coins. So reckoning each dowry as worth 10 thalers—a conservative estimate—then there is an emergency savings fund of six million florins, in this land without aristocracy or proletariat.

Besides these mobile private reserves, there is also a National Reserve Fund. Miloš established and bequeathed it, and though it has since grown rather lighter, it is still there, and will, let us hope, be replenished and increased, *ako Bog da*![1]

[1] If God wills.

4. CONSERVATIVE PEASANTS

M. Jovanović, *Die serbische Landwirtschaft* (Serbian Agriculture), Munich, 1906, pp. 25–94, selected.

Population and Land Ownership

THE total population of Serbia, according to the 1895 census, was 2,312,484, of which 319,375, or 14 per cent, were urban, and 1,993,109 or 86 per cent rural. The population occupied in agriculture was 1,932,660, or 84 per cent of the total. This proportion, and the fact that agricultural produce represents between 80 and 86 per cent of total exports, shows that Serbia is by nature a purely agrarian country.

As to property in land, the farm census of 1897 gives a total of 375,196 households, of which 293,421 or 78 per cent possessed their own land. Of the total rural population, nearly 90 per cent own land. Almost every peasant is an independent proprietor. There is no class of farm-tenants, and tenancy is seldom found, apart from market-gardens which are rented on a crop-sharing basis.

As to the distribution of ownership, Serbia is a land of medium-sized and small properties; there are no large estates such as exist in other countries. The largest proprietor is the state, which owns 2·3 million hectares,[1] or 48 per cent of the area, mostly forest. Private property accounts for 2·5 million hectares. This total includes communal and church property; the extent of the latter is small, amounting only to 23,889 hectares, but the area of common land is large, though its extent is not known.

Serbia is also a land of small farms, the average farm size being 8·6 hectares. The largest number of farms are in the size group between two and five hectares. Fifty-five per cent of the total, or 160,695 farms, have less than five hectares, and 73 per cent of the farms are between one and ten hectares in size. Only 86 farms, or 0·023 per cent of the total number, exceed 100 hectares. . . .

Fragmentation of land has gone to extremes, the total number of parcels amounting to 3,802,939, with an average of 14 parcels per farm. The most fragmented land is found in the regions which were incorporated in Serbia after the last war (Niš, Pirot, Leskovac), where the average size of a parcel is only 0·2 hectares, the average for Serbia being 0·62 hectares.

One of the causes of fragmentation is the law of inheritance, according to which property is divided equally among sons, the daughters receiving a dowry. Usually the landholding is divided up

---

[1] 1 hectare = 2·47 acres.

between the heirs, because the farmer has too little capital and cannot raise loans, so it is seldom possible for the heirs to agree to keep the holding undivided under the management of one son who would pay off the shares of the others. Another reason for sub-division is the lack of employment outside agriculture. Free division of the holding was rare before 1850, for so long as the zadruga tradition was respected the land was owned by the family communities in perpetuity. Their dissolution inevitably led to the splitting up of property.

In a country of predominantly small holdings such as Serbia, the farm family carries out all the work on the farm and outside workers are hired only in exceptional cases. Usually farmers help each other out. As there are no landless, there is no class of farm labourers; everyone has the opportunity of acquiring land, and the law provides that every farmer must have at least 2·8 hectares as an inalienable minimum holding. Townspeople who own land are obliged to hire workers, but these are peasants with insufficient land to employ themselves fully, not landless people. In the most fertile and advanced regions, there is a great shortage of labour, but in the regions of poor soil and backward farming, such as Vranje, Timok and Pirot, there are large numbers of peasants who cannot find enough work on their own farms and so look for work elsewhere. In 1898, the daily wage of an ordinary farm labourer averaged 1·13 francs.

Crops

Of the total area of 4·8 million hectares, nearly half, or 2·2 million, is forest; the area used for agriculture is 1·8 million hectares, of which one million is under field crops.

Maize is the chief bread grain and takes up nearly half the area under crops; it is also used to fatten pigs. Yields are high, averaging 16 quintals to the hectare [12½ cwt. per acre]. It is almost all consumed within the country. The area under wheat is expanding rapidly; average yields are 12 quintals per hectare for winter wheat; 10 quintals for spring wheat [9½ and 8 cwt. per acre].

Other crops cultivated are oats, barley and rye; tobacco (the area of which is restricted by the State Tobacco Monopoly); hemp and flax, vegetables, potatoes, clover and lucerne. Among fruit crops, plums are of importance, for distilling slivovitza, and for export as prunes. Vines are cultivated, but the wine is of poor quality, which could be improved by better selection. Phylloxera first appeared in 1882, causing much devastation, which has reduced production. To prevent its recurrence, the state has propagated American stocks for grafting on local stocks.

Backward Farming

So long as the population was small, land abundant and capital scarce, extensive farming was suited to the needs of the farmer and of the state, but now that these conditions are changing a transition to more intensive type of farming is desirable and necessary. Yet the transition is slow, simply because the peasants are ignorant of its advantages and adhere to what they know. In the more advanced districts, on good land and near the towns, crop rotations are practised, with considerable outlay of capital and labour; manure is brought from the towns, and primitive irrigation systems are installed. But the farther from the towns, the more extensive is the system of land use (recalling the circles of von Thünen). The three-field system is the most general, with fallow in the first year followed by maize in the second, then wheat, oats or barley in the third year. (A four-field system is also practised.) After the three-field system the most commonly practised rotation is annual alternation of maize and wheat or rye, with no interval of fallow. In the many river lowlands and valleys, the land is often cropped continuously with maize, because these lands are flooded in spring, so that no other grain crop can be sown, and the high fertility of the soil, aided by the floods, allows this permanent cropping.

Shifting cultivation, the most primitive of all systems, is unfortunately still fairly common. The land is cropped till it is exhausted and then let go back to grass; new land is then ploughed up in forest clearings or rough pastures. As the abandoned ploughland provides poor grazing, this system reduces the pasture available for cattle. This process of soil exhaustion is occurring in the more remote regions, particularly Krajina, Rudnik, Toplica and Pirot.

Extensive grazing predominates in the mountain regions, where the cattle spend most of the year in the upland pastures, and come down to the stall in winter. Though unsystematic, this type of farming is highly profitable.

These backward methods of land use are accompanied by rather primitive methods of cultivation. Though gradual progress has undoubtedly been made over the last twenty years or so, the improvement still falls far short of the desirable standard.

Why do the farmers cling to primitive methods and archaic implements?

To this question peasants gave a stereotype answer: that the best implement—the iron plough—was too dear, and that the old implements were better suited to the nature of the land, which could never be altered by man and must remain as it was created.

The main obstacle to the use of better implements is, in my view, the well-known peasant conservatism, which holds fast to tradition and mistrusts every innovation as contrary to the nature of things. It is strange that the Serbian peasant, so liberal in other ways, should be such a stubborn conservative in this respect. Political leaders and educated people enlighten him on everything except agricultural questions, and the political interests of the various parties completely ignore the economic interests of their members.

Another drawback, of course, is lack of education, since the most primitive methods and tools are found mainly in the remote regions. The high cost of the iron plough in relation to the small size of the farm and the low price of farm produce is an obstacle, as the peasants themselves emphasized, and yet another is the shortage of skilled workmen capable of undertaking repairs.

Three forms of plough are in use:

1. The most primitive is the scratch plough [or ard[1]] which lightly breaks up the surface of the soil without turning it, and so gives a poor return.
2. The wooden plough is an advance on the above in that it turns the furrow and goes deeper, but owing to its weight it requires twice as much draught power as the iron plough, which should replace it.
3. The iron plough, now coming into use, achieves much higher yields because it turns the soil and ploughs much deeper. The Agricultural Society and the Union of Agricultural Co-operatives have done much to encourage its introduction. . . .

At present there are in use 96,514 scratch ploughs, 34,859 wooden ploughs, and 65,792 iron ploughs, so that the most primitive type almost outnumbers both the others together.

Fertilization of the soil is much neglected, partly because of shortage of manure and partly because the peasants are on the whole ignorant of its benefits. Artificial fertilizers are not used, although recently the Congress of Agricultural Co-operatives has encouraged societies to undertake experiments under expert guidance.

Livestock Production and Exports

Until the eighties of the last century, livestock production was the farmers' chief occupation, with arable farming coming second in importance. Livestock exports up to that time amounted to more

---

[1] The prehistoric implement of the Mediterranean and other regions of Europe. See Grahame Clark, *Archaeology and Society*, London, 1960, pp. 192–3. For its use in Bulgaria, see p. 217 above, and in Montenegro, p. 368 below.

than half of the total value of exports, but since then the export of
other agricultural produce has increased, while exports of livestock
have remained stable, though they still exceed the export of grain in
value and represent about two-fifths of total exports.

From 1866 to 1895 all kinds of livestock, with the exception of
horned cattle, declined in numbers in relation to the cultivated area.

The causes of the decline of livestock production are, firstly, the
continuous clearing of the forests to gain new arable land, which
reduces the area for pasture; secondly, the new forest law which
controls grazing in the state forests, formerly considered as 'people's
forests' and free for all, as the laws regulating their use were not
enforced; and thirdly, the division of the former zadruga holdings
into small farms which have too little labour to care for livestock.
Finally, Serbia's unfavourable geographical and political position
plays a part; as an inland country, without access to the sea, its
export markets are confined mainly to Austria-Hungary, a situation
exploited by the Hungarian government which has restricted livestock imports (and so reduced prices) under the pretext of veterinary
control—a piece of political chicanery, since the alleged diseases do
not exist.

Although pigs have declined considerably in numbers for the
reasons given above, they are still the most important export and
the most important food. In winter the peasants eat pork almost
exclusively. The pig is the mainstay of the small farm, because it
grazes in the oak forests, consumes scraps, and multiplies fast. . . .
Attempts to improve the best native breed, the hardy heavy Shuma-
dinka, by crossing with imported Berkshire, Yorkshire and Manga-
litsa stock, have increased fertility and quickened growth, but at the
same time have reduced resistance to disease and climate.

Credit and Co-operatives

Credit facilities for agriculture are quite inadequate. The only institution for long-term credit is the so-called Public Fund, founded as
a mortgage bank in 1862, a public institution under the Ministry of
National Economy. For several reasons it has failed to meet the need:
the minimum loan, 1,000 francs, is much too high for the small
farm; most peasants do not know of the Fund's existence; and the
absence of a land register is a drawback. Only a small proportion of
the farmers make use of it. The majority of the peasants still rely on
money-lenders who borrow from the Fund to relend to peasants at
usurious rates—a regrettable abuse. Though the rate of interest is
restricted by law to 12 per cent, peasants in fact pay much higher
rates. . . .

To overcome the credit shortage, agricultural co-operatives have been established. The first agricultural co-operative was founded in 1893; in 1903 there were 335 societies, of which 328 were concerned mainly with the supply of credit, two with supply of farm equipment, two with marketing wine, one with marketing dairy produce, and one with purchase of consumer goods. As they are generally small, almost all societies are really multipurpose, since the credit societies also undertake to purchase farm equipment and consumer goods for their members.

Under the 1900 law for the Support of Agricultural Co-operation the state is pledged to contribute 25 per cent of the proceeds of the public lottery and 50,000 francs from the state budget towards a fund placed at the disposal of the Union, to finance it until such time as it is in a position to dispense with state assistance.

The late development of the co-operative movement in Serbia can be attributed to the low educational level of the peasants. Another cause, in my opinion, is the political conflict which flared up in the eighties and has since prevented all combined activity for the common good by carrying political divisions to extremes. Those who by reason of their position and ability should have taken the lead in joint action have been absorbed in political activity, at the expense of the economic welfare of their fellow citizens. Governments have changed with such rapidity that no coherent policy or economic plan could be carried out. Recently, things have taken a turn for the better, as is shown by the legislation mentioned above. But leadership is still the problem; a co-operative society will exist so long as the teacher or priest or whoever started it still lives in the village, and will break up when this leader dies or is transferred. Ten societies have dissolved for this reason. The hostility of money-lenders or retailers also dissuades people from founding or joining co-operative societies.

Government Policy

Until quite recently the activity of the state in agriculture was minimal, considering that 85 per cent of the population live by this occupation. Something was done to encourage agricultural education, but not much, though the need was immense, since agricultural progress depends on it. The first agricultural school was established as early as 1852 in Topchider near Belgrade, which took in one or two young men from each district and gave practical instruction in farming. But for political reasons the school was closed seven years later, in 1859, and fourteen years elapsed before a new agricultural school was founded at Požarevac in 1872, only to be closed in 1882 on account of its bad organization. Two secondary agricultural schools have since been opened, one in 1882 in Kraljevo for arable farming, the other in 1891 at Kloster Bukovo for vine and fruit growing. The former takes pupils of 14–18 for a three-year course; in 1899 it had 109 pupils, half of whom were on state scholarships. The latter had 86 pupils, of whom 67 were state scholars. Both have model farms and good modern equipment. . . .

Unfortunately it cannot be said that these schools have fulfilled their purpose of producing better farmers, through training the sons of well-off farmers in modern methods. State scholars were selected from the sons of artisans or poor peasants, who from the first intended to become civil servants after finishing their studies. New posts were created under the law of 1898 which appointed state agronomes, under the law for the establishment of agricultural stations for fruit growing and livestock breeding, so that even the worst pupils could hope to get a job through influence rather than ability. Since they were concerned only with finding a job and had no genuine interest in agriculture, such people could not make good practical farmers. So the schools have produced not farmers but officials. . . .

II. International Trade

5. ZEMUN AS A CENTRE OF EAST-WEST TRADE

Ignaz Soppron, *Monographie von Semlin und Umgebung* (Monograph on Zemun and its Environs), Zemun, 1890, pp. 363–4; 381–3; 384; 437; 438–9; 469–70.

GUILDS were established in the Frontier Province on the same pattern as that of the Crownlands of Austria and Germany, and offered artisans the same privileges. In the Syrmian-Slavonian Generalate[1] all masters and journeymen formed a single privileged guild, with its headquarters in Peterwardein[2] and branches in other communities and garrisons, including Semlin.[3] Here as far back as the Schönborn period[4] the craftsmen had formed a special class, under a president elected by themselves; the more prosperous they grew, the more exclusive they became.

Most craftsmen in Semlin were Germans, generally of the Catholic faith, which explains why they watched so jealously to ensure that only Catholics should be authorized to practise certain trades. For half a century they adhered to their custom of not accepting any Serb as apprentice, and of not giving work or granting the title of master to any craftsman of Serbian nationality. Of course there were exceptions, but only in certain crafts, as for example the soap-boilers, copper-smiths and a few other trades; some crafts were reserved for German masters only, others were purely Serbian. The latter included soap-boilers, sandal-makers, honey-bakers, national-dress tailors, furriers, mattress and bedcover-makers, Turkish-dress tailors, slipper-makers, cake-bakers and carpenters. The authorities however were concerned only to attract craftsmen, regardless of whether they were Germans or Serbs. . . .

The foreign merchants were Greeks,[5] mostly Turkish subjects who had escaped to become subjects of Austria, for reasons explained above. . . . In Serbia also there were at that time many Greek merchants who disposed of enormous assets in liquid capital. Kyriak Barboglu complained that on the night of 1 November he had been

---

[1] See below, pp. 328–9. Syrmia = Srem. [2] Petrovaradin. [3] Zemun.
[4] 1705–34. [5] Including the Hellenized Cincars; see following extract.

robbed of 8,000 gold ducats by his servants; but this accusation was not made until a fortnight after the alleged deed, because Kyriak had not noticed before that the money had gone!

The richer Greek merchants were not only engaged in forwarding goods and suchlike business with Turkey, but also took part in the grain trade and were wholesale dealers in colonial goods.[1] Some were also bankers and money-dealers. . . . All these trading enterprises also carried on exchange and credit dealings, and so were of service to the public on account of the confused currency situation which always prevailed on the Turkish frontier. . . .

Greek immigrants were far too numerous to be able to confine themselves to the branches of trade stipulated by the Treaty of Požarevac,[2] and so carried on other trades, becoming craftsmen and shopkeepers. Some traded in livestock, particularly pigs, as for example the brothers Karamat, who were among the first immigrants. In consequence some of them evaded the treaty stipulations and acquired house property. The Greeks or Macedonians engaged in crafts or the livestock trade were the first to abandon their Greek national status and become Serbs, while the forwarding and commission agents held fast to their Greek nationality, no doubt because of the nature of their business. Commission agents and dealers in colonial goods maintained uninterrupted relations with the Greeks, and so kept their books and carried on correspondence in Greek; but the livestock dealers came into contact with the country folk, and kept books in Serbian, if at all, as they made more use of the wooden tally. . . .

Some years after the signing of the peace treaty,[3] conditions here on the frontier gradually improved, and in the second half of the decade no more is heard of the acts of violence or violations of the frontier which had formerly occurred; nor were there the previous hindrances to trade. In legal matters there was reciprocity, and on the Turkish side a willingness to encourage trade. . . . 'Serbia prospered and grew rich through cattle-raising . . . in its trade with Austria alone it gained over 1,300,000 guilders a year.'[4] Of this trade the merchants of Semlin took the lion's share. . . .

With the Turks there again appeared at the mouth of the Sava their evil companion, the oriental plague.[5] At first it was only sporadic, but then broke out with great violence in Belgrade in the summer of 1795 and claimed many victims daily. It invaded even the quarantine centre at Semlin, and as several cases were fatal a longer period of quarantine, 42 days, was introduced, which did not

---

[1] Chiefly sugar and coffee. [2] Passarowitz, 1718.
[3] Sistova, 1791, favourable to the Turks. [4] Source not quoted. [5] Cholera.

however prevent the spread of the disease in the town or allay the terror of the population. Cattle plague had a damaging effect on the cattle trade in general, but import of pigs from Serbia was allowed, and they came over in greater numbers than before. During the epidemic, traffic between Belgrade and Semlin was only disturbed, not interrupted, and it was in this very period that the import of raw cotton from Macedonia and Thessalonia began to increase enormously. . . .

The total population of Semlin in 1801 amounted to 7,089, an increase of 50 per cent over the total of 4,559 in 1781. By religion the population was divided into 5,642 Greeks, 1,266 Catholics, 157 Jews and 24 Moslems. . . . Occupations were much the same as before: there were 32 merchants, 85 shopkeepers, 396 craftsmen, 95 innkeepers, 559 craftsmen-journeymen and servants, 7 priests and 63 central and local government officials. Non-residents numbered 560, of whom 190 were foreigners. The classification 'Greek', hitherto used in the census, was no longer employed; the term 'foreigner' was used, which meant 'Turkish subject'. From the beginning of the century, more and more Jews came in from Turkey.

A memoir by Paul Sparta describes how formerly the treasures of the Orient all flowed into Semlin to make their way thence to the west. A whole caravan of sellers of oriental wares entered the quarantine centre, with their bales of goods, their foreign clothes and medley of languages. In addition to the articles which had to be dealt with immediately by the customs, there were also great quantities of red oriental thread, raw silk, soft leather and other coloured leather goods, Macedonian honey and wax, olives, oil, opium, essences, tortoise-shell, gold and silver wares, pearls from Constantinople, carpets from Persia, shawls from India, partly for import, partly for transit trade.

Ignaz Soppron (1820–94), printer, publisher, journalist and amateur historian, printed the work quoted above on his own press in Zemun.

THE CINCARS 317

6. TRADE ROUTES AND THE CINCARS[1]

D. J. Popović, *O Cincarima* (The Cincars), Belgrade, 1937, 2nd edition, pp. 114–17.

THE Cincars, both Hellenized and pure, flooded the Austrian Empire after the Peace of Požarevac. Practically the entire wholesale and retail trade of the Near East and Central Europe was in their hands. 'Many Cincar houses were in direct contact with the main European ports and industrial cities.'[2] 'The wholesale trade of Hungary, and most of the money was in the hands of the Greeks and the so-called Cincars.'[3] Their commercial companies hold in their hands all trade 'from Athens to Budapest and Vienna'.[4]

In some areas certain branches of activity were almost entirely in their hands, and Schwartner, for instance, who seems to have known them very well indeed, is full of praise for their success, their ingenious speculations, and the way in which these 'cunning Neo-Hellenes could create an enormous fortune from nothing'.[5] They traded with everything and everybody, sold, bought, rented, leased, exported, imported, in one word carried on any kind of business which brought gain.

They used every method from the most primitive barter exchange to the most complex monetary and financial affairs. In certain kinds of business they were unrivalled, and often they were able to monopolize certain commodities . . . (they traded in Hungary, Transylvania, Rumania, Bukovina and Turkey with ever-increasing profits). . . .

They kept in their hands also the trade up to Carantania[6] and Styria. They smuggled rifles from Carinthia to Turkey and in the Generalate of Varaždin they traded textiles for food, or tobacco from Požega for wax. They exported cattle and grain from Slavonia.

---

[1] The Cincars are a small ethnic group, also known as Vlachs, Kutzovlachs or Arumanians, living by pastoral farming in Northern Greece and adjacent parts of Yugoslavia and Albania. Those of them who came to Serbia in the seventeenth and eighteenth centuries achieved the commercial predominance described in this extract; they founded several of the leading business families of Vienna in the nineteenth century, including that of Baron Sina, the financier of the Hungarian magnates (see Hungary, extract 11). In Serbia and Central Europe generally they were known as Greeks, and 'Greek' or 'Cincar' became synonymous with 'merchant'. They believed themselves to be of Greek origin and in the nineteenth century supported the Greek national cause.

[2] F. Kanitz, *Das Königreich Serbien*, Leipzig, 1868, p. 336 (*Author*).

[3] Schwartner v., Martin, *Statistik des Königreichs Ungarn*, 2nd edition, Pest, 1809–11, I, p. 138 (*Author*). See p. 39 above, footnote 1.

[4] *Ibid.* (*Author*).   [5] *Ibid.* (*Author*).   [6] Carinthia and Carniola.

After 1770 they tried exporting grain to Italy which until then had met her needs from Hungary, England and Egypt. The attempt was most successful. The grain was taken by barge up the river Sava to Sisak and Karlovac, and then transported along the Carolina road[1] to Venice, Ancona and further to Naples, Genoa and Nice. The same route was used by the cattle trade. . . .

Among all our cities the most important commercial centre was Zemun. With its very convenient position, on the frontier between two empires, Zemun became an important factor in the commercial world, thanks to the Cincars. As early as 1754 the Greeks and Cincars had the bulk of industry and trade in their hands. Zemun soon became 'a large trading centre for all German and Turkish goods, and merchants built large storehouses and warehouses there'. 'By the rivers Kupa and Sava many ships and barges came from Croatia and Carinthia with German and Italian goods, and by the rivers Drava and Danube boats arrived from Styria, Hungary and Austria with Hungarian, German, French and English goods. When these goods had been unloaded from the boats Turkish goods were loaded in their place and the boats sent back. Sometimes however it was too difficult to send the boats upstream to Germany and so they were sold. Even greater amounts of German and Dutch commodities were brought by cart across Hungary via Peterwardein, and here unloaded, and goods from Turkey and Syrmia loaded. From Zemun anyone can send and change currency for all countries in Asia and Europe, which is a sure sign of a very developed commerce.'[2]

[1] From Karlovac to Rijeka (Fiume).
[2] F. W. Taube, *Beschreibung von Slavonien*, Leipzig, 1777, iii, 108 (*Author*).

III. Croatia-Slavonia

7. FARMING IN THE MILITARY FRONTIER OF CROATIA

J. A. Demian, *Statistische Beschreibung der Militär-Grenze* (Statistical Description of the Military Frontier), Vienna, 1806, vol. i, pp. 4–8; 40; 42; 44–5; 64–5; 81–5; 87–8; 91–3; 306–9; 313–14; 320–1.

THE Military Frontier, which was set up as a defence against Turkish invasion and has existed through two hundred years of history, extends from the Adriatic Sea along the Croatian, Slavonian, Banat[1] and Transylvanian frontiers as far as Maramuresh, where the left wing of the second Transylvanian Wallachian regiment is stationed.[2]

Along this frontier cordon, more than 230 miles[3] long, and guarded day and night by 4,380 men, lies the extraordinary military land whose inhabitants are at one and the same time soldiers and peasants—a system to be found nowhere else in Europe, and one which creates most difficult problems for the art of government, particularly at the present time.[4]

This large and powerful establishment is generally less known to us than the savage islands of South America, even to the highly educated, although for centuries it has been of the greatest importance to Hungary, the adjacent parts of Germany and indeed to the whole of Europe. In attempting to describe this Military Frontier, I believe that I have filled an important gap in Austrian geography and produced a work which will be useful to men of affairs. Doubtless many of my readers will believe that they are reading an account of a recently discovered American island, rather than that of a province which for over a century has been the object of more than paternal care on the part of the Royal House of Austria.

[1] i.e. the Banat of Temešvar.
[2] The position of the Military Frontiers of Croatia and Slavonia described below is shown on the map of Hungary facing p. 29.
[3] See Note on Weights, Measures and Currency, p. 387.
[4] The rights and duties of the farmers were first clearly defined in the basic law of 1807, issued after the publication of Demian's work. For its provisions, see J. Tomasevich, *Peasants, Politics and Economic Change in Yugoslavia*, Stanford and London, 1955, pp. 78–9.

The Military Frontier of Croatia

The present Military Frontier in Croatia came into existence and was organized in different districts at different times. Owing to the circumstances of its original foundation, it is still divided into three Generalates, Karlstadt,[1] the Banat,[2] and Varasdin.[3] . . .

The Karlstadt Generalate

Inhabitants

A census or conscription list of the inhabitants of the Military Frontier is taken every two years. In the year 1802 182,733 souls were numbered in the Karlstadt Generalate.[4] . . . As to the ratio of population to land area, there are 1,295 people to each of the 141 square miles[5] of the Karlstadt Generalate. . . .

In 1802 there were 16,572 houses in the four regimental districts. The Karlstadt Generalate contains few large concentrated villages, especially not in the hills, where the houses are mostly dispersed. Most of the houses in the Karlstadt Generalate are miserable huts, all, with few exceptions, built of wood. Their roofs are disproportionately high and heavy, and the farmsteads are usually too small for their inhabitants, since they often house between 30 and 60 people. There is limestone and building stone in plenty in the region, so that in future houses of more solid material could be built, for the use of wood as building and repair material makes heavy inroads on the forests. . . .

Characteristics of the Inhabitants

In a frontier house several married couples usually live together, making up one family (*Hauskommunion*). Some families have grown so large in the course of time that four generations, including 50 or 60 people, live under one roof, where once there dwelt only a father with four or five children. Then the joint household can no longer continue, as the natural bonds weaken and the community spirit is dissipated in quarrels, conflicting ambitions and envy. The house elder who presides over the community and rules and guides it, and whom all obey, can no longer control the swarm of inmates, and the wretched little house cannot provide adequate quarters. . . .

The frontiersman is as a rule not given to regular work and purposeful occupation; he has little enterprise or industry and is on the

[1] Karlovac.   [2] i.e. the Banat of Croatia, to the east of Zagreb.   [3] Varaždin.
[4] In 1802 the total population of the three Generalates of Croatia numbered 376,180, or 45 per cent of the total population of Croatia, estimated by the author at 800,000.
[5] See Note on Weights, Measures and Currency, p. 387.

whole lazy. He customarily spends the whole winter from November to March in idleness, and eats up most of his store of food in boredom, so that he must often go short of food in the exhausting farm work of summer. The women, by contrast, are so hard-working that they not only perform all the housework—the tasks proper to their sex—but do all the man's hard work as well, and really carry the whole burden of the day. The stranger travelling in these parts will be amazed, when he first meets a woman of the Lika, to see how she walks singing over the high mountains of the Velebit or Kapela, a full sack on her head, a child on her back and another in her arms, while the man swings along beside her, smoking his pipe, idle and empty-handed. One never sees a girl unoccupied; at every step they spin, carrying the distaff at their side, or with the flax or hemp bound to one side of the head, as is the custom in the Sichelberg[1] district.

The moral character of the frontiersman is a mixture of good and bad, vice and virtue.[2] He is generous to the point of extravagance, magnanimous, inquisitive, docile, contented in misfortune, patient and long-suffering. His hospitality is so lavish that everyone who arrives at a mealtime must be his guest, and he will be insulted if they decline his generosity. He would feel it a disgrace to turn a poor man from his door or to refuse shelter to a traveller. . . .

. . . The most fatal characteristics of these people are intemperance and thriftlessness. The frontiersman lives from one day to the next, unable to foresee his needs. If the food is there, he eats it, regardless of the future when he may have to pay for this waste by starvation. Great displays of extravagance are seen at weddings, family feasts (the so-called *keszno-ime*) or at the feast of the patron saint. Half a year's food supply may be eaten at a wedding-feast, in which half the village may share and which may last for weeks. Funerals are concluded with a banquet, in the Lika with Dalmatian wine as the mainstay. Wife, child or mother may be lying in the last extremity, while the man goes round borrowing money to buy Dalmatian wine.

Yet in this unthrifty way of life, which may bring a family to ruin, the frontiersman is content, and satisfied if need be with little or poor food; indeed he can endure indescribable hunger and exist for days on a piece of bread. Hacquet in his description of the Slav races gives us an illustration:

[1] Žumberak, near Zagreb.
[2] This account, which on its favourable side owes much to Hacquet, is reproduced in almost identical form in the author's account of the province of Croatia (*Darstellung der öst. Monarchie*, vol. iii, part ii) as also is the indictment of peasant farming. Accordingly we have not included extracts from this volume.

Y

When I last visited this region and Croatia in the spring of 1787, the poor people were suffering from famine. In April I was riding over the mountain, when I met a maiden of some sixteen years, who bore a sack on her head and in a scarcely audible voice asked me for bread. This seemed strange, for begging is not customary among them. I asked why she asked for bread, seeing that I could not carry any on horseback. I offered her a few groschen, which she took with a dejected look, and said that she had eaten nothing for three days and was too weak to go further, and could buy no bread with the money, for in her village it was not to be had at any price. She spoke the truth, for I took her pulse and found that the rate was only 16. Then I asked her whence she came and what she had in her sack? It was perhaps flour, I thought, but when she opened it I found crushed tree-bark, for baking bread with clay. By good fortune I had some bread in the saddle-bag, which I at once gave to her, at which the poor creature was so overcome that I feared she might swoon.[1]

Agriculture

The area of land in the Karlstadt Generalate amounts to 279,148 joch.[2] But only 21,464 joch are good land, while 114,848 are of medium quality and 241,047 are poor and infertile. . . . In the Lika valley, which includes the districts of the Lika and Ottochan regiments, most of the arable land yields nothing in a dry summer, while in a wet summer it will give only a little hay; so these lands are cropped only once in every four, five or even ten or twelve years. In addition to the fact that in the Karlstadt Generalate the best soil is not even as good as the medium-quality land in the Varasdin Generalate, the climate is anything but favourable. It is subject to such frequent and extreme variations that scarcely a year passes without one crop or another being destroyed. . . .

The most common rotation is the three-field system. In the first year the good land will be sown with maize or wheat, after manuring, in the second with buckwheat, barley or spelt and in the third year with millet or oats; after which the land is manured again and the rotation repeated, or the land left fallow, for one or two years on the good land, for three years on the land of medium quality, with mixed grain or spelt in the first year and millet or oats in the second. The worst land is left fallow for four, six or twelve years, during which it is used for grazing, and then is sown with oats or millet for two years.

---

[1] Balthasar Hacquet, *Abbildung und Beschreibung der südwest- und östlichen Wenden, Illyrer und Slaven*, Leipzig, 1802–5, part i, vol. iv, chapter xi, p. 152. The passage describes the territory inhabited by the western Uskoks, on the borders of Carniola and Croatia; other passages from the same work are quoted in extract 16 below.

[2] See Note on Weights, Measures and Currency, p. 387.

The frontiersman as a rule only manures the ground or garden lying nearest his house, called the *podkuchniczi*, which is planted with potatoes and cabbages; if he has enough manure then he will put it on the nearest field before planting maize. The distant fields are rarely manured owing to lack of dung, for which the long fallows are a substitute. . . . One great weakness in the farming system is the great distance of the fields from the farmsteads. There are some households in this Generalate whose fields lie from three to six hours distant from the farmstead, and are broken up into between four and sixty pieces, which lie scattered in different parts. The fields therefore cannot be properly farmed or cultivated because man and beast are exhausted even before they reach them.

Another great defect is the lack of manure, which is due to the fact that the cattle are usually not kept in the stall, but graze on remote pastures, remaining in the mountains till the snow falls. What little manure there is does not get proper treatment; it is not kept in pits, but left under the open sky to be dried up or washed out. . . .

Yet another great weakness in the economy of the Karlstadt frontiersman is the absence of barns with a proper threshing floor for the corn. As there is no protection for the corn against the frequent storms, much of the harvest is lost, even if it does not go rotten in the fields or get sodden and grown out in the conical shocks. So immediately after the harvest the farmer must begin threshing, which is carried out in the open by the horses treading out the corn. In consequence he is held back from the autumn ploughing and sowing. This could be avoided if he had a proper threshing floor where he could spend the winter at work, instead of idling the winter through, devouring his food in boredom.

Adding up these obstacles—unfavourable climate, poor soil, laziness and ignorance—it is not surprising that the Karlstadt Frontier never covers its annual needs of food, and that there is often great scarcity. The grain deficit is made good partly through barter trade with Bosnia, in which the frontier people buy salt and exchange it for grain, partly through the transport of grain from Karlstadt to Zengg.[1] There were harvest failures in the region in 1762, 1764, 1774, 1784, 1785 and 1802.

The Varasdin Generalate

[With a total population of 101,902 in 1802], the Varasdin Generalate has only 1,500 people for each of its $67\frac{3}{4}$ square miles. The population is therefore very sparse in this Generalate, which is only half as densely peopled as the Banat District, which is the more

[1] Senj.

surprising, since the land of the Varasdin Generalate is among the most fertile in Croatia. . . .

As mentioned above, the Varasdin Generalate includes 265,145 joch of arable land. Taken as a whole, it has more land than can be cultivated by its small labour force. Most of the frontier households of this district own property in land far in excess of their capacity to work; many have up to 150 joch, while the manpower available is barely sufficient to cultivate 20. This is certainly one of the main reasons why most of the land is not cultivated, particularly in the hilly districts. . . .

There is anything but a surplus of grain in the Varasdin Generalate; even in good years the needs are not always covered and if the weather is bad there is a large deficit. . . . The main reason why even this fertile part of the Military Frontier offers such a poor living to its people, and rarely provides enough for their sustenance, lies in its faulty and negligent cultivation. How can the land be well cultivated if the workers available in most households are too few to carry out the field work?

Johann Andreas Demian (1770–1845) as an officer in the Austrian Army was officially charged with the collection of statistics on the Military Frontier. His first work, *Statistische Gemälde der österreichischen Monarchie* (Vienna, 1796), was the first methodical statistical survey of the Monarchy. It was followed by fuller treatment in *Darstellung der österreichischen Monarchie* (Vienna, 1804–7), including two volumes on the Military Frontier.

8. Under-populated Slavonia

(a) The Province

J. A. Demian, *Darstellung der österreichischen Monarchie nach den neuesten statistischen Beziehungen* (Description of the Austrian Monarchy according to the most recent statistical data), Vienna, 1805, vol. iii, part ii, pp. 441–3; 449; 456–7; 472; 482; 486–7; 515–19; 526.

THIS beautiful country Slavonia, which in Roman times was well cultivated and densely populated, has come to life again only in our own day. For more than two hundred years Slavonia was a theatre of ceaseless warfare, an empty desert, and a habitation for animals rather than men, until at the Peace of Karlowitz[1] after 150 years of terrible conflict it again fell to Hungary. Under the Turkish yoke its original inhabitants were almost wholly exterminated through the

[1] Karlovci, 1699.

continual ravages of war, but it has now been repopulated by foreign settlers, Illyrians who emigrated from the Turkish Empire in swarms, and other colonists from Germany and Hungary. . . .

The present population of Slavonia, including the provincial as well as the military districts, numbers at least 458,044 souls. . . . So the population is still small for such a large and fertile country, since it has not more than 1,659 people to the square mile (estimating the area at 276 square miles). It is true that in Carinthia there are only 1,424 people to the square mile, and in Tyrol only 1,270; but what are Carinthia and Tyrol, with their high mountains and uncultivable rugged soil, compared with fertile Slavonia, endowed with all the gifts of nature? . . .

As recently as sixty years ago, almost no villages were to be found in the whole of Slavonia. The few that did exist in the plains were no more than groups of about twenty mud-huts, called *szemonize*,[1] and these often stood half-empty. In the hills the inhabitants lived in isolated houses, rarely in group settlements. But today the Slavonians build villages of our own type, because the estate-owners force them to maintain public and private security. For this purpose the people of each village keep watch by turns through the night, and in the centre of each village there is a little hut, where the sentry can shelter in bad weather.

Social Classes

The number of the Slavonian nobility is not large in relation to the size of the country. In 1785, the number of nobles was only 314; in the province of Slavonia, only one person in 846 is a noble, while in Hungary the proportion is one in $21\frac{1}{2}$.[2] The nobility, apart from two German families and one Italian family, are partly Slav and partly Hungarian by origin, as the family names clearly indicate. . . . Almost all the land in Slavonia belongs to the nobility; the Crown possesses only two properties, Essek and Dallja, the latter leased to the Greek archbishop of Karlowitz. . . .

After the nobility come the burgesses, whose number in Slavonia is extremely small, since they are confined to the royal free city of Posega[3] and the three military settlements of Peterwardein, Semlin, and Karlowitz. The inhabitants of the free market-towns cannot be considered as belonging to the burgess class.

Thus the great majority of the inhabitants of Slavonia belong to

[1] Zemunice.
[2] For Croatia the author estimates the proportion at one in 42. (*Darstellung der öst. Monarchie*, vol. iii, part ii, p. 60.)
[3] Požega.

the peasant class. In relation to the small number of townspeople the size of the peasant class is excessive, and this disproportion is unfavourable for the economy of the country. But of course the peasants carry on many of the trades which in other countries are practised by townspeople. . . .

Agriculture

Slavonia ranks among the best farmlands of the Austrian Monarchy. Wheat, maize, buckwheat, millet, barley and oats are the crops grown. Wheat and maize thrive best in Syrmia and the lower districts of Posega county, in the military districts of the Brod and Gradiskan regiments, while millet is the main crop in the hilly regions and in the districts of the Peterwardein regiment. Verötz[1] county has the best corn land. . . .

In general there is a lack of balance between grain production and cattle-raising; there is too little livestock and so too little manure. But under the present system of farming, shortage of fodder and pasture of course limits the amount of livestock that can be kept, and the lack of manure is due to free-range grazing and neglect of manure conservation, showing that the Slavonian peasant is partly too lazy, partly still too ignorant. Here and there indeed, and particularly in Syrmia, there is a prejudice against the use of fertilizer,[2] the idea being that the soil is too fertile to require it, and that it would injure the seed, although experience proves the contrary.

Another fault of the Slavonian farmer is that he sows the seed too thick, so that it comes up into empty ears. Instead of a harrow he drags a thorn bush across the field,[3] so that the seed is not covered and instead of germinating is eaten by birds.

Because agriculture in Slavonia still remains on a low technical level, the peasants of the region do not produce grain over and above their annual needs. If they have a good harvest, then they feed the surplus to cattle, or squander it. Only the estate owners produce a sufficient quantity to export their grain through the seaports or to Inner Austria. The frontier soldiers, by contrast, do not sell their surplus, but store it against bad years, or feed it to animals, particularly pigs, for the market.

On the whole it can be expected that agricultural production in Slavonia will increase with the increase in population and the removal of these obstacles. But one obstacle will still remain—

[1] Virovitica.

[2] A prejudice which survived in this region as late as the 1930s.

[3] A practice which continued in the south of England in the 1890s.

the absence of towns in most of the province, which means that the countryman cannot dispose of his output quickly or in small quantities. The lack of an easily accessible market reduces profits and the incentives required by these idle people.

How the proximity of the market can influence agriculture is strikingly demonstrated by the Csepin estate, where farming is organized completely on the German model, and the peasants have cattle stalls and barns with threshing floors, manure their crops, and often send as many as thirty wagons laden with grain or timber to Essek[1] on one day. Another example is the Daruvar region, which now has an excellent farming system and is the most advanced part of Slavonia, owing to the influence of the well-frequented spa, flourishing trade and the settlement of German artisans. The same is true of Verovitiz,[2] where the surrounding region is exceptionally advanced, owing to the improvements made by the landowner and the lively trade with Croatia. . . .

Grain exports consist of wheat and rye. The grain trade first became important in 1770, when it was stimulated by the demand from Italy. But this demand was effective only when there was a harvest shortfall in Italy, which occurred every three or four years, so that in the intervals grain surpluses piled up on the estates, and there might be as much as 20,000 florins'[3] worth of grain held in store. On the average, crop exports from the country then amounted to half a million gulden.[3] Since the French revolutionary war, however, the grain trade of Slavonia has been drawn steadily to the markets of Inner Austria and the Austrian littoral. At present wheat and grain exports to the value of 250,000 florins a year from Verötz county alone go up the Drava and Mur to Inner Austria.

Peasant Crafts

In a country where everyone is occupied in agriculture and where even that is short of manpower, the people have no needs which they cannot supply themselves, and the countryman must necessarily ply the trades that are normally carried on by townspeople. Where there are very few officials whose expenditure can create a demand for goods and services, there is no stimulus to domestic industries or the development of manufactures and factories. There is scarcely a peasant in Slavonia who would not rather make his wagon, carts, ploughs and other implements himself than buy them from artisans. He knits his own woollen stockings, belts and gloves, weaves linen and cloth and makes all his own linen and woollen clothing.

[1] Osijek.   [2] Virovitica.
[3] See Note on Weights, Measures and Currency, p. 387.

Even dyeing the Slavonian women carry out with great success, though they have not a wide range of dyes and confine themselves to the primary colours. For red they use madder, crushed to powder and heated, though not boiled, in water to which they add a little decoction of Brazil wood to brighten it. . . . They can also dye cured white lambskins blue, so that they can be worn as furs. Such a fur costs up to ten ducats, and the beautiful blue colour does not fade. From certain roots they make a cosmetic rouge, which is more natural and prettier than the French, does not cost half as much and does not rub off. With this art a fortune could be made in Vienna, but the Slavonian women keep it a close secret, which money will not persuade them to disclose.

Since the peasants of Slavonia make everything they require in dress and household utensils, the few manufactures and trades that exist cannot develop, and in consequence the artisans and craftsmen of the main towns must depend partly on agriculture and cattle-raising for their livelihood.

(b) The Military Generalate

J. A. Demian, *Statistische Beschreibung der Militär-Grenze* (Statistical Description of the Military Frontier), Vienna, 1807, vol. ii, pp. 32; 48–51; 72–3.

THE Slavonian Military Frontier has a very small population.[1] Although the soil is so fruitful that it gives a rich yield even with poor cultivation, this land has not more than 1,685 people to the square mile, while the cold and infertile Karlstadt Generalate has 1,300 people to the square mile. . . .

The area of land used for agriculture (including forests), according to the 1804 returns, is 987,462 joch, of which 310,378 are arable and 360,980 forest. So the area of agricultural land per head amounts to five joch, while in the Karlstadt Generalate there are seven, in the Banat district only $3\frac{3}{4}$, and in the Varasdin Generalate $5\frac{3}{4}$ joch per head. . . . The disproportion between population and productive area is specially striking in this frontier district, because most of the land is fertile, and there are 626,482 joch of land consisting of arable and pasture, vineyards, orchards and gardens to provide food for man and beast. . . .

The chief reason why the yield per acre is so low in this Generalate, although from the fertility of the soil much better results could be expected, is insufficient labour. The quantity of labour available is

[1] 189,208 in 1802, or 44 per cent of the total population of Slavonia, estimated above at 458,044.

too small, partly because there are too few workers, and partly because of the laziness of the frontiersman and his distaste for work. What I said above about the disproportion between the supply of labour and the land area in the Varasdin Generalate holds good to a great extent of this Military District also. Most households have landholdings far too large in relation to their manpower, so that the great expanses of the region cannot be properly cultivated. And since laziness and various other factors prevent the existing labour force from being well-used, even the most fertile land cannot produce good harvests.

9. FEUDAL CONDITIONS IN CROATIA

I. Tkalac, *Uspomene iz Hrvatske* (Reminiscences of Croatia), *1749–1823, 1824–1843*, Zagreb, 1945, translated into Serbo-Croat from the original German by Josip Ritig, pp. 219–20; 239; 221–2.

(a) 'Optima flens'

ALTHOUGH Hungary and Croatia are in the real sense of the word agricultural states which cannot exist without a numerous peasantry, up to the reign of Maria Theresa no thought was given to improving the social condition of those who were the foundation of the whole life of the state. The peasants were allowed to grow up like ignorant animals so that they could be more easily robbed and exploited. The peasantry was called 'misera contribuens plebs'—the wretched tax-paying poor—and the attitude of the nobility towards the peasants is shown by the saying that the peasants were best when crying, worst when laughing—*optima flens, pessima ridens*. Therefore to maintain the peasants in a position to bear the full burden of the state, care had to be taken that they were always crying. The relationship between the lord of the land and his serfs was based not only on law, but also on commonly accepted customs which were very different in different parts of the country. The serf was not a bondman, but he was bound to the soil, and was subjected to the patrimonial jurisdiction of the lord of the manor who could inflict corporal punishment and imprisonment; if he had *ius gladii* (the right of the sword) he could, in the presence of judges, condemn him to death on the scaffold. The barbarous misuse of patrimonial power caused Charles VI to limit the oppression of the serfs in the urbarium[1] for Slavonia

[1] This was the first of several such laws promulgated by Habsburg rulers during the eighteenth century, to regulate the rights and duties of the serfs by determining the size of the landholding which the serf was entitled to occupy and

in 1737. But since this urbarium was not law no one observed it. Maria Theresa in the state parliament in 1764 proposed that a commission should be nominated which would draw up a general law on the same lines. . . . The Urbarial Law was issued in 1767, but since it was not constitutionally promulgated it was only a temporary solution, and no one kept it strictly. There were many lords, some of whom I knew, who treated their serfs in the same way that West Indian plantation owners treat their negro slaves. They behaved as if there was no law for them. In addition to the *ius primae noctis* they indulged themselves without fear of punishment in every kind of outrage against the serfs. Not until the 1832–6 parliament was an urbarial law passed which was slightly more human and which considerably improved the lot of the serfs. This law, however, only lasted a short time, because the epoch-making parliament of 1847–8 abolished all rights of manorial law, and took away from the lords all feudal rights, against compensation. In addition it ended patrimonial jurisdiction, and restored to the peasants those rights as citizens of which they had been deprived for a thousand years.

(b) *House-to-house Trading*

The women of the house made all the household linen and clothing at home from materials which they prepared themselves, the only exceptions being footwear and fur garments. From the Jewish house-traders people only bought trimmings and decorations, and these not for money but in exchange for plums, honey, raw silk and rags.

In villages and hamlets distant from the towns, house-to-house trading was an absolute necessity and was carried on entirely by Jews. The Jew who called on the house was a welcome visitor both to peasants and nobility. He brought all that was needed in a household—and indeed many things that were not really necessary—and did not take money, which neither nobles nor peasants had, but instead products which would otherwise have had to be carried to the town. The most sought-after products were plums and the stalks and skins left from wine making, which were used for brandy distillation, and above all rags for export to England where Croatian flax and hempen rags were particularly highly prized and fetched a good price. This trading of 'goods for goods' was exceptionally advantageous for the travelling Jew because he could sell his wares at a

the money or produce-rent and labour services which he was obliged to render to the landowner. See J. Tomasevich, *Peasants, Politics and Economic Change in Yugoslavia*, Stanford and London, 1955, pp. 61 and 71. For the legislation in Hungary, see pp. 39–41 above.

high price, but it was not disadvantageous for the peasants either, who in any case did not know what to do with their rags. In this way they managed to exchange them for some of the things that they needed and were unable to buy because there was no money.

(c) Over-spending

People constantly spent more than they had. And so they sold, at any price, the wheat in the ear, the uncut hay in the field, the grapes on the vine and the plums on the tree, and when all this proved insufficient, they raised loans at usurious rates of interest. In Croatia there was then no institution for giving loans; the only one that could be considered as a mortgage bank in even a rudimentary way was the Chapter of the Zagreb Bishopric. This Chapter, which efficiently managed the huge estates of the bishopric, gave mortgages to the large landowners, the main security being property. But even the considerable funds of the Zagreb Chapter were insufficient to satisfy the increasing number of people seeking credit, and so very few landlords profited. The Public Funds Agency was even less in a position to meet demands for mortgages. Those who could not slake their thirst at either of these springs fell into the merciless hands of the usurer. The big estate owners had in abundance all they needed to live off, but they never had any money, and so their estates deteriorated with increasing rapidity.

Imbro Ignatijević Tkalac (1824–1912) was a writer of strong liberal principles, and the editor of several periodicals in Zagreb and Vienna. He was for a time secretary of the Chamber of Commerce in Zagreb, and died in Rome as an official of the Italian Ministry of Foreign Affairs, in exile because of his determined stand against Austrian and Hungarian rule in Croatia. His book, *Jugenderinnerungen aus Kroatien*, originally published in Leipzig in 1894, gives his recollections—written later in life—of his youth in Croatia. It was not published in Croatian till 1924.

10. SOCIAL EXTREMES

Hippolyte Desprez, *Les Peuples de l'Autriche et de la Turquie*, Paris, 1850, vol. i, pp. 6–10.

I ENTERED Illyrian territory at the beginning of autumn in 1845, by the majestic granite roads of Tyrol. I had been told that Agram,[1] the

---

[1] Zagreb.

capital of Hungarian Croatia, was the cradle of Illyrianism, the privileged spot where it was born and could grow without too much constraint. I went to Agram . . . I travelled slowly through Carinthia and Carniola, listening intently for the first sounds of the Illyrian[1] tongue, which in these two provinces is still mingled with the less harmonious notes of the German language. The people had changed, and I began to notice in increasing numbers the true dynamic sons of the Illyrian race. Here a peasant returning from the town would be driving his horses at a gallop; farther on, young barefooted highlanders would be racing down the steep mountainsides, their long hair streaming in the wind. As soon as I had passed through the customs barrier which separates the Austrian provinces from Croatia and Hungary, this impression of vivacity, of buoyant and impetuous gaiety, was intensified. What was the source of this content, this open expression of all-pervading happiness? It evidently originated, not in the standard of living, which far from having improved showed a marked deterioration, but in the possession of a little more liberty. Imperfect as this is, one would not exchange it for the greater material welfare in the adjacent provinces under direct Austrian administration.

In summer in the Croatian villages the children play naked in the sun in the front of the houses; they wear clothes only when it is really winter. The women rarely wear shoes and their clothing ordinarily consists only of a Hungarian sleeveless jacket over a long shirt. The men are a little better dressed; in all seasons of the year they wear heavy boots, wide breeches of cloth and a sort of blouse caught in at the waist with a belt. In cold weather they wrap themselves up in a woollen or sheepskin coat. Such is the luxury of the peasants of Croatia.

The houses stand separately, each surrounded by an enclosure, but have a poor appearance. Some have no chimneys; their hearths are in the middle of the room, and lacking wood, the peasants burn straw. The smoke escapes by the open door or through a hole in the roof. Sitting on wooden benches round this primitive hearth, the Croatian peasants spend their evenings listening to amusing tales recalling the age of chivalry in old Illyria. Sometimes rakia revives the inspiration of the story-teller, but they know when to stop, unless, of course, they are celebrating the feast of some great saint or of the blessed Virgin.

I travelled through several villages in succession which belonged to some powerful magnate with an income of several millions, whose name I no longer remember. He had a magnificent house built on

[1] Serbo-Croatian.

the side of a hill and surrounded by an English park. His coach-and-four was standing beside the portico. Several superbly mounted out-riders and lackeys, wearing a kind of semi-Albanian uniform, with swords at their sides, were awaiting the order to start. An old man appeared, leaning on the arm of a young man who showed him much deference; both were dressed in the latest fashion of Paris and Vienna. They took their seats in the splendid equipage which set off at full tilt on the road to Agram, and soon disappeared, although the cart in which I was travelling was moving reasonably fast. I had already seen the two extremes of Illyrian society in Croatia.

11. Serf Emancipation

(a) The Jelačić Manifesto of 25 April 1848

J. Šidak (ed.), *Historijska čitanka za hrvatsku povijest* (Croatian Historical Reader), Zagreb, 1952, vol. i, pp. 206–7.

We, Baron Josip Jelačić of Bužim, Ban of Croatia, Slavonia and Dalmatia, true Privy Councillor of his Apostolic Majesty Ferdin-and I, Emperor of Austria, King of Hungary, Bohemia, Lombardy, Venice, Dalmatia, Croatia, Slavonia and Galicia, Vladimiria and Illyria, etc., Field Marshal-Lieutenant and General in command of the entire army and the Military Frontier in the Kingdom of Croatia, wish the whole nation and people of Croatia and Slavonia God's help and salutation.

Although it has already been proclaimed in the Kingdom of Croatia and Slavonia that all urbarial dues[1] and labour services and church tithes have been abolished, yet, nevertheless, you might stand in doubt and fear regarding this, your newly acquired right; because except for the above-mentioned proclamation, you have not in your possession any written document. Wherefore, we, Ban of Croatia, Slavonia and Dalmatia, as the highest authority appointed and placed over you by our illustrious King, and acting as the defender of your rights, wish to pacify and reassure you. We, then, address to all of you who belong to the Croat-Slavonian nation, and who, hitherto, have been serfs and subjects of your lords, this our Ban's letter, in order to assure you, by virtue and privilege of our Ban's honour and power, of your newly acquired rights and freedom, according to which you and your descendants are for all time exempt from labour-duties and all urbarial taxes[1] and church

[1] Money or produce-rents due from serf to landowner under the urbarial laws. See p. 329 above, footnote 1.

tithes. We promise you that no one, at any time, now or in the future, can or may deprive you of such rights and freedom as are now accorded to you by law and confirmed by our Gracious King.

Moreover, we give and accord to you and to your descendants of both sexes this our open letter, signed by our own hand, and confirmed by the Great Ban's seal, in Zagreb on St. Mark's day, to wit the 25th of April, 1848.

Signed: Baron Jelačić, Ban

Seal

Josef Jelačić (1801–59), traditionally the liberator of the serfs, was appointed Ban (Governor) of Croatia by the Emperor in March 1848, to counteract the Hungarian national movement and bring Croatia directly under Austria. He encouraged the Croatian separatist movement, and in September 1848, in alliance with the Serbs, attacked Hungary. After Hungarian resistance had been quelled by the Russian army sent by Tsar Nicholas to the aid of Francis Joseph, Austria suppressed the national movement in Croatia. Jelačić, though hurt by this betrayal, remained as Ban.

(b) Law XXVII: On the Abolition of Urbarial Lands and Services, 1848

Šidak, op. cit., pp. 228–9.

1. All urbarial services and dues[1] previously in force are abolished for ever. In addition the independence is hereby proclaimed of both individual serfs and whole communes which have hitherto been under the authority of landlords.

2. The force and validity of the charter of the Ban by which the abolition of urbarial services and dues and church tithes were previously assured is confirmed by this law.

3. All those who were previously serfs are the undisputed owners of their urbarial lands[2] which they are free wholly or in part to exchange, lease or sell.

4. The so-called minor royal rights (jura regalia), i.e. tavern keeping, hunting, fishing and butchery, from henceforth will not be the sole prerogative of the landlord so that:

(a) The right of tavern keeping from St. Michael's Day to St. George's Day will in the future continue to belong to each commune; and in addition each commune will have the same rights from St. George's Day to St. Michael's Day in one place.

[1] See p. 329 above, footnote 1.
[2] i.e. serfs are to become freehold owners of the farm holdings to which they had held rights of occupancy under the urbarial laws.

(*b*) Tavern-keeping rights are understood to include the right to sell all kinds of drink, i.e. wine, beer, and brandy. These rights belong to the community as a whole, and the commune will have the right to lease them for the benefit of the whole community.

(*c*) Each peasant is allowed to fish, shoot birds and slaughter animals on his own land.

(*d*) Hunting is also free to all except in forests owned wholly by the landlord or on allodial lands.[1]

5. The state guarantees to compensate landlords for the loss of urbarial dues and services and also for loss incurred by tavern keeping passing to the commune. A special state commission will determine the method and means for this compensation, and make recommendations at the next meeting of the Diet.

6. Each commune and each individual in it has the right on his own land, without payment of tax, to distil brandy, fire bricks, burn lime and operate any kind of mill or saw-mill, and, within the existing laws, to build or inherit. If it is ascertained that any mill is working to the detriment of neighbouring land this will be prohibited by the local authorities and not by the landlord.

General Note. Although this law emancipated all serfs from rent payment and labour service, it granted ownership of land only to the urbarial serfs, i.e. those whose rights of occupancy were laid down in the urbarial laws, while the serfs on allodial land, which was not subject to these laws, received no land in freehold ownership and so became farm labourers. In principle therefore the law resembled the laws of serf emancipation in Hungary (p. 33 above) and in Rumania (p. 187(1) above), which similarly granted ownership rights to the serfs whose rights had previously been recognized in law, leaving the remainder landless.

12. THE LIBERATION OF THE SERFS IN 1848

Rudolf Bićanić, 'Oslobođenje kmetova u Hrvatskoj, 1848' (The Liberation of the Serfs in Croatia, 1848), in *Djelo* (Action), Zagreb, 1948, pp. 198–200.

ALL THE measures taken to improve the position of the serfs in Croatia were the outcome of peasant revolts. The impact of these revolts shook and finally shattered the centuries old edifice of feudalism, and fear of revolt wrought panic among the feudal lords. During

---

[1] 'Allodial lands' refers to estates in absolute hereditary ownership which had never been subject to the urbarial laws. On such estates serfs had no legal rights of occupancy.

the eighteenth century, every Austrian enactment beneficial to the peasants resulted from one or another peasant revolt. The Empress Maria Theresa proclaimed the Slavonian urbarium of 1756 because of 'turmoil among the peasants'; this turmoil was in fact the great rising of some twenty thousand peasants near Kalnik (a mountain near Zagreb). She produced the Hungarian urbarium of 1767 after revolts and unrest in Hungary. The Croatian urbarium, of which the aim was 'to prevent unrest, forestall disturbances and bring peace and general pacification', was proclaimed in 1780, a short time after the peasant revolt in Bohemia and Moravia. The same was true of the law of Joseph II concerning personal freedom and the serfs' right to move. This was issued immediately after the rebellion of Rumanian serfs in Transylvania in 1785, which caused the death of four thousand people.

The same story was repeated again and again. First the serfs would send petitions and complaints to the emperor; the revolt would be forcibly suppressed by the nobility and the emperor's troops. Thereafter the conscience of emperor and empress would be awakened and they would make concessions to the serfs in order to deny them their rights in more important matters in the future.

The preparation of the Hungarian urbarial law of 1836 began in 1832,[1] a year after the rising of the Polish nobility against Russian rule. But the Polish nobles did not win the support of the peasants, and their own serfs killed them and burned their castles. In the Polish rising of 1846, the Kraków rebellion, the same thing happened. It was against this background that the Hungarian Diet met in 1847 to consider the question of peasant liberation.

At the beginning of the nineteenth century the attitude of the Hungarian and Croatian nobility towards serf emancipation was that the serf liked his position; he was sub-human, a kind of beast of burden, and so did not feel his subjugation. It was in such terms that a Hungarian jurist described serfdom.[2]

By the thirties of the nineteenth century, however, the landed gentry had come to respect the serf but were concerned to defend

---

[1] This law, advocated by Széchenyi, Wesselényi and others after 1825, was the first attempt to lighten the burden of the serfs. The Diet in 1833 agreed on a draft law which would have had this effect: its chief provision was to grant serfs the right of appeal against nobles, but the Emperor refused assent. The law was then revised, but the Lower House refused assent to the revised version. When finally placed on the statute book in 1836, the law was so emasculated that it made little difference to the position of the serfs in Hungary. Tkalac, however, considers that its effects in Croatia were beneficial. (P. 330 above.)

[2] A. W. Gustermann, *Die Ausbildung der Verfassung des Königreichs Ungarn*, Vienna, 1811, pp. 311 ff. (*Author*).

their own class interests. The idea of freeing the serfs was considered as an attack on the sanctity of property and as a concession to terrorization. Among the ruling class the idea of the natural sub-ordination of the serfs gave place to a purely self-regarding desire to preserve the system from which it derived its income. By 1847 feudalism had no defenders: it was obviously decaying, and the only questions were how and at whose expense it should be abolished. That the ruling class did not intend to foot the bill was quite evident from the ideas and arguments discussed in the Hungarian and later in the Croatian Diet. The instructions to the Croatian delegates to the Hungarian Diet in 1847 stated that 'if the principle of liberation from urbarial dues and tithes is proclaimed, the delegates should endeavour to secure full compensation for the landlords', and added that, if emancipation were made obligatory, it should be accom-panied by full compensation, and that a mortgage credit should be arranged for the purpose.[1]

In the Hungarian Diet the question was discussed from the angle of ruling-class expediency and advantage. Stress was laid on the fact that at that moment the nobility possessed power, but that later they might lose it, and that it would therefore be better to enact emancipation while the interests of the landowners were still upper-most (Kossuth). It should be carried out in such a way that 'the state should not be shaken' (Szemere). The serfs should be freed because freedom was an antidote to revolt (Széchenyi). Among the economic issues, it should be noted that discussions centred on the payment of compensation, and not on the question of liberation itself. The main concern was whether emancipation should be obli-gatory or optional. Landlords must be given compensation to the full value of the capitalized feudal rent, and since the peasants had no capital the state must help. Serfs who wished to buy their freedom could be permitted to do so by giving up part of their land to the landowner. As land values and other prices were rising, owing to the improvement in communications, it was to the landowners' advan-tage that emancipation should be completed as soon as possible, because the purchasing power of the money received as redemption payments would later fall. This money would provide the land-owners with considerable capital and enable them to solve their immediate financial problems and invest in their estates. The debate ended in disagreement between the Upper and Lower Houses of the Diet on the question of compulsory versus optional emancipa-tion.

[1] *Novine Dalmatinsko-horvatsko-slavonske* (Dalmatian-Croatian-Slavonian News), 1847, p. 362 (*Author*).

z

As we see, the Hungarian Diet of 1847–8 prepared for the abolition of serfdom in what Lenin called an openly 'Prussian manner',
with the interests of the landowners protected in every way, by
imposing the costs of redemption partly on the serfs, to be paid off
in instalments, and partly on the state, i.e. the taxpayer. Finally, in
February 1848, a committee was appointed to discuss the formula-
tion of the law, by the long procedure which normally lasted for
several years.

In March 1848, however, the outlook was radically changed by
the revolution in France. The proletariat of Paris pushed the wheel of
history forward with such force that they drew our serfs along with
them. The revolutionary movement among the people, seething but
long suppressed, gained strength with enormous rapidity in Vienna,
Prague, Hungary and Croatia. 'The peasants are getting ready for
bloody work. God forbid . . . there is no resistance', wrote Gaj's
Novine from Pest. Now the liberation of the serfs took on quite
another and a revolutionary meaning. In the Hungarian Diet on
15 March 1848, Kossuth said, 'Time is flying . . . we must prevent
disorders', and demanded the immediate enactment of serf emancipation. The law was formulated and enacted on 18 March 1848, in
both houses of the Diet, and the conservatives could do nothing
but agree to everything 'unanimously and in terror'. Serfdom in all
its forms was abolished with the passing of the law. 'Compensation
to the landlords will be secured by the general national justice, and
the state will provide capital for full compensation.' The cost was to
be borne by the state, i.e. the taxpayer. On 11 April 1848, the law
ending urbarial relations was sanctioned by the Emperor and promulgated.

The revolutionary mood spread to Croatia and Slavonia; the
peasants were influenced by it and refused to perform labour service
any longer. Data concerning the landowners' estates show that serf
labour stopped in the main about March, that is to say, even before
the law abolishing urbarial relations had been promulgated. The
serfs themselves ended their dues, and 'what was once the work of
centuries is now the work of two or three days'. At the heart of this
revolutionary action lay the idea that 'for long enough the lazy
gentlemen have fed themselves on our blisters and our sweat, now
let them feed themselves by themselves . . . the peasants from now
on will see to it that everybody works'.[1]

The break-up of feudal relations and the peasant movement
developed independently of the policy of the Croatian ruling class.
After the great popular meeting in Zagreb on 25 March 1848, the

[1] *Novine Dalmatinsko-horvatsko-slavonske*, 6 April 1848 (*Author*).

Croatian delegation carried a petition to the Emperor containing the Croatian national demands, among them the demand for the abolition of serfdom. But they found as they travelled through Croatia that this was already an accomplished fact, and that the people had decided to wait no longer. In the memorandum of the delegates to the Emperor the position in Croatia was described in these significant terms: 'The nation is threatened by the secret incitement of communism coming from abroad, by peasant revolt and general internal revolution. For these reasons a Ban with a strong hand is needed, the soldier Jelačić.'

In agreeing to the abolition of serfdom, the Croatian ruling class was motivated by fear, as was openly admitted. 'Were we to wait until some Gubec[1] or other appeared and stirred up the peasants in revolt against the nobility? . . . Were we to wait for a repetition of the scenes of Galicia? . . . We granted what we could no longer withhold.'[2] From the provinces of Croatia the voices of the terrified landowners were heard: 'What in heaven's name are they doing in Zagreb? Why do they not give us protection?'

All the efforts of the ruling circles were concentrated in an attempt to pacify the people, to slow down or divert the popular movement for liberation. The entire apparatus of the feudal state, the municipal councils, and the Catholic and Orthodox Churches, was directed to this end.

A month after these events, on 25 April 1848, Jelačić published his famous letter, around which the untrue legend has grown up that Ban Jelačić freed the Croatian peasants from serfdom. Jelačić in this manifesto says only that the law concerning the abolition of serfdom had already been proclaimed in Croatia and gave his word that 'No one, at any time now or in the future, can or may deprive you of the rights accorded to you by this law.' On the same day, however, Jelačić issued his second manifesto, proclaiming martial law against 'wicked and lawless elements who go among the people inciting them'. Jelačić tried to pacify the people and confine the movement within the bounds of legality, and asked people to trust him. Meanwhile, within the bounds of legality, a deceitful and perfidious game was played, in an attempt to reverse the situation brought about by the peasants themselves.

In June 1848 the Croatian Diet had recognized the validity of the Hungarian law for the abolition of serfdom, but in July it passed a bill of its own, i.e. a second law for the same purpose. According to this second bill, as in the Hungarian law, 'all urbarial

[1] Matija Gubec, leader of the savagely suppressed peasant rising of 1573.
[2] *Novine Dalmatinsko-horvatsko-slavonske*, 30 March 1848 (*Author*).

dues and services are discontinued for ever, but the state guarantees that the nobility will receive compensation'. The bill did not say that the state itself would provide the capital. The motive of this bill we consider to be the anxiety of the Croatian nobility as to who would pay them compensation once relations with Hungary had been severed. This interpretation is supported by the fact that the problem of compensation was the chief issue under debate in the Croatian Diet. The radical members took the view that the feudal lords were not entitled to any compensation from the state or the serfs, because they had exploited the serfs for centuries, and held that on the contrary the serfs should demand compensation from the landowners.

The majority of the Diet accepted the view that the state should guarantee compensation to the landlords for the loss of their 'acquired rights'. The Croatian bill was published, but a year elapsed before Jelačić and the Ban's Council sent it to the Emperor for his assent. In 1850, when the Emperor gave assent to all the other bills of the Croatian Diet, he did not confirm those on the abolition of urbarial relations, so that from a legal standpoint the liberation of the serfs had no validity. The Hungarian bill was not recognized, and the Croatian bill had received no legal sanction. The Emperor did not give assent to the Croatian bill and make it law, because negotiations had started between Jelačić and the commissioners, most of them landlords, appointed to settle the payment of compensation. The Croatian delegation demanded that compensation should be paid by the serfs.[1] Indeed the Austrian minister Bach defended the interests of the serfs of Croatia better than Jelačić and the Croatian nobility. Jelačić and the delegation made a special petition to the Emperor requesting that he should not give his assent to certain clauses of the Croatian Diet's bill concerning the forests and pastures in Slavonia, which were favourable to the serfs. These clauses, they said, were shameless, and had been included in the bill only because otherwise it would have been impossible to maintain peace in Slavonia at that time, but now they were no longer necessary.[2]

Finally, after three years of negotiations, a third regulation was passed in 1853 concerning freedom from labour service and the

[1] In the event, the landlords as a rule received compensation amounting to the annual rents from their properties or other rights, capitalized for twenty years; the former serfs paid these indemnities over twenty years, together with the land tax. See J. Tomasevich, *Peasants, Politics and Economic Change in Yugoslavia*, Stanford and London, 1955, p. 86.

[2] See Milivoj Vežić, *Urbar hrvatsko-slavonski* (The Croatian-Slavonian *Urbar*). Zagreb, 1882, pp. 539–40 (*Author*).

regulation of urbarial relations. This again liberated the serfs and laid down principles concerning compensation for the landowners. But this imperial patent was issued during the period of absolutism, and was not considered valid under the Croatian constitution. Thus it was not until the law of 1876, twenty-eight years after they had gained their freedom, that the liberation of the serfs acquired legal validity. The legal course of serf emancipation shows that the land-lords carried on a long and persistent struggle for the maintenance of their privileges, endeavouring by the use of legal weapons to turn back the wheel of history and reverse the situation which the people had brought about by their own acts. By keeping the question unsettled in law, they at first hoped that an opportunity of re-establishing serfdom might perhaps present itself,[1] and afterwards they used legal pressure to try and gain as much as possible for them-selves and retain what survived of their feudal privileges.

It was the Croatian peasants themselves who, without waiting for the law, and apart altogether from the regulations and manifestoes of the Ban, broke up the thousand-year-old system of serfdom, put fear into the hearts of the nobility, and resolutely showed that they would no longer accept serfdom. By this action they liberated them-selves and their descendants from the thraldom of feudalism. So it is not true to say that the Croatian peasants were liberated from serf-dom by Ban Jelačić, by the Emperor Francis Joseph, or by the Hungarian or Croatian Diets. The facts show that the Croatian peasants liberated themselves when they took the road of the great European revolutionary movement started by the French workers in 1848.

13. Attitudes to the Zadruga

Rudolf Bićanić, *Hrvatska ekonomika na prijelazu iz feudalizma u kapitalizam, I, Doba manufakture u Hrvatskoj i Slavoniji (1750–1860)* (The Croatian Economy in Transition from Feudalism to Capitalism, I, The Period of Manufacture in Croatia and Slavonia), Zagreb, 1951, pp. 357–60.

Once serfdom had been abolished in Croatia, the next main ob-stacle to the development of capitalism was the joint family, or

---

[1] When the most reactionary of Croatian politicians, Baron Kulmer, proposed the re-establishment of feudalism after the victory of the counter-revolution of 1849 Vraničan replied, 'God forbid, that would be the surest way to provoke another revolution, and we have had enough of the first.' Thus it was fear of the people which prevented the landlords from taking this step (*Author*).

zadruga. The question as to whether the dismemberment of these zadrugas should be allowed or prevented was the touchstone in every circle of political life. According to whether the answer given was positive or negative we can differentiate the liberal and conservative economic ideologies of Croatia at that time. . . . This was the most controversial question. Around it seethed discussion and polemics and about it were written newspaper articles, pamphlets and books. Questionnaires were circulated concerning it, and projects for laws drawn up and redrawn.

1. *Liberal circles* were for getting rid of all barriers to the development of capitalism. They therefore advocated the free entry of Austrian capital, a customs union with Austria, and the abolishment of the zadrugas. They were against the old Croatian constitution. Croatian autonomy was considered, at least for the moment, as a secondary problem. The main problem was that of the capitalist economy, and this, they considered, could be centrally solved from Vienna, that is, largely in the interests of Viennese capital.

The liberals were made up mainly of two groups of people. First there were liberals of the Austrian brand, civil servants and those who favoured Austrian absolutism, Bach's 'hussars', the Germanized 'Kulturträger' trying to bring culture to a backward, feudal Croatia. With these were lined up the capitalists, who, on a purely practical level, and without any ideological discussion, wanted to find a solution to their immediate problems of lack of manpower, credit and railway communications, etc. For different reasons both these groups were against zadrugas. The capitalists, and with them some of the landowners, simply needed workers, the former for their factories and forests, the latter for their estates. They did not want to get them by paying higher wages, but from peasants proletarianized by the forced break-up of the zadrugas.

The ideas of the first group were set forth most clearly by an Austrian civil servant, an excellent lawyer, who wrote anonymously, and whose name Utiešenović will not disclose. Summing up the advantages of the dismemberment of the zadrugas and the creation of individual peasant holdings, this anonymous writer lists the benefits of the latter as a more intensive tilling of the soil, a firm basis for credit, a greater desire for education, fewer infringements of the law and higher morale in individual families; in addition individual families would not be subject to the pressure of the headman, and this would assist in their political emancipation. The writer in particular drew attention to the advantages of creating individual family holdings because of the 'prosperity which would result from the existence of a large proletarianized working class as a basis for introducing rational business methods and as an industrial lever favouring the large landowner and capitalist'.[1]

The point of view of the liberal capitalists was most clearly set forth by the Chambers of Commerce and Industry which demanded that the zadrugas should be allowed to divide legally and that they should be forced to provide manpower.

In 1859 the Zagreb Chamber demanded a law for the division of zadrugas 'so necessary for economic and moral reasons . . . to increase manpower on the land. . . .'[2]

The Osijek Chamber of Commerce in 1860 demanded that an end be put to the patriarchal system which was the main reason for shortage of manpower and high wages. 'We are not against zadrugas . . ., but they must be changed so that we can work. . . .'[3]

2. *Conservative circles* wanted to keep the zadrugas for many complex reasons, ranging from political to economic. Their approach was not so immediate and practical as that of the liberals under absolutism, but more subtle.

Among the conservatives were found some of the nobility—the more reactionary and politically aware; those who upheld absolutism, not foreigners, but Croatian counter-revolutionaries; and also a large number of merchants and intellectuals. All these varying elements were held together by fear of social revolution and inability actively to support Austrian absolutism.

The changed outlook on social and economic questions after the 1848 revolution, and the sharpening of class conflict after the ending of serfdom, are shown in the writings of Vukotinović, the editor of *Gospdarski list*,[4] which was the voice of the Agricultural Society of Zagreb ,the largest Croatian agricultural organization. Vukotinović had been an Illyrian and radical liberal before 1848, but under absolutism he had withdrawn and occupied himself with agriculture and economic studies. In 1856 he gave his final judgement on the question of zadrugas in the controversy between the supporters and opponents of the patriarchal system, i.e. the zadrugas: 'My opinion is that the advancing culture of our century is of itself a disintegrating force in our patriarchal life, and, whatever we write about it, it will—if the laws do not help—in about ten years' time have completely disintegrated. . . . Morale will be worse, poverty greater and the country will find it has proletarians, vagabonds, ruffians

[1] O. M. Utiešenović, *Die Hauskommunionen der Südslaven*, Vienna, 1859, p. 109 (*Author*).

[2] *Bericht der Handels- und Gewerbekammer für Kroatien 1858–1859*, pp. 12 ff. (*Author*).

[3] *Bericht der Handels- und Gewerbekammer für Slavonien 1860*, p. 34 (*Author*).

[4] Agricultural Journal.

and a considerable number of idlers. . . . Many people think that
the dissolution of the patriarchal way of life will mean more hands
for agriculture and industry, but this belief is held only by those
who do not know our people. The lazy and useless will remain
lazy and useless even when left on their own; and for this reason
our peasants will starve like dumb animals, will be ragged, wander
the roads and sleep beneath the limes, if you like will even perish
rather than work when they have no urge to work. . . . It is appropriate, and indeed necessary for the supreme government to take
into account the lack of discipline in our peasant class. . . . Our
ordinary people need education, tutelage and strong leadership;
only thus—and even then not until half a century has passed—will
they be able to understand the principles of a higher way of life.'[1]
This bitter attack on his own people, and the call to discipline the
peasant, show the characteristic development of the mentality of the
middle-class and its liberal democracy even in the circles of those
opposed to Austrian absolutism.

The zadrugas began to disintegrate fast immediately feudalism
ended, but in 1848 Jelačić forbade zadruga division. In 1852 a
committee of Croatian and Slavonian officials was nominated which
drew up a report recommending the retention of zadrugas for the
following reasons: 'Zadrugas have shown themselves to be in every
way the firmest centre of support for the state. Because in them
military service, tax collection, compulsory public works, religious
duties, morals and obedience to superiors are far better preserved
than in the individual peasant family, dismembered and weakened
as a result of zadrugal division. Zadrugas are the strongest bulwark
against an impoverished peasantry and a corrupt proletariat.'[2]

This fear of creating a proletariat which would be a force of social
revolution was one of the main motives in the struggle to retain the
zadrugas. It is the reason why conservatives fought against their
dismemberment.

The full reasoning of the conservatives was given most systematically by Utiešenović in his book concerning the zadrugas, which is a
textbook of conservatism and counter-revolutionary arguments.

In favour of their retention a whole series of arguments was
employed, ranging from zadrugas as a specific form of Slav social
organization to zadrugas as a kind of Christian communism. In fact
the real reason was the following.

The argument concerning manpower was not so naïve as it may at
first seem. The conservatives hoped, with the power of the law

[1] Quoted from Utiešenović, *op. cit.*, p. 249 (*Author*).
[2] *Ibid.*, pp. 139–40 (*Author*).

behind them, to keep the zadrugas and use them for the benefit of the bourgeois order in a way similar to that which had been followed by the feudal landowners. Utiešenović admits this openly. He says that 'a large number of workers cannot be expected to be available in the first generation after the break up of the zadrugas; only later will there be any considerable increase of manpower, for many of the zadrugas have not enough land'. Then comes the characteristic passage: 'The Military Frontier system and feudalism constantly made use of national customs in order to create a surplus population and manpower to use for their own ends. It should be borne in mind that it is in the interests of industry, too, to retain this particular national custom and to reach a position of excess manpower that cannot be made use of in agriculture.' 'Unused labour', writes Utiešenović, a little later, 'is the result of lack of legal regulation of this question and lack of understanding of the position among the heads of the communes and superior authorities.' The proletarianized peasant would go out into the world to find a job. Labour would become a commodity, and the proletarian would go and work for whoever paid more. And this was his reason for retaining the zadrugas with government support: the zadruga's function should be to ensure a monopoly of local manpower for the local capitalists and landowners.

The aim therefore was to use manpower in a semi-feudal way for capitalist enterprises and former feudal estates by bolstering up the zadrugas.[1]

14. Grain Exports and the Railway

E. A. Joanelli, *Die kroatische Eisenbahnfrage mit besonderem Hinblick auf die allgemeinen Verhältnisse des österreichischen Ausfuhrhandels an's adriatische Meer* (The Croatian Railway Question, with special reference to the general conditions of Austrian export trade on the Adriatic), Zagreb, 1852, pp. 4, 19–20.

THE construction of the railway line from Steinbruck[2] to Agram and thence to Sissek[3] and Karlstadt, which was sanctioned and immediately started in the year 1850,[4] has had a generally favourable reception here; this popular and well-timed action on the part

---

[1] The Civil Code of 1853 allowed division, and the joint family holdings broke up rapidly. The law of 1889 prohibited division if the majority of the members objected, and if the divided holdings fell below the minimum size laid down by the law (areas varied according to regions). Sub-division continued and the law was evaded. (J. Tomasevich, *Peasants, Politics and Economic Change in Yugoslavia*, Stanford and London, 1955, pp. 87–8.)

[2] Zidani Most.   [3] Sisak.   [4] Completed 1862.

of the government has done more to allay the widespread unrest existing in Croatia than any other measure.

It is indeed high time that the obstacles which prevent the marketing of Banat grain in the Adriatic were removed. Only an improvement of the means of communication can reduce transport costs sufficiently to allow our grain to compete successfully with the enormous increase in grain exports through Odessa and the Wallachian Danube ports. Up to the present the transport of grain from the Banat and adjacent territories by the river Sava up to Sissek, although it leaves much to be desired in speed and security, has proved by far the cheapest mode of transport, and is likely to remain so. But from Sissek to the Adriatic the costs of transport are extremely high, and represent the main obstacle to effective competition with the grain from the Black Sea or Danube ports. The construction of the $22\frac{1}{2}$-mile[1] line from Sissek to Karlstadt will provide a connection with the Karlstadt–Fiume Line, and the great reduction in the costs of transport thereby achieved will allow a very large expansion in our export of grain to the Adriatic. For such an important purpose the expenditure of the six or seven million gulden[1] needed to construct the line should appear a relatively small sacrifice.

On the basis of present experience, the annual average exports of grain that pass through Semlin for onward freighting can be estimated as below:

From Neu Bece [Novi Bečej] about	300,000 centners[1]
From Temesvar and Beckerek [Bečkerek]	400,000 ctrs.
From Panceva [Pančevo]	750,000 ctrs.
Total	1,450,000 ctrs.

To this quantity must be added the crops from Syrmia assembled in Mitrovitz, estimated at about 150,000 tons, so that the total annually exported from the region amounts to about 1,600,000 centners.

Thus in an average year a considerable quantity of grain will be shipped upriver from the Banat and Slavonia to Sissek. Unfortunately not all of it is destined for export overseas. Yet fifty or sixty years ago, before Odessa had driven us out of the Adriatic and Mediterranean ports,[2] a much greater quantity was exported. At present the above trade is consigned as follows:

About half the total, or 800,000 centners, are despatched to

---

[1] See Note on Weights, Measures and Currency, p. 387.
[2] After the opening of the Straits in 1830.

Karlstadt, of which 500,000 are sold there and 300,000 are sold for export by sea. The other half of the total remains in Sissek and thence is consigned as follows: 400,000 to Laibach,[1] 100,000 to Agram, 200,000 for sale in the surrounding districts, and 100,000 for export by sea.

In addition to these regular consignments the merchants of Sissek and Karlstadt buy several hundred thousand *metzen*[2] of grain at their own risk, and can deliver up to about one and a half million *metzen* to the seaports, if the state of the export market makes prices sufficiently attractive.

15. THE SLAVONIAN TIMBER INDUSTRY

Bericht der Handels- und Gewerbekammer zu Essek über die volkswirtschaftlichen Zustände Slavoniens bis zum Schlusse des Jahres 1881 (Report of the Osijek Chamber of Commerce and Industry on the Economic Conditions of Slavonia to the end of 1881), Osijek, 1882, p. 63.

TIMBER and timber products are the outstanding industry in Slavonia and take first place in her export trade. The production of timber has increased enormously in the past two decades. The exploitation of the rich supplies of hardwood, oak, etc., in the Slavonian forests began to be developed only towards the end of the first half of this century; firewood was also cut for the neighbouring countries. But the timber industry could only be developed within the limits of a local trade; on the one hand the foreign market was accustomed to get its timber supplies from Hungary, and in the second place, Slavonia's bad communications defeated all attempts at exploitation of the industry. Then again the Slavonian industry was affected by the timber trade carried on by Bosnia, which at that time had some splendid oak available.

Not until the seventies of this century did the Slavonian timber industry really come to life. It obtained a communications link with Trieste when the southern railway line Sissek–Steinbruck was built; and subsequently a second port was made accessible by the opening of the Karlstadt–Fiume line. Then, as a result of the increase in railway lines and the competition that this brought about, the Danube steamship companies reduced their freight charges and

---

[1] Ljubljana.
[2] See Note on Weights, Measures and Currency, p. 387.

improved the connections with Germany, France and Italy. Germany sent increasing numbers of buyers into this country, for they had realized the importance of the Slavonian forests. When the forestry industry was rationalized and regulated, bigger railway lines were built, and soon Slavonia was in a position to satisfy the rapidly increasing demands of foreign countries.

IV. Slovenia

16. Margins of Existence

Balthasar Hacquet, *Abbildung und Beschreibung der südwest- und östlichen Wenden, Illyrer und Slaven* (Portrayal and Description of the South-Western and South-Eastern Wends, Illyrians and Slavs), Leipzig, 1802–5, vol. i, chapter ii, pp. 19; 20–3; 31–2; 39–40; vol. ii, chapter iv, pp. 57–9.

(a) The Krainians (Upper Carniola)

THESE Wends are to some extent mixed with other Slav peoples, such as the Belochorbati. Their specific name, from the Slav word *kraj* (borderland), shows that they are people of the marchlands, or inhabitants of the farthest boundaries of the Slavs to the west, just as those Russian peoples who inhabit the regions reaching down to the Black Sea, the Zaporozhe Cossacks or Haidamaks, are known as Ukrainians or Ukraini, because they inhabit the farthest boundaries to the south-east. . . .

To the north and east this small race is bounded by the Wends described above, to the south by the Dolenzi, or so-called Lower Krainians, and to the west by the people of the Karst,[1] known to the ancients as the Japidians, and partly by the sea of Friuli[2] and the Adriatic.[3]

This tall and well-built race, whose women are endowed with beautiful red and white complexions and black eyes and hair, lives happy and content with frugal fare. Water from snow and ice-crowned Alps, springing pure and fresh from the rocks, provides their drink. Their daily food is buckwheat flour, though they also eat some rye-bread (*kruh*). From the former they make a kind of porridge by boiling, straining and then stirring it into a mash, flavoured with a little butter, bacon, or milk and salt.

[1] Barren limestone region to the south and west of Ljubljana.
[2] The Gulf of Venice.
[3] Linhart, *Versuch einer Geschichte von Krain und den übrigen Ländern der südlichen Slaven Oesterreichs*, 2 Parts, Laibach, 1791 (with maps). Weichard Valvasor, *Die Ehre des Herzogthums Krain*, Laibach, 1689, 4 Parts, with many copperplates (*Author*).

This dish, known as *sterz*, gives the peasants an excellent sustenance. Buckwheat, as is generally known, has a peculiar smell rather repugnant to those unaccustomed to it, but in summer their sweat makes this smell unnoticeable. Sour cabbage (*kislekapus*) is much eaten in its fermented state. They keep the leaves through the winter, then dry and boil them with some fat for Easter. This they call *Alleluja*, but whence the custom comes I could not learn, and even Valvasor, the indefatigable universal recorder, does not tell us.

Meat and brandy they consume very rarely. But as their neighbours to the east and south have wine in plenty, wine is a common drink, even for the poor.

The houses, as is usual among the Slavs, are built of wood, though in the plains there are villages with houses of stone. In the mountains they are poor scattered huts, with little windows (*okna*), no more than air-holes, since a man can scarcely put his head through them. When such a house (*hisha*) is built, they use whole or half fir-tree trunks, and build the four walls on a single foundation stone. Then they put a thatched roof (*streha*) on top, cut out the little windows, stop up the cracks in the walls with clay, divide up the rooms (*izby*) and whitewash the whole interior. They have stoves (*petsch*), but like all the Slavs make little use of chimneys.

However poor a village may be, its churches are usually clean, well-found and strongly built, especially the steeple. One church does not suffice for a village; many parishes have as many as seven or nine such temples, standing on mile-high mountains and dedicated to various saints. Yet as a rule such churches are visited only once a year. As there is usually no priest's house at the temple, all the vestments for the church ceremonies are carried up. On the feast-day the innkeepers set up in huts of branches or tents; there is a sermon and a feast, and then, since there is no shelter other than the temple of the Lord, all the faithful crowd into it together to spend the night, which for many a passionate boy or girl does not pass without fulfilment of desire. An unedifying example of such ways of spending the night in church is given by the above-mentioned anonymous author of the journey through South Germany.[1] I could give many instances to corroborate this licentiousness, but that they are better consigned to oblivion. It has often been proposed to close these superfluous churches, and a beginning was made in the salutary reign of the Emperor Joseph, but under his successors the intention has been abandoned, because it ran counter to the self-interest of the priests (*fari*); for, says the reverend father (*tajmashtr*),

[1] *Reise durch einige Theile vom mittäglichen Deutschland und dem Venetianischen*, Erfurt, 1798 (*Author*).

'the more churches, the more collections, and the more for my bag'.

This excess of churches is a bad thing, not merely because building them costs many their best working days and is a useless expense, but also because it gives rise to licentious gatherings which levy contributions on the whole countryside. The priests encourage the well-to-do young men to collect for the church. Winter comes, when the highlanders have little work, and six or eight of them set out like a band of gipsies to journey through the country. Their begging begins with music, followed by lusty dancing with buxom wenches. The money collected is intended to be used for the new church, but the collectors must also live on it, which is anything but edifying. As they are more or less drunk all the time, these parties usually end in brawls and the like. . . .

Agriculture is carried on most laboriously by the Upper Krainians[1] (*Gorenzi*, highlanders), as they have no vineyards. The fields are narrow, and as the soil is shallow they are ridged up with deep furrows, to drain the land and hold it together. The crops are hung out to dry in the fields on long high railings (*kosotz*). These, as the above-mentioned Mr. Anton rightly supposes, go back to an ancient nomadic life;[2] I have seen the same among the wandering Zaporozhe Cossacks and Bessarabian Tartars.

Trades and crafts are carried on mostly by the Germans among the population, for the Krainians lack application, though not ability. But under discipline they excel the Germans in industry and skill, as the miners of Hydria[3] proved to my complete conviction. The pit-worker there is a carpenter and mason as well, and thoroughly understands his work, and so is welcome in other state mines.

In small industries these people show some skill. The little workshops for weaving kersey (*meslanka*) clothe the country and its neighbours, and such cloth can be sold at a good price. The same is true of the horse-hair sieves and the straw hats which are much exported. Many centners of nails and all kinds of iron[4] and steel goods are exported to Italy, where they can face competition from Swedish and other iron, because the products are made in an

[1] Inhabitants of the northern and eastern districts of Carniola.

[2] Uncertain summers, not nomadic habits, are the explanation. The practice still continues in Slovenia, as also in Scandinavia.

[3] The Idrija quicksilver mines were at this period the largest mines in Yugoslav territory, employing 918 miners in 1801. See M. Mirković, *Ekonomska Historija Jugoslavije*, Zagreb, 1958, pp. 182–90.

[4] Small iron-works, smelting with charcoal at Železniki, Kropa, Tržič and Kamnik, grew into large-scale enterprises during the nineteenth century.

assortment of sizes which can be used in the small Italian fur-
naces. . . .

The attachment of the Krainian—of the peasant, that is—to his
fatherland is very great; he will endure every ill, even starvation,
rather than abandon it. To be convinced of this it is necessary only
to travel in the southern parts, where the wretched huts stand on the
bare crags, and the poor peasant has gathered a little earth into a
pot-shaped hollow to grow some crops there. When even this is
lacking he must live off goats and sheep, and in the dry season
drives them miles to find water, for the uplands are denuded of tree
cover and soil, and the water runs off into underground channels.
As if nature were not chary enough, the climate is also harsh; the
prevailing north-east wind, called the *Bora*, strips soil and plants
from the rocks, can overturn a cart with a 60-centner load, and
blows men and beasts down the rocks to perish helplessly—and yet
these people will not leave their stony Arabia.

More than once I have seen in anguish the people of this region
dying of hunger. It is a desperate death: the mother, with her child
crying of hunger at her breast, sinking to the ground in despair
because she can give no milk. To me the attachment to this desert
was incomprehensible; yet their old habit of a free patriarchal life,
pure air and water, and often a weakness in their lungs, which I
have described elsewhere,[1] make them afraid of low-lying land
where the air is heavier than in their hills, and cause homesickness.

(b) The Japidians or Zhitzes (Southern Carniola)

The Japidian is strong, tall, well-built, with brown complexion and
black hair; his pastoral life hardens him against the climate. Poor,
indeed very poor, he is, since never a decade passes in which many
do not die for want. So barren is Japidia! The first letter of its name
should be an L instead of a J, for the whole country is strewn with
stones.

The trade and occupation of these people consists in a little cultivation, carried on with admirable diligence in the declivities between
the crags, for on the heights the wind would carry seed and soil
away. But even in the most fruitful years the soil can never produce
enough sustenance. Here and there vines are grown, but the wine
they yield is of little worth and, as it usually ferments sour, is sold as
vinegar by the Zhitzes throughout the Duchy of Carniola.

The people of the Karst and the Poiks[2] live by a miserable carrying trade, because the trade routes from the seaports of Trieste (Trst)

---

[1] *Nova acta Academiae nat. curiosorum*, Norimberg, 1785, vol. vii, p. 95 *(Author)*.
[2] Inhabitants of the marsh region round Ljubljana.

and Fiume (or Rijeka) traverse their country. Their small wagons are drawn by double-yoked oxen; no iron goes to their making, and their drivers use no grease—not, like the Nogai Tartars, in the belief that to be heard afar is to warn off robbers—but because they have nothing to use to prevent friction and the horrible grinding sound. Nowhere in Europe have I seen such a wretched carrying trade as this, or such poor people; they are like the Alans, who would rather starve than leave their rocks.

On this rugged soil, where water is scarce, there are few or no water-mills, and windmills are out of the question. To grind corn for the small amount of bread they eat they use little querns or mortars, like the Hebrews in the time of Abraham, and many use Sarah's method of baking in the ashes. Their wine-presses are the most primitive imaginable, and so are the stone huts which they inhabit. Wine is often carried in sacks of hide. There are no craftsmen among them, and the more necessary domestic utensils they make themselves; everything of stone, wood, hide, etc., is men's work, while spinning, linen and wool-weaving is the work of the women. Apart from food, they buy little or nothing, and had they not the misfortune to have acquired a harmful and useless habit—namely tobacco—they would be in somewhat better circumstances. I shall always remember a rapacious tobacco official who came to the bad end he deserved, together with his family. One day he said to me, 'Look at this bare rocky country and half-starved people! Through my influence (power) I exact thousands from them for the state', etc., etc. To this tyrant who cheated his fellow-men and the government, under a semblance of piety and patriotism, I replied that the beneficent Joseph II would not allow the corruption of these poor people, did he but know of it.

Balthasar Hacquet (b. Brittany 1739, d. Vienna 1815), philologist, botanist, geologist, physician and ethnographer, served as a doctor in the Austrian army during the Seven Years War; in 1780 became a teacher at the Laibach Lyceum, and in 1788 Professor of Natural History in the University of Lemberg (Lwów). The work quoted above describes travels in Carinthia and Carniola in 1779–86, which were followed in 1788–9 by travels in the Carpathians. His other works include *Oryctographia Carniolica* (Geology of Carniola), 4 vols., Leipzig, 1778, 1781, 1784, 1789; the frontispiece of which is reproduced on the cover of this book.

17. FRAGMENTATION

Bericht der Handels- und Gewerbekammer für das Kronland Krain über den Zustand des Handels und der Industrie im Jahre 1852 (Report of the Chamber of Commerce and Industry for the Crownland of Carniola on the State of Commerce and Industry in 1852), Ljubljana, 1853, pp. 6–7; 9–10; 28–31.

LAND is more fragmented in Carniola than in any other province of the Austrian Monarchy, with the exception of the coastal region. For example, 229,847 joch[1] of arable land are divided into 609,600 parcels of land; 1,382 joch of meadows into 3,250 parcels; 2,876 joch of pasture into 2,700 parcels; 2,649 joch of vineyards into 9,108 parcels, while the whole area of land in holdings is divided between 73,469 owners. As the farmers wish to produce as many varieties of crops as possible, they raise many different crops on one small area, and there are therefore many different rotations, in which buckwheat, the main crop in this region, is usually planted as a second crop in the stubble of winter wheat and barley. Necessity drives the smallholder to grow on one and the same field the greatest possible quantity of a variety of crops, and to use methods which could not be approved in more advanced larger-scale farming. . . .

The chief food of the people is buckwheat, then millet, potatoes, cabbages and turnips, and in the mountains even oats. Bread is rarely eaten every day in the households of the small peasants, sometimes not for weeks at a time. Potato cultivation formerly extended to a much larger area than at present, but has declined because farmers have been discouraged by the rot which reached its culmination in 1849.

As a result of the steady encouragement of the Agricultural Society,[2] the cultivation of maize is being greatly extended, but is far from being as important as it should be. Since maize is a crop with a very high gross and net return per acre, and $\frac{5}{12}$ of the land is suited to its cultivation, a great extension of the present small area of 5,280 joch would be possible and highly advantageous, because it would enable Carniola to cover its food requirements and dispense with imports of foreign grain.[3] As proof of this assertion there is the fact that since the cultivation of maize was introduced into the

[1] See Note on Weights, Measures and Currency, p. 387.
[2] Founded in 1767; the first agricultural school was opened in 1771, but existed only until 1780.
[3] The second half of the century saw a great extension of the area under maize, but in spite of this advance grain imports were still necessary.

NEED FOR FARM PROGRESS 355

mountain valley of Bohinj by the Reverend Father Jacob Pagon, the import of grain into the region has declined by almost half.

Maize, millet, beans and pumpkins are often grown on one and the same piece of land. Maize and beans provide food for the peasant, pumpkins feed his pigs, and millet is his cash crop, because he makes besoms from it and with this craft can make enough money to purchase his requirements of salt. . . .

An outstanding obstacle to agricultural progress is the excessive fragmentation of land. As already mentioned, there are very few provinces in Austria where the land is divided into a chessboard of such tiny parcels, for in Carniola $23\frac{1}{2}$ square miles[1] of arable land is divided among 73,000 owners, and for tax purposes the area is divided into 120,000 parcels. It is inevitable that in such conditions many families must live very poorly, and evident that an intelligent and progressive management of the land cannot be expected from such people.

So it appears urgently necessary that limits should be set to this unrestricted fragmentation, and that the physiocratic system, which was introduced during the French occupation of Carniola and received legal sanction under the decree of 17 January 1815, should be abolished.[2]

18. NEED FOR AGRICULTURAL PROGRESS

Dr. Johann Bleiweiss, *Was hätte in Innerkrain bei dem in Folge der Laibach-Triester Eisenbahnen aufhörenden Fuhrwerkverdienste zur Hebung der Produktion zu geschehen?* (What should be done to increase production in Inner Carniola to make up for the loss of the carrying trade resulting from the Ljubljana–Trieste railway?) Speech at General Meeting of the Royal Agricultural Society, Ljubljana, May 1856, pp. 3–15.

THE railway from Laibach[3] to Trieste, which is shortly to be opened, will have serious effects for our country and particularly for its poorer regions, because it will deprive most of the population of their main source of earnings, namely the carrying trade.

This is generally known, and much has been written on the subject, particularly on the Karst afforestation project.

All members of the Agricultural Society for Inner Carniola[4] are

[1] See Note on Weights, Measures and Currency, p. 387.
[2] The Code Napoléon, which enforces equal division of property among heirs, was introduced during the French occupation of Illyria.
[3] Ljubljana.
[4] The central lowland, in the valley of the Sava and its tributaries.

unanimously agreed that because farms are so small only a few peasant proprietors in Inner Carniola can produce enough food for themselves and their families, even in years of good harvests, and even if the potato rot can be checked. The cadastral survey under-lines this clearly, for in eight districts, with a population of 96,476 souls, there are only 39,179 joch of arable land, giving an average of $\frac{2}{5}$ of a joch per head. Undoubtedly the same ratio holds for the rest of Carniola.

From this it inevitably follows that the peasants are forced to buy food with the money they earn in the carrying trade; this source of income, together with their earnings from forestry and recently from work on the railway, also enables them to pay their taxes.

Through the sudden loss of this income, a catastrophe will face the population, particularly those living near the highways. . . .

But though the local population will be seriously affected by the disappearance of these earnings, in a few years' time it should result in an improvement of agriculture and welfare in Inner Carniola. The road carrying trade is everywhere harmful to agriculture, since it leads to neglect of cultivation, wastage of manure, exhaustion of livestock instead of better breeding, farm debts and the demoraliza-tion which always accompanies life on the roads.

A second important problem for Inner Carniola is the forests and pastures. The destructive system of forest management which has prevailed, particularly during the last eight years, results in progressive advance of the arid Karstland, although at the same time plans are discussed for its reafforestation.

The third calamity for Inner Carniola is the great floods in the same districts, which often reduce the population to dire need.

From these three standpoints, conditions in Inner Carniola deserve the most serious consideration. The question to be considered is:

'In view of the loss of earnings from the carrying trade resulting from the opening of the Laibach–Trieste railway, what needs to be done in Inner Carniola to increase agricultural production, and how shall the Agricultural Society participate in such action?'

So far as agricultural production is concerned, the main questions to be answered are:

(a) Is it possible to bring additional land into cultivation?

(b) Are there means of making the land more productive?

Both questions can be answered with an emphatic affirmative, and therein lies reassurance for the future of Inner Carniola.

I find in the cadastral survey that in the eight districts of Inner Carniola there are 100,900 joch of pasture land and 16,020 joch of wooded pasture. Amongst these there must certainly be many thousands of joch—perhaps even the greater part—of pasture in common ownership. According to official documents, communally owned pastures represent dead capital, which can be made productive by conversion into arable or meadow. At present, three or four cows per joch are grazed on land which could at best support one cow on two joch, and the cattle go short of food and their manure is wasted, though the pastures if improved could support more cattle. . . .

. . . Thus the dividing up and improvement of the common pastures is the first necessity in winning more productive land, and my first proposal is therefore that the provincial government should enforce the subdivision of all communal pastures within one year, making due allowance for cases of hardship.[1]

At the same time as more productive land is obtained in this way, the coming of the railway will make it possible to devote to the improvement of the land a considerable amount of capital in the form of manure which is now wasted in cattle and horse droppings on the roads. At present, with the exception of a few excellent farms, small farmers have no manure pits, but simply throw the manure up against the stable or house wall, so that it is dried by heat and washed out by rain. Moreover, with few exceptions, the farm houses have no closets. It has been proved that cholera is spread by human excrement, and this is the reason why the disease proves so intractable in these regions. On both agricultural, sanitary and moral grounds, it should be made compulsory for every farmer to build a manure pit and a closet.

A third means of raising farm incomes is by the cultivation of fruit and mulberry trees, the latter for silk-worm breeding. All Inner Carniola is suited to fruit growing; the Poik region[2] and the Karst produce excellent fruit, and the mulberry, which likes chalk soil, thrives on the limestone. The Agricultural Society can help to develop these cultures by providing instruction and free distribution of fruit and mulberry saplings.

A fourth aim, which to some extent will be achieved automatically as a result of the railway, is the improvement of cattle-breeding.

---

[1] This main recommendation was unrealistic as a substitute for the loss of the carrying trade, since no estimate of the extent of these pastures is made by the author; much of the area lay in the mountains and could not have been subdivided among individual owners. As to the fate of some of these pastures, see p. 363 below. Though the other recommendations as to fruit-growing and cattle breeding were wise and, as extract 20 below shows, were practicable, they were obviously too long-term to provide a sufficient remedy for the loss of earnings from cartage. As the following extract shows, the loss was still felt thirty years later.

[2] Round Ljubljana.

When earnings from the carrying trade cease, and agriculture must make good the loss, the farmer will find cattle-breeding the means of increasing his supply of manure and the fertility of his land. The Agricultural Society should do everything in its power to assist and encourage better breeding. . . .

Johann Bleiweiss (Janez Bleiweis) (1808–81), physician, veterinarian, economist and Slovene nationalist, had a great influence on the Slovene peasants.

19. HELP FOR HOME INDUSTRIES

Bericht über die am 17. und 18. April in Laibach abgehaltene Agrar-Enquête (Report of Enquiry into Agricultural Conditions, held in Ljubljana on 17 and 18 April), ed. J. Vošnjak, Ljubljana, 1884, pp. 40–5.

Johann Murnik: The Committee of the Diet[1] has addressed various questions to the District Offices and other local authorities, in particular the question of whether the population is occupied in any kind of domestic industry. According to the reports, such industries are more or less advanced in 32 districts and in 20 are of considerable importance. Scarcely any district exists which has no domestic industry of any kind. The most important are the following:

1. Horse-hair sieves[2] in Stražišče near Kranj.[3]
2. Pillow-lace in Idrija and a few other places.
3. Straw hats[2] in Kamnik.
4. Straw mats and baskets in Sv. Marjetina, Lipoglava, Polica, and Sv. Lenhart near Ljubljana.
5. Wood-turning and carving in Ribnica, Kočevje, Lašče Velike, Lož, Bled, and other places in the districts of Idrija, Loke, Kranj, Kamnik and Ljubljana.
6. Basket-making in the districts of Ljubljana, Brdo, the Bohinj valley, Ribnica, where withies can be cut in great quantities along the river banks.

[1] In 1883 the Diet of Carniola appointed a committee to investigate 'the causes of the economic decline of the peasantry in Carniola' and make proposals for action to improve the peasants' position. In April 1884 the committee reported to a conference of representatives of the Diet, the government, the Agricultural Society and experts on peasant economy. On the question of where and how domestic industries should be encouraged, the chairman of the sub-committee reported as above.

[2] See p. 351 above.

[3] Slovene place names have been substituted for the German in the text, a translation from the original Slovene.

7. Besoms of birch and other trees, all over Carniola, but especially in Polhov Gradec, Dobrova and Ig.
8. Frieze cloth in Idrija.
9 and 10. Mats and rugs in Kranj.
11. Flannel and wool jackets in Bled.
12. Linen weaving and spinning almost everywhere, the best quality in Smlednik, Mengeš, Medvode, Škofja Loka, Metlika, Kranj and Kočevje.
13. Headcloths in Radovljica, Kamnik, Zatičina and near Ljubljana.
14. Caps and jackets in Kamnik.
15. Stockings and jackets in Idrija, Kranj, Tržič, Bled, Javornik and Jesenice.
16. Bandages in Smlednik, Gameljne, Mengeš.
17. Woven cloth slippers (sandals) in Kranj.
18. Headdresses in Kranj.
19. Brushes in Ribnica and other places.
In addition to these, all the implements used by farmers are made at home.

The questions to be considered are which of these industries is to be encouraged, in what districts and by what methods. In view of the present position of our peasantry any kind of domestic industry deserves support.

The horse-hair sieve industry enriches the owners more than the workers, but even this industry needs support, for it will collapse if tariff duties are too high. The same is true of the remaining industries. Our business today is to make general recommendations, leaving the detailed provisions to be worked out by the Diet under the guidance of the Provincial Government. I therefore move that the committee should recommend the following measures.

1. Assistance to the pillow-lace industry in Idrija. This is making fairly good progress, as there is a lively demand for lace. Last year the sale of lace realized over 30,000 florins,[1] while a few years ago its sales amounted to only 5,000 florins. The reason for this increase is that the lace-makers have received good patterns, and they now need a designer who would produce patterns, not only for the school in Idrija, but also for their own use at home. But such a designer is hard to find in Carniola, and even in all Austria. Efforts should therefore be made to ensure that the lace-makers receive good patterns.

2. The second most widespread home industry is straw-hat

[1] See Note on Weights, Measures and Currency, p. 387.

making. Since 1866 the factories have been taking over this industry and are certainly bringing it up to a higher level. But the profit goes in the main to the factory-owners. Our task should therefore be to assist the home workers to weave better and to obtain finer quality straw. . . . A training school should be established in the centre of the province for this purpose.

3. The weaving of bread baskets in Bystrica, and along the Sava to Beričevo and Šmarno Goro continues to decline. And why? Because in spite of our railway connection, ordinary bread baskets find no buyers, because they are uniform and tasteless. If we had a training school, people could learn to make baskets in good taste and colours, and they could be sold in Vienna, where the price at present paid for an ordinary basket barely covers the cost of carriage.

4. For the pottery industry, the establishment of a special school is not necessary, because it would be too costly; but the potters, who are otherwise highly skilled workers, should have instruction in better glazing.

5. For wood-working and carving a school should be set up in Ljubljana.

6. A special committee should be appointed to decide which domestic industries should be established, and in which districts.

7. The government should include in the provincial budget an appropriate sum for the encouragement of such industries and vocational training.

It is important that such industries should be introduced where they do not at present exist, so that people can earn during the off-season. The peasants lead a hard life, and in recent years have been unable to pay their taxes, so that everything is undermined. If a domestic industry is introduced, then they can earn something, however little, but perhaps as much as 20 crowns a day, instead of sitting by the stove in winter drinking brandy. But money is needed for our last recommendation, and that is why we propose that the government should include an adequate sum in the Budget. . . .

[In the course of discussion,] *J. Potepan*, Mayor of Zemun Dolnji, said: In our district, the railway has done great harm, for since it came there is nothing to be earned in the carrying trade. And now they will take from us even the small earnings which remain, because it is intended to sell the Bystrica water to the city of Trieste. Our people who go abroad to work usually come back as beggars. I should therefore like to propose that some industry, no matter what, should be introduced in our district, so that we should have something to live on. The most suitable would be a cloth factory, so that people would get cheap clothing. Basket-weaving and straw-hat making would also be suitable, and pottery could be started very easily, because in the Bystrica district there is a good supply of clay for making earthenware. . . .

20. Causes of Agricultural Depression

G. Pirc, *Krain im Jahre 1893* (Carniola in 1893), in symposium *Die Land- und Forstwirtschaft in Österreich-Ungarn* (Agriculture and Forestry in Austria-Hungary), ed. H. H. Hitschmann, Vienna, 1894, pp. 64-71.

In the year 1893 the situation of agriculture in Carniola has in no way improved. On the contrary, as a result of the shortage of fodder, it has much deteriorated. For several reasons our farmers—who with the exception of a few 'smaller' large estate-owners belong exclusively to the peasantry—are in a desperate situation.

The almost continuous bad harvests, together with various natural disasters, would alone have prevented economic progress, and since in agriculture more than in any other sphere standing still means going back, we can speak only of a decline in agricultural welfare, which is much aggravated at present by several other adverse influences. Shortage of agricultural labour, the 'unsolved farm servant problem', continued emigration, phylloxera in the vineyards of Lower Carniola, drought in the Karst—all these must necessarily have a very strong negative influence. All in all, it is not surprising that the farmer lacks confidence and regards the future with indifference.

But one thing should not be forgotten: universal education and a higher degree of literacy have raised the intellectual level of our peasantry, and their mental outlook has undergone a great change. The farmer now begins to understand that he is not alone responsible for his precarious position and that this is due to circumstances which could be avoided if various kinds of action were taken in time. He also begins to realize the obstacles which the costly and complex legal system causes for him, and is filled with distrust and discontent. So let us hope that the authorities responsible will come to his assistance in time, for otherwise the farming class, the pillar of the state, will become too unstable to carry its burden! . . .

By comparison with the past, the amount of assistance and encouragement now given to agriculture is enormous, and the success of the attempts to improve farm management seem truly astonishing when one recalls how backward the country was in this respect. The admirable activity of the flourishing Royal Agricultural Society in

Laibach is supported by the Ministry of Agriculture, and the provincial government annually votes a large sum for agricultural improvement, while the wealthy Savings Bank of Carniola assists local agricultural societies with substantial advances.

Among various measures taken in 1893 the following must be mentioned.

A model farm of the size typical in the province was started by the Laibach Agricultural Society in the vicinity of Laibach, to be used as an experimental station and demonstration farm.

As propaganda for artificial fertilizers, 200 tons of basic slag and kainite were distributed to farmers.

Although our country cannot make full use of agricultural machinery owing to the predominance of small and tiny holdings, there is a great need for wider use of machinery suitable for small holdings. Threshing machines, both hand- and horse-driven, chaff-cutters and winnowing machines are now in use in all parts of the country. The agricultural societies have made more than 100 machines available for the use of their members. Better implements, particularly ploughs and grass harrows, are coming into more general use.

The Agricultural Society has introduced better varieties of seed in large quantities, chiefly flax, oats and buckwheat, and also seed potatoes, the more resistant varieties of which are now supplanting the exhausted local varieties. It has also distributed about 15,000 standard fruit trees from its nurseries, either free or at low prices; every member has the right to receive four standard trees free of charge. The big cider press in Bled has been enlarged; two other villages have built presses and individual farmers received loans to buy them; the Horjul Society has built an American fruit-drying plant.

The hopeless situation of the vine-growing peasants due to the irresistible spread of phylloxera has been improved through the rapid introduction of American stocks, and there is welcome activity in many new vineyards. The activity of the Agricultural Society, aided by the Central Savings Bank, has been most praiseworthy, in establishing new nurseries and aiding farmers to buy stocks.

Cattle-breeding received great attention in 1893, for it is indeed the chief branch of agriculture in Carniola. . . . Mürzthal and Mölltal breeding cattle have been imported. For regions that need good milking cattle and must breed the grey cattle which are the only type required by Italian dealers, eight Swiss pedigree bulls have been imported and one genuine Simmental bull for the Laibach district. In all 46 bulls were imported.

Cattle-breeding in the last two decades has made enormous

strides; the improvement in quality may be estimated at 50 per cent. Production increased in the vine-growing districts devastated by phylloxera. But in the alpine districts—predestined for this branch of production—there has been a decline. The reason for this distressing fact is that the alpine pasture lands belonging to the former Church properties have been bought up for game preserves by owners of large estates, through whose intrigues the peasants have been forced or persuaded to yield their rights; another reason is in the preference shown to hunting as compared with agriculture. For these reasons the cattle population in all these districts during the last decade has fallen, in the Radovljica district, for example, by as much as 3,000 head.

Unfortunately those responsible do not understand the serious effects of this abuse, which will mean the ruin of many hundreds of peasants. Can no one see that the taxpaying capacity of these districts depends on the prosperity of the local peasants, and not on the number of buck chamois?

Finally, the lax enforcement of the law for the increase of cattle-breeding is much to be regretted. It seems as if this law—like all other legislation for the improvement of agriculture—is doomed to remain only on paper. . . .

Agricultural organizations in Carniola are concentrated in the Royal Agricultural Society and its branches. The only other unions are the eleven cheese co-operatives in the alpine regions and a fruit-marketing co-operative in Slap near Vipava. In 1893 this made progress and now has 2,653 members (against 436 in 1883 and 2,317 last year) who are divided into 63 branches as against 50 last year. The society's annual turnover in 1893 amounted to 140,000 florins.[1]

As to agricultural education, there has been an increase in the number of pupils at the School of Agriculture and Viticulture in Standen; the travelling teachers have been so successful that their work deserves every encouragement.

The credit needs of the country are well and reliably supplied through four Savings Banks and numerous Loan Banks; several new Loan Banks organized on the Raiffeisen principle were established in 1893.

Gustav Pirc (1859–1923), agricultural economist; as secretary of the Peasant Union did much to raise the technical and educational level of the Slovene peasants through the agricultural co-operative movement.

[1] Co-operative organization reached an extremely high level by the end of the nineteenth century, chiefly as a result of the efforts of the Catholic clergy. Credit societies handled a large proportion of all credit business, and marketing societies were important in dairy produce, cattle, eggs, fruit and vegetables.

V. Dalmatia

21. TRADE AND AGRICULTURE

Sir John Gardner Wilkinson, *Dalmatia and Montenegro*, London, 1848, vol. i, pp. 215–17; 233–4.

IT is to be regretted that the Austrians, with all their paternal care, do so little to better the condition, and advance the useful acquirements, of the Dalmatian peasantry, who are left in entire ignorance of any system of agriculture, and know as little about the advantages or improvement of land, as their ancestors in the days of medieval darkness. For the encouragement of schools the Austrian government deserves credit, and, after the neglect of their Venetian rulers, the Dalmatians have reason to rejoice in a wiser and better system; but something more is wanting for the instruction of an agricultural population, whom a limited knowledge of reading will not teach skill in husbandry, nor the mode of improving land, nor the importance of new and useful productions.

Their implements of husbandry are on a par with those of the unenlightened inhabitants of Asia Minor, and the primitive waggons used in the neighbourhood of Knin called to mind those of the plains about Mount Ida; the land is tilled as in the remote provinces of Turkey, and the ploughs of the Morlacchi are often inferior to those of Herzegovina. Nor has Dalmatia any manufactures really deserving that name; and the quality and dye of the common cloth, called Rascia, used by the peasants, are of the worst description. Nor is the production of silk sufficiently encouraged, though the soil is well suited to the growth of the mulberry tree; and I have seen some of immense size, about Fort Opus,[1] as well as near Perasto[2] and Risano,[3] in the Bocche di Cattaro.[4] Hemp, and many other useful productions, might also be extensively cultivated in Dalmatia. But even the great fall of water in the rivers is unheeded, though so well suited to the establishment of mills; and there are none on the strong streams of this country, except those for grinding corn, some of which

---

[1] Opuzen.   [2] Perast.   [3] Risan.   [4] The Gulf of Kotor.

were made by the Turks; and however incredible it may appear, all the wheat of the valley of the Narenta is sent to be ground in Herzegovina. . . .

Sign[1] contains about 2,000 inhabitants. It was long the bulwark of the Venetians against the Turks, whose frontier is now seven miles off. A bazaar or market is held twice a week, on Monday and Thursday, at a place called Han, about five miles from Sign,within the Dalmatian territory. Ever since the plague of 1815, Han has been appointed for the reception of the Turkish caravans, which, according to the treaty of Passarovitz,[2] had until then the privilege of going to Spalato.[3]

The caravans are escorted by soldiers from Billibrig, on the confines, to Han, and are taken back in the same manner; in order to prevent smuggling, or an infringement of the quarantine regulations. Another bazaar is held about four hours from Sign, on Wednesdays and Fridays; and there is another, distant about six hours. Formerly, these points of intercourse with Turkey were more numerous than at present: the trade has now passed into other channels; and the Turks find it more profitable to send the greater proportion of their exports at once to Zara,[4] than to supply the limited consumption of the small towns, in the interior of the country.

Salt, and a few other productions of Dalmatia, are sought by the Turks at the bazaar of Unka, near Metcovich; and Imoschi, and a few other places, are still frequented by them; but the principal trade is with Zara; which has succeeded to most of the advantages once enjoyed by Spalato, in the visits of the caravans.

John Gardner Wilkinson (1797–1875), explorer and Egyptologist; author of several works on Egyptian archaeology, of which the most important was *Manners and Customs of the Ancient Egyptians*, London, 1837. In 1844 he travelled through Dalmatia, Montenegro, and Bosnia-Hercegovina.

22. BENEFITS OF TOBACCO CULTIVATION

M.J.D., *Dalmatien im Jahre 1893* (Dalmatia in 1893), in symposium quoted in extract 20 above, pp. 196–7.

TOBACCO, which in 1893 was planted on a larger scale than in 1892 because the State Tobacco Monopoly approved larger acreages, was cultivated with great care, so that the harvest of 1893 can be

[1] Sinj.　　[2] Požarevac, 1718.　　[3] Split.　　[4] Zadar.

considered fairly good both in quantity and quality. In Imotski and Vrgorac districts tobacco cultivation is now exemplary; but as a result of the laudable efforts of the officials of the Monopoly, progress has also been made in other regions, such as Ragusa,[1] Cattaro,[2] Trau[3] and Sinj. In the district of Budua,[4] where conditions favour the growth of fine aromatic varieties, the population felt a great aversion to its cultivation; this was due, as we have learnt from a reliable source, to a malicious agitation on the part of the neighbouring Montenegrins, and also to the not always entirely tactful behaviour of some sections of the Financial Control.

In November 1893, the State Tobacco Monopoly purchased 100,000 florins'[5] worth of tobacco from the Montenegrins, and paid 75 florins per kilogram. This astonished the tobacco-growing peasants in the adjacent Boka,[6] and it is to be hoped that they will now understand why their Montenegrin neighbours advised them against growing tobacco, and that in 1894 they will take up its cultivation in earnest.

Tobacco cultivation is a source of great prosperity for Dalmatia. The author of these lines, who has inspected the districts of Imotski, Sinj and Vrgorac, can testify that the past six years there has been a complete revolution in economic conditions in all the districts where the peasants are diligently growing tobacco. Where previously there were dirty wretched huts, there are now pretty one- and two-storeyed houses. The peasants have paid off all their debts, and are free from anxiety, while the money-lenders—the vampires who live on the poor in these parts—have completely disappeared.

In Dalmatia, one hectare of tobacco gives a gross output of 1,200 to 2,000 florins, so that a peasant family which can do the whole work itself has a certain annual income of 900–1,700 florins. Since the Tobacco Monopoly now procures larger quantities of tobacco from Dalmatia and will in future take still more, it is very desirable that a tobacco factory should be established as soon as possible in one of the coastal towns, so that girls and women of poor families could earn money by working there.

---

[1] Dubrovnik.   [2] Kotor.   [3] Trogir.   [4] Budva.
[5] See Note on Weights, Measures and Currency, p. 387.
[6] Boka = Gulf (of Kotor).

VI. Montenegro

23. VILLAGE LIFE AND TRADE

Sir J. G. Wilkinson, *Dalmatia and Montenegro*, London, 1848, vol. i, pp. 406–7; 415–17; 420; 424–5; 426–31.

MONTENEGRO contains few towns. It may indeed be doubted whether any deserve that name; for a town there would be a village in any other country, and the largest does not contain a population of 1,200 souls. None of them are walled, and few can be said to have any streets; the houses are frequently detached, and in some so scattered, and distant from each other, that they appear rather to be farm-houses, or cottages, than the component parts of one village. Those, however, which stand close together, have only a common wall between them, as in towns in other countries; and they are generally better built, than when detached in the scattered villages; where, in some of the most mountainous, and secluded, parts of the country, they are of the rudest construction.

The total number of towns, and villages, in the country is between two and three hundred. They are principally situated in hollows, and on the slopes of mountains, but none on the points of hills difficult of access, as in the neighbouring provinces of Turkey; plainly indicating the fearless independence of the Montenegrin, who feels secure in the natural strength of his country, and requires no measure of defence beyond his own courage. . . .

The houses are of stone, generally with thatched roofs; but many are covered partly, or entirely, with wooden shingles, a mode of roofing very common in Slavonic countries. Some of the better kinds are roofed with tiles, on which large stones, the primitive nails of Montenegro, are ranged in squares, to keep them from being torn off by the wind. Each house generally contains one or two rooms on the ground-floor, with a loft above, occupying the space between the gables; where they keep their Indian corn, and other stores. The ascent to it is by a ladder, applied to a square hole in its floor, calling itself a door; and this floor, which performs the part of ceiling to the lower room, is frequently of wicker work, laid on rafters running from wall to wall. . . .

Whether in or out of the house, in a bed or on the ground, the Montenegrin always keeps on his clothes; his arms are close to his side; and when roused by any alarm, or by the approach of morning, he is up at the shortest notice; and no toilette intervenes, on ordinary occasions, between his rising and his pipe. . . .

Both men and women are very robust; and they are known to carry as much as 200 *funti*, (about 175 pounds,) on their shoulders, over the steepest and most rugged rocks. All appear muscular, strong, and hardy in Montenegro; and the knotted trees, as they grow amidst the crags, seem to be emblematical of their country, and in character with the tough sinewy fibre of the inhabitants. . . .

Agriculture is in a very primitive state, and except in the valley of Bielopavlich, and a few other parts of the country, the land is all cultivated with the spade. The plough is very simple, consisting of a wooden share, with long sloping slides, or cheeks, reaching to the holder, and placed at a very acute angle with the horizontal foot.[1] It has only one handle, or holder, like that used in Greece, about Nauplia and Argos; which is equally simple, though the position of the few parts it is composed of varies a little; and both are drawn by two oxen, yoked to the pole.

No cultivable soil is neglected; every piece of land, a few feet square capable of tillage, is planted with Indian-corn, potatoes, or some other useful produce; and no means are left untried by the Montenegrins, to obtain a livelihood by labour, and augment the exports of their country.

Notwithstanding all their efforts to multiply its productions, the means of obtaining a sufficiency of food does not keep pace with the increase of population; and though they export provisions to foreign markets, many, who are poor, find themselves destitute of the necessaries of life. Frequent migrations, therefore, take place, especially after years of scarcity; and now that the Vladika has put a stop to their former unlimited system of robbery, those who hold the rank of poor, in that poor country, are forced to seek a livelihood, and a home, in more productive regions. They mostly go into Servia, which may be called the parent of Montenegro; but those who have been distinguished in war are retained by their compatriots, and subscriptions are raised to furnish them with the means of subsistence. . . .

The principal market for the produce of Montenegro is Cattaro; some is also sold at Budua, and Fortenuovo, near Castel-Lastua,[2] as

---

[1] See p. 310 above.   [2] Petrovac.

well as in the towns of Turkey, during the casual truces with that country; but dried fish, and a few other articles, are sent to more distant places.

Though so near the sea, that a stone might almost be thrown into it, from the mountains overhanging Cattaro, the Montenegrins have no port; nor does their territory, in any part, come down to the shore; and they are dependent on the Austrians for permission to pass all goods intended for exportation, or received from abroad, by the Adriatic. This is a great disadvantage to the Montenegrins; and it would certainly be highly conducive to their prosperity, and to their progress in civilization, if their territory reached to the sea, and enabled them to enjoy the advantages of direct commercial communication with other people. It would not, however, be desirable, either for themselves or others, that they should have possession of any stronghold, like Cattaro, which they once greatly coveted; and nothing would be required, but a port for the purposes of trade. . . .

The promotion of civilization there may, some day, be of importance, and be attended by very desirable results; far more than could be hoped for from an intercourse with the adjoining province of Albania, which has not the same prospect of coming in contact with other nations as the Slavonic race. It would indeed be difficult to civilize, or improve, the Albanians; whose savage habits are so little suited for the encouragement of industry, and who frequently outrage the common feelings of humanity; and few hopes can, as yet, be entertained of a country, where excesses are committed, similar to those that happened four years ago; when some Moslems, having attacked a Christian village, were not satisfied with the murder of the men, but actually obliged the women to roast their own children at the fires, kindled from their burning houses.

The numerous sheep and goats reared by the Montenegrins afford them a very profitable supply of wool, and cheese, for exportation; their smoke-dried mutton (called *Castradina*) pays an annual duty at Cattaro, of from 2,000 to 2,600 florins; and the mutton hams of Montenegro are highly esteemed, and are sold for exportation to Istria, Venice, and Ancona.

The Exports of Montenegro are: smoked mutton (*Castradina*), salt fish (*Scoranza*), wax, honey, hides, tallow, cheese, butter, *Scottano* wood and leaves (for yellow dye and tanning), fire-wood, charcoal, cattle, sheep, pigs, and pork, fowls, (a few horses, and tobacco, brought from Turkey,) wool, ice, tortoise-shells, quinces, figs, olives, walnuts, and various fruits, Indian corn, potatoes, cabbages, cauliflowers, and other vegetables, silk (to Turkey), common tobacco grown in Montenegro, etc.

2B

The Imports are cattle, and some horses, as well as tobacco, from Turkey, and meat, for exportation; salt, copper, iron, oil, *baccala*,[1] salt fish, wax candles, wine, brandy, coffee, sugar, arms, gunpowder, lead, flints, glass, shoes, *opanche* sandals, cloth, linen and cotton stuffs, handkerchiefs, Fez caps, rice, grain, (sometimes, when the harvest is bad,) leather, etc.

Taxes. The taxes are levied on each hearth, or family. The custom has been to divide them into three classes, which paid one, two, and three florins a year for every house, or family; and the total now amounts to about 28,000 or 30,000 florins a year. There is also an *appalto* of tobacco, which brings in annually about 200 florins.

The revenue amounts to from 76,450 to 78,450 florins,[2] including the 10,000 sequins, about 47,000 florins, given by Russia, for the government expenses; Montenegro being under the protection of the Czar.

	Florins	
The Family, or house, tax	28,000 to	30,000
Duty on salt	200	200
Duty on fish	250	250
Duty on dry meat	200	200
Land of different convents let by the Vladika to peasants	600	600
Appalto of tobacco	200	200
	29,450	31,450
Given by Russia	47,000	47,000
	76,450 or	78,450

The price of a sheep is about four *zwanzigers*, or 2s. 8d. English; and the daily wages of a man in Montenegro are twenty *carantani*.[3] They coin no money; all that is current there being dollars, *zwanzigers*,[4] and other Austrian coins, as well as Turkish *paras*; though these last are generally used as female ornaments.

The manufactures of Montenegro, if they can be so called, are confined to some of their household furniture, and wearing apparel; and may be on a par with the manufactures of the Bedouins, or Arabs of the desert. The principal are the *strucche*, woollen stuffs, answering the same purpose as the Scotch plaid, and the Spanish *Manta*, and performing the office of cloak and blanket, to men and women. The coarse woollen coloured aprons of the women, some of the sandals, the socks, and other parts of their dress, are made by

---

[1] Dried cod.
[2] £7,645 to £7,845 English (*Author*).
[3] Or one *zwanziger*, eight-pence English (*Author*).
[4] Pieces of 20 *carantani*, the third part of a florin (*Author*).

members of the family: the women also embroider with the needle; and the shirt sleeves, and borders of their cloth dresses are neatly worked in silk, and patterns of coloured cloth.

There are few Montenegrins who exercise any trade; though some perform the offices of blacksmiths, farriers, or whatever else the immediate wants of a village may require; and their principal occupation, next to agriculture, is fishing, which they find very profitable; particularly in the Lake of Scutari. Guns, and other arms are of foreign manufacture; and the skill of the Montenegrin is confined to mending them, when slightly injured. He also contrives to make some gunpowder, when unable to purchase it at a foreign market; and the charcoal he uses is from hazelwood, which abounds in the country.

VII. Bosnia-Hercegovina

24. UNDEVELOPED RESOURCES

Anon., *Historisch-topographische Beschreibung von Bosnien und Serbien mit beson-
derer Hinsicht auf die neuesten Zeiten* (Historical-topographical Description of
Bosnia and Serbia, with special reference to recent times), Vienna, 1821,
pp. 5–7; 12–14.

THOSE writers and travellers who assert that in comparison with
other countries Bosnia has few cattle are wrong; there is plentiful
evidence to the contrary. The thieving Uskoks (Turkish deserters
who fled first to Dalmatia and were then on account of their depre-
dations resettled in Carniola), and other gangs of robbers from
Croatia and Slavonia, have stolen much from Bosnia. But every year
many ox-hides and lambskins are exported from Bosnia to Spalato
and Sibenik; and when the Venetians held Dalmatia they took much
livestock by way of Zara to Italy and grazed it on the rich pastures
of the Adige which produce fine meat. The Bosnian horses are
spirited and strong, and difficult to control unless their wildness is
tamed in youth. In Bosnia's forests there is game in plenty, both
four-footed and winged, above all the falcon. All rivers and ponds
are full of fish. Thus Bosnia lacks nothing for necessity or convenience. If the forests were not so excellent, how should the cattle
produce such good hides and such good tallow for export abroad?
How should the wool of the numerous herds of sheep produce an
export commodity?

Pig-feeding is extensive, owing to the prevalence of oak forests.
Wild beasts from the forests provide skins, furs, rugs and other
articles, and bees produce wax and honey, not only for local consumption but also for export.

Though the land is mountainous, the climate is on the whole warm
and the land most fertile. Grain is cultivated to supply the needs of
the country. There is an abundance of plants which could be used
for medicinal, domestic and technological purposes (such as dye-
stuffs), if the region were not inhabited and governed by such wild

and barbarous people. And what treasures of unused but useful minerals are locked away in these rough mountains! The author of this book was astonished to learn of them from a friend who had business in these parts. First and foremost, according to all accounts, there must be much silver. Gold is found in the river beds, and orpiment;[1] there are also sulphur, copper, lead, rock and spring salt; and there are mineral springs, of which the best are at Kiselipan, on the river Lepnica between Bosna-Serai[2] and Travnik. At present the only mineral worked is iron. Judging from the quality of the local produce, the quality of fruit could be much improved. The trade in fox-skins is worthy of mention. Because it is so mountainous, the province is specially rich in timber. . . .

If the Bosnian does not do as much as he could in agriculture, trade, commerce and industry, the fault lies only in the ruling race, the Turks. In order to maintain a large permanent army, they oppress their subjects in every way, and never allow them to attain even a modest level of prosperity. By seizing every means to this end, they think to achieve another object, namely, the maintenance of the fighting spirit of their subjects. They believe that so long as the people are destitute they will be ready to fight anywhere and for anything, and fear lest this readiness should be diminished if they are softened by the cares and toils of cultivation and become attached to the soil of their fatherland. The inhabitant of the provinces subject to Ottoman rule is aware of this attitude on the part of his rulers, and so cultivates the soil only in so far as is needful for his own sustenance, for he knows that his oppressors will rob him of anything that might promote his comfort or prosperity.

It is for this reason that the Turkish Empire is one of the worst cultivated of Empires, in spite of its rich provinces and smiling pasture-lands. The medicinal plants and the glorious minerals awaiting the day when they will be surveyed and worked are now neglected, for under the present government nature offers her treasures in vain to the inhabitants. This is why huge forests cover the country and stretches of wasteland are everywhere visible, while the best soils are neglected, and cattle-raising remains the main source of food for the people of this Pashalik.

[1] A mineral, used as yellow dye.   [2] Sarajevo.

25. THE LAND QUESTION, 1878–1910

K. Grünberg, *Die Agrarverfassung und das Grundentlastungsproblem in Bosnien und
der Herzegowina* (The Agrarian Structure and the Land Redemption Problem in Bosnia and Hercegovina), Leipzig, 1911, pp. 28–40; 48–50; 51–8;
82–5; 88–90; 96–7; 99–102.

(a) The Existing Land Tenure System

A NEW era began in the history of Bosnia and Hercegovina when the
provinces were invaded by the Austro-Hungarian army in 1878. But
although the occupation has brought many changes to the country,
the foundations of the land system have remained unaltered.

If we attempt to describe these institutions as they now exist, we
get the following picture.

The agricultural land belongs to large landowners, who own most
of the area, and free peasants.

Landowners' estates consist of large properties, farmed in part in
numerous peasant holdings under kmet[1] tenure, and in part under
the owner's direct management. In distinction from the kmet lands,
the area under the owner's direct management is known as the
beglik (from Tk. *beylik*, estate). The latter usually includes a few
arable fields and meadows, the owner's house, and barns and corn-
racks for the storage of the crops delivered as tribute. The beglik is
cultivated either by the labour service of the peasants, so far as this
still continues, or by paid labourers. Landlords' properties are often
very large, their size being reckoned by the number of kmet holdings
which they include. Many landlords 'own as many as 400 or 600
peasant farms'.[2]

The landlord, if a member of the nobility, is usually described as
the aga—now also used of non-Moslems—or the beg, if the estate is
large. In many districts he is called the spahija (from Tk. *spahi*),
recalling the time when the landed aristocracy held land in military
fiefs.

---

[1] The word *kmet* (pl. *kmetovi*) has different meanings in different parts of Yugoslavia. In Croatia it means a serf, in Serbia an independent peasant proprietor. In
Bosnia it means a dependent peasant under the system described in the following
pages, and in this context has no precise English equivalent. In translation, *kmet*
has been retained where legal aspects are in question; elsewhere 'peasant' or
'dependent peasant' is used.

[2] Cf. Eduard Ritter von Horowitz, *Die Agrarfrage in Bosnien und der Herzegowina*,
Vienna, p. 28, and *Die Bezirksunterstützungsfonds in Bosnien und der Herzegowina*,
Vienna, 1892, p. 7 (*Author*).

Corporate bodies can also be landowners: in the first place *vakuf*;[1] also monasteries, 'particularly Franciscan monasteries which here and there own dependent peasants',[2] for in the last years of Turkish rule the right to own land had become independent of religious denomination;[3] and finally the state itself, in respect of the *miri* lands[4] which have reverted to its ownership and are let out under the kmet system.

In many regions, especially on the Bosnian-Dalmatian frontier, the peasants' hereditary holding on a landlord's estate is called the bǎstina, as of old.[5] But the usual term for it is chiftlik,[6] which is best translated as 'yoke holding'. In Turkish times the farmer was called the chiftchija, which literally means 'yoke peasant'. These terms were and are still used to describe small farms and peasants in general, while the terms 'kmet' and 'kmetsko selište' have come into use since the occupation to describe the dependent peasants and their holdings.

The area of land belonging to a peasant holding is nowhere defined. It varies from district to district according to the configuration of the land and the type of farming. The essential is that it should be large enough to maintain and fully employ a peasant family. Building land and small plots therefore cannot be let on kmet tenure.

With the many thorny controversies as to the juridical nature of this tenure system—whether it should be described as a relationship of tenancy, hereditary tenancy or serfdom—we are not here concerned. It is pointless to force a social relationship which has developed under special conditions into the categories of Roman law which are familiar to us. All that is necessary is to describe the actual nature of the kmet tenure system.

From the standpoint of the peasant, his tenure consists in an hereditary or rather a permanent right of use of the holding, which cannot be alienated. Since the introduction of land registration in the provinces, it has been made obligatory to 'record each kmet holding in such a way that it represents a unit in the Landbook'.[7]

---

[1] Moslem religious endowments.

[2] Cf. Horowitz, *Die Agrarfrage*, p. 23 (*Author*).

[3] The imperial firman of 12 December 1875 laid down that in future 'there shall be no distinction between our subjects in regard to the possession of lands sold by auction or in regard to the possession of land or property sold by individuals'. (Reproduced in Documents from the Correspondence, etc., pp. 150–3) (*Author*).

[4] In this context, lands left uncultivated, to which the state reassumed the full right of ownership,

[5] Horowitz, *Die Agrarfrage*, p. 28 (*Author*).

[6] From Tk. *chiftlik*; from *chift*, the pair (of draught animals understood) (*Author*).

[7] Paragraphs 10 and 18 of the Land Registration Law for Bosnia and Hercegovina of 13 September 1884, promulgated by decree of the Provincial Government

New kmet relationships come into existence through contracts for which no special form is prescribed. The Sefer decree,[1] as we have already mentioned, required a written contract, determining the obligations of the kmet on the basis of previous customary relationships. But the bad results which followed from the application of this standard after the occupation have caused the administration to abandon it;[2] the contract must be in accordance with special agrarian law and is otherwise invalid. Thus there is freedom of contract only within the framework of this special law.

The subject of kmet rights and duties is not an individual person, but the 'peasant family'. This may be and usually is a zadruga, i.e. a co-operative including up to 80 or more interrelated people, engaged in joint farming of the holding; or it may be the ikonoština, the family in our narrower sense, i.e. a household consisting of parents and unmarried children, which normally grows into a zadruga as the children marry.[3] The head of the family, the 'house father' or 'house elder', is certainly described as the 'kmet'. Yet since the head of the family is not necessarily the father, but may be the eldest or indeed any man of the family group, he is only the representative of the household and is at one and the same time its partner and director. He is appointed by the household, which can replace him by another member if he proves incapable of fulfilling his functions. His death therefore does not affect the rights and obligations of the group which survives him; only the head is changed. The land registration law recognizes this family right by providing that in the index of owners 'in the case of kmet holdings, the name of the kmet family is to be recorded'.[4] It is clear that division of the kmet holding through inheritance is neither practised nor permissible.

The peasant family has the right of undisturbed use and cultivation

of 28 September 1884 (Collection of Laws 1886, pp. 60 ff.). Cf. Explanatory Memorandum on the Draft Law on Land Registration in Bosnia and Hercegovina, Sarajevo, 1890, p. 10. Registration in the Landbook had been carried out in the whole country with the exception of four districts by 1907, and was completed in these in the course of the year 1908 (Administrative Report for 1908, p. 248) (*Author*).

[1] The decree of 12 September 1859 (14 Sefer 1276), which codified the existing customary agrarian law, was intended to protect the peasants. In Bosnia, according to Grünberg, it was ineffective in this aim and was used as a pretext for increasing their obligations.

[2] Ordinance of the Provincial Government of 18 August 1880 (Collection of Laws, vol. i, pp. 537–8) (*Author*).

[3] Author's footnote omitted, listing sources from the voluminous literature of this subject.

[4] Paragraph 50a of the Land Registration Law (*Author*).

of the holding. The landowner may not interfere with its management, nor may he expel the family and live in the house while forcing the peasants to support him (a practice forbidden in the Sefer decree, but actually continued much later). The landowner is responsible for repairs to the house and buildings, and may also meet part of the farming costs by supplying seed, cattle and fodder. Improvements on the holding, such as new buildings or the planting of fruit trees or vines, cannot be undertaken without the landlord's consent. The peasant family has no right of ownership in the holding; it cannot be divided without the landowner's consent, nor may he divide it without theirs. Transfer by sale or bequest is also precluded by the nature of the system.

The chief obligation of the peasant family consists in the *hak*,[1] 'the just share', i.e. a tribute in kind levied on the produce of the soil, though not on the livestock. It amounts as a rule to one-third,[2] in many places to one-half, while in others it is only one-quarter or one-fifth. In quite exceptional cases it amounts to only one-sixth or one-seventh.[3]

A levy in excess of one-third is taken if the landlord performs any special service such as the supply of seed, working livestock, or fodder, the digging of ditches, etc., or if the soil or climate is specially favourable, or in the case of special crops requiring little labour. Thus the tribute is usually not the same for all kinds of field and garden crops; on the same holding different quotas will be levied for crops, hay, fruit, vegetables and industrial crops.

Tribute is sometimes levied as a fixed instead of a variable payment. When this is the case, payment can be made by substituting another product for the one on which the levy is due, e.g. butter instead of hay, a lamb instead of fruit and vegetables, or payment may be made in money. In these cases payment is known as *kesim*.[4] The conversion of a proportionate tribute in kind into a fixed payment in goods or money may be complete or partial; various combinations are possible. However, since the Austro-Hungarian administration has enforced payment of tithe in money, the payment of *kesim* in money has declined 'because the peasant is seldom able to make both payments in cash'.[5]

[1] From Arabic *haq*, the right. The Slavonic term is aginski dohodak, i.e. the income of the aga or danak, the tribute (to the landlord understood) (*Author*).

[2] Author's footnote omitted listing the shares prescribed in different districts by the Sefer decree of 1859.

[3] Cf. Horowitz, *Die Agrarfrage*, p. 31 (*Author*).

[4] As in the Kyustendil district of Bulgaria; see p. 250 above.

[5] Cf. Karszniewicz, *Das bäuerliche Recht in Bosnien und der Herzegowina*, i, *Das Agrarrecht*, Tuzla, 1899 (*Author*).

Usually the landowner's share is separated out on the threshing floor in the presence of the landowner or his agent and then handed over there, unless the agreement requires delivery to another place. Where the half or third share is taken, the tithe is deducted beforehand. From the early eighties up to 1905, when the tithe was converted to a fixed payment, the landowner had the right of calculating his share of the produce according to the official assessments for tithe.

In addition to the *hak*, all kinds of supplementary dues are levied, which vary inversely with the proportion taken as the main tribute. Of these the most important is labour service. This does not mean the services which were obligatory on the *raya* in Turkish times, though these have not disappeared entirely and still survive (as for example the levy of beaters for a shoot, which is generally made and always fulfilled). But such services are now voluntary, or at any rate cannot be required by law, since they have been expressly prohibited since 1859. The labour services now required are in the nature of payment for the use of the kmet land, consisting of transport of the produce-share to the landowner's house or the nearest market, or work on the beglik. These services are prescribed according to the job or the time taken, and may be fixed as the collective obligation of several families or of an individual family. . . .

The peasants can at any time abandon their holding and leave the estate. This however must not occur at the 'wrong time', and peasants must give notice of their intention to leave at the end of the threshing season; otherwise they must pay compensation to the landowner. On the other hand, they can be evicted from their holding if they neglect cultivation for two successive years, provided that they have been given warning under an official notice.

The peasants' right of occupation lapses in the interest of both parties if the family has so diminished in size that it is incapable of farming the holding. If this incapacity arises from the reduction of the number of working members of the family or for other reasons, such as shortage of livestock, the landlord can enforce a reduction in the size of the holding to an area which the family can culti-vate. . . . Kmet families which leave their holdings voluntarily or under compulsion are entitled to receive compensation for any improvements which the landowner has approved. When a holding has been abandoned, the landowner regains full rights of disposal and is under no obligation to cultivate it or to let it again under kmet tenure.

It must be emphasized that the peasants can buy themselves free from their obligations if the landowner agrees, i.e. they can acquire ownership of the land that they cultivate and 'become their own landlord', to use an expression from the old Austria.

Since the occupation, the settlement of disputes arising from the kmet relationship (for which there was no legislative provision at all in Ottoman times) has become a function of the political authorities, in the first instance the district office, in the second and final the provincial administration. This procedure was first established in 1895. It is oral, summary and very cheap. In the first instance the case is conducted and adjudicated by the district administrator, assisted by two persons, one representing the landlords, the other representing the peasants.

There is a very evident contrast between the agrarian structure of the two provinces and that which existed in the Monarchy before the reforms of Maria Theresa and Joseph II, or even after them in the period up to 1848.[1]

The landowner in Bosnia-Hercegovina has no position of public authority or responsibility like that of the landowner in the old Austria; he exercises no judicial or administrative functions; he has no disciplinary authority over the peasants; he does not stand between them and the state. Moreover, the kmets are not 'subjects' like the serfs; their freedom in law and contract is in no way limited; their rights and obligations in relation to the beg are entirely a matter of private law. . . . In short 'landlord' in these provinces means no more than a large landowner, and one who is restricted in his choice of the method of managing his property by a kind of tenancy right which is far stronger than that of an ordinary tenancy agreement and forces him to follow a system of peasant farming; though only so long as the rights of the kmets occupying his land continue. If these rights lapse, then he gains complete freedom of action and can go over to farming his land under direct management to the extent that he succeeds in getting rid of his kmets. So there are no safeguards to protect the peasant class and keep peasant land in peasant hands such as existed in the old Austrian legislation.[2] Thus there is nothing to prevent 'clearances' of kmet holdings by the landowner to make large farms, if legislation is not introduced to prevent such action or to abolish the kmet relationship entirely by a general enfranchisement of the land.

Up to the present, however, the Austro-Hungarian administration has taken no action in either direction and in particular has rejected any idea of compulsory enfranchisement.

[1] Cf. Grünberg, *Die Bauernbefreiung und die Auflösung des gutsherrlich-bäuerlichen Verhältnisses in Böhmen, Mähren und Schlesien*, Leipzig, 1893–4, vol. i, pp. 1–94, 358–68; and the article *Bauernbefreiung in Österreich-Ungarn, Handwörterbuch der Staatswissenschaften*, 3rd edition, vol. ii, pp. 562–73 (*Author*).

[2] Author's footnote on this legislation omitted.

(b) Official Policy and the Kmet Strike

Immediately after the occupation the attitude was entirely different. How could it be otherwise? Had not Count Andrássy, like so many other Austrian statesmen before him, always rightly regarded the land system as the real cause of the perpetual risings and of the ultimately chronic state of civil war in Bosnia and Hercegovina?[1] Long before the Congress of Berlin, he had demanded a comprehensive and compulsory agrarian reform which would secure the land to its cultivators free of produce-levies and labour services. He did not, however, consider the Turkish central government as capable of carrying out such a reform, nor did he believe that the autonomous or provincial administration proposed in the Treaty of San Stefano could undertake it, owing to the tension created by religious hatred and the desire for social vengeance. This opinion was respected by the other Powers, which gave expression to it by according the mandate of occupation to Austria-Hungary.

Consequently in the first years of the Austro-Hungarian administration there was strong pressure to 'create as quickly as possible a new, permanent and beneficial landlord-peasant relationship'. . . . Many proposals were put forward for a bold legislative solution for the agrarian problem. . . . It was believed that the civilizing mission that the Monarchy had undertaken to improve the living conditions of the population liberated from the Turkish yoke could be fulfilled only by an agrarian reform 'to expropriate the landlords against proper compensation and grant the tenant occupiers the right of

---

[1] Author here quotes passages urging the necessity of agrarian reform in Bosnia-Hercegovina, from Andrássy's speech at the Congress of Berlin and from his diplomatic correspondence. Count Julius Andrássy (1823–90), Hungary's first constitutional premier (1867), and later Austro-Hungarian Foreign Minister (1871–9), was chiefly responsible for the Austro-Hungarian occupation of Bosnia-Hercegovina. After the outbreak of the revolt of 1875 in Bosnia-Hercegovina, Russia, Germany and Austria-Hungary, supported by France and Britain, jointly presented to Turkey a note, drafted by Andrássy, demanding religious equality and fiscal and administrative reforms in the two provinces. Turkey's rejection of the Andrássy Note and the 'Bulgarian atrocities' of 1877 precipitated the Russo-Turkish War, which ended in Russian victory. The Treaty of San Stefano (March 1878) granted independence to Serbia, Rumania and Montenegro and autonomy to Bulgaria, while Bosnia-Hercegovina was to receive an autonomous administration under joint control of Russia and Austria-Hungary. At the Congress of Berlin, Andrássy succeeded in reducing Russian influence and securing the mandate of occupation for Austria-Hungary alone, under the Treaty of Berlin (July 1878). The occupation was unpopular in German Austria and Hungary and in 1879 Andrássy was forced to resign.

ownership of their houses and of an adequate part of the land in their cultivation'.[1]

But this zeal did not last. Barely six months after the occupation the proposal of the Bosnian Commission for an immediate enfranchisement of the land was no longer approved in Vienna. . . . As so often happens in Austria, the provisional became the definitive. . . . The legal system which existed in Ottoman times was still maintained. The Austro-Hungarian administration has avoided any profound change in the traditional structure, and has not even attempted to codify agrarian law. The legislative changes in this sphere since 1878 are—as the preceding description shows—of a formal nature, not affecting the real situation.

The government justifies this policy by the argument that it has no right 'to recast customary land law into the rigid mould of unalterable legality and so possibly obstruct future development'.[2]

Of course there is something to be said for this argument. In fact, so long as the axe is not laid to the root of the prevailing landlord-tenant relationship, all attempts at legal regulation must encounter great difficulties arising from local variations in the land system. But why has the kmet system not been entirely abolished? Why was it impossible to carry out 'the various projects for a general and final solution of the agrarian problem'?[3]

Surely there is no need for further proof of the fact that the *hak* is a corrupting economic influence? In a subsistence economy, with extensive cultivation and poor communications, there are advantages both for giver and receiver in a system of fixed share produce-rents, varying in quantity with crop production. But these merits become defects when the need for more intensive agricultural production increases as population grows, and the market for farm surpluses expands. Then the fixed levy weighs more heavily on the more productive farms than on the less productive. With every increase in the intensity of cultivation, the ratio of the levy to the net output becomes more unfavourable to the farmer; it is therefore an obstacle to better cultivation and reinforces the peasants' lively aversion to technical progress. The efforts of the peasants to increase quantity at the expense of quality hinder the development of specialized types of farming. Moreover, the harvest control is burdensome for the peasants and costly for the landowners, owing to the heavy losses

[1] Ordinance of the Joint Ministry of 4 February 1879 concerning the Regulation of the Agrarian Question. (Collection of Laws, vol. i, p. 514) (*Author*).

[2] Administrative Report for 1906, pp. 55–6. Cf. also Horowitz, *Die Agrarfrage*, pp. 153 ff. (*Author*).

[3] Administrative Report for 1906, p. 56 (*Author*).

involved in collection and delivery of the produce-levy. The effort to produce bad results to spite the landowner and oneself has a demoralizing effect. 'Thin as a rent hen, bad as a tithe wine' is always a true saying! . . .

There are many reasons why the government has set itself steadily against any radical interference with the agrarian structure of the provinces, and has adhered rigidly to the principle of voluntary emancipation and moreover established it by law.

Most important are the juridical considerations. 'Obligatory redemption could only with difficulty be reconciled with existing rights over property in land', and therefore 'the legally enforceable rights of property must not be prejudiced'.[1] [2]

This argument, however, is not to be taken seriously. No legal system has ever recognized private property as an eternal right, in the sense that the relation between property and its owners can never be modified. Every day—to leave the past entirely out of account—offers us examples of legal and administrative changes in one direction or another. How could it be otherwise, if all economic and social progress is not to be obstructed? And in what civilized country is legal expropriation foreign to the Civil Code? Such action, and on a large scale, would certainly be involved in a compulsory redemption of kmet obligations, for which the landowners would of course be fully compensated.

But the government objects that such redemption 'would be accompanied by so great an economic upheaval that the interests of neither peasants nor landowners would be protected and the economy of the country would be weakened, possibly even severely damaged'![3]

This would occur because 'a compulsory enfranchisement of the land would require a large credit operation', and this would impose 'a considerable burden on the peasantry, now struggling to make the transition from a subsistence to a money economy'.[4]

This argument proves too much, or nothing at all.

---

[1] Explanatory Introduction to the Government Draft Law (*Author*).

[2] In 1910, during the first session of the provincial parliament, constituted after the annexation of the provinces by Austria-Hungary in 1908, the provincial government proposed a draft law on the issue of loans to peasants for voluntary redemption, which was enacted with slight modifications in April 1911. Its provisions are quoted in the author's text, pp. 76 ff.

[3] *Ibid.* (*Author*).

[4] Administrative Report for 1906, p. 56; Documents on the Negotiations for the Foundations of the Agricultural and Commercial Bank of Bosnia-Hercegovina, Vienna, 1909, vol. iv, p. 132 (*Author*).

Why, if it is true, has the payment of tithe in kind been abolished? Moreover, the government has not only encouraged voluntary redemption in the past, but is actively promoting it now. It has recently granted a monopoly to a bank in order to supply the moneyless peasants with the funds needed to purchase their redemption, and it has guaranteed state credit to an equivalent amount. It is true that the government intended to limit credit to an élite among the peasants, i.e. to those 'whose economic efficiency appeared to ensure their independent existence after redemption'.[1] This limitation, however, was set aside in principle by the provincial parliament, and also the government itself did not regard it as absolute, but only as coming into operation when state credit was claimed. For the peasant is still justified in acquiring the means to buy himself free in the same way as before. If for any reason bank credit is not available to him, he will not hesitate to use the old way. We are told that the peasants, who hitherto hardly ever disposed of cash, 'are now prepared, since they can borrow more than half the value of the holding from the bank', to get the rest 'by selling some of their livestock' and 'borrowing at usurious rates'—regardless of the danger of 'often irreparable economic harm'![2] Of the 11·15 million crowns collected from the peasants for redemption in the years 1898–1909, 4·64 million, or almost 42 per cent, came from 'their own resources'.[3]

The growth of a money economy is as inevitable in Bosnia as elsewhere. It will proceed whether or not there is redemption, though redemption will encourage it, and maintaining the principle of voluntary redemption will not prevent it. This can at most relieve the government of responsibility for the economic disadvantages of free purchase and shift it to the peasants who undertake it recklessly. Any adverse effect that may arise will be far greater if the enfranchisement comes about solely through free purchase and not by compulsory official measures.

The economic results of the previous voluntary redemptions[4] are described by the government as extremely unsatisfactory from the standpoint of the peasantry, particularly because they desire above all to break their bondage to the landlord, and for this end will make any sacrifice, however excessive. They are hopeful and therefore reckless. Accustomed to a subsistence economy, they cannot fully understand the significance of the cash liabilities incurred, nor

---

[1] Paragraph 8 of the Draft Law and Explanatory Introduction (*Author*).

[2] Documents, *op. cit.*, vol. ii, p. 22 (*Author*).

[3] Administrative Report for 1909, p. 16, 1910, p. 14; Documents, *op. cit.*, vol. iv, p. 126 (*Author*). See Note on Weights, Measures and Currency, p. 387.

[4] The total number of redemptions in 1879–1909 was 26,219, of which 21,595 were complete and the rest partial (p. 67 of Author's text).

balance them against the benefits they hope to gain. 'Even small redemption payments, which it seems as if they should be able to afford, do not always benefit the peasants, but often lead to ruin.'[1] 'Some farm redeemed land with insufficient livestock and capital and a burden of debt, and so cannot pay the interest and the instalments of the purchase price, so that the redeemed land must be sold.'[2] So 'many a wholly impoverished peasant who formerly paid one-third of the produce for his hereditary tenancy is glad to obtain land at a rent of half the produce with insecurity of tenure'.[3]

There is too little material to enable us to judge how far this sombre picture accords with reality. In fact, an analysis of official statistics shows only a small percentage of failures to pay the taxes due. Of course this is not to assert that no peasants have been ruined through redeeming their holdings. The number of those who have had to abandon house and holding is certainly not small. But this is neither the fault of emancipation in itself, nor of the inability of the peasant to adjust himself to it, but to the combination of voluntary redemption with an inadequate credit organization. This drives the peasants into the arms of the money-lenders or to the sale of their farm stock, and at the same time allows the beg to raise the purchase price at the cost of the peasants.

The recently enacted redemption law has brought less change on these two cardinal points than appears at first sight. Certainly the new credit organization represents an advance, the greater in that it is retroactive. But the advance is formal rather than real. Certainly state credit could hardly be cheaper; the conditions of payment are favourable, and take into account the effect of harvest conditions on the debtor's ability to pay. But whether the peasant can benefit from all this is entirely dependent on the will of the landowner. . . . The legal and economic power of the landowners, which is in no way diminished, will retard the scale and rate of redemption as before, and will allow them to raise the purchase price of the holding, so that the law will remain a dead letter. Its benefits will probably be limited to the provision of credit to peasants who have already purchased their redemption. So long as the voluntary principle is maintained, no genuine remodelling of the decaying agrarian structure is to be anticipated. It can only be achieved through compulsory emancipation, for which the necessary administrative machinery has now been created and lies ready for use. . . .

[1] H. Lanter, *Die fakultative Kmetenablösung in Bosnien und der Herzegowina*, Österreichische Rundschau, Vienna, 1 January 1911, p. 7 (*Author*).

[2] Explanatory Introduction to the Government Draft Law (*Author*).

[3] Lanter, *op. cit.* (*Author*).

We now come to the 'political' argument of the government against compulsory emancipation: the fear of a mass emigration of the Moslem population.

In this connection, one thing is—most surprisingly—overlooked. The agrarian conflict is not between Moslems and Christians, but between landowners and dependent peasants. According to the statistics of 1895, the former included 5,833 families (with whose interests the majority of the 17,256 'sundry heads of families' were identified), and the latter 103,508 families, of which almost four-fifths were dependent peasants and the remainder semi-dependent, with some land of their own. The 98,081 free peasants, the majority of whom are Moslems, and represent the bulk of the Moslem population, would not be in any way affected by the compulsory enfranchisement of kmet land, and their sympathies would not thereby be alienated, since they are independent farmers and have no kmets. Clearly the interests of a small group of landowners should not outweigh those of the comparatively huge number of dependent peasants, among whom discontent is politically a far more dangerous factor. . . .

But does the prospect of the destruction of the nobility as a land-owning and ruling class mean nothing?

Such a question takes us back about a century. We might well suppose that we have advanced beyond the idea that a community must be socially stratified and have a landed aristocracy as its peak. Apart from that, the peasants do not consider the beg as their political leader and the representative of their interests. For five hundred years he was the oppressor and they the oppressed, each divided from the other by religious opposition and religious hatred. It would be otherwise if the landowners were well equipped with capital, professionally trained, intelligent, managing their own farms and leaders in technical progress. But the large agricultural enterprise does not exist in these provinces, and the government tells us that the landowners do not know what to do with the capital they receive for redemption, apart from consuming it.

What is politically far more important [than the opposition of the landowners to compulsory emancipation] is that in neighbouring Serbia and Bulgaria the liberation from the Turks brought the peasants complete emancipation, which thirty-three years of Austro-Hungarian rule have not yet produced.

Beyond doubt the agrarian policy in these provinces has been a grave, indeed the gravest mistake of the Austro-Hungarian administration. It in fact overshadows all the benefits which this has brought to the two provinces. These benefits are certainly neither few nor small. The indirect effects of peace, law and order are extremely favourable, especially for the peasant class. The occupation put an end to ceaseless civil war, the Christian population's lack of civil rights, insecurity of person and property, and the brutally capricious rule of an overbearing landed aristocracy and bureaucracy. No objective thinker will dispute the progress which has been achieved since 1878. It is attested by the 64 per cent increase in the population, and to an even greater extent by the comparatively slight emigration movement, despite the tendency of the Moslem population to move out with the Crescent from the former Turkish provinces. But men commonly take for granted the good in which they participate; it does not compensate for that which they forgo. Indeed, if a burden long endured is lightened, they may well find the remainder is harder to endure than the whole. That the peasants are discontented with the continuance of their traditional dependence on the landowner is therefore not surprising, nor can it be expected that they will accept as final the solution of the land emancipation problem proposed in the first elected provincial parliament.

How great this discontent is and what the peasants hoped to gain from representative government came clearly to light in the autumn of 1910.[1]

In June of that year, the Serbian peasants in Upper Bosnia refused to pay the *hak*. Such an event was in itself nothing unusual. What gave their action special significance was its solidarity and widespread support. This first flare-up of a revolutionary movement in the Gradiška district was instantly quelled, chiefly, it seems, by a compromise agreeing that the valuation of the harvest should be made by the knez (the elder of the district) instead of by the landowner's agent. But scarcely had order been restored when much larger demonstrations began in many villages in the Banja Luka and Tuzla districts. Thousands thronged together and flocked from village to village, quite peaceably, with no violence, as had to be acknowledged even by the Bosnian press, though it strongly condemned this attempt to influence the decisions of the provincial parliament.[2] 'These manifestations were accompanied by the most exemplary compliance with official regulations in other ways. Taxes, even the tithe, were promptly paid, even by people who usually reckoned on remissions. No one should be able to say that the movement was directed against the Emperor or his authorities.'[3] But the *hak*, the

---

[1] For the following, see Lanter, *op. cit.*, and *Bosnische Post* of 4–18 October 1910, in particular the series of articles on 'The Kmet Movement' (*Author*).

[2] *Bosnische Post*, 5 October 1910 (*Author*).

[3] Lanter, *op. cit.*, p. 5 (*Author*).

marchers declared, they could not and would not pay in the future. 'They also sang a song: "Puče puška s pečine, nema begu trečine" [From the rocks the rifles roar, the beg shall get the third no more].'

The provincial government took comprehensive measures, including military action, 'to give the agas full support in claiming their legal share of the harvest', and was soon in control of the 'peaceable rising'. The peasants acquiesced in the imposition of the tribute, in the conviction that it was for the last time. That this conviction is fed by agitators, who can doubt? But as the general in charge of the repression of the peasant revolt in Russia said in 1774: 'Pugachov does not matter; what matters is the universal hostility.' May it not be concluded that the universal hostility among the peasants will be increased by the disappointment that they have now experienced?

Karl Grünberg, b. 1861 in Focşani (Rumania), d. 1940; 1909–24, Professor of Economic History in the University of Vienna. Author of several authoritative works on agrarian reform and also on the history of socialism.

Note on Weights, Measures and Currency

Weight
   The *Centner* (of Vienna) = 56 kg. or 123·48 lbs.

Capacity
   The *Metze* (of Austria-Hungary) = 61 5 litres = 45 kg. or 99 lbs. (wheat).

Length and Area
   The (German) mile = 7·5 km. or 4·6 statute miles.
   The square mile = 57·5 sq. km. or 22·24 English sq. miles.
   The *Joch* (*Jutro*) varied with locality (see Hungary: Note on Weights, Measures and Currency, p. 112). In the texts quoted, it may be taken as equivalent to one acre.

Currency
In the late eighteenth and early nineteenth centuries:
   1 Thaler (dollar) = 2 Florins (or Gulden).
   1 Florin = 60 Kreutzer (Krajcer).
The rate of 1 florin to 2 English shillings (quoted by Lloyd Hodges, p. 300, footnote 3) was maintained for most of the nineteenth century.
After 1892:
   1 Krone (crown) = 10d at parity.
   1 Florin = 2 crowns (unofficially).

INDEX OF PERSONS

INDEX OF PLACE NAMES

INDEX OF SUBJECTS